Studies in the History of Art
Published by the National Gallery of Art, Washington

This series includes: Studies in the History of Art, collected papers on objects in the Gallery's collections and other art-historical studies (formerly Report and Studies in the History of Art); Monograph Series I, a catalogue of stained glass in the United States; Monograph Series II, on conservation topics; and Symposium Papers (formerly Symposium Series), the proceedings of symposia sponsored by the Center for Advanced Study in the Visual Arts at the National Gallery of Art.

[1] *Report and Studies in the History of Art*, 1967
[2] *Report and Studies in the History of Art*, 1968
[3] *Report and Studies in the History of Art*, 1969
[In 1970 the National Gallery of Art's annual report became a separate publication.]
[4] *Studies in the History of Art*, 1972
[5] *Studies in the History of Art*, 1973
[The first five volumes are unnumbered.]
6 *Studies in the History of Art*, 1974
7 *Studies in the History of Art*, 1975
8 *Studies in the History of Art*, 1978
9 *Studies in the History of Art*, 1980
10 *Macedonia and Greece in Late Classical and Early Hellenistic Times*, edited by Beryl Barr-Sharrar and Eugene N. Borza. Symposium Series I, 1982
11 *Figures of Thought: El Greco as Interpreter of History, Tradition, and Ideas*, edited by Jonathan Brown, 1982
12 *Studies in the History of Art*, 1982
13 *El Greco: Italy and Spain*, edited by Jonathan Brown and José Manuel Pita Andrade. Symposium Series II, 1984
14 *Claude Lorrain, 1600–1682: A Symposium*, edited by Pamela Askew. Symposium Series III, 1984
15 *Stained Glass before 1700 in American Collections: New England and New York (Corpus Vitrearum Checklist I)*, compiled by Madeline H. Caviness et al. Monograph Series I, 1985
16 *Pictorial Narrative in Antiquity and the Middle Ages*, edited by Herbert L. Kessler and Marianna Shreve Simpson. Symposium Series IV, 1985
17 *Raphael before Rome*, edited by James Beck. Symposium Series V, 1986
18 *Studies in the History of Art*, 1985
19 *James McNeill Whistler: A Reexamination*, edited by Ruth E. Fine. Symposium Papers VI, 1987
20 *Retaining the Original: Multiple Originals, Copies, and Reproductions*. Symposium Papers VII, 1989
21 *Italian Medals*, edited by J. Graham Pollard. Symposium Papers VIII, 1987
22 *Italian Plaquettes*, edited by Alison Luchs. Symposium Papers IX, 1989
23 *Stained Glass before 1700 in American Collections: Mid-Atlantic and Southeastern Seaboard States (Corpus Vitrearum Checklist II)*, compiled by Madeline H. Caviness et al. Monograph Series I, 1987
24 *Studies in the History of Art*, 1990
25 *The Fashioning and Functioning of the British Country House*, edited by Gervase Jackson-Stops et al. Symposium Papers X, 1989
26 *Winslow Homer*, edited by Nicolai Cikovsky, Jr. Symposium Papers XI, 1990
27 *Cultural Differentiation and Cultural Identity in the Visual Arts*, edited by Susan J. Barnes and Walter S. Melion. Symposium Papers XII, 1989
28 *Stained Glass before 1700 in American Collections: Midwestern and Western States (Corpus Vitrearum Checklist III)*, compiled by Madeline H. Caviness et al. Monograph Series I, 1989
29 *Nationalism in the Visual Arts*, edited by Richard A. Etlin. Symposium Papers XIII, 1991
30 *The Mall in Washington, 1791–1991*, edited by Richard Longstreth. Symposium Papers XIV, 1991
31 *Urban Form and Meaning in South Asia: The Shaping of Cities from Prehistoric to Precolonial Times*, edited by Howard Spodek and Doris Srinivasan. Symposium Papers XV*
32 *New Perspectives in Early Greek Art*, edited by Diana Buitron-Oliver. Symposium Papers XVI, 1991
33 *Michelangelo Drawings*, edited by Craig Hugh Smyth. Symposium Papers XVII, 1992
34 *Art and Power in Seventeenth-Century Sweden*, edited by Michael Conforti and Michael Metcalf. Symposium Papers XVIII (withdrawn)
35 *The Architectural Historian in America*, edited by Elisabeth Blair MacDougall. Symposium Papers XIX, 1990
36 *The Pastoral Landscape*, edited by John Dixon Hunt. Symposium Papers XX, 1992
37 *American Art around 1900*, edited by Doreen Bolger and Nicolai Cikovsky, Jr. Symposium Papers XXI, 1990
38 *The Artist's Workshop*, edited by Peter Lukehart. Symposium Papers XXII*
39 *Stained Glass before 1700 in American Collections: Silver-Stained Roundels and Unipartite Panels (Corpus Vitrearum Checklist IV)*, compiled by Timothy B. Husband. Monograph Series I, 1991
40 The Feast of the Gods: *Conservation, Examination, and Interpretation*, by David Bull and Joyce Plesters. Monograph Series II, 1990
41 *Conservation Research*. Monograph Series II, 1993
42 *Conservation Research: Studies of Fifteenth- to Nineteenth-Century Tapestry*, edited by Lotus Stack. Monograph Series II.*

*Forthcoming

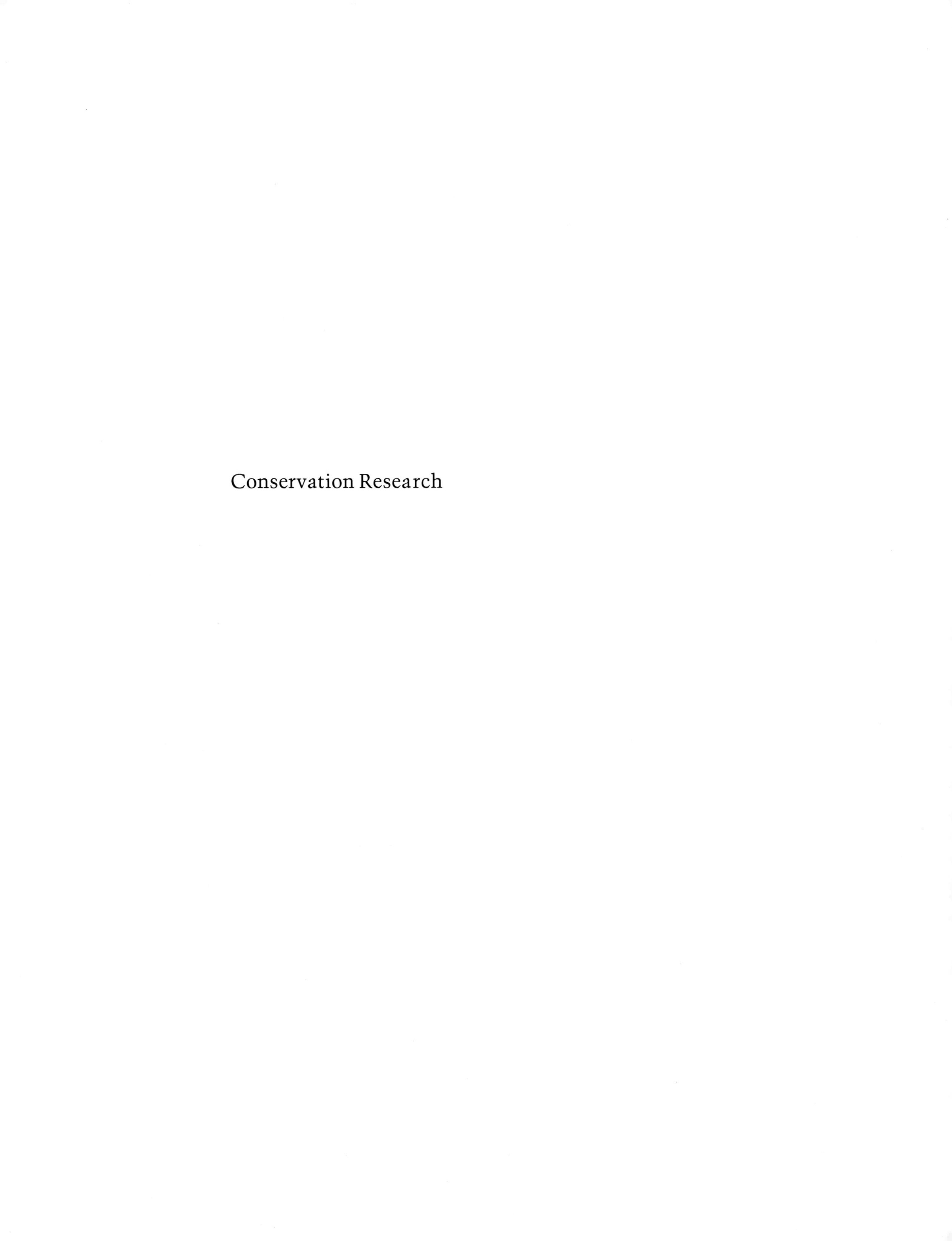

Conservation Research

STUDIES IN THE HISTORY OF ART • 41 •

Monograph Series II

Conservation Research

National Gallery of Art, Washington

Distributed by the University Press of New England

Hanover and London

This publication was produced by the Editors Office, National Gallery of Art, Washington
Editor-in-Chief, Frances P. Smyth

Printed in Hong Kong

The type is Trump Medieval, set by BG Composition, Baltimore, Maryland

Distributed by the University Press of New England, 23 South Main Street, Hanover, New Hampshire 03755

Abstracted by RILA (International Repertory of the Literature of Art), Williamstown, Massachusetts 02167

ISSN 0091-7338
ISBN 089468-178-8

Cover: Detail, Paul Gauguin, *Parau na te varua ino* (Words of the devil), 1892, National Gallery of Art, Washington

Contents

Foreword

With the inaugural volume of *Conservation Research*, the National Gallery of Art begins to report regularly on the research and technical studies pursued by its conservation division. The National Gallery periodically has published technical studies, beginning in 1973 with a contribution to *Studies in the History of Art* on the construction, treatment, materials, and scholarly studies of Peter Paul Rubens' *Deborah Kip, Wife of Sir Balthasar Gerbier, and Her Children*; this was one of the first publications jointly undertaken by a scholar, conservator, and conservation scientist. More recently, another volume of this series was devoted to a single work, *The Feast of the Gods* by Giovanni Bellini and Titian. In addition, the National Gallery, under the auspices of the conservation division, published in 1986 the first volume of a series, *Artists' Pigments: A Handbook of Their History and Characteristics*, edited by Robert L. Feller. The second volume, edited by Ashok Roy, will be released in 1993; volume three, edited by Elisabeth West FitzHugh, is in process, and plans are under way for volume four. The Gallery also has reprinted important technical works such as *On Picture Varnishes*. Two recent publications, *Art in Transit: Studies in the Transport of Paintings* and the *Handbook for Packing and Transporting Paintings*, incorporate the research of major conservation institutions and museums and establish a new understanding of packing procedures.

In this publication, research by Andrew W. Mellon Fellows from 1984 to 1988 and by members of the conservation staff at the National Gallery of Art is reported. Readers are introduced to analyses forming the basis for a greater understanding of Renaissance bronzes; techniques that produced obscure and charming medieval pasteprints; the mystique and realities behind Gauguin's choices of canvases and painting materials; characteristics of Japanese papers selected by Whistler; the painting methods of El Greco; and insight into the impressionists' attitudes toward varnish coatings on paintings.

In the format of *Conservation Research*, we look forward to making available scholarly information pertaining to our collection, and others, not only to conservators but to a wide audience of curators, scientists, and connoisseurs.

EARL A. POWELL III
Director, National Gallery of Art

Introduction

The publication of technical studies is not new to the National Gallery of Art, although for many of the authors this is a first effort to bring their research to print. This initial volume of *Conservation Research* marks the culmination of intensive effort by the conservation staff and fellowship recipients. Accumulating technical data is a painstaking process, and preparing it for publication is even more so, especially when research is not the primary endeavor of the Gallery conservator. Conservation scientists often pursue ongoing research for many years, posing the dilemma of when to stop and articulate findings and when to probe further for that last, elusive bit of data that irrefutably confirms their findings.

Technical studies and research based on the National Gallery of Art's extensive permanent collection form an integral part of the Conservation Fellowship Program. In addition, special exhibitions afford staff members and fellows the opportunity to assemble information on objects from other institutions and collections. The subjects addressed in this volume, and to be addressed in future volumes, are wide-ranging. While all of the papers are written from the viewpoint of the conservator or conservation scientist, the intended audience is not only those in the conservation field but also those who may apply the information to their particular branch of art or scientific interest. The general reader as well will find articles of interest. Daphne Barbour and Lisha Deming Glinsman's study of Renaissance casting practices forms an important foundation for recognizing spurious works. Antoinette Dwan's classification and examination of Japanese papers of the nineteenth century focuses on the prints of James Abbott McNeill Whistler. Monographic study of an artist's materials and working techniques underlies Susanna P. Griswold's comparison of two paintings by El Greco, while the more general research of a painter's oeuvre is at the heart of Carol Christensen's analysis of Paul Gauguin's materials and technique. The student of medieval prints will find clarification by Sarah Bertalan of a long-disputed issue of materials and process used in medieval pasteprints, based on study of pasteprints in the Gallery's collection and others. Michael Swicklik provides factual foundation to speculations on attitudes of French artists beginning in the eighteenth century toward the use of varnish coatings on paintings, with emphasis on how impressionists viewed their use.

Conservation research, with its focus on the material structure of works of art as revealed through modern technology, has drawn scholarly interest, as well as general interest for its application of exotic technology. The absence of extensive technical research in scholarly museum publications heretofore should not suggest that up-to-date analytical and research techniques are not applied by many museums, but rather it indicates the difficulty of bringing a technical investigation to publication without reducing a great work to a simple material artifact. Technical studies may be regularly cited by scholars, but seldom have been published by their authors. As their informative contributions are becoming recognized, however, investigations by conservators and conservation scientists are finding new outlets in monographs and exhibition catalogues. We even find our academic colleagues taking up applied science in their research.

The conservation division encourages collaborative projects by conservation scientists, conservators, curators, and our academic colleagues. Future issues of *Conservation Research* will present articles resulting from these collaborative investigations.

Acknowledgments

The groundwork for this publication was laid by John Wilmerding, past deputy director of the National Gallery of Art, and was enthusiastically implemented by his successor, Roger Mandle. Foremost in his support of our conservation fellowships, staff research, and other conservation programs has been the National Gallery's director emeritus, J. Carter Brown. We are grateful for the continuing support and encouragement of the National Gallery leadership.

This publication is made possible through the ongoing efforts and patience of the conservation division's department heads, the division editor, Janice Gruver, and Michael Skalka, conservation programs coordinator. We are also grateful to those who have given generously of their expertise and time in reviewing our research.

The sponsors of the Conservation Fellowship Endowment, principally the Andrew W. Mellon Foundation, as well as the Charles E. Culpeper Foundation, have provided fellows with the opportunity to pursue research projects. This publication serves as a forum for their work and that of staff members who have undertaken special research projects. We also are indebted to the Publications Fund of the National Gallery for support.

ROSS M. MERRILL
Chief of Conservation, National Gallery of Art

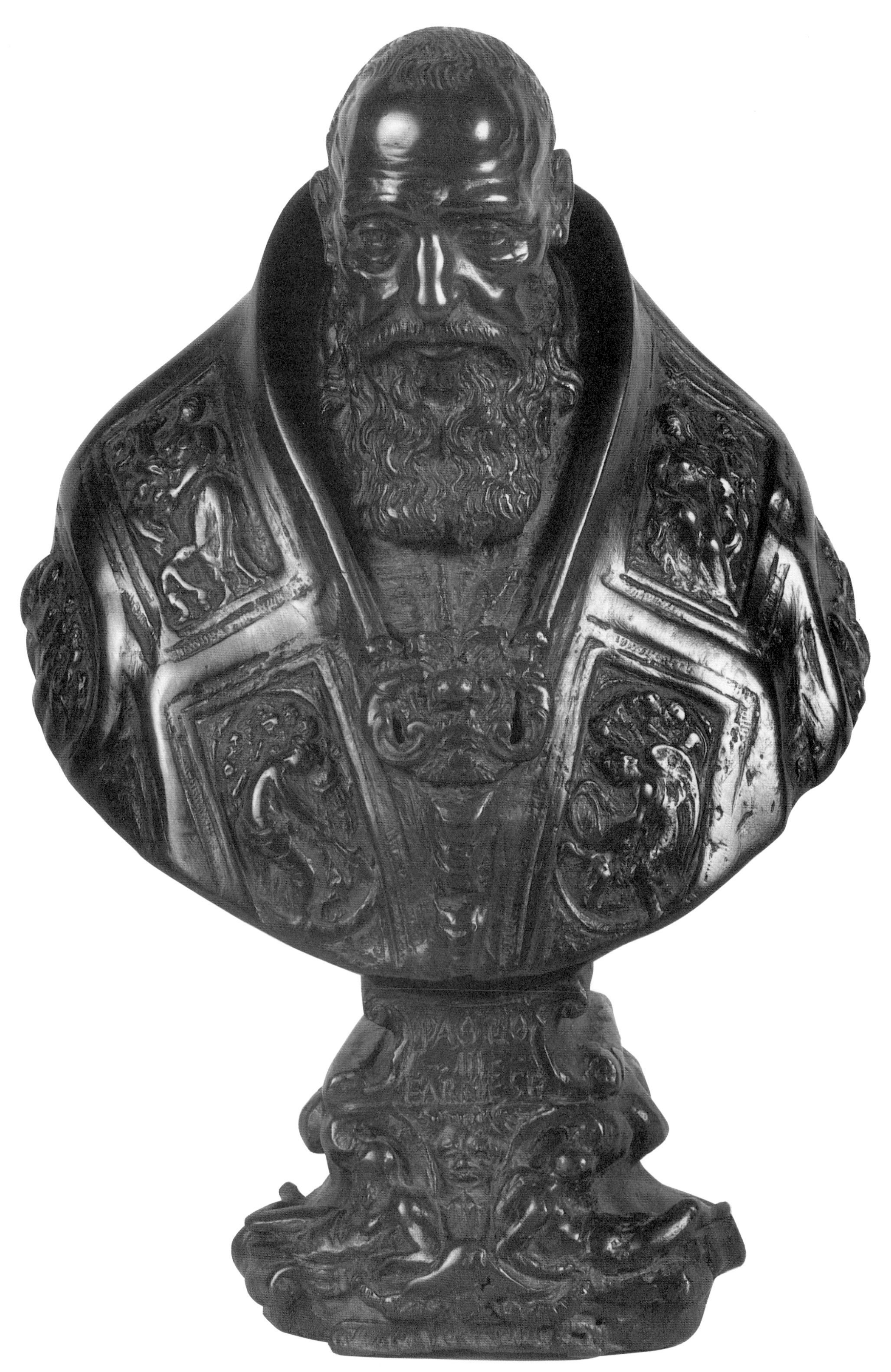

DAPHNE BARBOUR and LISHA DEMING GLINSMAN

An Investigation of Renaissance Casting Practices as a Means for Identifying Forgeries

A series of seven small bronze busts of Pope Paul III Farnese, attributed to Guglielmo della Porta (c. 1516–1577), was assembled at the National Gallery of Art, Washington, for technical study (fig. 1).[1] National Gallery curators had questioned the attribution and authenticity of this unusual series, since no precedent for a group of small-scale portrait busts is known to exist in the Renaissance.[2] In addition, the blatant lack of documentation for any of these busts prior to 1936,[3] although they ostensibly date from an era well known for its meticulous record keeping, prompted the effort to validate or refute the attribution by investigating the casting methods and materials of these busts.

The seven small bronze busts were first examined visually to determine whether the method of manufacture was consistent with sixteenth-century casting practices. They were then analyzed to determine whether the composition of the metal was in accordance with that of other Renaissance bronzes or what is known about Renaissance metallurgical practice.

HISTORICAL BACKGROUND

First attributed to Guglielmo della Porta by Werner Gramberg,[4] the bronze busts depict Pope Paul III, Alessandro Farnese (1468–1549) (fig. 2). Guglielmo della Porta was a Lombard artist who worked in Milan and Genoa before moving to Rome. Giorgio Vasari claimed that he moved to Rome in 1537,[5] but the earliest documented date for his presence there is 3 May 1546, when he was paid for marble doors of the Sala del Ré in the Vatican.[6] John Pope-Hennessy describes him as a "sculptor of genius" who helped mark the transition in Italian sculpture after 1550 from Florentine supremacy to Lombard artistry.[7]

In Rome, Guglielmo was introduced to Michelangelo and, through him, to the Farnese family. It was Michelangelo who, according to Vasari, "conceived an affection for him, and before any other thing, caused him to restore some antique things in the Farnese Palace, in which he acquitted himself in such a manner that Michelangelo put him into the service of the Pope [Paul III]."[8] When Paul III's reigning *piombatore apostolico* (the individual charged with making lead seals for papal bulls) died in 1547, Guglielmo procured this prestigious position against such acclaimed competitors as Benvenuto Cellini. As *piombatore apostolico*, Guglielmo was further granted the honor of designing and executing the pope's tomb. Between 1547 and 1567 he is not known to have completed many sculptures, but as Vasari wrote, "It is the characteristic of those who hold that office to become sluggish and indolent."[9]

The attribution to Guglielmo of the small busts considered here is not unfounded. He executed several portrait busts of Paul III and received payment in 1547 for one cast in

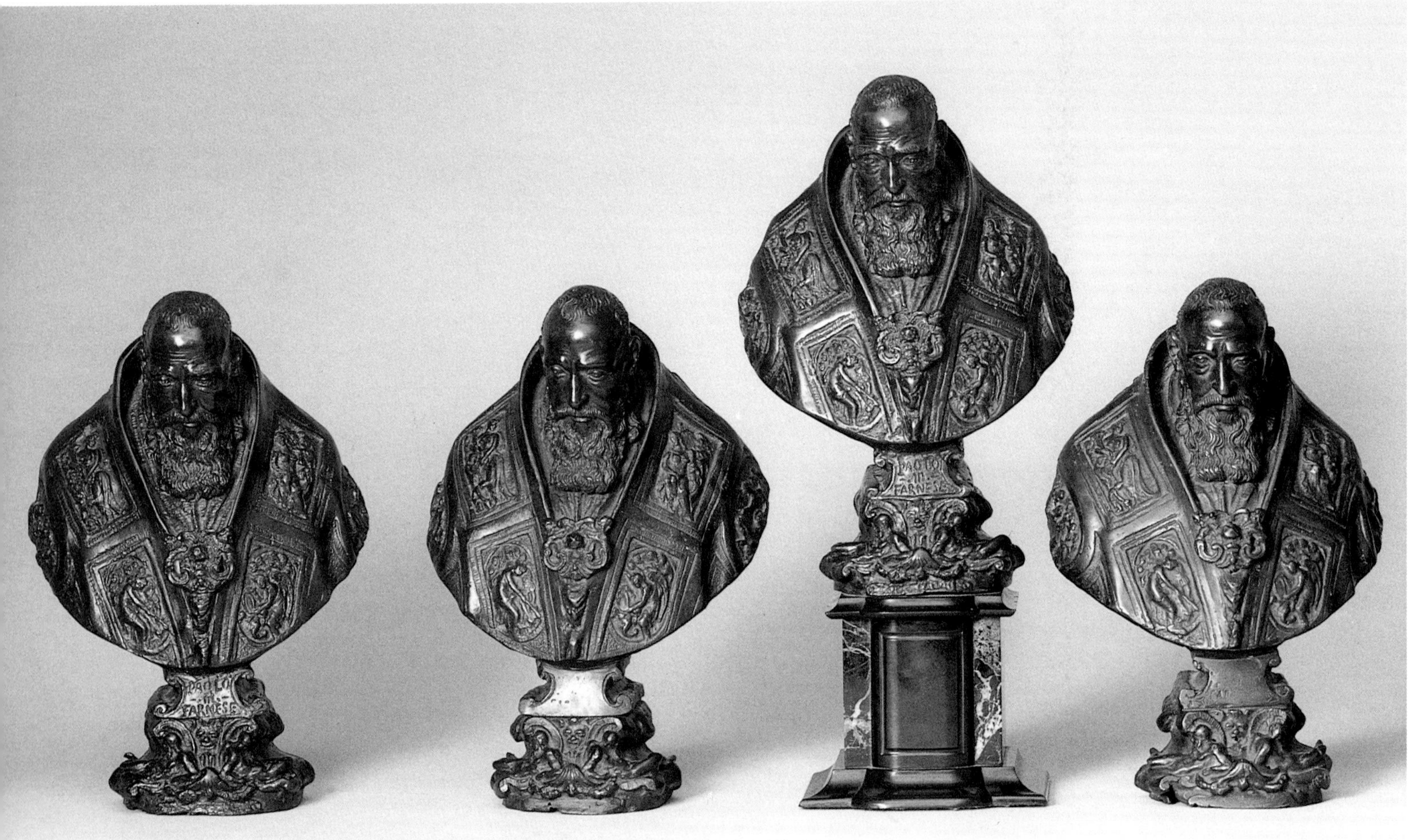

1. Attributed to Guglielmo della Porta, *Pope Paul III Farnese*, bronze (copper alloy)
From left to right: Herbert F. Johnson Museum of Art, Cornell University, Ithaca, New York; Virginia Museum of Fine Arts, Richmond; Sotheby's, New York; Willard B. Golovin Collection (A and B); J. B. Speed Art Museum, Louisville, Kentucky; National Gallery of Art, Washington

bronze.[10] He also cast a seated portrait of the pope for his tomb. Two over-life-size marble busts of the same sitter were also reported as having been executed by Guglielmo around 1550. Today they are in the Museo Nazionale di Capodimonte, Naples. Gramberg considers only one (10514) to be the work of Guglielmo (fig. 3), however; the second (10524) is considered to be a workshop piece (fig. 4).[11] Henceforth they will be identified as Guglielmo's bust or the workshop piece, based on Gramberg's attribution.

The series of small busts appears to have been derived, if not copied, from Guglielmo's marble at the Capodimonte (see fig. 3). Except for their size (the marble is considerably larger than the small bronzes), they are identical. It has even been suggested of one of the small bronzes that it was a *bozzetto* (study) for the Capodimonte marble,[12] but the high degree of detail and the finished quality of the surface of the bronze busts is atypical for *bozzetti*.

Based on his observation that some of the nicks and minor losses on the bronze bust in the Museum für Kunst und Gewerbe, Hamburg (not available for this examination), appear to have occurred prior to casting, Gramberg believes that it was cast from a wax model made by Guglielmo c. 1544. He also suggests the wax model was saved from destruction to be cast later for documentation purposes. He considers the finished quality to be characteristic of Guglielmo's oeuvre.

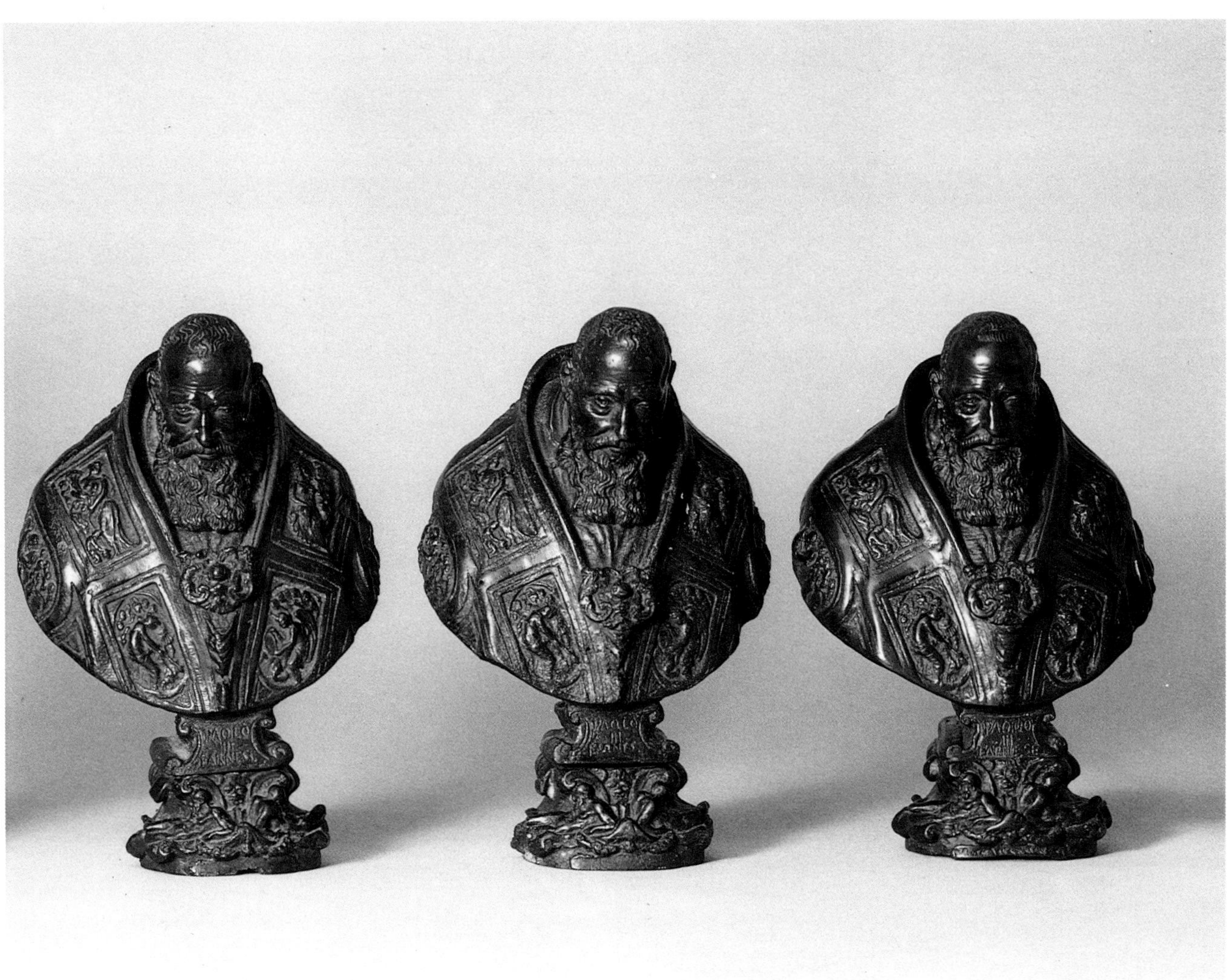

Furthermore, he interprets the casual inscription, "Paolo III Farnese," excluding the compulsory "PONT MAX.," to mean that Guglielmo added it later, probably after the pope had died (fig. 5).[13] It could be argued, however, that the inscription was merely written by an individual unfamiliar with the proper way to inscribe a papal title and therefore could not possibly have been done by Guglielmo. It could also be argued that what is in fact incongruous is that the inscription is not in Latin. "PONT MAX." would not be added to an Italian inscription.[14] This study is not intended to prove or disprove questions pertaining to a nonextant wax or lost-wax model and when and who inscribed it. They are raised to show how these bronzes, and similar ones, have been interpreted in relation to Guglielmo's oeuvre.

DESCRIPTION

The small bronze busts depict a bare-headed, bearded Paul III clothed in an ornamental ecclesiastical cope clasped at the neckline by a heavy brooch. On the front of the cope are four rectangular fields, each containing an allegorical scene. The proper right fields show Abundance (fig. 6) and Peace, while the proper left fields represent Justice (fig. 7) and Victory. These four concepts, extremely important to Paul III, are frequently depicted in his portraits. Scenes from the Pentateuch—

the Tablets of the Law and the dead Egyptians—on both shoulders reflect the pope's attempt to strengthen the Catholic church against the Protestant Reformation; they exist in the identical configuration on Guglielmo's marble in the Capodimonte.[15]

The bases of the bronzes, which differ from that of Guglielmo's marble, contain an inscription identifying the sitter (see fig. 5). Flanking the inscription are reclining river gods, perhaps inspired by Michelangelo's river gods intended for the Medici tombs. On several of the bronzes, the inscription is effaced; however, excepting superficial variations, design elements remain consistent throughout the series. The busts with legible inscriptions all read, simply, "PAOLO III FARNESE."

Gramberg points out that the workshop piece has a base similar to those of the bronzes under examination. In fact, except for a missing inscription area in the former, the bases of the small bronze busts and the workshop piece are identical. In contrast, Guglielmo's marble portrait rests on a cylindrical base that appears to be almost too narrow at the top to support the bust. It is conceivable, as Gramberg suggests, that the bases of Guglielmo's bust and the workshop piece were inadvertently switched. In fact, even the rectangular inscription area that is absent from the workshop piece is present on Guglielmo's marble. Thus, if Guglielmo's marble portrait of Paul III originally rested on the marble base that is similar to the bases portrayed under the small busts, the busts would be entirely analogous to the marble bust's original condition. If this is correct, the artist who created the small bronze busts must have done so before the bases of the marble portraits were exchanged.[16]

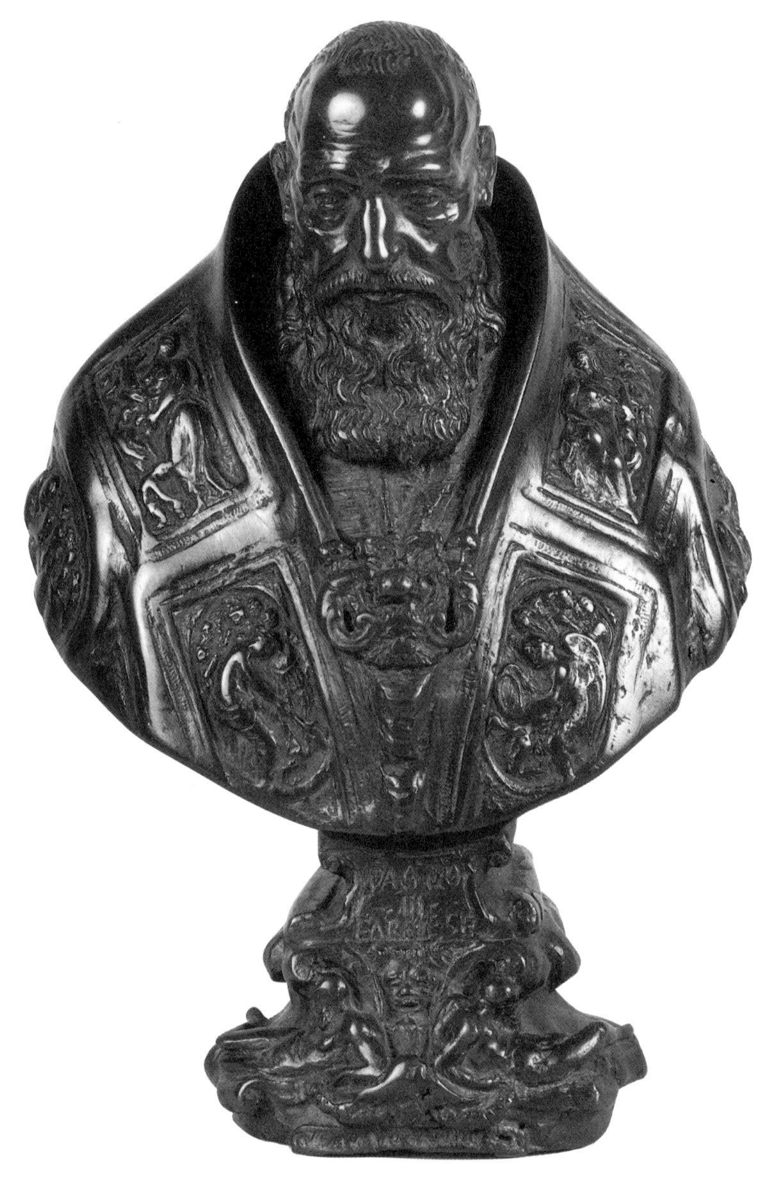

2. Attributed to Guglielmo della Porta, *Pope Paul III Farnese*, bronze (copper alloy)
National Gallery of Art, Washington

METHOD OF MANUFACTURE

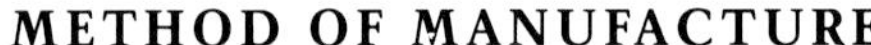

Fabrication

All the bronze busts appear to have been cast by the lost-wax method, a technique well known and well documented in the Renaissance. Benvenuto Cellini, Guglielmo's contemporary and competitor, recorded his own casting methods in great length. First he described how to prepare a core, the material that fills the center of the model enabling the sculpture to be hollow once cast: "I made a model in clay of just the size the figure was to be; . . . Then I gave it a good baking, and after that I spread over the whole an even coat of wax of less than a finger's thickness."[17]

A core need not be made from the complex recipe described by Cellini, which included, among other things, oxhorn and dung. In fact the only criterion is that it be made from a refractory material, specifically one that will

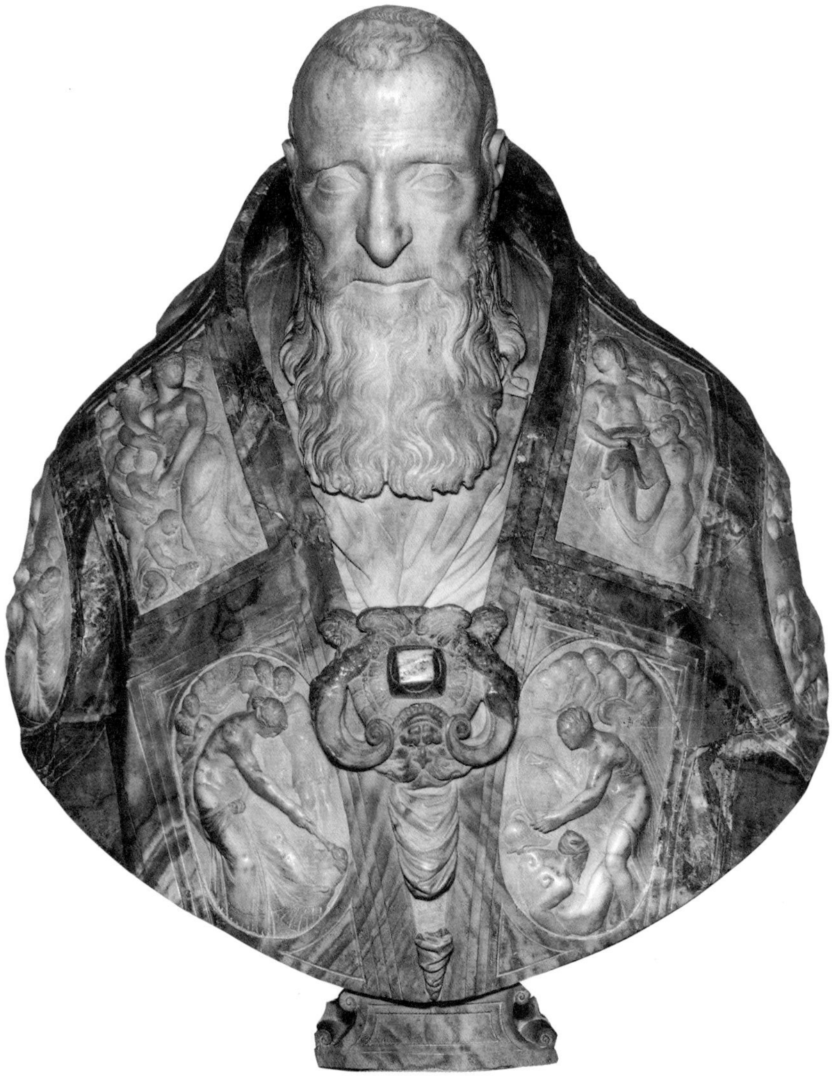

3. Guglielmo della Porta, *Pope Paul III Farnese*, c. 1550, marble
Museo Nazionale di Capodimonte, Naples

retain its shape and composition even when subjected to high temperatures. Wax painted over the core, in the way recounted by Cellini, served as a model with the qualities sought in the final bronze. Sprues (rods) made of wax were then attached in strategic locations throughout the model. It was through channels created by the wax sprues that molten metal was ultimately poured. Other wax rods attached at this time, which were not used as channels for the molten metal, provided vents or holes. These in turn enabled gases to escape and eliminated back pressure and subsequent bursting of the bronze. Cellini perceptively recommended that all such attachments point downward:

You fashion in wax . . . all the vent holes for the bronze casting, and mind that they all slant downwards to the bottom; later when the figure has its last and earthen mould on, these vents may easily be turned up with clay [or mold material].[18]

Core pins (chaplets), used to hold the core material in place during casting, were also inserted at this stage. The wax model and core would have next been covered (invested) with a refractory material to form a mold. When the mold had dried, it was placed in an oven and heated slowly until the wax model was melted out, or "lost." The investment continued to be baked until all moisture was removed:

In melting out the wax your fire be so tempered that the wax does not boil in the mould, but comes out with the greatest patience. When the wax is all out give the mould yet another but very moderate firing, in order to rid of any moisture that may be left in the mould.[19]

The mold was then placed in a "pouring pit" dug into the ground. Finally, molten metal was poured in through a pouring cup at the top of the mold into channels left by wax sprues and allowed to cool.

In general, the lost-wax manufacturing technique appears the same on all the busts. That they all originated from the same source is implied, not only because they are visually alike but also because internal and overall measurements of all the portraits are comparable. The measurements differ only slightly, and their variations are random; no overall shrinkage is noted. For these reasons, it is impossible to claim one was cast after another.

There is, however, one notable difference between the method Cellini described and that used on the small busts. Unlike Cellini's method, where wax is brushed over a clay model, the wax models used for the small busts under examination appear to have been slush cast, as evidenced by the drip marks on the reverse of the bronzes. Slush casting is a technique of hollow casting that does not require a core; it is analogous to slip casting in ceramics. A molten medium is simply poured into a mold. In this case, hot wax was poured into a mold of the busts. After those areas that were in contact with the cooler mold surface solidified, the remaining liquid wax was slushed around to ensure that it had made contact with all areas of the mold and then poured out. The principles involved in slush casting were recorded in the Renaissance by Vannoccio Biringuccio in 1540, who described this method in conjunction with the manufacture of tin sheeting, lead roofing, and organ pipes.[20] Though not often associated with casting procedures used on Renaissance sculpture, the technique of slush casting certainly existed in the sixteenth century.[21]

When the hollow wax model had cooled, it was removed from its mold and polished in the same manner used to finish the final bronze. Likewise, superficial changes or enhancements could be made to the wax model at this time. A core would then have been added to the center of the model so that the final bronze could be hollow once cast.

The remainder of the busts' casting process is entirely analogous to the procedure Cellini described. Core pins were inserted on both sides of the cope, on the top of the head, and, in some busts, behind each ear. These were easily detected in the laboratory as they created superficial holes after the pins were removed (fig. 8). Remnants of mold and core materials from the busts were analyzed using x-ray diffraction (XRD) and were identified in all cases as gypsum.[22]

Wax sprues, whose placement was identified by their small projecting remnants, were then attached along the reverse edge of the cope and neckline, on the top of the head, and on the bottom edge of the base. Lastly, molten metal was poured through the base while the sculptures were overturned.

Similar placement of chaplets and sprues on the busts reflects the work of an individual or workshop that had achieved a working method capable of yielding consistent results. However, visible superficial differences do exist. These appear to have been made to wax models prior to casting. For example, bases were added and removed from the wax model; some sculptures were cast as a single unit with the bases and others, like those from the Virginia Museum of Fine Arts, the Speed Museum, and the Golovin Collection, B, were cast in two pieces and the bases were attached with screws. The inscription, done by hand, could be easily traced or effaced on the wax model as desired (figs. 9–10).[23] The manipulation of striations around decorative fields on the cope further suggests that the wax models were constantly reworked. Eyebrows, forehead wrinkles, and other superficial features disappeared from and reappeared in individual busts. Yet in general, the overall workmanship and the type of surface deviations remain comparable on each piece. It is possible that the minor changes were intentionally introduced to create the illusion that each bust had aged separately.

Casting flaws are numerous. Many of these

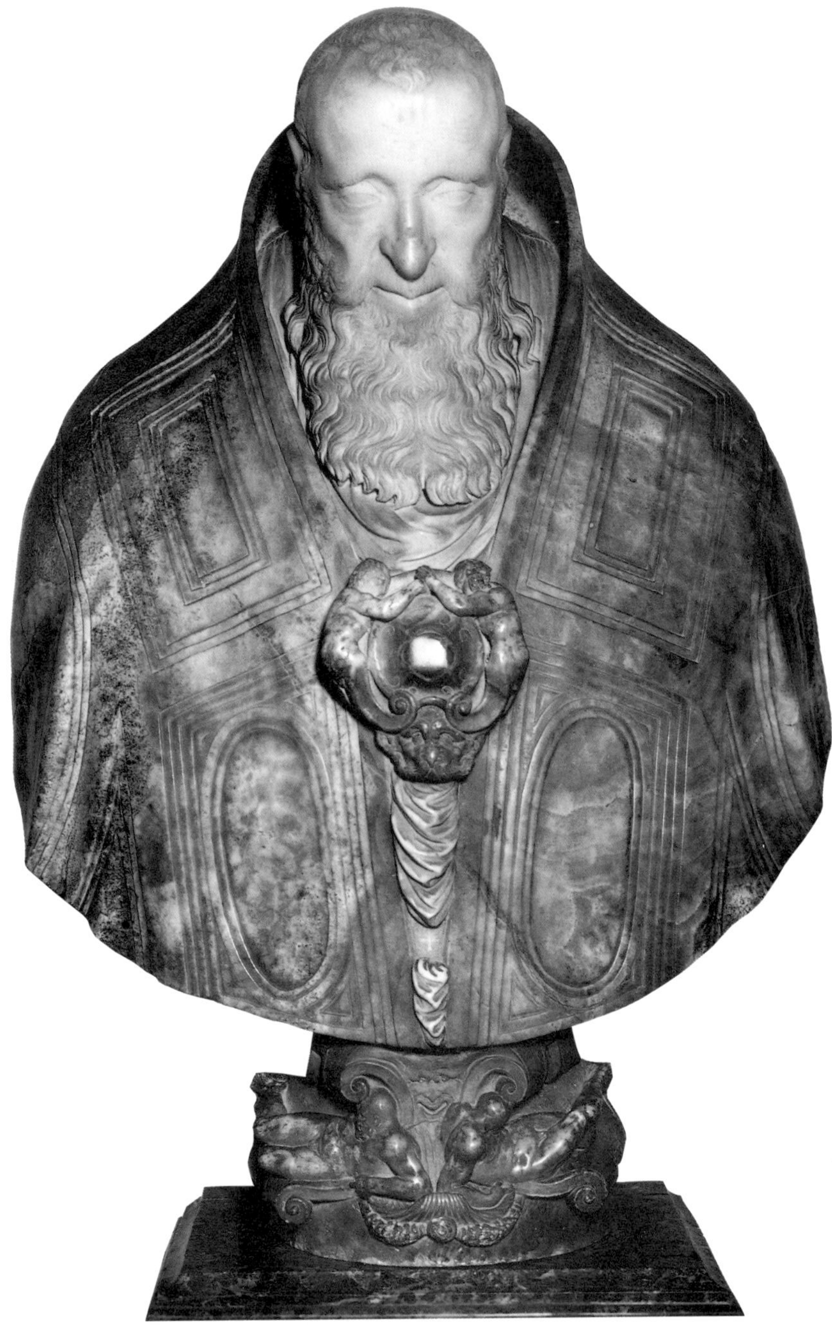

4. Workshop of Guglielmo della Porta, *Pope Paul III Farnese*, c. 1548–1549, marble
Museo Nazionale di Capodimonte, Naples

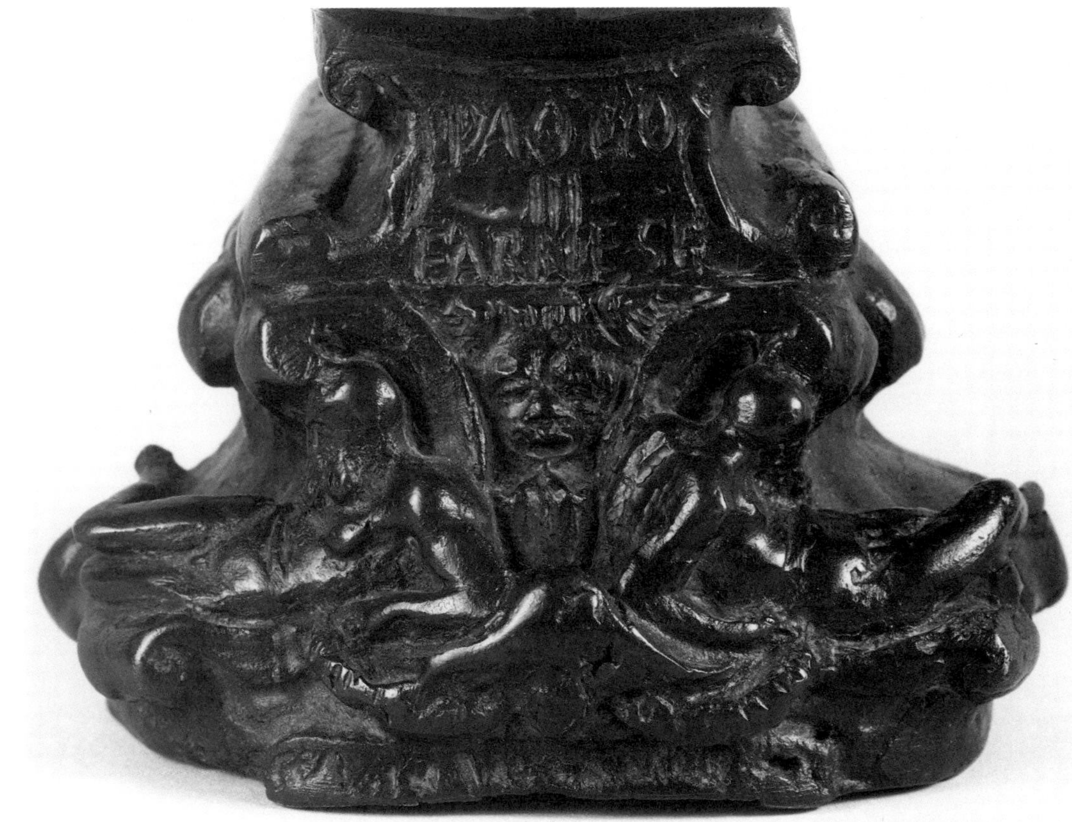

5. Detail, fig. 2, showing the inscription in the base

6. Detail, fig. 2, showing the cope, proper right upper field, containing allegorical scene of Abundance

7. Detail, attributed to Guglielmo della Porta, *Pope Paul III Farnese*, bronze (copper alloy), showing the cope, proper left upper field, containing allegorical scene of Justice
Golovin Collection, B

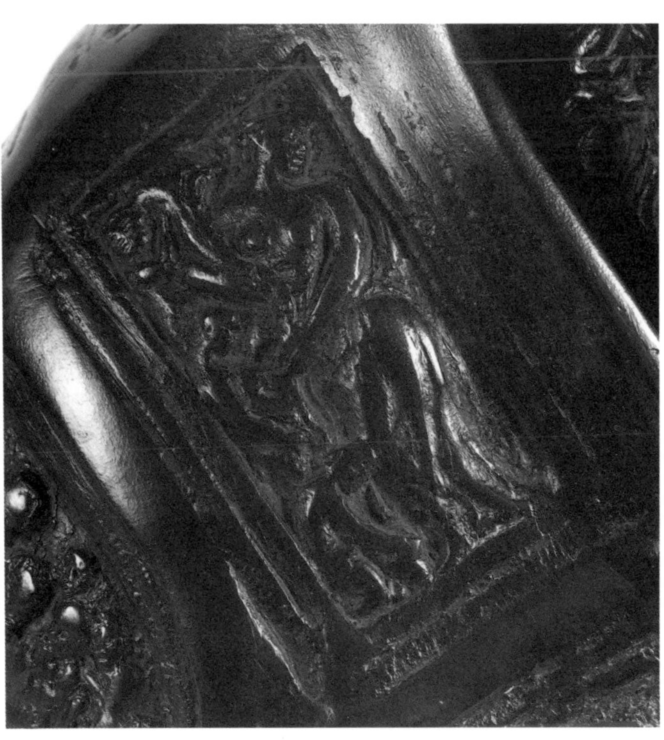

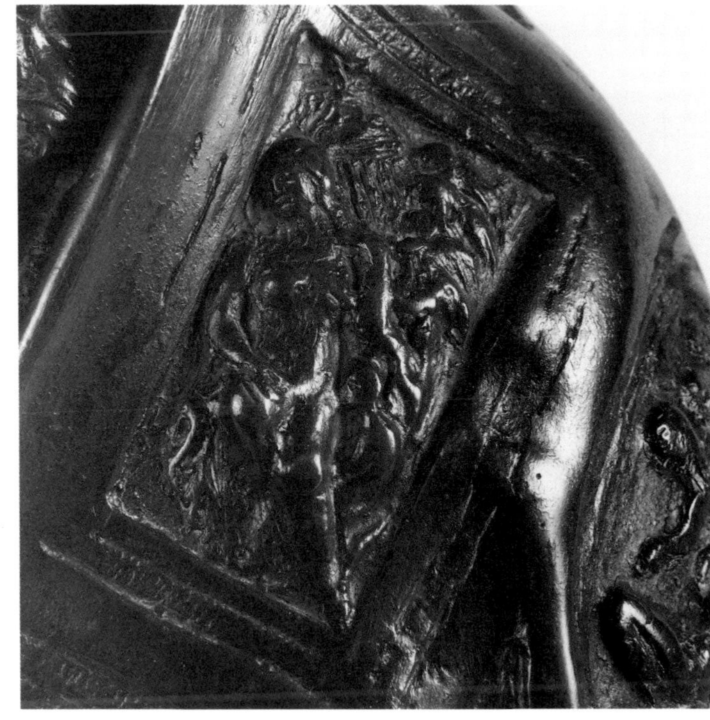

were plugged with wax. In the Sotheby bust, however, a large flaw in the proper left shoulder appeared as a hole. Pitting, the result of gases trapped in the molten metal, is noted repeatedly on all the busts. None of these "flaws" is unusual, although casting imperfections are frequently corrected in the foundries to improve the final appearance of the piece. Furthermore, foundries often repaired large losses with metal rather than wax plugs.

The patination varies significantly from piece to piece. Most surfaces display brushstrokes indicating brush coating, and most display several campaigns of patination, the underlayer being very red-brown in color. Over this, patinas that range from green-brown to black-brown were applied. Patination, or rather repatination, can be applied at any time, and therefore surfaces examined now may not resemble those created at the foundry.[24]

Surface finishing after casting appears negligible. Spherical metal deposits like those on the base of the Golovin B bust, particularly around the river gods, were caused by air bubbles in the mold and were not chased—finished to remove or repair casting flaws. Fins (raised, threadlike bits of metal), resulting from cracks in the mold or where a piece mold was not tightly joined, have not been removed on many busts, specifically along the back of the head of the Golovin B and Speed Museum pieces.

Examination under magnification (16×) confirmed that surface working of all the busts was completed prior to casting. No cold working was noted in any area, including those with sharp incisions such as the hair, beard, or moustache. There were, however, file marks executed on the surface of the busts after casting. These tended to correspond to areas of wear and appeared to have been used to expose a red patina below the darker upper patination (fig. 11). In cases where filing was too rigorous, the bare metal was exposed. Most frequently this occurred on the knees of Justice (proper left upper field), though numerous incidences were observed on all the busts. The fact that the wear was erratic and did not always correspond to areas of highest relief suggests that filing was intentionally employed to create the impression of age and wear. On the Speed Museum piece, for example, the central portion of the proper left ear was much more "weathered" than its outer edge.

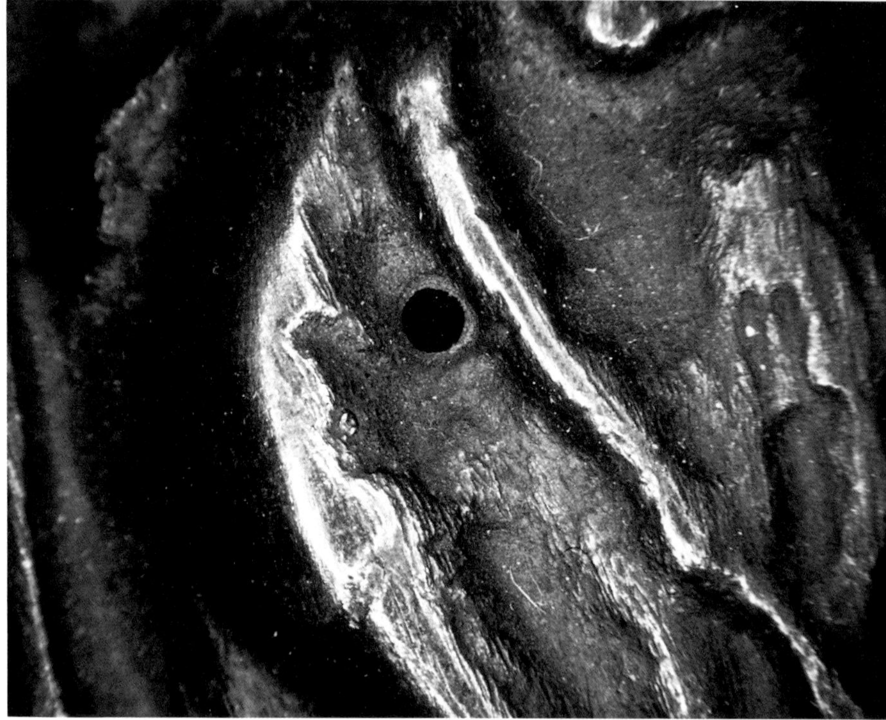

8. Detail, attributed to Guglielmo della Porta, *Pope Paul III Farnese*, bronze (copper alloy), showing the chaplet or core pin hole, proper left lower field
Golovin Collection, A

What is unusual about the manufacture of the small busts when compared to Guglielmo's recorded working method is that they are riddled with flaws. Vasari noted that Guglielmo devised a special casting method so that his seated portrait of Paul III would be as clean as the wax model. Clearly the final appearance of the bronze was important to him:

But doubting, on account of the size of the casting, lest the metal might grow cold and the work therefore not succeed, he placed the metal in the vessel below, in such a way that it might be gradually sucked upwards. And with this unusual method that casting came out very well, and as clean as the wax.[25]

Despite the apparent incongruities between the small busts and Guglielmo's personal preferences, the lost-wax method by which the small busts were cast is very much in accordance with Renaissance casting procedures. Yet their superficial wear is erratic, and the sculptures do not appear to exhibit high-caliber workmanship. These facts do

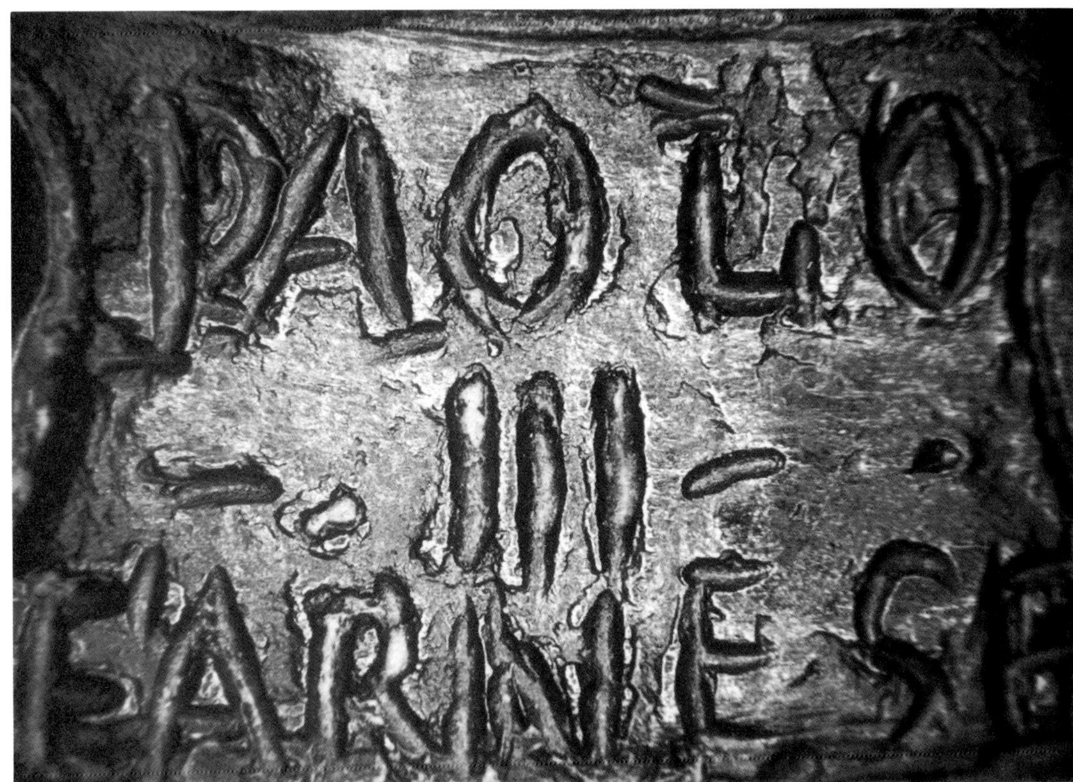

9. Detail, fig. 2, showing the inscription

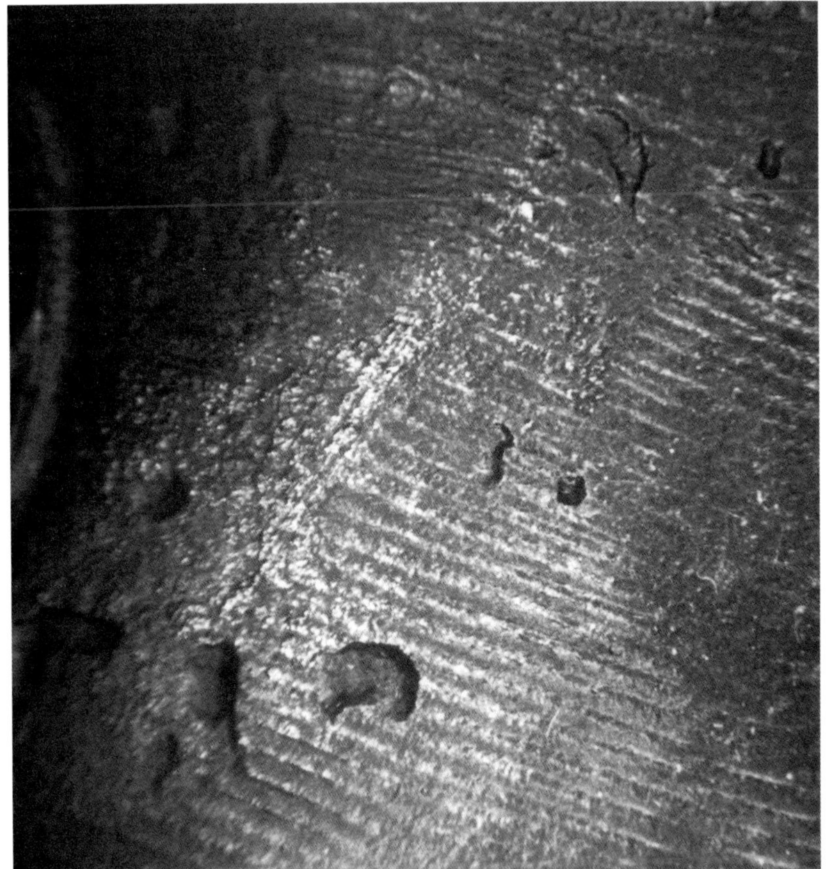

10. Detail, attributed to Guglielmo della Porta, *Pope Paul III Farnese*, bronze (copper alloy), showing the inscription. Note the remnants of the letters "FAR" in the lower left corner as well as file marks overall
Virginia Museum of Fine Arts, Richmond

not preclude their having been made by Guglielmo della Porta, but they certainly raise questions that require closer scrutiny.

Composition

The compositions were analyzed by nondestructive means to further establish whether the busts originated from the same workshop and whether their alloys were comparable to other known Renaissance pieces. If the busts had closely similar alloys, then the assumption could be made that they originated from the same workshop. Likewise, alloy composition can, on occasion, be used to date metal objects, since methods for producing brass or bronze changed with technological advancements. Brass-making techniques in Renaissance Europe could achieve an alloy no more than 28 percent zinc. Consequently the zinc content in a copper alloy can, in some instances, be used to determine the earliest possible date of manufacture.

The busts were analyzed using x-ray fluorescence spectroscopy (XRF).[26] Compositional analysis of the surface revealed that the alloys are high-zinc brasses, with 2–3 percent lead, 1 percent tin (except for the Speed Museum bust, in which tin was not detected), and less than 1 percent each of iron and nickel (except for the Virginia Museum of Fine Arts bust, in which iron was detected at 1 percent). The table presents XRF data in percent composition by weight.

The implications of the metallic composition of the busts can be better understood with background information on the history of metallurgy, particularly as it applies to brass production from the Renaissance to the industrial revolution.

Renaissance Brass Production

In the Renaissance, copper was alloyed with tin or lead to make bronze simply by melting and mixing the metals together. Brass, an alloy of copper and zinc, could not be prepared in this simple way, since zinc boils well below the melting point of copper[27] and oxidizes and evaporates before alloying can occur. Technically bronze is understood to be an alloy of copper and tin with other elements in smaller quantities sometimes present. However, the term "bronze" is commonly used in the museum field to describe sculptures composed of any copper alloy, including brass, an alloy of copper and zinc.[28] The Pope Paul III busts are, in fact, brasses.

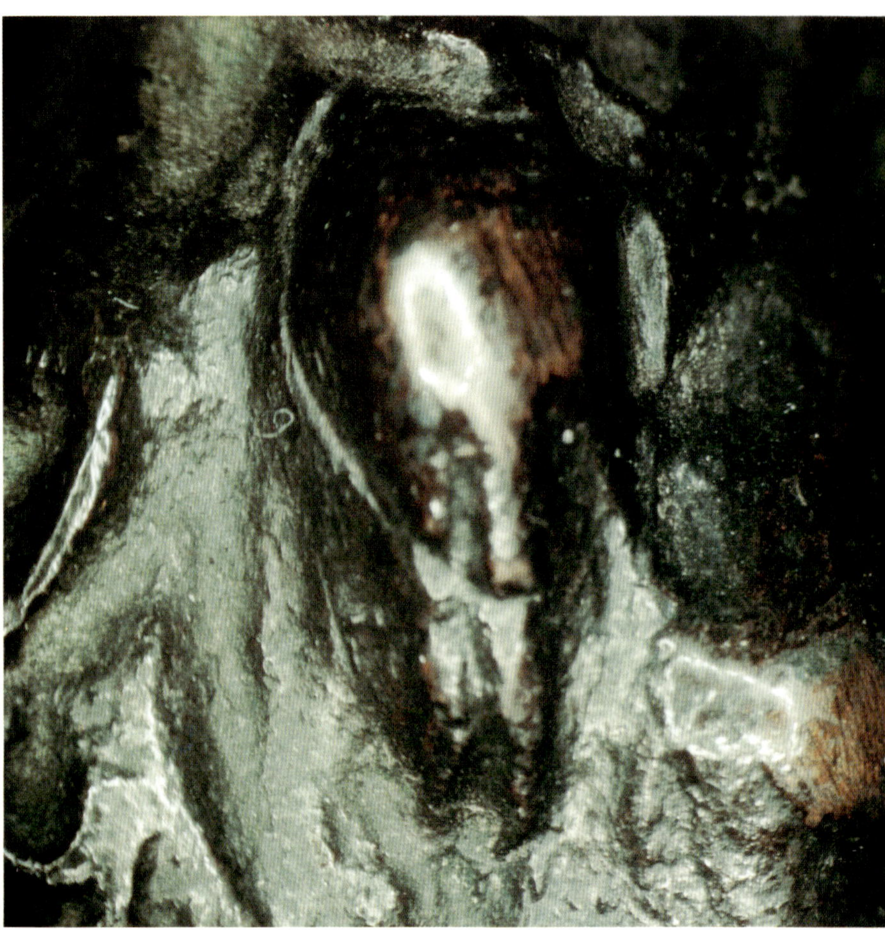

11. Photomicrograph, fig. 7, showing the knees of Justice. Note how the green patina has been intentionally filed to expose the red-brown underlayer.

Percent Composition by Weight of Surface Alloy of Pope Paul III Busts

	Copper (Cu)	*Zinc (Zn)*	*Lead (Pb)*	*Tin (Sn)*	*Iron (Fe)*	*Nickel (Ni)*	*Silver (Ag)*	*Antimony (Sb)*	*Arsenic (As)*
National Gallery of Art	73	24	2	1	0.5	0.2	†	†	†
Willard B. Golovin Collection, A	72	24	2	1	0.5	†	†	†	†
Willard B. Golovin Collection, B	72	23	3	1	0.5	0.1	†	†	†
Herbert F. Johnson Museum	68	28	3	1	0.2	0.1	†	†	†
Virginia Museum of Fine Arts	67	29	2	1	1	0.1	†	†	†
J. B. Speed Art Museum	62	35	2	†	0.2	†	†	†	†
Sotheby's, New York	60	36	2	1	0.3	0.1	†	†	†

† below detectable limit (approximately 500 ppm)

Even though the alloying of copper with zinc was a more complicated process than manufacturing bronze, brass could be made more cheaply than bronze because zinc was more abundant and readily available than tin. The standard method for European brass production from the first century B.C. to the nineteenth century A.D. was the cementation process.[29] As described by Theophilus in the eleventh century, the zinc ore, generally calamine (zinc carbonate), was calcined (oxidized) by placing the ore on wood and roasting it until the ore glowed, thus forming the zinc oxide:

A kind of stone is also found of a yellowish colour, and sometimes red, which is called calamine, which is not broken up, (but as it is dug up it is placed upon wood, heaped up and very glowing, and is burned until it quite glows. This stone, afterwards cooled and broken very small,) is mixed with coals finely divided, and is mingled with the above-mentioned copper in the furnace.[30]

Small fragments of copper were then combined with the calcined zinc ore (zinc oxide) and charcoal, packed into a sealed crucible, and heated to a temperature between 900°C and 1,000°C. This temperature was hot enough to vaporize the zinc but not hot enough to melt the copper. Maintaining this temperature was crucial. Below 917°C the zinc would not vaporize, while above 1,080°C, copper would melt to form a pool of metal at the bottom of the furnace. The sealed crucible prevented most of the zinc vapor from escaping, allowing the zinc to be dissolved into the copper fragments to form brass. After this had been accomplished, the temperature was raised and the molten brass was mixed to make a uniform alloy.[31] This process was also described by Theophilus:

When they are glowing, take calamine [zinc carbonate] . . . very finely ground, with coals, and arrange them in each cup about one sixth part full, and fill it quite with the above-mentioned copper, and cover with coals. . . . And when the copper is altogether melted, take a slender iron, long and curved and fixed to a wooden handle, and carefully stir it, that the calamine may be mixed with the copper.[32]

Laboratory experiments by Otto Werner established that this process resulted in an equilibrium among the zinc oxide, charcoal, and copper and formed a brass with a maximum zinc content of 28 percent.[33] Even when a brass containing 40 percent zinc was used in these experiments, the overall zinc content in the resulting brass was reduced to 28 percent. Generally, the zinc content obtained by this procedure ranged between 22 percent and 28 percent.[34] Temperature, surface area, and the presence of other metals dictated the amount of zinc that could be absorbed by the copper. The closer the temperature was to the melting point of copper, the greater the amount of zinc that could be absorbed. Increasing the surface area of the copper by making the fragments as small as possible also increased the amount of zinc that could be absorbed. Ensuring the use of relatively pure copper was important because the presence of other metals, especially tin and lead, reduced the amount of zinc absorbed. Paul T. Craddock described a simplified formula:[35]

$$\text{theoretic zinc maximum} = 28 \text{ percent} - [(1 \times \text{tin concentration}) + (2 \times \text{lead concentration})]$$

For example, the presence of 2 percent tin would reduce the absorption of zinc in the copper by 2 percent, while the presence of 2 percent lead would reduce the absorption of zinc by 4 percent. Therefore, under optimum conditions, the maximum amount of zinc in a brass produced by the cementation process containing 2 percent tin and 2 percent lead would be 22 percent. It is important to remember that the formation of a pure brass alloy with as much as 28 percent zinc could take place only without the presence of any other elements, for example tin or lead, elements that are present in the busts of Pope Paul III.

Comparison of the brass alloys for each of the busts examined, in relation to copper and maximum zinc concentrations, suggests that the Sotheby and Speed Museum busts, with 36 percent and 35 percent zinc respectively, could not have been produced in the sixteenth century. At first glance, the compositions of the Johnson Museum and Virginia Museum of Fine Arts busts, with zinc contents of 28 percent and 29 percent respectively, appear to have been technically possible. Yet considering that the absorption of zinc in the copper is reduced by the presence of lead and tin, the maximum zinc concentration in the Johnson Museum bust could have been no more than 21 percent and in the Virginia Museum of Fine Arts bust no more than 23 percent. In other words, these alloys contain at least 6–7 percent more zinc than could have been achieved using sixteenth-century Italian alloying practices. These percentages are actually conservative since they refer to brass used directly from the smelters. If, however, the busts had been cast from remelted brass (scrap), then some zinc (approximately 10 percent) would evaporate from the metal with each remelting.[36] The zinc concentration of the National Gallery of Art and both Golovin busts appear to have been technologically possible in the Renaissance. The absence of impurities in the alloy, however, makes them also suspect.

Electrolytic Refining

Even more revealing than the high zinc contents was the absence of impurities in detectable amounts in the busts examined. The presence or absence of impurities within the alloy can also in some instances be used to date metal sculptures. From Theophilus' time until the industrial revolution, metal refining was performed by a process of fire refining, involving oxidation and reduction. This lengthy process consumed a great deal of fuel. Although furnace design improved, the process remained virtually unchanged until the second half of the nineteenth century, when electrolytic refining began to be used for purifying metals. When this process is used for copper refining, an electric current is passed through an acidified copper sulfate solution (electrolyte), causing the unpurified copper to pass into solution at the anode and be deposited as pure copper at the cathode. Impurities such as silver, arsenic, and antimony are left behind in the sludge.

Charles Watt, in his patent dated 1851,[37] first suggested the use of electricity to refine copper. The first person to carry out Watt's process of electrolytic copper refining on an industrial scale was James Elkington of the Birmingham firm of electroplaters. He patented his method in 1865 and 1869. In 1869, he founded the first electrolytic copper refining facility at Pembrey in South Wales.[38]

The principal demand for copper at this time came from the expanding electrical industries, which used copper wire as a conducting material. Even minute impurities in the copper would increase the resistance of the copper wire and reduce its conducting power. The older process of fire refining, if carried out very carefully, could achieve a copper purity of 99.25 percent.[39] Early electrolytic refining resulted in a copper purity of 99.96 percent. The remaining .04 percent generally consisted of a combination of arsenic, antimony, and silver.[40]

The absence of these impurities in detectable amounts in the brass alloys for each of the busts examined suggests the use of electrolytic refining of the metal. This conclusion implies that all the busts postdate 1869.

CONCLUSION

This study was undertaken to answer several questions and define the facture of the small sculptures in relation to one another. Visual examination reveals that all seven busts were cast by the traditional lost-wax method, that they appear to originate from the same source, and that their metallic compositions are similar. Furthermore, the manufacturing techniques are consistent on all seven busts. There is no evidence of cold working to reinforce surface details; and basic casting flaws such as excess metal deposits, fins, and large losses were left untouched. The presence of these flaws is at variance with Vasari's account, which suggests that Guglielmo della Porta was concerned with the final appearance of a cast sculpture. Cold working does appear in the form of file marks and coincides with areas of wear, indicating it was intentionally employed to create the appearance of aged, worn surfaces.

Likewise, the relationship of the busts to Renaissance bronze sculptural practices is aberrant. The compositions are inconsistent with those achievable using sixteenth-century Italian metallurgy. The high zinc content of most of the busts would have been technologically impossible to achieve in Europe until the early nineteenth century. In addition, impurities generally found in Renaissance bronzes were not detected in any of the seven busts examined. These impurities could not have been removed until the advent of electrolytic refining in 1869. From the assembled evidence, it is apparent that this series of portraits did not originate in Guglielmo della Porta's workshop or in any sixteenth-century European workshop.

NOTES

The authors are grateful to the institutions and individuals for their generous loans of the objects that made this study possible. They are the Herbert F. Johnson Museum, Cornell University; the Virginia Museum of Fine Arts; Willard B. Golovin; the J. B. Speed Art Museum; and Sotheby's, New York. We are indebted to Douglas Lewis, curator of sculpture, National Gallery of Art, who initiated this study and arranged the loan of these pieces. Thanks are also due to other National Gallery staff, including Barbara Berrie, conservation scientist; E. René de la Rie, head of the scientific research department; Suzannah Fabing, managing curator of records and loans; and Janice Gruver, editor for the conservation division, for reviewing our manuscript. Philip Charles, photographer, kindly photographed the sculpture many times. Susanna P. Griswold, conservator of paintings, assisted with the translation of articles from German. In addition, we should like to acknowledge Janet Snyder from the Freer Gallery of Art, Smithsonian Institution, for her atomic absorption analyses and Paul Craddock from the British Museum research laboratory, for taking the time to discuss the compositional results of the busts. Finally, we are indebted to Shelley Sturman, head of objects conservation, and Alison Luchs, associate curator of sculpture, both at the National Gallery, for their unflagging encouragement and support throughout this endeavor.

1. The busts assembled for study included (in the order shown in fig. 1) Herbert F. Johnson Museum of Art (1967.26); Cornell University, Ithaca, New York; Virginia Museum of Fine Arts (1986.163), Richmond; Sotheby's, New York (22 June 1989, lot 95); Willard B. Golovin Collection, A and B; J. B. Speed Art Museum (1968.33), Louisville, Kentucky; and National Gallery of Art (1975.6.1), Washington. All are 29–31 cm high and 20 cm wide. In addition to the seven works illustrated in figure 1, two similar busts exist in the Museum für Kunst und Gewerbe, Hamburg, and Muzeum Narodowe Warszawie, Warsaw, but were not available for comparison.

2. A series of small bronze portraits of Marie de' Medici and Henri IV, c. 24–25 cm high, by the French sculptor Barthélemy Prieur, which date to approximately 1600, are perhaps the earliest known examples. See, for instance, Meribell M. Parsons, *Sculpture from the David Daniels Collection* [exh. cat., Minneapolis Institute of Arts] (Minneapolis, 1979), 40–43.

3. The Warsaw piece was donated to the museum in 1936. Dariusz Kaczmarzyk, "Portrait de Paul III Farnese–Un Bozzetto di Guglielmo della Porta," *Bulletin du Musée National de Varsovie* 2, no. 3 (1961), 85, mentions that the will of the donor, Monsignor Adolf Jelowicki, bishop of Lublin, refers to the bust as "un bronze de l'ancienne collection bien connue" but does not identify the collection. She proposes that Jelowicki might have acquired it as early as 1886, when he traveled to Italy after completing his studies. But this early journey would presumably not have been the only trip to Italy that contributed to his eventual collection of some three hundred objects.

4. Werner Gramberg, "Die Hamburger Bronzebüste Paul III Farnese von Guglielmo della Porta," in *Festschrift für Erich Meyer zum Sechzigsten Geburtstag* (Hamburg, 1957), 160–172.

5. Giorgio Vasari, *Lives of the Most Eminent Painters, Sculptors and Architects* (1511–1574), trans. Gaston Du C. Vere, 10 vols. (London, 1912–1915), 9:234.

6. John Pope-Hennessy, *Italian High Renaissance and Baroque Sculpture* (New York, 1986), 396. For a detailed bibliography on Guglielmo della Porta, see 397, 462.

7. Pope-Hennessy 1986, 88.

8. Vasari 1912–1915, 9:235.

9. Vasari 1912–1915, 9:237.

10. Pope-Hennessy 1986, 396.

11. Gramberg 1957, 160, mentions that the workshop piece has an alabaster *Bruststück* (breast piece). Kaczmarzyk 1961, 89, says that both busts in the Museo Nazionale di Capodimonte, Naples, are partially marble and partially alabaster, as does Aldo de Rinaldis, *Pinacoteca del Museo Nazionale di Napoli* (Naples, 1911), 556. A marble head of Paul III (10517), attributed to Guglielmo, probably intended to form part of a bust, is also in the Capodimonte.

12. Kaczmarzyk 1961, 85. She also proposes (95) that the Hamburg bust is a replica from a mold of the Warsaw piece, worked up in greater detail. Its higher degree of finish probably results from the difference in the final working of the wax model prior to casting. The seven busts we examined exhibit the same range of differences.

13. Gramberg 1957, 164.

14. Caroline Elam, editor of the *Burlington Magazine*, personal communication, 21 August 1990.

15. Gramberg 1957, 167. Pope Paul III chartered the Jesuit Order (1540), established the Tribunal of the Inquisition (1543), and convened the Council of Trent (1544). Counter-Reformation references are prolific on his portraits. For a detailed discussion of Paul III and the iconography related to his ideology, see Fredrika H. Jacobs, "Studies in the Patronage and Iconography of Pope Paul III (1534–1549)" (Ph.D. diss., University of Virginia, 1979).

16. Gramberg 1957, 170–171. Two other small bronze portrait busts of the Farnese family members with bases identical to those of the small bronze busts under study were analyzed about the same time. The two busts, one of Marguerite of Austria (private collection), and the other of Ottavio Farnese (private collection), were similar in size, subject matter, and alloy composition.

17. Benvenuto Cellini, *The Treatises of Benvenuto Cellini on Goldsmithing and Sculpture* (1568), ed. C. R. Ashbee (London, 1898), 111–112.

18. Cellini 1898, 118.

19. Cellini 1898, 118.

20. Vannoccio Biringuccio, *The Pirotechnia of Vannoccio Biringuccio*, ed. Derek Price (New York, 1959), 376.

21. Cyril Stanley Smith, "The Early History of Casting, Molds and the Science of Solidification," in Smith, *A Search for Structure* (Cambridge, Mass., 1981), 147. A date for the origins of this technique has yet to be established; Richard E. Stone, "Antico and the Development of Bronze Casting in Italy at the End of the Quattrocento," *Metropolitan Museum Journal* 16 (1982), 105, noted that Antico used slush casting for some of his sculptures.

22. JCPDS, *Powder Diffraction File Search Manual* (Swarthmore, Pa., 1982). The presence of gypsum cannot be used to date the objects since its use as an investment material is not unique to the Renaissance; in fact, it is still used today. If a larger sample of the core material were available, the sample might have been dated using thermoluminescence. The analyses were performed on a Philips x-ray generator (XRG) 3100 equipped with copper target and nickel filter to provide Cu Kα radiation, 45 kV anode voltage, and 25 mA current. Exposure time ranged from four to six hours.

23. The inscriptions on the busts from the Virginia Museum of Fine Arts and the Golovin Collection, B, are effaced. All the others are legible.

24. Richard Hughes and Michael Rowe, *The Colouring, Bronzing and Patination of Metals* (London, 1986). It is virtually impossible to identify the materials employed for patination, especially when a surface has been chemically patinated. Chemical patinations are frequently applied with heat and fuse with the metal substrate. They cannot, therefore, be isolated from the substrate for identification purposes.

25. Vasari 1912–1915, 9:235.

26. The analyses were performed on a Kevex 0750A energy dispersive XRF spectrometer equipped with a $BaCl_2$ secondary target, 6 mm collimators, 60 kV anode voltage, and 0.4 mA anode current. Several areas were investigated from each of the seven busts. Kevex XRF Quantex-Ray Software, using the EXACT fundamental parameters program provided by Kevex Corporation, was used for calculating the elemental surface composition. It should be emphasized that this particular technique analyzes only the uppermost surface (up to 100 microns), and bulk values may vary considerably. To confirm the bulk values, a sample was removed from the interior of the National Gallery of Art bust and examined by Janet Snyder, Freer Gallery of Art, Smithsonian Institution, Washington, using atomic absorption spectroscopy (AA). The surface was determined to be of virtually the same composition as the bulk values. The copper, zinc, tin, and lead values obtained using AA were within 1 percent of the XRF values. The elements less than 1 percent were within 40 percent.

27. Zinc boils at 905°C. Copper melts at 1,080°C.

28. Eugene Farrell, "Non-Destructive Instrumental Analysis of Medals," *Studies in the History of Art* 21 (1987), 35–43.

29. Ronald F. Tylecote, *A History of Metallurgy* (London, 1976), 96.

30. Theophilus, *An Essay upon Various Arts in Three Books by Theophilus* (11th century), trans. Robert Hendrie (London, 1847), bk. 3, 307.

31. Paul T. Craddock, "The Composition of the Copper Alloys Used by Greek, Etruscan and Roman Civilizations: The Origins and Early Use of Brass," *Journal of Archaeological Science* 5 (1978), 9.

32. Theophilus 1847, bk. 3, 311.

33. Otto Werner, "Über das Vorkommen von Zink und Messing im Altertum und im Mittelalter," *Erzmetall* 23 (1970), 259–269.

34. Craddock 1978, 13. A few postmedieval brasses have been reported to have up to 33 percent zinc. See H. K. Cameron, "Technical Aspects of Medieval Monumental Brasses," *Archaeological Journal* 131 (1974), 215–237. The accuracy of these numbers cannot be evaluated since no information regarding the method of analysis on these objects was reported. Assuming these analyses were indeed performed on authentic pieces and the zinc values reported are accurate, then it may have been possible to achieve a zinc concentration as high as 33 percent. Even if the zinc content could have reached 33 percent, the fact that the absorption of zinc in the copper is reduced by the presence of lead and tin indicates that the zinc content in the majority of the busts under examination still appears too high to have been achieved in the Renaissance.

35. Paul T. Craddock, "Medieval Copper Alloy Production and West African Bronze Analyses," pt. 1, *Archaeometry* 27, no. 1 (1985), 23–25.

36. Craddock 1978, 12.

37. John Kershaw, *Electrometallurgy* (New York, 1908), 101. No industrial development resulted from this patent for more than a decade, since electric currents could not be obtained in sufficient quantities to perform metallurgical refining until the development of the dynamo, an early generator.

38. Kershaw 1908, 101.

39. Tylecote 1976, 151.

40. Kershaw 1908, 117.

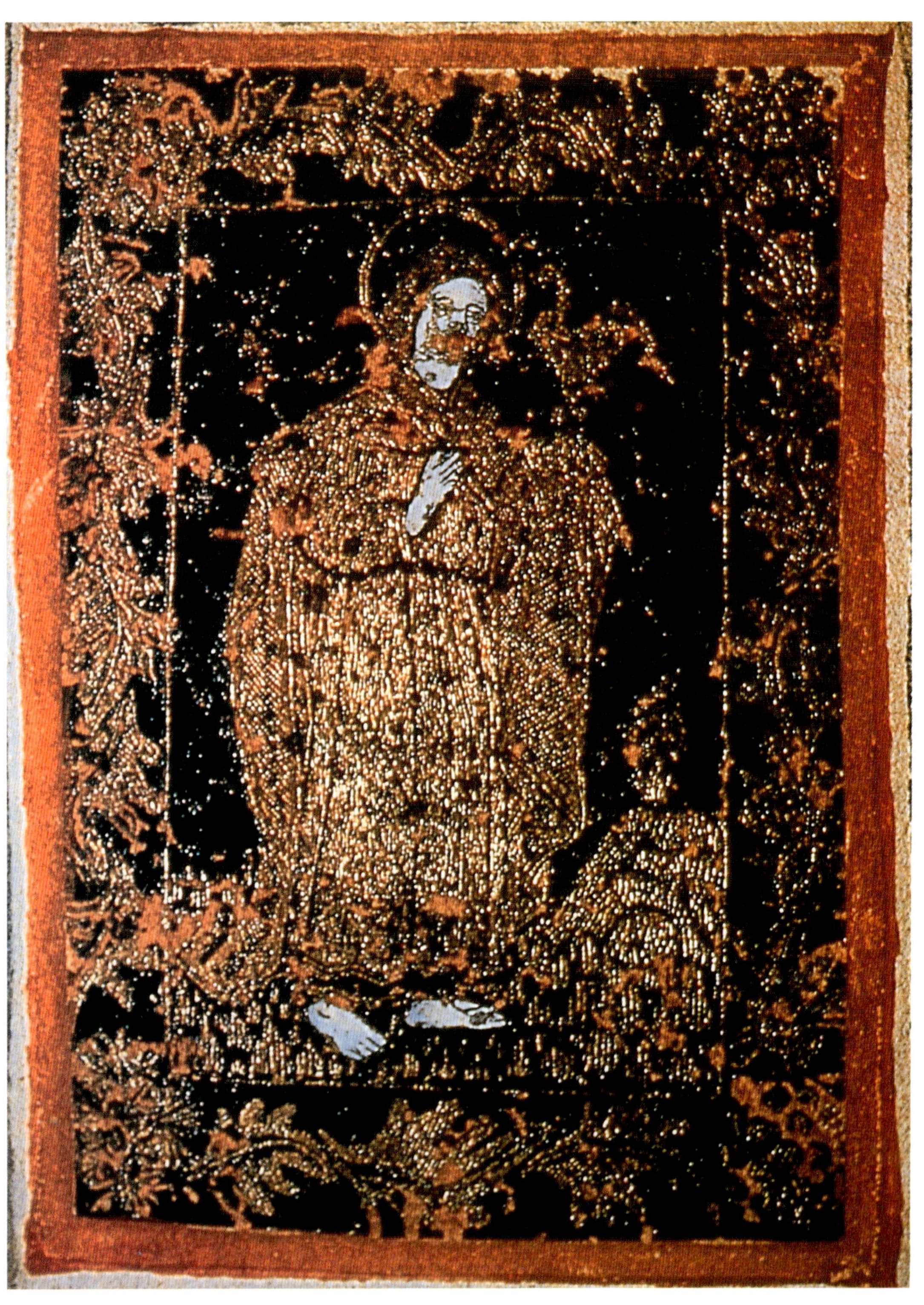

I. *Saint John the Evangelist*, pasteprint
Staatliche Graphische Sammlung, Munich

SARAH BERTALAN

Medieval Pasteprints in the National Gallery of Art

Medieval pasteprints have long been the subject of inquiry and controversy. The major issues regarding these tiny, fragile reliefs—their damaged appearance, their composition, the problematic relationship with identical but reversed images printed on paper, and the questions regarding technique—seem to have generated new theories whenever print curators and cataloguers encountered them in the great print collections. As a result, most of the literature offers a thoroughly confusing picture to even the most attentive reader.

Most pasteprints have been found affixed to the covers of fifteenth-century handwritten codices, many with provenances traced firmly to some of the great medieval monastery libraries in Germany. Some of their compositions reflect those of printmakers active in Germany in the latter half of the fifteenth century, such as the Master E. S. or the Master of the Dutuit Mount of Olives. Thus, pasteprint making is generally considered to have taken place in southern Germany in the latter half of the fifteenth century. Catalogued early in this century by Wilhelm L. Schreiber, approximately 195 are known to exist, most still housed inside the book covers that have preserved them.[1]

No record of pasteprint technique has survived and very little is known about their production. One important clue to their method is the fact that some pasteprint images also exist as prints on paper. In each matching set, the pasteprint represents an identical but reversed image of the print. It is therefore likely that pasteprints were made using an intermediate cast from the matrix used to print the image on paper. The practices of casting and stamping from dies were well developed in medieval workshops, and their application produced not only the odd and fragile pasteprint but the world-changing invention of movable type at about the same time. Rather than viewing pasteprints as curios of print collections, it is appropriate to consider them in the context of the widespread experimentation and lively technical exchange made possible by itinerant craftsmen in the latter half of the fifteenth century.

The most comprehensive study of pasteprints to date is *Pasteprints: A Technical and Art Historical Investigation* (1986) by Elizabeth Coombs, Eugene Farrell, and Richard S. Field. In this publication, the materials of three pasteprints in the Harvard University Art Museums have been fully identified, the appearance of pasteprints has been incontrovertibly explained, and great strides have been made in understanding these rare objects in the context of fifteenth-century religious life.[2] The present study has taken the exhaustive technical analysis conducted by Coombs and Farrell as a point of departure and has relied upon Field's connoisseurship for the history of pasteprint scholarship and sources in the related areas of medieval piety and popular culture.

The group of pasteprints at the National Gallery of Art, gathered by Lessing J. Rosenwald, afforded an opportunity to scrutinize many more examples. Only limited nondestructive analysis and sampling were used in this study, and the results concurred with those published by Coombs and Farrell. However, new information has been gained regarding the questions of composition and technique. Most of the National Gallery of Art pasteprints and the eighty-one examined in other collections (see app. 1) are in relatively good condition and more informative than the Harvard University Art Museums' examples. The preparation of cross sections, a method often used to reveal the layer structure of paintings, was applied to pasteprints for the first time in this study. The cross sections taken of two pasteprints in the National Gallery of Art collection demonstrate a simpler structure than that proposed by Coombs and Farrell, one that is consistent in all the National Gallery of Art examples and those examined in other collections. Finally, mock-ups were executed that convincingly recreate the appearance of the originals. It is hoped that the present study will add to the understanding of these unusual documents of fifteenth-century conception.

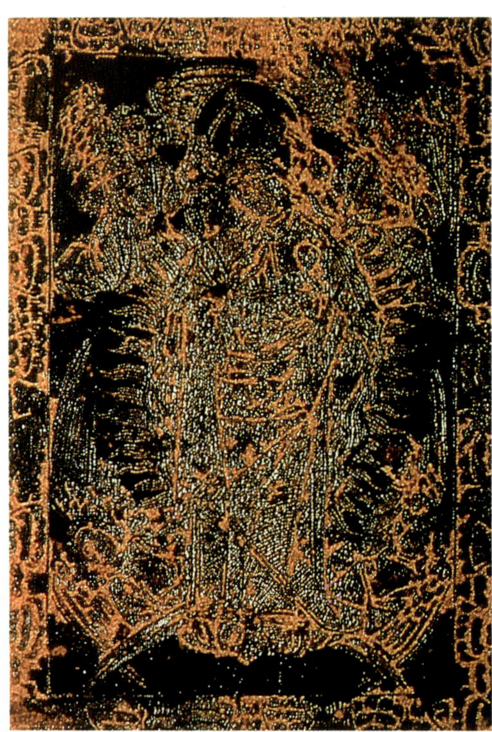

2. *Madonna in Glory with Four Angels*, pasteprint
Germanisches Nationalmuseum, Nuremberg

APPEARANCE

Now darkened and damaged, the pasteprints we see are woefully unlike their original state. The best-preserved examples, *Saint John the Evangelist* (S2850) in the Staatliche Graphische Sammlung, Munich, and *Madonna in Glory with Four Angels* (S2827) in the print room of the Germanisches Nationalmuseum, Nuremberg, attest to their intended appearance as precious objects in which the contrast of black and gold created a glittery image (figs. 1–2). In fact, as suggested by several authors and as Coombs and Farrell have shown, the original pasteprint was a composite of metal foil, ink, and varnish. The foil was shaped by molding to the contours of a matrix, probably a metal plate, creating an image in relief. The metal relief surface was decorated with ink and toned glazes and, occasionally, with detailing in paint. The images were readable because the raised relief lines of the foil surface were inked (black) while the (sunken) recesses of the foil surface were uninked and toned with glazes that made the metal appear gold.

Pasteprints generally depict saints and other religious subjects. The images originally read clearly due to the contrast of black-inked lines against a gold-colored ground as described above. However, physical damage caused by compression of the relief surface, chemical deterioration of the inherently incompatible materials, and the effects of high humidity have altered their appearance. Because of their condition and without the benefit of analysis, the speculation that they were composed of brown paste appeared early in the literature, hence their name.

Good examples are indeed rare. Most surviving pasteprints exhibit the confusing problem we see in one of the best-known examples, *Christ Crucified between Two Thieves* (S2791), in the collection of the Guildhall Library, London (fig. 3). The image is a negative one, that is, the principal lines are light (blank paper) against a gray-brown layer that many authors have described as

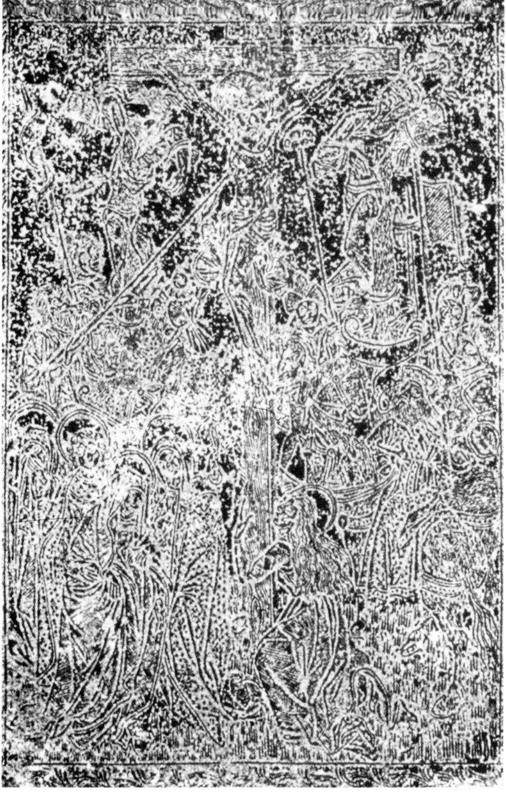

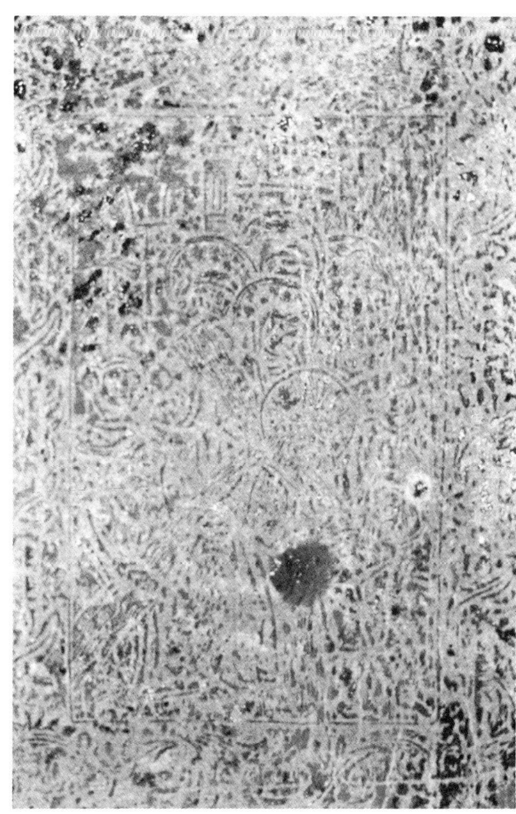

3. *Christ Crucified between Two Thieves*, pasteprint
Guildhall Library, City of London, Willshire Collection

4. *Christ Carrying the Cross*, pasteprint
National Gallery of Art, Washington, Lessing J. Rosenwald Collection

paste. The problematic negative image was formerly interpreted as a deliberate feature of pasteprints, and in the past several scholars, unaware of well-preserved examples, were prompted to propose that the "paste" was displaced by the action of printing, producing a white-line image.[3] Only a few authors understood that this puzzling phenomenon was the result of deterioration, and the most considered solution was offered by Coombs, Farrell, and Field in 1986. During the printing process, raised portions of the printing plate compressed the "paste" and enhanced adhesion to the paper support. Although originally gold or silver in color, the layer has oxidized to gray-brown, a reversal of the original appearance. Those lines that now appear as bare paper were originally inked passages, which appeared dark against the gold layer. The lines were raised and therefore vulnerable to loss, ultimately revealing the paper beneath.[4]

Looking at an example in the National Gallery of Art that is in poor condition, *Christ Carrying the Cross* (S2788, variant) (fig. 4), we can perhaps understand scholars' earlier misinterpretations of pasteprint composition. Virtually nothing is left of the artifact, and the bright orange tone may easily be interpreted as the residue of a paste that has stained the paper substrate. The National Gallery of Art also possesses examples that are only partially deteriorated and therefore clearly illustrate the fact that the light areas of worn pasteprints were formerly in relief. Such raised lines of embossed tin are well preserved in an image of *Saint George and the Dragon* (S2845a) (fig. 5). Under magnification, the surviving relief of the saint's face, his sword, the decorative emblems of his armor, and the wings and limbs of the dragon are readily visible. They are best read by examining the contours of the face and the lines forming the nose, mouth, proper left eye, and chin, which are still intact (fig. 6). Also visible in this detail is the contrasting color of the raised lines against the yellow pigmentation in the recessed areas. The losses in the relief are apparent as well; for example, the line delineating the proper left eye and nose suddenly breaks off, exposing what is clearly the paper substrate. Similarly, the line of the saint's helmet has disappeared. Where the relief has broken away, not only the thin raised line but a significantly wider area of the pasteprint structure is lost as well.

COMPOSITION AND LAYERED STRUCTURE

Authors have generally guessed about pasteprint composition without the benefit of magnification and analysis. The layered structure of pasteprints has been described as a brown paste of bird lime and glue, bone glue with egg white and tin foil, and, according to one author, black bread dough.[5] Additional confusion is due to their name. In fact, pasteprints are not made by typical printmaking techniques, nor is paste an ingredient in their composition. The misnomer can be traced to Johann D. Passavant, who in 1864 described several relief impressions, which he called *empreintes en pâte* (impressions in paste). He used the term to distinguish these objects from sulfur casts or niello, convinced that they could not be composed of metal because attempts to remove several examples from book covers using water had completely dissolved the impressions. He speculated that a colored mixture with the consistency of paste was used to fill the engraved lines of a heated metal plate. The plate was then printed on paper that was prepared with a yellow ground, and parts of the paste mixture melted, producing stains on the paper. This misleading explanation was corrected only many years later using analytical techniques available in the conservation field.[6]

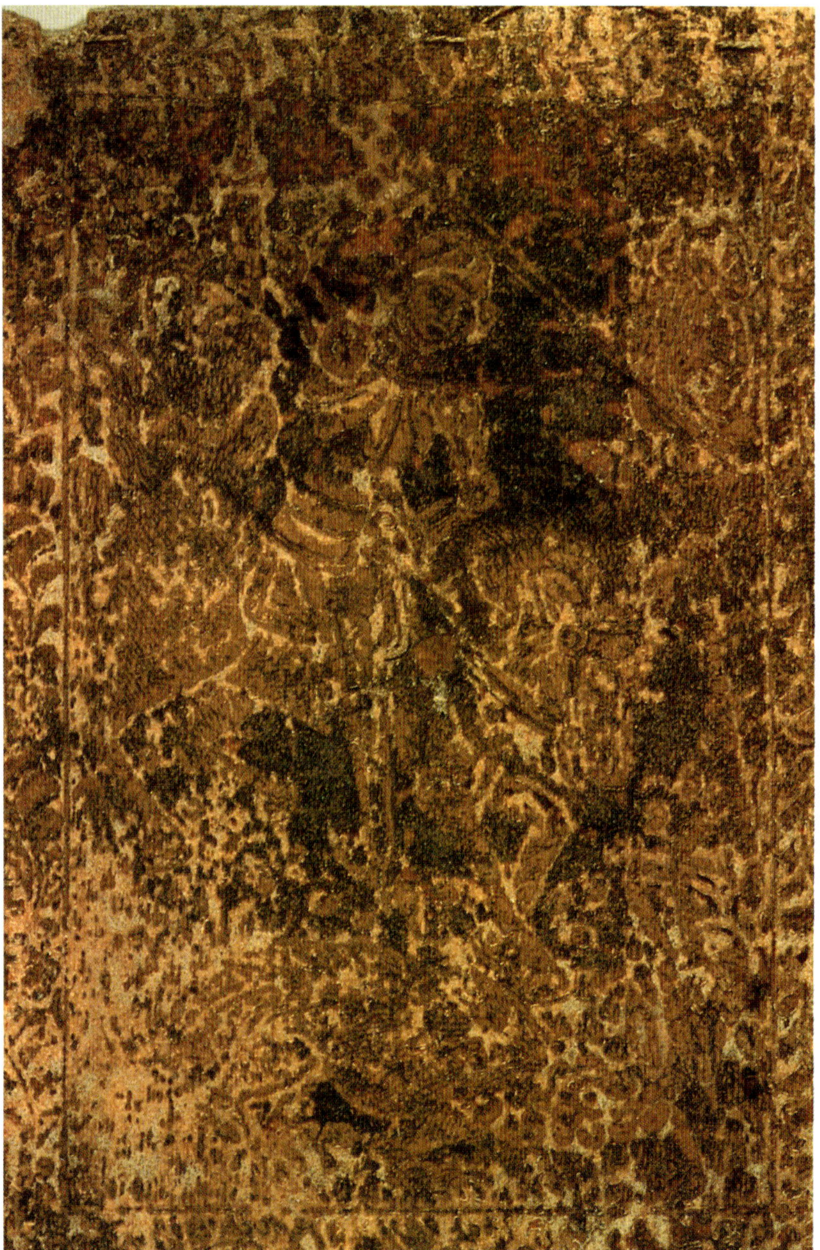

5. *Saint George and the Dragon*, pasteprint
National Gallery of Art, Washington, Lessing J. Rosenwald Collection

In 1942, Rutherford Gettens offered a clue to pasteprint composition when he analyzed four examples then in the private collection of Lessing J. Rosenwald using x-ray diffraction (XRD) and microchemical testing. He examined *Saint Catherine* (not catalogued by Schreiber), *Saint John the Baptist* (S2850m), *Madonna and Child* (S2824c), and *Madonna and Child* (S2825). Based on his analyses, Gettens described the structure of all four pasteprints as a vegetable gum sizing layer over the paper substrate, a principal layer of tin sulfate, an orange or brownish layer of resin over the tin, and an ink layer. He postulated that the tin sulfate was an oxidation product of tin foil or stannous sulfide, a substance known to have been used during the Middle Ages to imitate gold.[7] Gettens was the first to clarify that the so-called paste was actually a complex layered structure, thereby linking pasteprints to the general use of tin as a less precious replacement for gold in medieval workshops. His mention of a size layer is misleading, however. As we have seen on better-preserved examples, there is no evi-

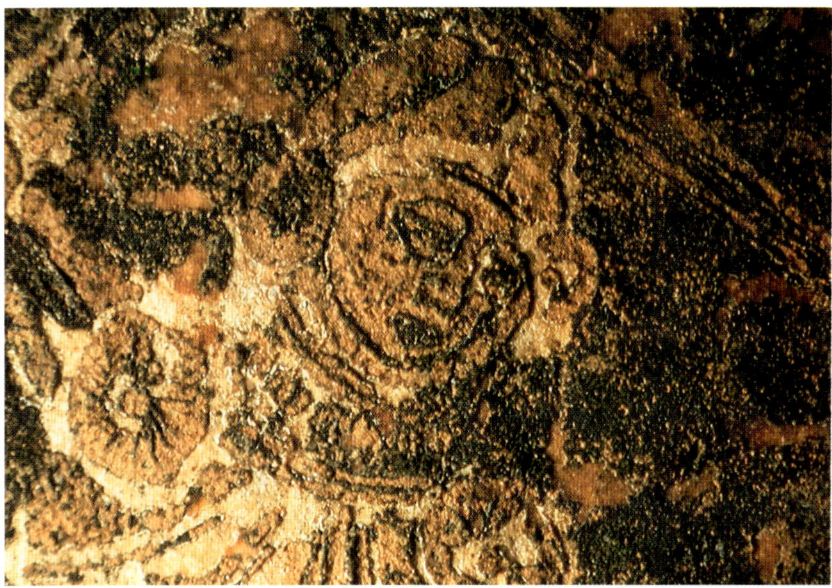

6. Detail, fig. 5, showing face, shoulders, and sword of Saint George

dence of a separate sizing or adhesive layer; rather a single resin layer both reinforces the foil relief by filling gaps where the foil is not in direct contact with the paper and adheres the foil to the paper support.

Gettens' analyses were cited in 1985 by Cynthia Bowman, who drew attention to the similarities between the materials he identified and those used to create the imitation brocades found on fifteenth-century German sculpture. Bowman's note was based on studies made by German conservators who sought to recreate the fragile pressed brocades using instructions outlined in the *Liber Illuministarius*, a fifteenth-century artists' recipe book from the Benedictine abbey at Tegernsee. Bowman likened the composite structure of pasteprints to that used in the fifteenth century to create relief on sculpture using a mordant layer, tin foil, gold leaf or silver twist, and paint.[8] The like materials demonstrate the widespread use of tin in medieval workshops to imitate gold. Her citing of the Tegernsee manual is intriguing because many pasteprints have survived from this monastery. She conducted no additional analysis, however, and referred to some unrelated medieval recipes for "paste" mixtures, so that, rather than clarifying the misunderstandings already stated in the literature, the nature of the "paste" was further confused.

In the most recent study of pasteprints, Coombs and Farrell carried out extensive analysis on three pasteprints in the collection of the Harvard University Art Museums. They identified the lower pasteprint layer as an oil-resin varnish because of its insolubility in cold and warm water, reactivity to a test for resin acids, and violent positive reaction to a test for saponifiable oils. The red lead pigment in the varnish was identified by x-ray fluorescence. Coombs and Farrell concluded that the layer was an oil-resin varnish containing red lead, used either to color the varnish or to enhance drying. The next layer, a fine white powder, was identified as tin oxide using scanning electron microscopy (SEM) and x-ray diffraction. The authors considered this a deterioration product of an original tin leaf layer. They attributed this deterioration to contact with layers of acidic varnish and conducted experiments exposing tin foil to glacial acetic acid vapors, identifying the resulting white powder as tin oxide. A second layer of varnish appeared to be identical to the first. Next, a gray-brown layer was found to be tin foil coated with an organic yellow glaze. The glaze was analyzed with inconclusive results. Based on Auger spectroscopy, the authors ruled out egg or animal glue as media because of the absence of nitrogen but were unable to identify the coloring substance. The foil layer was identified, using x-ray diffraction, as beta tin. The black

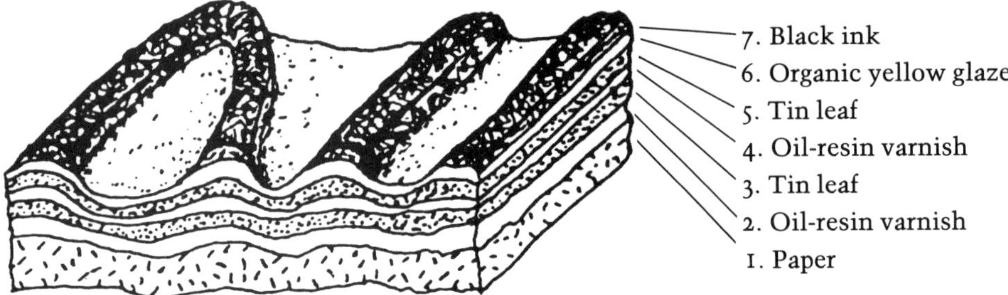

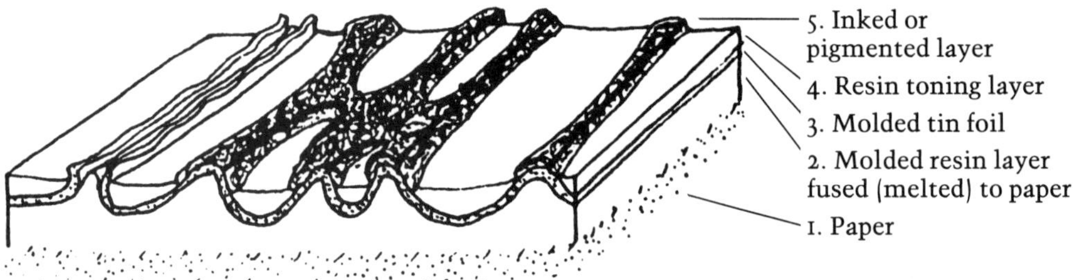

7. Cross section of a pasteprint of the type observed in the Harvard University Art Museums
From Elizabeth Coombs, Eugene Farrell, and Richard S. Field, *Pasteprints: A Technical and Art Historical Investigation* (Cambridge, Mass., 1986), 4.
Courtesy of the Center for Conservation and Technical Studies, Harvard University Art Museums

8. Cross section of pasteprint layer structure observed in the present study
Drawing by author

ink was analyzed using SEM and energy-dispersive x-ray fluorescence (EDX). No calcium or phosphorus was detected, ruling out bone black. Under magnification, a distinction could not be made. The authors relied on Gettens' microchemical tests and identified this layer as printing ink.[9] Based on the evidence of the three examples, the authors described a layered structure as diagrammed in figure 7.

Observations of the structure of nearly one hundred pasteprints examined for this study differ from the findings of Coombs, Farrell, and Field. There was no evidence of two layers of tin foil in any of them. Moreover, cross sections taken from two pasteprints in the National Gallery of Art follow the structure diagrammed in figure 8.

The first layer in figure 8 is paper, followed by a layer of resin that varies in thickness, confirming the relief of the foil layer. Under magnification the granular nature of this layer—an amalgam of resin, red lead, and other pigment particles—is evident. A stain caused by the application of the resin to the paper is also present. The stain is usually buff or orange in tone, depending on the color of the resin.

The third layer is deteriorated tin foil. This layer is present in all examples. In many areas it appears as a gray-brown layer, but in some places it appears to be composed of a fluffy white powder. This variation suggests that in some places the tin foil has turned completely to tin oxide powder, while in others it has deteriorated but remained intact.

Layer four is a toning glaze for the tin foil. This layer varies. In one example a yellow powdery layer is apparent in the recesses of the foil and appears to have been used to color the tin. In all other cases a thin, reddish glaze appears to have served to tone the foil with no sign of any other coloring material. This glaze tends to make the remaining gray deteriorated tin foil appear brown in color, no doubt contributing to its misidentifications as "paste."

On all but one pasteprint, layer five is shiny black ink that is now quite brittle.

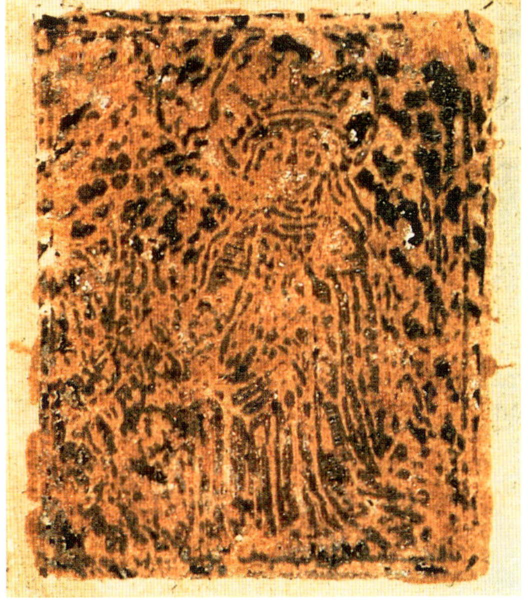

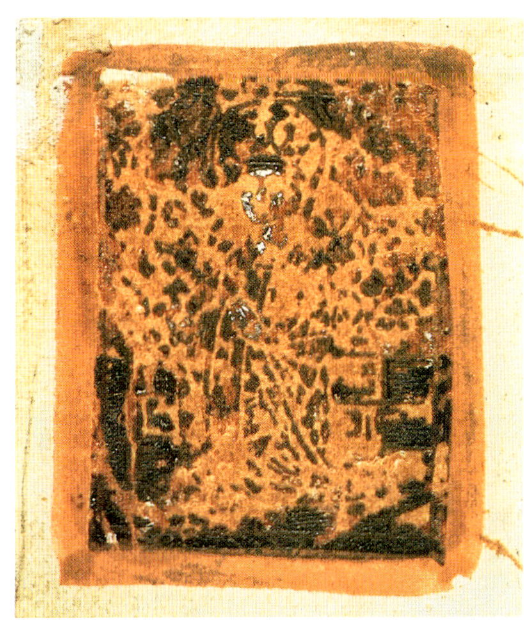

9. *Unknown Saint* (S2861n), pasteprint
National Gallery of Art, Washington, Lessing J. Rosenwald Collection

10. *Unknown Saint* (S2861m), pasteprint
National Gallery of Art, Washington, Lessing J. Rosenwald Collection

11. *Madonna and Child* (S2826a), pasteprint
National Gallery of Art, Washington, Lessing J. Rosenwald Collection

12. *Saint Margaret*, pasteprint
National Gallery of Art, Washington, Lessing J. Rosenwald Collection

EXAMINATION OF THE NATIONAL GALLERY OF ART EXAMPLES

Close scrutiny of the sixteen examples of pasteprints in the National Gallery of Art (see app. 1) has yielded valuable information for an overall understanding of pasteprint composition. One group of eight small images came from a codex from the monastery of Saint Peter in Salzburg.[10] They depict two unknown saints (S2861n, S2861m), *Madonna and Child* (S2826a), *Saint Margaret* (S2854d), *Saint Catherine* (S2837a), *Pietà* (S2822b), *Trinity* (S2811m), and *Sudarium* (S2811z) (figs. 9–16). They follow the structure shown in figure 8, all bearing a bright orange stain resulting from a molded and heavily pigmented resin layer, a tin foil or tin oxide powder layer, a reddish glaze over the foil, and shiny

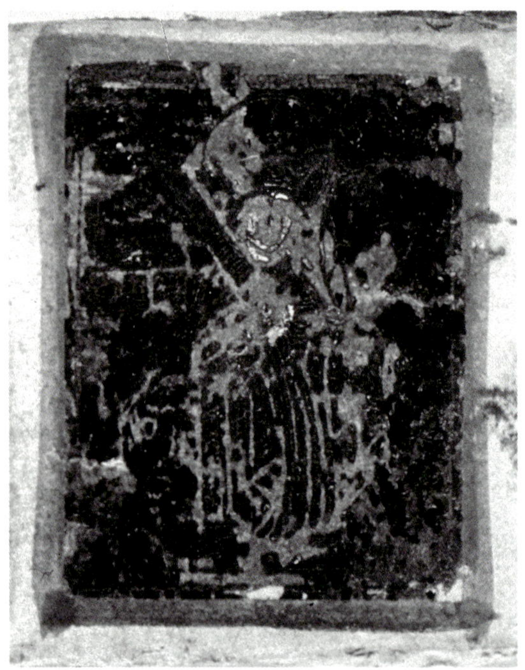

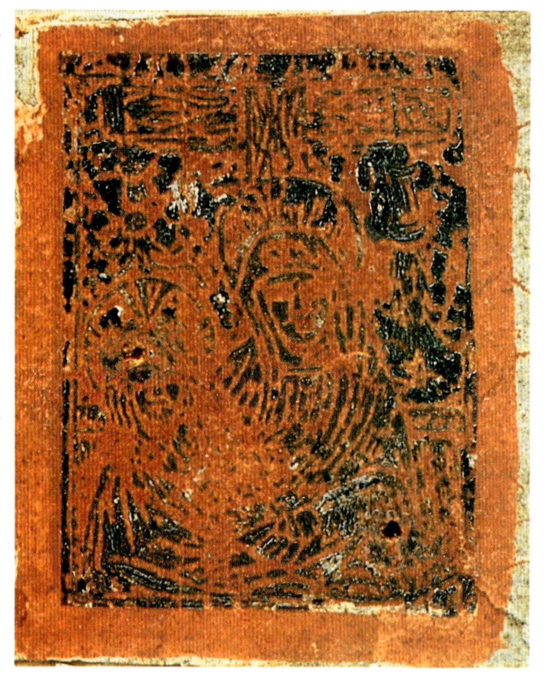

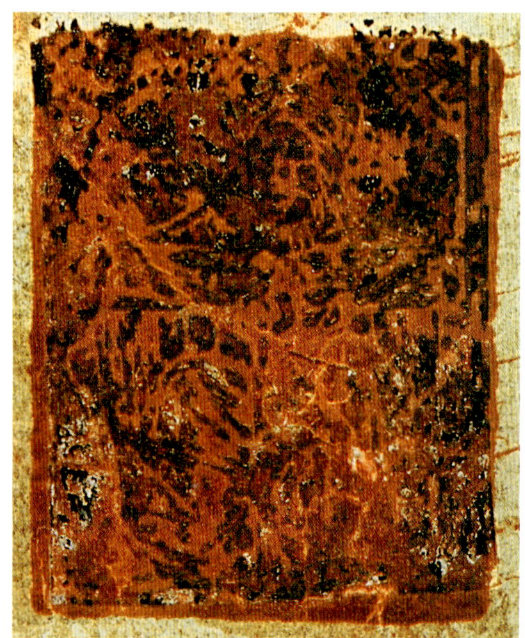

black ink (fig. 17). Painted borders containing mixtures of red lead, bits of tin, and other pigments were added to neaten the edges on four of the pasteprints, disguising the mismatched foil and resin layers (figs. 18–19).

The structure of *Saint John the Baptist* (S2850m), also from the monastery of Saint Peter in Salzburg, is the same as the other Salzburg pieces, although the pasteprint is about four times as large (fig. 20).[11] It has a brown stain caused by the brownish molded resin layer (heavily pigmented with red lead), a tin foil layer, the toning glaze, and the ink layer. In the figure of Saint John, the golden areas of glazed tin are well preserved in the recesses of the relief, though darkened (fig. 21).

In *Madonna and Child* (S2825), formerly in the collection of the Prince Oettingen-Wallerstein in Mahingen and cited by Passavant, we see a buff-colored stain, the result of the relatively thin, molded resin layer that is pigmented with red lead (fig. 22).[12] This resin layer is now deteriorated, embrittled, and blanched around the edges (fig. 23). The ogival arch in the background still displays a brilliant green varnish (fig. 24), but no general toning layer is apparent on the foil, which simply appears gray. One reads the design of the image, which was created using

13. *Saint Catherine*, pasteprint
National Gallery of Art, Washington, Lessing J. Rosenwald Collection

14. *Pietà*, pasteprint
National Gallery of Art, Washington, Lessing J. Rosenwald Collection

15. *Trinity*, pasteprint
National Gallery of Art, Washington, Lessing J. Rosenwald Collection

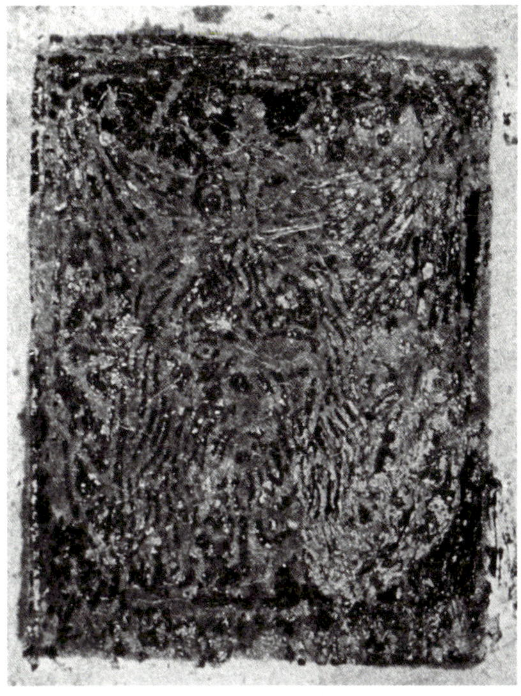

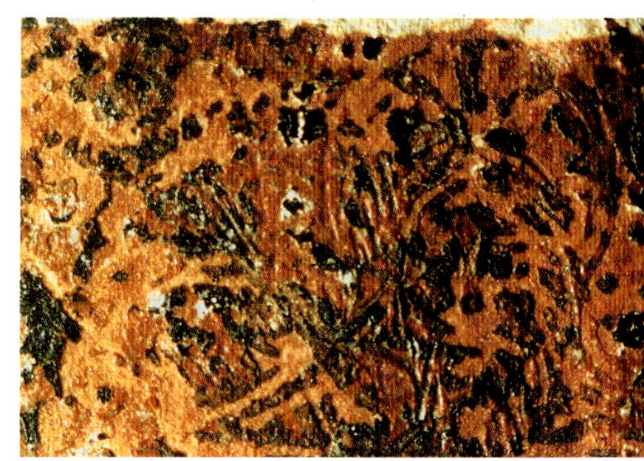

16. *Sudarium*, pasteprint
National Gallery of Art, Washington, Lessing J. Rosenwald Collection

17. Detail, fig. 15, showing layered structure with the stain, molded varnish, glazed tin foil, and black ink

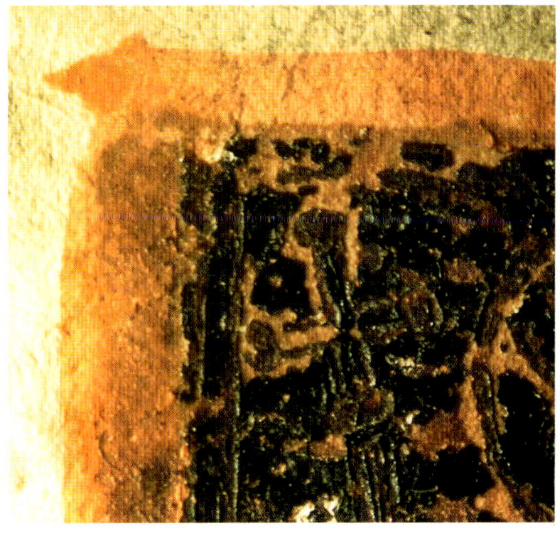

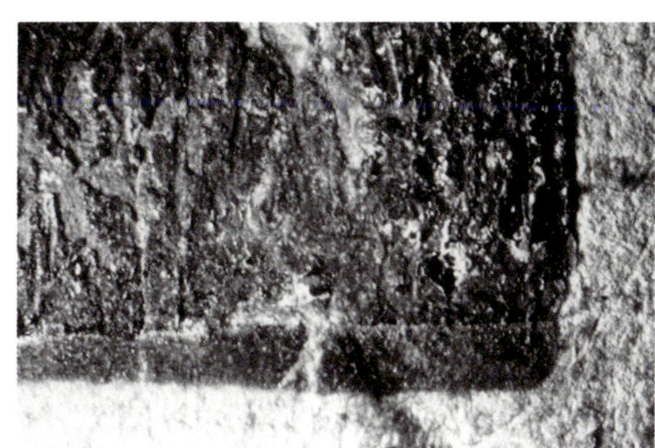

18. Detail of upper left corner, fig. 12, showing painted border that disguises the mismatched edges of the layers

19. Detail of lower left corner, fig. 15, showing how the varnish stain and the metal foil layer are mismatched

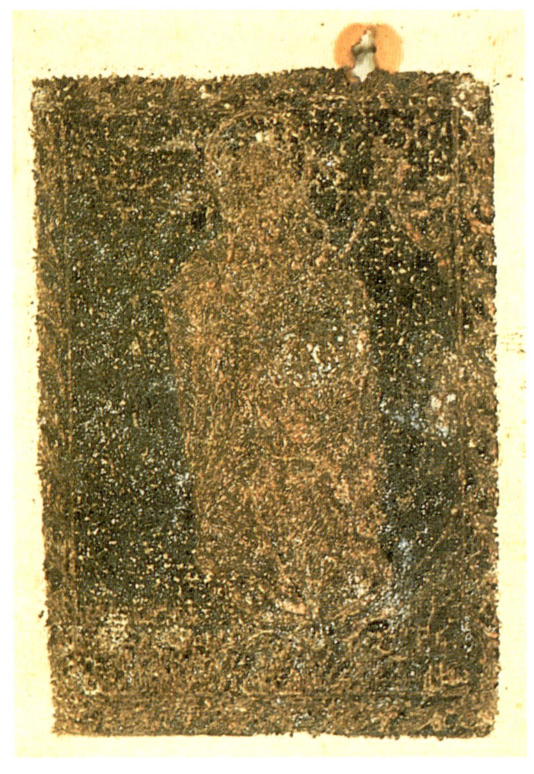

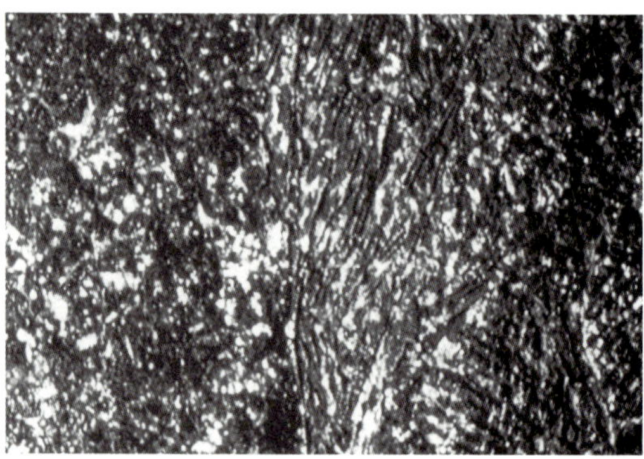

20. *Saint John the Baptist*, pasteprint
National Gallery of Art, Washington, Lessing J. Rosenwald Collection

21. Detail, fig. 20, shows shining glaze still visible

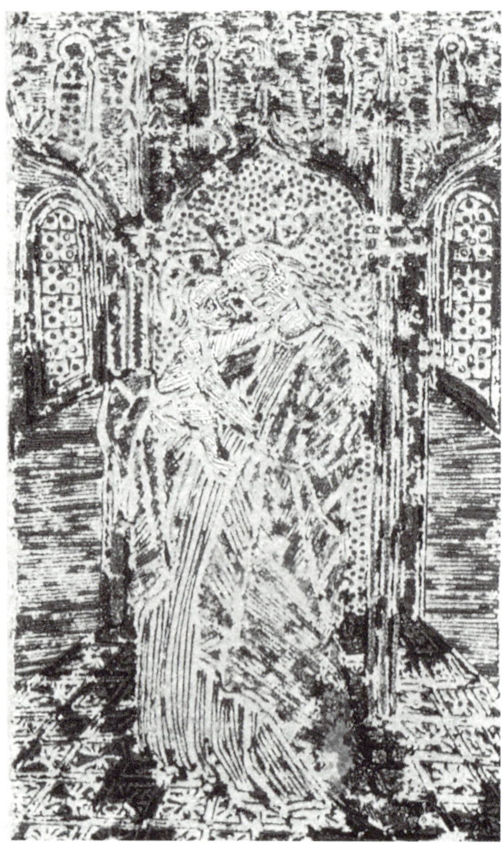

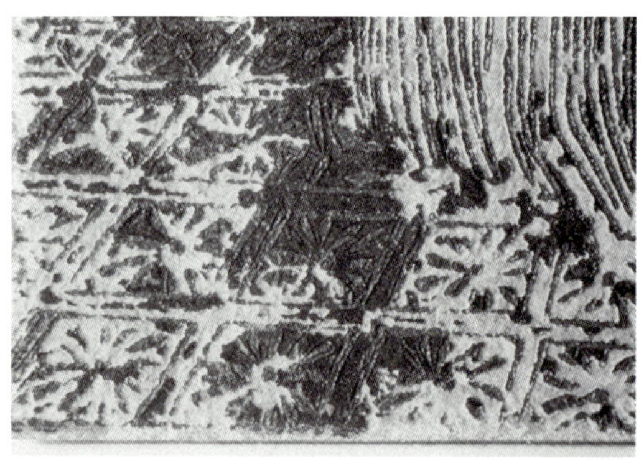

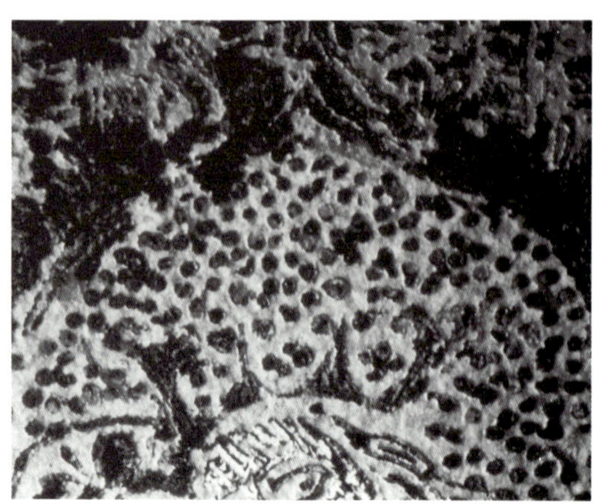

22. *Madonna and Child* (S2825), pasteprint
National Gallery of Art, Washington, Lessing J. Rosenwald Collection

23. Detail, fig. 22, showing the deterioration and blanching of the resin

24. Detail, fig. 22, showing the area where a green glaze was applied to tone the metal foil around the arch only. This green color is unusual in the pasteprints in the National Gallery of Art, Washington

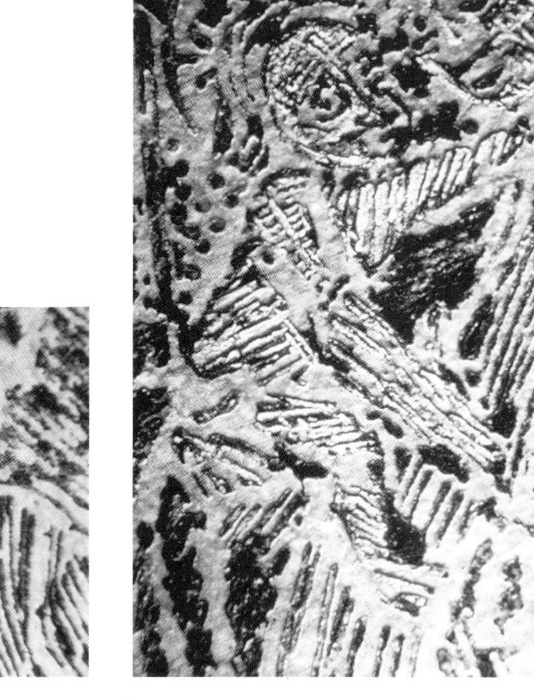

25. Detail, fig. 22, showing the otherwise untoned metal foil. The contrast of the black ink against the gray foil is evident

26. Detail, fig. 22, showing the applied flesh tone

27. Detail, fig. 5, showing the deteriorated and blanched resin layer

28. Detail, fig. 5, showing the powdery layer presumably intended as a gold toning layer for the metal foil

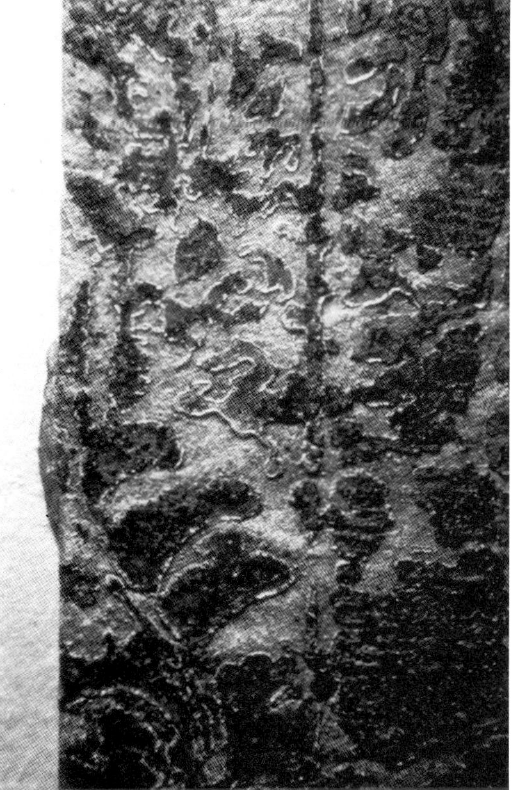

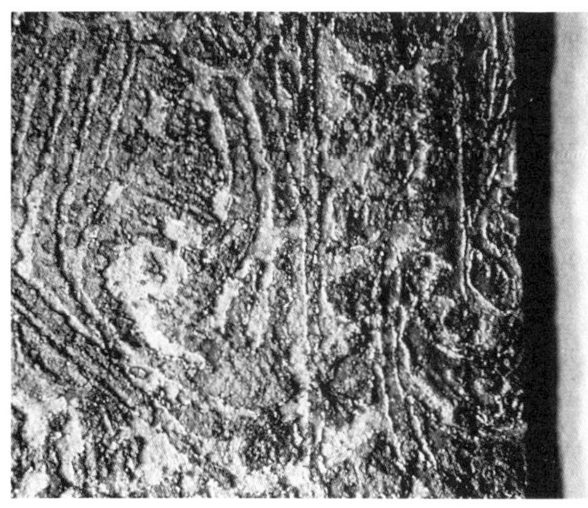

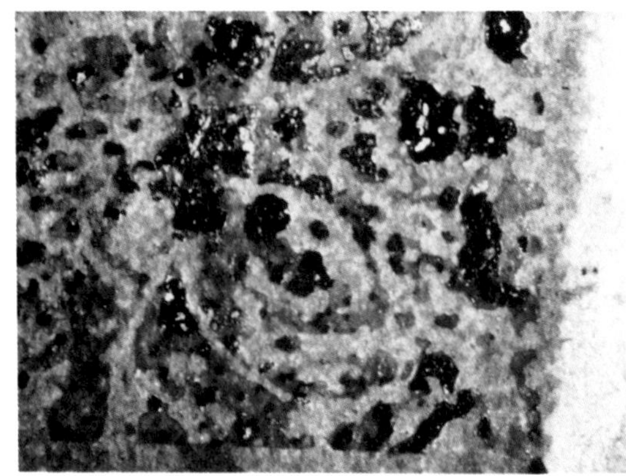

punches and implements as characteristic of dotted prints, by reading the contrast of the gray foil against a light application of shiny black ink (fig. 25). The face and hands of the Madonna and Child were painted with flesh tone (fig. 26). There is no powdery tin oxide on this pasteprint, although the foil is indeed tin.

Saint George and the Dragon (S2845a), formerly in the collection of the Albertina, Vienna (see fig. 5), shares the same molded resin layer as all the examples in the National Gallery of Art and exhibits similar deterioration and blanching as *Madonna and Child* (S2825) (fig. 27).[13] A powdery yellow layer is intact, presumably the gold toning layer for the tin (fig. 28). This may be an "unfinished" pasteprint or an unusual variation, as it lacks the shiny black ink layer. There is also no powdery tin oxide in this example.

Little is left of *Christ Carrying the Cross* (S2788, variant), formerly in the Trau Collection (see fig. 4). The structure is again consistent with the other examples. We see the brilliant stain from the red-orange resin layer (pigmented with red lead), the foil (which in certain areas of the same layer appears as white powder, that is, the foil layer deteriorated further to tin oxide), a reddish glazing layer, and a shiny black ink layer (fig. 29).[14]

Another *Madonna and Child* (S2824c), purchased in Munich in the 1920s (fig. 30), has a brownish stain with a great deal of red lead left by the thin dark resin layer, of which very little remains intact (fig. 31).[15] The metal foil again appears in places as a powder layer. This example also has a reddish glazing

29. Detail of upper left corner, fig. 4, showing all layers

30. *Madonna and Child* (S2824c), pasteprint
National Gallery of Art, Washington, Lessing J. Rosenwald Collection

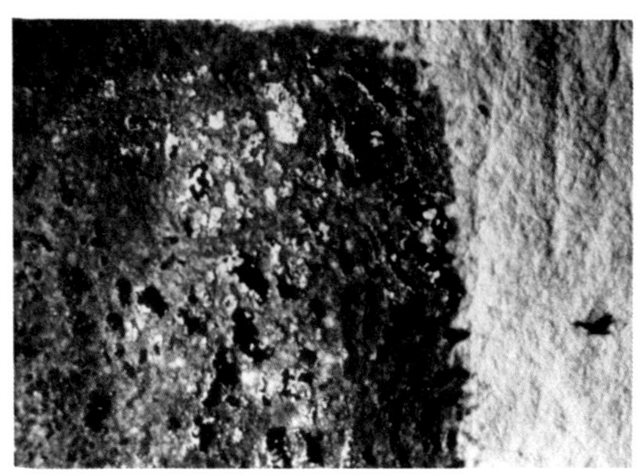

31. Detail, fig. 30, showing pigment particles scattered in the thin resin layer

32. Detail, fig. 30, showing the advanced stage of deterioration of the metal foil layer

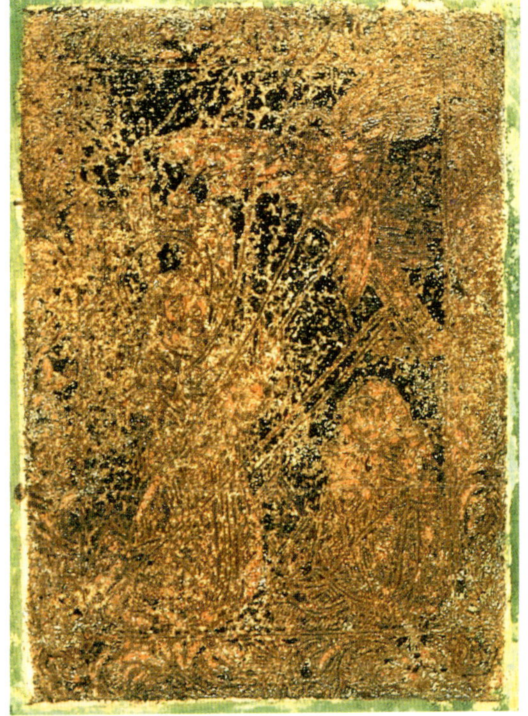

33. *Saint Francis*, pasteprint
National Gallery of Art, Washington, Lessing J. Rosenwald Collection

34. *Saint Michael*, pasteprint
National Gallery of Art, Washington, Lessing J. Rosenwald Collection

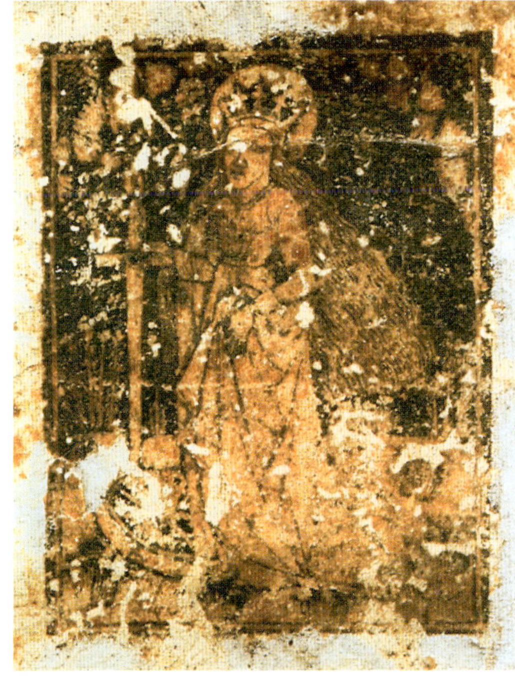

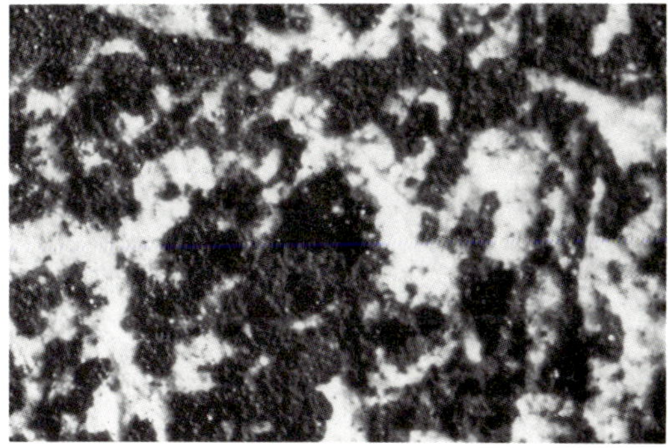

35. *Saint Catherine*, pasteprint
National Gallery of Art, Washington, Lessing J. Rosenwald Collection

36. Detail, fig. 35, showing correct order of the structure on the original support

layer and a shiny, brittle black ink layer. A great deal of grayish powder and white powder lies on the surface of this very deteriorated pasteprint (fig. 32).

Saint Francis (S2843), formerly in the E. Schultze Vienna Collection (fig. 33), and *Saint Michael* (S2856), from Mahingen (fig. 34), also exhibit the diagrammed structure shown in figure 8.[16] The edges of *Saint Francis* have been painted over with a bright green border.

The final, somewhat puzzling pasteprint of

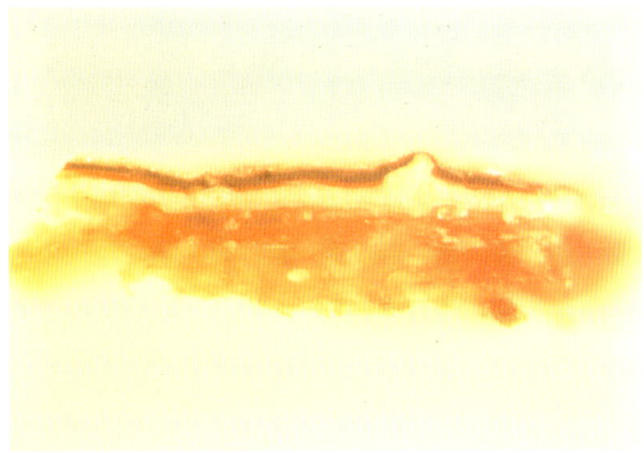

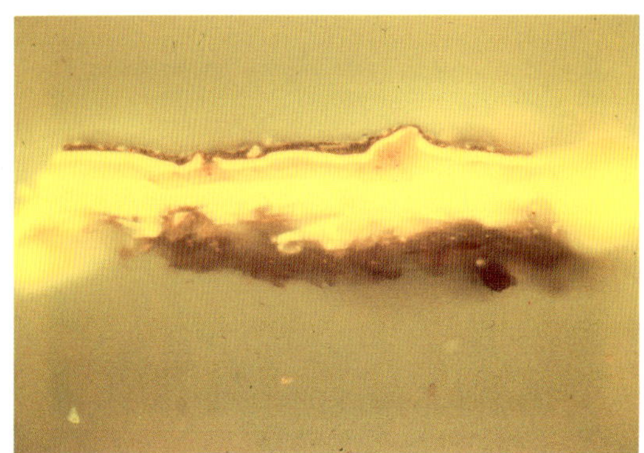

37. Cross section, fig. 20, prepared from the broken edge of the pasteprint *Saint John the Baptist* and shown top lit, confirming the layered structure we have observed

38. Cross section, fig. 20, prepared from the broken edge of the pasteprint *Saint John the Baptist* and recorded using Leitz Orthoplan microscopy equipped with a Ploemopak

Saint Catherine (not catalogued by Schreiber) (fig. 35) was discovered on the reverse of a metalcut, *Monogram of Christ*, when *Monogram* was removed from an old frame in the 1940s.[17] *Saint Catherine* was analyzed by Gettens, and the findings were published by Elizabeth Mongan in 1943. Mongan suggested that the pasteprint was unrelated to the metalcut and had become transferred to the reverse of the metalcut support when the *Monogram* was adhered over it.[18] Examination of the pasteprint indicates this is entirely possible, as the layers diagrammed in figure 8 are adhered to the support of the metalcut in reverse order, with the ink layer closest to the paper and the metal layer on top. What remains of the layers is in correct order on its former support (fig. 36). There was no adhesive layer on the former support, and the pasteprint was easily transferred to the reverse of the metalcut when the latter was adhered with an abundant amount of glue.[19]

ANALYSIS

Because of the rarity of these small objects, only limited sampling was done to confirm the observations made under magnification and using ultraviolet light. The preparation of cross sections using a sample from the damaged edge of *Saint John the Baptist* (S2850m) and a detached fragment from *Madonna and Child* (S2824c) (see app. 2) confirmed our visual observations that the structure of pasteprints differs from that proposed by Coombs and Farrell. In the toplit cross section of *Saint John the Baptist* (fig. 37), the paper and resin layer are difficult to distinguish, but the tin layer shows up clearly as a discrete white layer. When examined using the Leitz Orthoplan microscope equipped with a Ploemopak (fig. 38), the layers are more distinct. In this illumination, samples are exposed to ultraviolet rays of c. 500 nanometers and certain substances fluoresce, or emit light. Here, the molded resin layer appears yellow and can be easily distinguished from the dark paper. We can also note that no separate adhesive layer is detectable. The tin foil layer is still distinct, now showing as a dark, grayish layer. The cross section also reveals the toning layer for the tin—a thin, even layer directly on top of the tin that emits a bright orange fluorescence when illuminated with the ultraviolet rays of the Ploemopak. The top dark layer consists of ink and other pigments used to decorate the image. Except for the paper support, these layers are also shown on the cross section prepared from *Madonna and Child* (fig. 39). When illuminated as above, we see the fluorescence of bits of the molded varnish layer, the dark tin layer, the bright orange toning layer, and the dark decorative top layer.

Early in our study, analytical methods were used to attempt to identify a wax component or another low-melting substance in the resin layer. It was speculated that the melting property may have been exploited to adhere the tin foil to paper support. The results of using simple microchemical tests and heating were inconclusive. Aged materials no longer respond characteristically to their original solvents or melting and charring temperatures. It later became apparent that resin itself is heat fusible.[20]

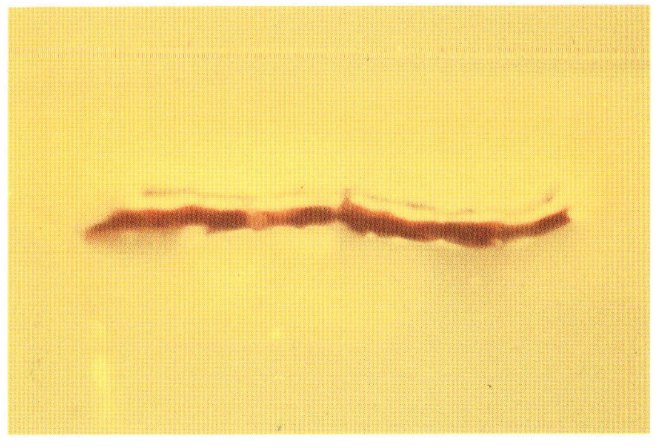

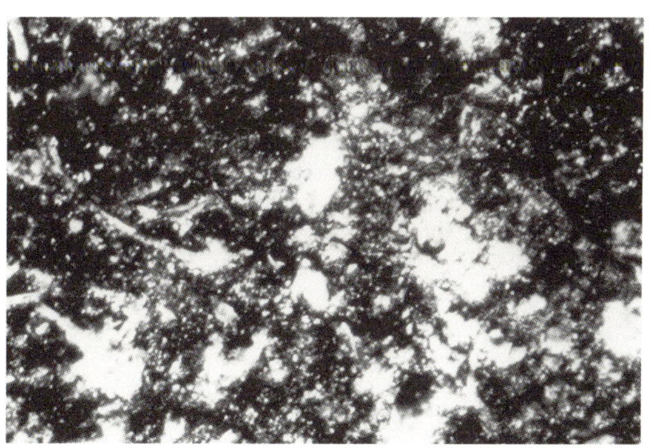

39. Cross section, fig. 30, prepared from a broken area of the pasteprint *Madonna and Child* and shown using Leitz Orthoplan microscopy equipped with a Ploemopak

40. Detail, fig. 20, showing the white powder of the deteriorated tin foil layer under the broken layer. Samples were taken from two broken sites near the center

41. Detail, fig. 20, showing how the white powder of the deteriorated tin foil layer effluoresces to the surface of the pasteprint

42. Ultraviolet light photograph, fig. 9, showing yellow-orange fluorescence of stain and molded resin layer under ultraviolet illumination in the 300–400 nm range

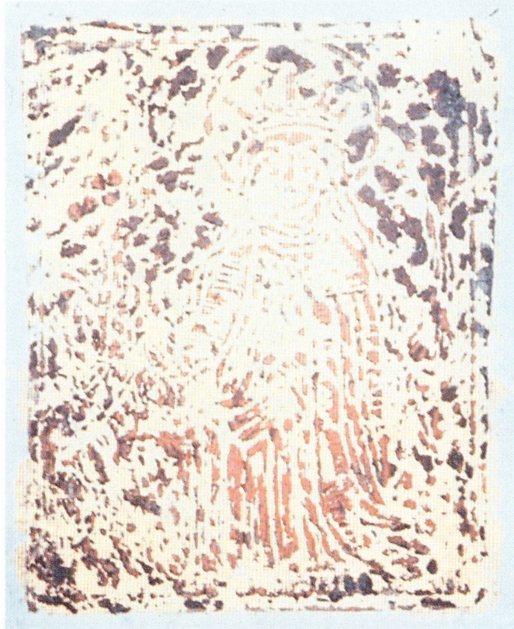

Nondestructive testing of five of the pasteprints showed that the metal foil layer on each example was tin, even in cases where the deteriorated powdery white tin oxide layer was not observed.[21] The ubiquitous shiny white powder was sampled just beneath a broken site in the ink layer of *Saint John the Baptist* (S2850m) (fig. 40). This sample, analyzed by x-ray diffraction (XRD), clearly exhibited the pattern of stannic oxide (SnO_2). To identify the white accretions we observed on the surface of many of the National Gallery of Art pasteprints, a sample was taken from the surface of *Saint John the Baptist* (fig. 41). This accretion proved to be stannic oxide with an additional pattern that closely matches that of sodium hydroxide. The sodium hydroxide may be present due to handling or as a by-product of attempts to conserve the object. (For patterns on stannic oxide and sodium hydroxide, see app. 2).

X-ray diffraction analysis of a sample of the gray-brown surface of *Saint John the Baptist* (S2850m) revealed the mixed patterns of stannic oxide and stannous oxide, the secondary deterioration product of tin (see app. 2). The color of the deteriorated tin in these areas is influenced by oxidation and the organic toning glaze, which accounts for the brownish cast. The presence of both the relatively intact, brown oxidized layer and the white powder underneath represent various phases of corrosion of a single tin layer.[22]

Based on analysis and the close examination of the National Gallery of Art examples, it is evident that the coated tin foil deteriorates actively from beneath. Stannic oxide effluoresces to the surface of the pasteprint, breaking through the brittle, fragile, oxidized and coated layer and contributing to surface deterioration of glazing and ink layers. This activity is comparable to that of tin in sculpture composed of metal alloys, where stannic oxide is the most abundant corrosion product and is often observed to leach out from the alloy and form deposits on the surface. Because the pasteprint structure is so thin, the powdering of the tin and embrittlement of aged resins constitute a fragility that could not withstand the uncontrolled fluctuations in humidity, compression, or handling to which these objects were certainly subjected.

No further analysis was done; however, some interesting observations were made while studying the pasteprints under ultraviolet light. All the pasteprints revealed a bright yellow-orange fluorescence of the stain and molded resin layer under ultraviolet light in the 300–400 nm range, illustrated here in one example, *Unknown Saint* (S2861n) (fig. 42). This fluorescence again suggests that the stain and resin layer are the same material and the unusual color may be a clue for a more specific identification of the oil-resin varnish suggested by Coombs and Farrell. Although identification on the basis of ultraviolet fluorescence is not reliable, it is interesting to note that while fresh samples of dammar and mastic show little fluorescence, the yellow-orange fluorescence seen here is closest to that exhibited in fresh samples of rosin or a substance called Burgundy pitch, a tree exudate often referred to in artists' manuals of the Middle Ages.[23]

To Coombs and Farrell's extensive but inconclusive analysis of the top toning layer, we can add that under ultraviolet illumination this layer fluoresces red-orange. This fluorescence is characteristic of aged samples of two organic materials known to have been used by medieval craftsmen—shellac and saffron. Shellac, or "lac," was commonly used in Europe as early as the thirteenth century and was valued as a clear red for rendering the folds of garments and drapery over gold foil. Shellac is one of several organic preparations recommended by Cennino Cennini for toning silver or tin foil.[24] Saffron was often used in fifteenth-century German workshops for fabric dyeing, as discussed by Emil Ernst Ploss, and is mentioned as a yellow pigment in the *Strasburg Manuscript*.[25]

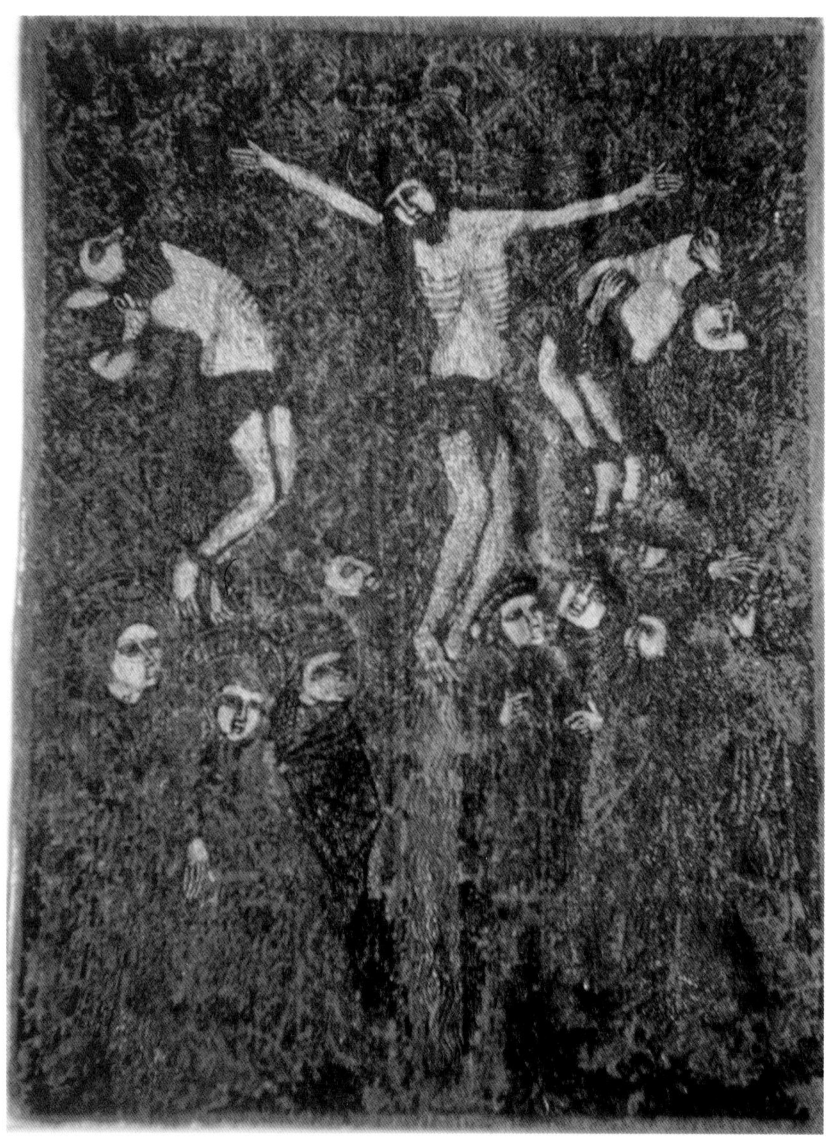

43. *Crucifixion* (S2801), pasteprint created from a punched metal plate
Germanisches Nationalmuseum, Nuremberg

THE NATURE OF THE PASTEPRINT PLATE AND THE RELATIONSHIP BETWEEN PASTEPRINTS AND METALCUTS

The nature of the plate used for pasteprints became a subject of speculation early on in the literature. Schreiber noted the relationships between pasteprints and certain metalcuts on paper, suggesting that some metalcut images with black backgrounds were printed from plates intended for "printing in paste."[26] Max Geisberg was the first to discuss prints on paper and pasteprint pairs that represent identical but mirror images, that

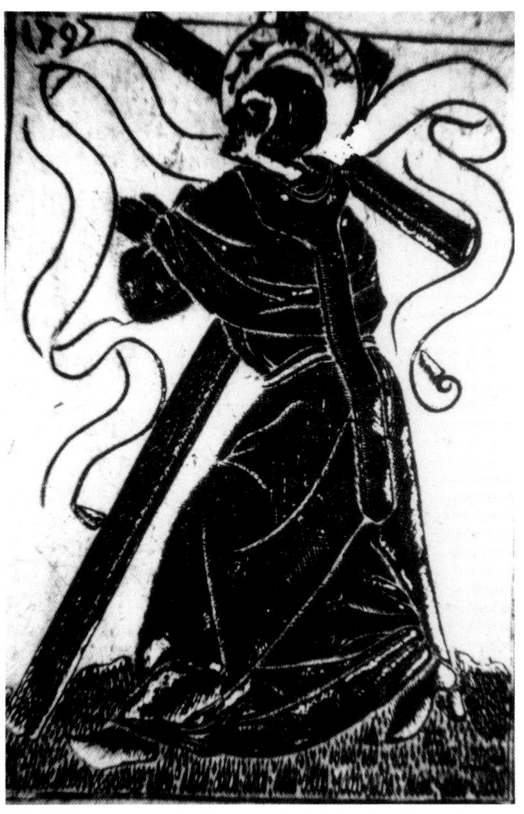

44. *Saint Simon*, eighteenth century, print on paper pulled from an intaglio inked plate (which no longer exists)
Germanisches Nationalmuseum, Nuremberg

is, the images are reversed from left to right. He characterized the plates used for such metalcut prints, explaining that the essential white line image, the use of parallel lines for hatching, and the lack of punchwork were typical.[27] Geisberg's study of metalcut prints, pasteprints, and two existing plates for a metalcut and pasteprint (subsequently lost) led to his observation that the metalcut plate surface remained largely intact, unlike woodcuts, where the surface is cut away except for the slim contour lines. He concluded that metalcut plates were used to make pasteprints. He also observed that pasteprints were relief images that reproduced all of the depth of the plate and noted that pasteprints were attempts to print an image on gold.[28]

If Geisberg intended to exclude plates executed in the dotted manner from the repertoire of potential sources for pasteprints, he is contradicted by the series of jewellike pasteprints in the Germanisches Nationalmuseum, Nuremberg, of which *Crucifixion* (S2801) is but one example (fig. 43). All nineteen that survive from a series of presumably twenty-eight scenes of the passion decorating a fifteenth-century codex from Nuremberg were formed from plates executed in the dotted manner. The images were rendered using punches in various patterns or tools, which removed most of the surface. There is hardly an engraved line anywhere. These images, published by Martin Weinberger in 1925, may have been executed by the Dominican nuns in the cloister of Saint Katharine, a hypothesis that is supported by the provincial nature of the work.[29]

Based on this series and other examples, the matrix for pasteprints could have been executed using punches or burins to break up or cut away the plate surface. More important, the execution of all pasteprints bears no relation to the sophistication exhibited in contemporaneous printed engravings, except in the borrowing of motifs for compositions. The relationship between pasteprint imagery and early engravings on paper demonstrates the manner in which prints provided a visual vocabulary for many decorative arts. Similarly, metalsmiths often borrowed compositions from the Master E. S. and Israhel van Meckenem to decorate plates and liturgical ware.[30]

Several pasteprints bear reversed inscriptions or present an image in the reverse of its iconographic formula. Considering these puzzling reversals, authors have suggested that the metalcut plates from which such compositions were printed were the product of metalsmiths and may have been prepared as decorative plates in their own right.[31]

In the course of the present study a new cognate pair has been discovered that supports the suggestion that decorative plates were used to produce certain pasteprints. No pasteprint pair is known for the printed image of *Saint Simon* (S2874) in the Germanisches Nationalmuseum, Nuremberg (fig. 44); however, its simple image is useful for illustration. It is an unusually highly embossed impression pulled from an intaglio inked plate.[32] The plate was not engraved with a burin but was worked with tools to create broad lines and voids. The drapery and figures were rendered in a cross-hatching technique typical of fifteenth-century metalwork decoration. Varying degrees of depth and relief were created as well. Because of the broadness of execution, when such a plate is inked intaglio and its surface wiped, the ink is easily removed from the broad lines. Characteristically, such plates produce a halo of ink around the edges of a given shape, while the broad shapes remain uninked. This result is seen in the details of the saint's shoes and in random spots where the paper is embossed but uninked.

The printed image of *Mass of Saint Gregory* (S2871) (fig. 45) in the Germanisches Nationalmuseum, Nuremberg, shares the same characteristics as the *Saint Simon.*[33] The plate surface was heavily worked to produce the foliate pattern in the border and the lines that delineate the garments in the figures. Similar haloing of the ink is evident in the broad shapes of the flowers at the four corners where the ink could have been easily removed with surface wiping. It is very likely that this plate, too, was a decorative metal plate that has produced an unsatisfactory image when inked. That such plates were used for pasteprints is confirmed by the exact but reversed pasteprint versions of *Mass of Saint Gregory* in the Staatsbibliothek, Munich (S2848), and the Bibliothèque Nationale, Paris (S2848b) (fig. 46).[34]

The corresponding print and pasteprints also illustrate another aspect of pasteprints that has long puzzled many authors. In every case where there is a printed and pasteprint version of an image, the pasteprint is the mirror image of the print. Moreover, those lines or areas that are uninked in the printed version and would have been voids on the printing plate are conversely those areas that were printed or impressed on the pasteprint surface. This relationship indicates that not only the image direction but the pasteprint relief is the opposite of the printed version. The flower petals, vines, halo of Saint Gregory, as well as the punched dots decorating the altar (obviously created when an instrument cut away the surface of the plate) are identical to the printed version but were impressed on the pasteprint. Initially better adhered to the paper than the inked lines, these are the areas that have survived.

Other pasteprint and printed cognate pairs illustrate this reversal. Over the course of this study, the printed partner of the tiny pasteprint image of *Pietà* (see fig. 14) in the National Gallery of Art (S2822b) was examined in the collection of the Bibliothèque Nationale, Paris (Ea. 5 rés) (fig. 47). The print, pulled from a metalcut plate that was surface inked, is a mirror image of the pasteprint. Again, the simple image offers an excellent opportunity for examining the details of the halo, eyes, and various other easily readable lines that confirm this is a reversed relief.

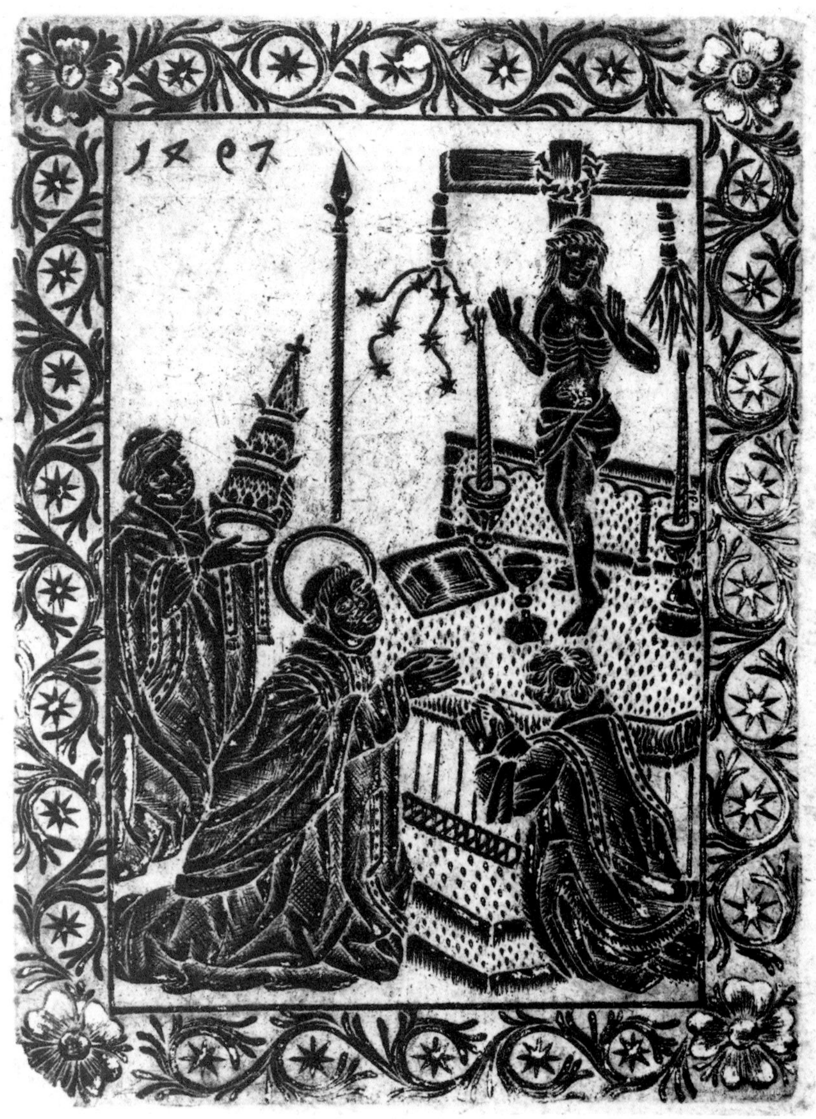

45. *Mass of Saint Gregory,* c. 1780, print on paper pulled from an intaglio inked plate (which no longer exists)
Germanisches Nationalmuseum, Nuremberg

This reversal of image and relief occurs in each case where a printed image and an identical pasteprint image exist. It is best explained by supposing that a cast of the printing matrix was used to produce pasteprints. This suggestion was first fully discussed by Wilhelm Molsdorf while examining the large

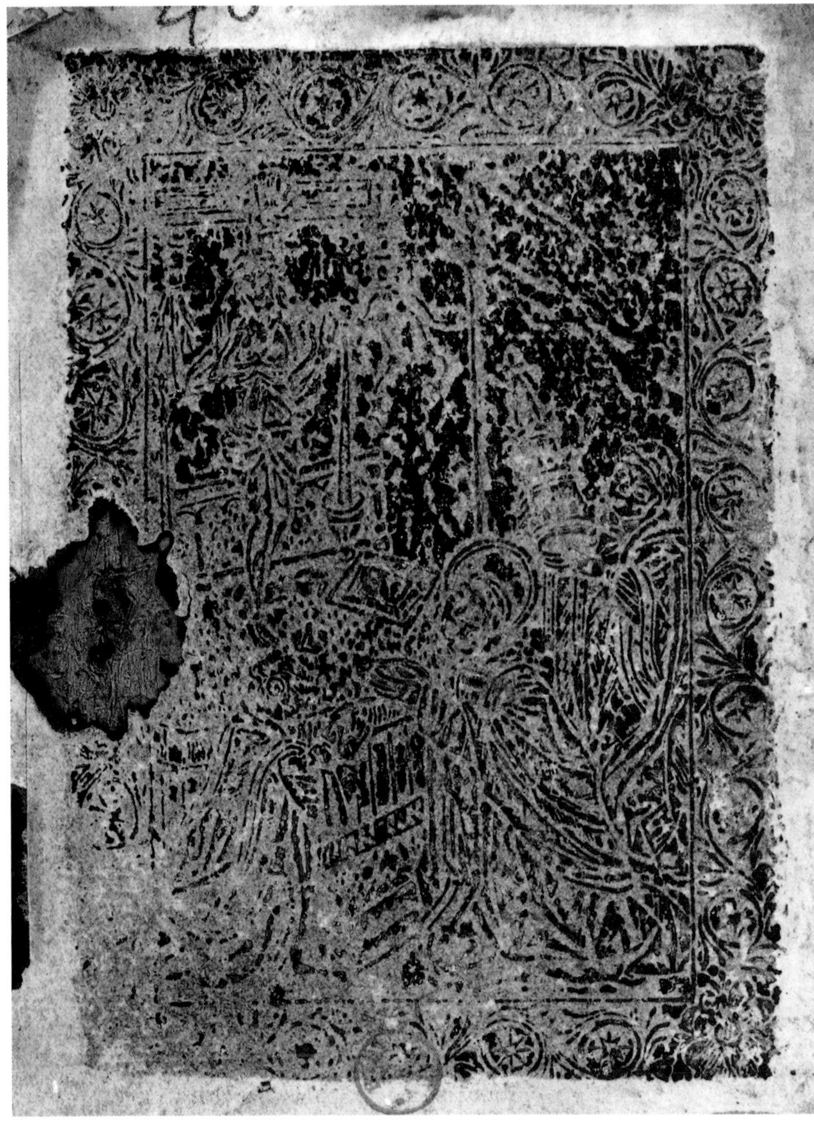

46. *Mass of Saint Gregory*, pasteprint. This is one of two pasteprints produced using the same plate as the Nuremberg print. The plate no longer exists
Bibliothèque Nationale, Paris

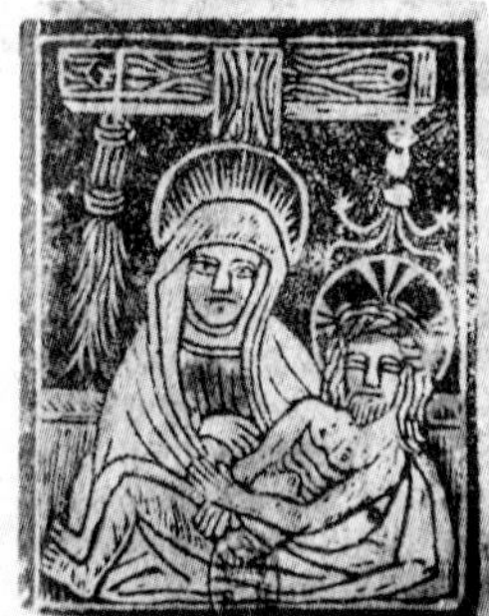

47. *Pietà*, metalcut print on paper. This is partner to the *Pietà* pasteprint, fig. 14
Bibliothèque Nationale, Paris

pasteprint in the Guildhall Library, London. He concluded that the pasteprint was without question printed from the same relief plate used to print its cognate (S2344) in the Staatliche Graphische Sammlung, Munich (fig. 48) and proposed an intermediate to account for the reversal of the image.[35] Field, illustrating the same large pasteprint, noted that the use of an intermediate cast of the original matrix explained not only the reversed direction but the reversal of relief from that exhibited in the print. As we see in the details he chose to illustrate (figs. 49–50), comparison of the pasteprint and printed images shows that the engraved lines that were not printed when the plate was surface inked are those preserved on the pasteprint.[36] Field remarked correctly that these voids would have been in relief on a cast of the metalcut plate and consequently would have pressed the tin foil more firmly in contact with the paper support. The recesses in the cast would have yielded raised portions on the pasteprint areas that would be fragile and easily broken away. Eventually, the pasteprint image would read as a reversed negative of the print.

TECHNIQUE

Only the most general suggestions appear in the literature regarding technique. Despite the fact that no pasteprint exhibits a platemark, it is usually assumed that a metal plate was used in a press to create the impression.[37] More recently, the technical discussion has been broadened to include comparison to techniques used in medieval sculpture. Close examination of nearly one hundred pasteprints has been sufficient to dispel some of the confusing suggestions in the literature. By also studying contemporaneous artists' manuals and fifteenth-century printing and book decoration, a plausible technique for pasteprint making can be proposed.

Tin was widely used as a less expensive substitute for gold in medieval workshops. The less precious metal could be used in more generous amounts, and as a result, tin was often used to create relief embellishments for panel and wall decoration by a process that is the reverse of and, it would appear, more expedient than that used for gilding. The gilding process is consistently described in manuals beginning with the time of Cennini. In all cases, it requires a mordant layer. Relief may be built up with several applications of a ground and by molding and stamping while the ground is still malleable. The mordant and thin leaf are then applied. Using tin, a thicker foil could be produced, which could be more extensively handled and treated than the relatively unmanageable gold leaf. Again, this process is consistently described over several hundred years.[38] Relief was achieved by molding the tin foil by stamping or beating it with a hammer against a carved matrix. Gesso was then applied as a paste to the reverse to fill the hollows of the molded shape. The foil-gesso composite was trimmed and adhered to the support with varnish, paste, or glue. Processes were also well known in which no gesso was used and varnish was brushed on to fill and reinforce the relief and act as an adhesive in one step.[39]

This combination of resin and the less precious tin foil are indeed closer to the materials used in pasteprints, which never contain gesso and exhibit a molded resin layer, a significant clue to their method of fabrication. Although Bowman cited the above techniques in relation to pasteprints,[40] she did so probably because of the confusing use of the term "paste" in many manuals. It is important to note that paper is never mentioned in the manuals as a support for these processes, and with good reason. Although it is possible to obtain a certain amount of relief using gesso for gilding on paper, resin is inevitably absorbed by paper when applied in liquid form. It is impossible to prevent even a viscous resin varnish from spreading and transparentizing paper. There is no sign of varnish or solvent absorption on any paste-

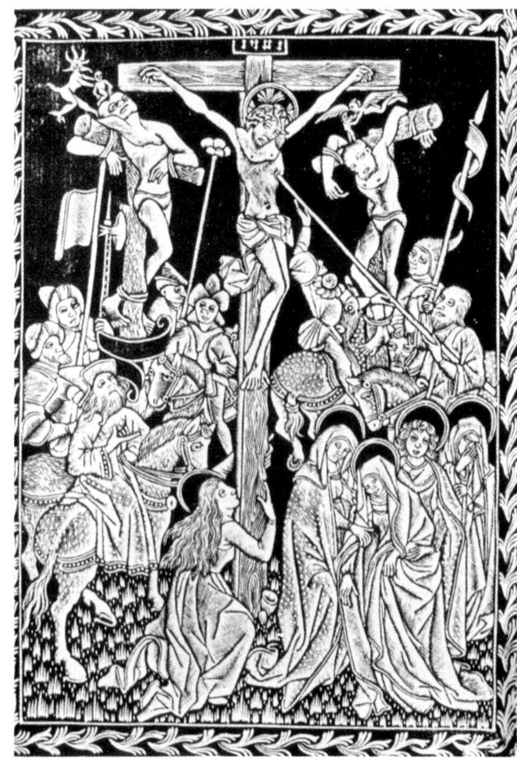

48. *Christ Crucified between Two Thieves*, metalcut
Staatliche Graphische Sammlung, Munich

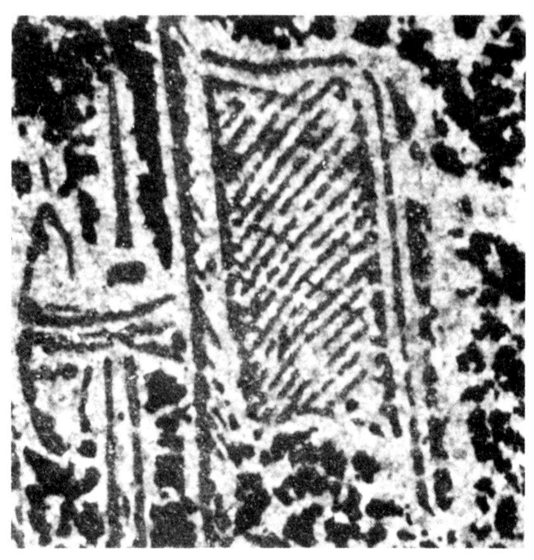

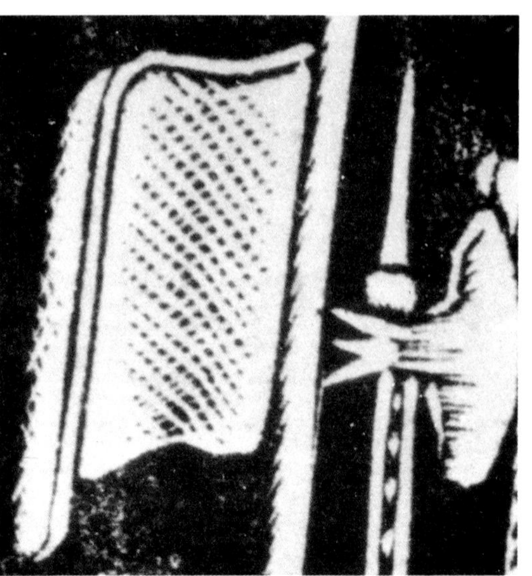

49. Detail, fig. 3, selected by Field to illustrate reversal of image and relief in pasteprint versus printed version
From Coombs, Farrell, and Field 1986, 38

50. Detail, fig. 48, selected by Field to illustrate reversal of image and relief in pasteprint versus printed version
From Coombs, Farrell, and Field 1986, 38

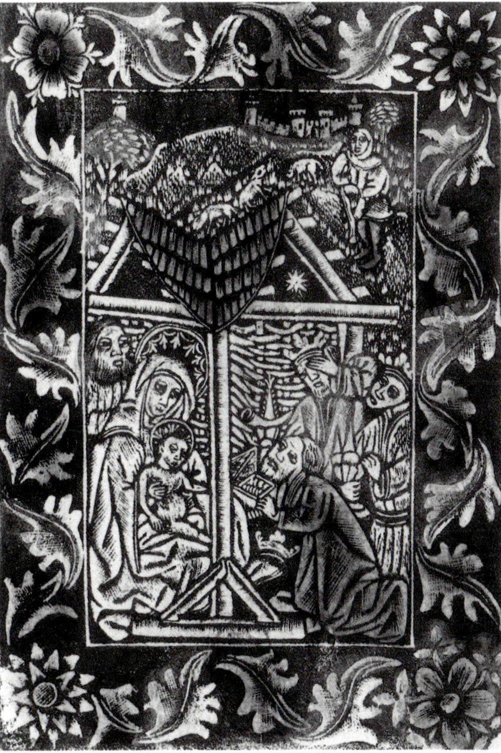

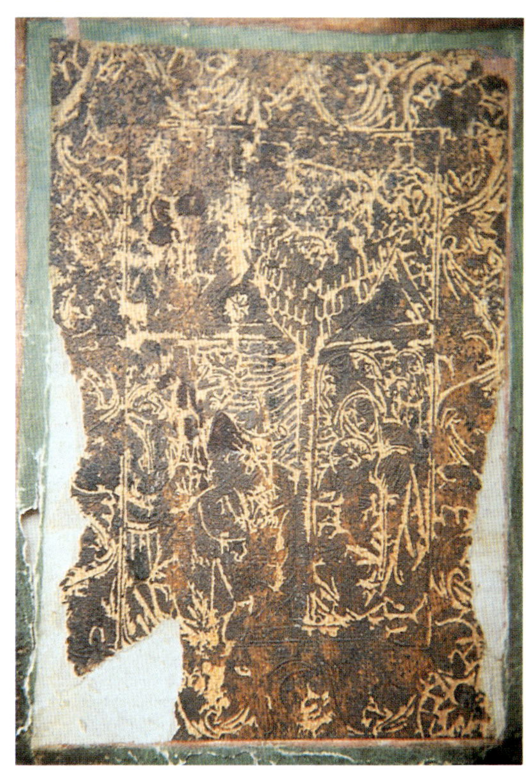

51. *Adoration*, metalcut print on paper. This is partner to the *Adoration* pasteprint, fig. 52
Bibliothèque Nationale, Paris

52. *Adoration*, pasteprint. This partner to the metalcut print on paper, fig. 51, exhibits a molded resin varnish layer
Staatsbibliothek, Munich

print. Yet the varnish layer is molded to follow the contours of the foil and slightly stains the paper.[41] The degree to which the resin layer was molded during the pasteprint making process is especially well illustrated by a metalcut and pasteprint pair of *Adoration* in the Bibliothèque Nationale, Paris (S2208), and the Staatsbibliothek, Munich (S2775), respectively (figs. 51, 52).[42] Although much of the upper layers of the pasteprint has fallen away, the raised lines have been unusually well preserved in the molded resin. If not applied in liquid form, how could this molded resin, characteristic of all pasteprints, be formed?

The use of resin affords a possibility over typical mordants—that of using heat to fuse the metal foil to the support. This innovative technology was introduced in the latter half of the fifteenth century for gold tooling on leather bindings and the early attempts to print with gold on paper. Evidence to support this consideration exists in the National Gallery of Art pasteprints.

Although the resin has not been absorbed into the paper, it has penetrated the surface to some extent, yielding the stain observed by most authors. The cross sections prepared for this study and the bright yellow-orange fluorescence of the stain on all pasteprints examined under ultraviolet illumination show that this stain is not a separate adhesive.[43] The application of heat would allow the resin to be fused to the paper by partial melting (and absorption, creating the staining of the surface) while simultaneously molding it to the contours of the heat-conducting tin foil. It is thus plausible to consider that pasteprints were made using a heated metal form, foil, and resin and that the foil and resin were molded in one step.[44]

The use of heat to fuse and mold the layers may explain another puzzling aspect of all pasteprints—the mismatched edges of the foil and resin layers. Generally, the edges of the tin and the molded resin layer match precisely within the image, but the resin extends beyond the decorated foil. Often the resin layer has a shape that is independent of the outline of the foil. Where the foil is out of square with the edges of the resin, there is no indication that the foil has shifted or that the resin has been squeezed out from under the foil, as may be expected if the resin were viscous and the layers were subjected to pressure. Where the foil is out of alignment and extends beyond the resin, only fragments of the tin layer survive. The foil is intact only where the resin has bonded it to the paper. Where this bonding has not been effected, the pasteprint stops, producing a skewed effect. That the foil does not survive intact beyond an adequate couch of resin may indicate that the resin not only adhered the pasteprint to the paper but was molded with it as well.[45]

The mismatched shapes of the foil and resin may also be explained by supposing that a heated plate was used. The resin would have also melted where it came into contact with the plate outside of the perimeter of the foil layer.[46]

As mentioned above, two other techniques introduced in the late fifteenth century used heated metal forms for adhering metal foil to a surface. Gold tooling, which appeared around 1480, employed powdered resin or glair to fuse gold leaf to leather with heated bookbinder's stamps.[47] Recent investigation of two early attempts to print in gold—the experiments carried out by the German Erhard Ratdolt and the Greek Zacharias Callierges working in Venice—surmised that these two printers used powdered resin (possibly the low-melting rosin) to adhere gold leaf to vellum and paper.[48]

Experiments conducted for this study with powdered rosin and the heated cast of an original carved matrix successfully reproduced the technical details observed in the National Gallery of Art pasteprints.[49] Both the tin and rosin molded convincingly to the contours of the plate. The rosin extended neatly just beyond the metal foil, and rosin particles that came in contact with the plate fused to the paper independent of the foil layer. There was no transparentizing of the support; however, a thin layer of melted rosin penetrated and stained the paper in a manner identical to what we observe in true pasteprints. The paper was not embossed, but a slight stiffening of the sheet is visible on the verso and the cockling of the paper around the pasteprint is comparable to that observed in the fifteenth-century prototypes. The need for a heat-conducting material, moreover, may further explain why all pasteprints appear to have been made using a cast taken from an original (possibly wooden) matrix used for printing on paper. In order to make use of the resin-molding capability of heat, a metal form would be required.

Although the exact method of production may still be in question, it appears that pasteprints relied on technologies that were quite well known and widely used by bookbinders and printers in the fifteenth century.[50] Their limited production, in both temporal and geographic terms, suggests that they fall within the realm of early, not entirely successful efforts begun late in the fifteenth century to replace the slow and painstaking labor of traditional methods with less expensive materials and more innovative techniques.[51] Further investigation may prove that their presence in books was not an accident of survival but a deliberate decorative scheme. In any event, their "safekeeping" in books is the very source of their deterioration. The pressure of the pages enhanced the bond of those areas in contact with the support while the same pressure compressed, bent, and finally broke the relief, obscuring forever their visual message.

NOTES

I was initially prompted to study the sixteen pasteprints in the National Gallery of Art collection by Shelley Fletcher, head of the paper conservation department. I would like to thank her for her encouragement of this project in all stages. I also wish to thank Barbara Berrie, then acting head of the scientific research department, for her willingness to take part in this project with enthusiasm, her suggestions regarding analysis of these unusual objects, and her contribution of a technical appendix. I thank Elizabeth Coombs for taking time to talk "yet again" about pasteprints and for sharing Rutherford J. Gettens' correspondence and reports. I am especially grateful to Claus W. Gerhardt for his thoughtful responses to my inquiries and for bringing to my attention his article and additional literature on early printing processes. I am also grateful to Shelley Sturman, head of the objects conservation department, National Gallery of Art, and Carol Grissom, objects conservator, Conservation Analytical Laboratory, Smithsonian Institution, for discussing metal corrosion, and to the artists Elizabeth Peak and William R. Bowser for their help in creating the mock-ups, from which we learned a great deal.

1. Wilhelm L. Schreiber, *Die Meister der Metallschneidekunst nebst einem nach Schulen geordneten Katalog ihrer Arbeiten*, 8 vols. (Strasbourg, 1926). Volume 6 contains the pasteprint (*Teigdruck*) information. All pasteprints discussed will be identified by Schreiber numbers; the numbers are grouped by category and within each category, by subject. In many cases one Schreiber number is given for pasteprints located in various collections.

2. Elizabeth Coombs, Eugene Farrell, and Richard S. Field, *Pasteprints: A Technical and Art Historical Investigation* (Cambridge, Mass., 1986).

3. According to Field, John Frederick Lewis and Georg Leidinger published this assumption (see bibliography). Coombs, Farrell, and Field 1986, 29.

4. Max Geisberg first suggested that parts of the plate had crushed the "paste," causing it eventually to fall away. "Teigdruck und Metallschnitt," *Monatshefte für Kunstwissenschaft* 5 (1912), 314. Richard S. Field first proposed that the negative image presented by pasteprints may be due to the loss of certain lines in *Fifteenth-Century Woodcuts and Other Relief Prints in the Collection of the Metropolitan Museum of Art* [exh. cat., Metropolitan Museum of Art] (New York, 1977). See also Coombs, Farrell, and Field 1986, 6–7, 35–38.

5. John Frederick Lewis, "Teigdrucke," *Proceedings of the Numismatic and Antiquarian Society of Philadelphia for the Years 1902–1903* (Philadelphia, 1904), 189–194; Erwin Kistner, "Studien an Teigdrucken aus dem Besitz des Germanischen Nationalmuseums in Nürnberg," *Festschrift Eugen Stollreither*, ed. Fritz Redenbacher (Erlangen, 1950), 71. According to Field, the last suggestion was made by Maximilian Pfeiffer in *Einzel-Formschnitte des fünfzehnten Jahrhunderts in der Königl. Bibliothek Bamberg*. Coombs, Farrell, and Field 1986, 29.

6. Johann D. Passavant, *Le Peintre-graveur*, 6 vols. (Leipzig, 1860–1864), 1:103; Friedrich von Bartsch, *Die Kupferstichsammlung der K. K. Hofbibliothek in Wien* (Vienna, 1854), 65, 77–78. Pasteprints present problems to the conservator both in terms of preservation and in the elucidation of artists' techniques. Passavant's text reveals that 130 years ago pasteprints were already deteriorated to such an extent that the metal foil layer was water soluble. It is the determination of the present study that, except for appropriate housing in controlled environments, no conservation methods can successfully halt the deterioration of the inherently unstable materials in these objects. Several examples in the collection of the National Gallery of Art have been fixed or varnished in an effort to preserve them. The effect is an unfortunate glossy surface or white, stringy accretions of consolidant. While more appropriate materials may currently be available as consolidants, other examples that have not been treated have survived comparatively well. Now, properly housed in a controlled environment, the pasteprints appear to have incurred no further damage.

7. Gettens found the size layer readily soluble in water and insoluble in alcohol. Vegetable gum was suggested because the sample tested negative for nitrogen, ruling out animal glue. When heated with hydrochloric acid, the residue turned greenish brown, suggesting gum arabic. Using x-ray diffraction, Gettens provisionally identified the metal as tin oxide. He subsequently changed this identification to tin sulfate and confirmed the presence of sulfate based on the formation of calcium sulfate crystals (gypsum) when hydrochloric acid and calcium acetate were applied to the sample. Gettens analyzed the "varnish" layer on the tin by heating it on a platinum spoon, noting that it turned cherry red at a low temperature and appeared to melt before charring. He found that it did not appear to melt in warm Canada balsam. Hot concentrated nitric acid dispersed the sample into small oil droplets, suggesting a resin or old dried oil film. He also noted scattered red lead in the medium-rich layer, confirmed by a strong positive test for lead. The ink layer was analyzed by Gettens and proved to be carbon black, probably in a soft resin binder. Gettens confirmed these findings on all four of the pasteprints he analyzed from the collection of Lessing J. Rosenwald. In addition, he found a green copper resinate varnish on *Madonna and Child* (S2825).

This information is based on Gettens' correspondence and reports, housed at the Center for Conservation and Technical Studies, Cambridge, Mass. His findings are also published by Elizabeth Mongan, "Two Undescribed Fifteenth Century Prints in the Collection of Lessing J. Rosenwald," *Art in America* 31, no. 2 (April 1943), 104. The correct identification—tin oxide—was published by Cynthia Bowman after consultation with Joyce Plesters of the National Gallery, London. "Pasteprints: A New Hypothesis about Their Production," *Print Quarterly* 2 (1985), 10–11. Extensive analysis conducted by Elizabeth Coombs and Eugene Farrell on pasteprints in the Harvard University Art Museums' collection identified tin oxide as a deterioration product of the original tin foil layer.

They also reviewed the x-ray diffraction pattern produced by Gettens' sample and confirmed the identification of tin oxide. Coombs, Farrell, and Field 1986, 1–26.

8. Bowman 1985, 4–11.

9. Coombs, Farrell, and Field 1986, 8–23.

10. These pasteprints are S2811z (NGA accession number 1943.3.795), S2822b (1943.3.794), S2826a (1943.3.789), S2837a (1943.3.791), S2854d (1943.3.790), S2861m (1943.3.792), S2861n (1943.3.793), and S2811m (1943.3.788). According to Schreiber, who saw them in Salzburg, the codex was handwritten about 1480 in the monastery of Saint Peter. Originally four additional scenes were represented. Schreiber noted two pasteprints (S2860b, S2862b) in the Staatliche Graphische Sammlung, Munich that were probably from the same series. Schreiber 1926, 6:15. After seeing these two pasteprints in June 1988, I am sure they are of the same series. A printed version of *Pietà* is located in the Bibliothèque Nationale, Paris.

11. According to Schreiber, this pasteprint was printed on the same sheet as a representation of *Saint George and the Dragon* (see n. 13). He found them in a small, handwritten Benedictine devotional book completed around 1474 at the monastery of Saint Peter in Salzburg. Schreiber 1926, 6:28, 30.

12. Schreiber saw S2825 at the Fürstlich Oettingen-Wallersteinsche Fideikommiss-Bibliothek in Mahingen, but Passavant had seen it in the collection of the Prince Oettingen-Wallerstein in Mahingen. Passavant 1860–1864, 1:104. According to Schreiber, the National Gallery of Art version is identical to pasteprints in Berlin and Vienna, lacking only a foliate border with rosettes at the corners, which is intact on the European examples. Moreover, the images are all identical to, but the reverse of, a metalcut print also catalogued by Schreiber, S2492x. Schreiber suggested that the pasteprints were printed from a cast of the metalcut plate. Schreiber 1926, 6:20. The edges of the National Gallery example have been trimmed, so it cannot be determined whether there was ever a border around it.

13. As stated in n. 11, the image of *Saint John the Baptist* was attached to the same page as a *Saint George and the Dragon* in a book found in the monastery of Saint Peter in Salzburg. Schreiber remarked that the *Saint George and the Dragon* was in very bad condition. This is not the version in the National Gallery of Art, Washington. A second identical *Saint George and the Dragon* example was also found at the monastery of Saint Peter, adhered to a manuscript from around 1470. This is the version in the National Gallery of Art catalogued by Schreiber (S2845a) when it was in the collection of the Albertina, Vienna. Schreiber listed a *Saint George and the Dragon* (S2845) in the Bibliothèque Nationale, Paris, separately, meaning that to his knowledge the image was distinct from other representations of Saint George. Schreiber 1926, 6:28. During the course of this study I have been able to ascertain that the image is identical.

14. This pasteprint was not catalogued by Schreiber, but its similarity to S2788 was noted when the pasteprint was in the collection of Lessing J. Rosenwald. Schreiber 1926, 6:9.

15. Schreiber saw S2824c in Munich at Weiss and Co. and noted the mismatched layers of the impression and the stain on the paper as well as the watermark of an ox head with crown. Schreiber 1926, 6:20.

16. *Saint Francis* was catalogued by Schreiber when it was in the Albertina, Vienna. He dated it around 1480 and noted that it was formerly in the collection of E. Schultze in Vienna. Schreiber 1926, 6:27. An identical version of the pasteprint exists in the print cabinet in Dresden. *Saint Michael* was also catalogued by Schreiber at the Fürstlich Oettingen-Wallersteinsche Fideikommiss-Bibliothek in Mahingen. He noted the similarity to an engraving by the Master of the Dutuit Mount of Olives. Schreiber 1926, 6:32.

17. The metalcut and pasteprint were adhered into a fifteenth-century manuscript. The pasteprint is not catalogued by Schreiber. According to Mongan (1943, 98), the metalcut was acquired in the 1930s by Rosenwald and had been in the possession of Colnaghi and A.S.W. Rosenbach. Nothing is known of its earlier provenance.

18. Mongan 1943, 108.

19. Mongan 1943, 101–102. Why the image of Saint Catherine would have been covered has to do with the preeminence of the religious movement that popularized the motif of the monogram of Christ, as Mongan has discussed. If the metalcut came from inside the cover of a book, it may also be due to the sixteenth-century practice of preparing pasteboards by pasting together paper scraps. D. Rogers, "A Glimpse into Günther Zainer's Workshop at Augsburg, c. 1475," in *Buch und Text im 15. Jahrhundert*, ed. Lotte Hellinga and Helmar Hartel (Hamburg, 1978).

20. The results and technique are reported in appendix 2.

21. This information is recorded in an analysis report prepared by Lisha Glinsman, conservation scientist, National Gallery of Art, Washington, 17 November 1987.

22. For references to tin deterioration, the following publications were consulted: S. Turgoose, "The Corrosion of Lead and Tin: Before and After Excavation," in *Lead and Tin Studies in Conservation and Technology,* United Kingdom Institute for Conservation Occasional Papers (London, 1985), 15–26; L. L. Shreier, ed., *Corrosion* (London, 1976).

23. Mary Philadelphia Merrifield discussed Burgundy pitch in the general introduction to materials, describing it as a purified pine resin, firmer and more solid than other wood resins. *Original Treatises on the Arts of Painting,* 2 vols. (London, 1849; reprint, New York, 1967), 1:ccli. Fluorescence of contemporary samples of Burgundy pitch and shellac were examined both in solid form and painted out.

24. See Cennino D'A. Cennini, *Il Libro dell'Arte: A Craftsman's Handbook* (1437), trans. Daniel V. Thompson (New Haven, 1933), 26. Merrifield (1967, 1:cxlix, cclix, 30, 686), also discusses the general use of shellac. Lac is mentioned as a red pigment in Strasbourg Staatliche Bibliothek, *The Strasburg*

Manuscript: A Medieval Painters' Handbook, trans. Viola Borradaile and Rosamund Borradaile (London, 1966), 99.

25. Theophilus used saffron to give tin a golden tone. *On Divers Arts*, trans. John G. Hawthorn and Cyril S. Smith (Chicago, 1963), 33. Emil Ernst Ploss discussed the preparation and use of saffron in *Ein Buch von alten Farben: Technologie der Textilfarben im Mittelalter mit einem Ausblick auf die festen Farben* (Munich, 1962), 62–63. Saffron is also discussed in *Strasburg Manuscript*, 1966, 21, 25, 45, 91.

26. This suggestion is noted by Field in Coombs, Farrell, and Field 1986, 32.

27. Geisberg 1912, 311–312, 314–316.

28. Geisberg 1912, 316.

29. Martin Weinberger, *Die Formschnitte des Katharinenklosters zu Nürnberg* (Munich, 1925). Kistner (1950) identified the pasteprints as the work of the Master of the Housemark ↥; however, I did not see the mark in any of the pasteprints I examined, and the workmanship differs significantly from other products of this workshop. Weinberger (1925) noted that the nuns in this convent were known to illustrate the books there.

30. The use of contemporary engravings by metalsmiths is discussed in Johann Michael Fritz, *Gestochene Bilder: Gravierungen auf deutschen Goldschmiedearbeiten der Spätgotik* (Cologne, 1966), 383–439.

31. Another plausible suggestion, supported by evidence of fifteenth-century workshop practices, is that they were intended for use with casts in order to print the inscriptions and compositions properly. This explanation was first proposed by François Courboin and further discussed by Pierre Gusman early in this century. See Coombs, Farrell, and Field 1986, 30–31, for the history of this discussion. Authors have also suggested that the copyist workshops that proliferated prints in the sixteenth century were probably responsible for pasteprint production. Schreiber was the first to identify the pasteprints of the workshop of the Master of the Housemark ↥. The oeuvre of this workshop was further investigated and expanded by Kistner. Field also discussed the pasteprint making activity of copyist workshops in "A *Passion* for the Art Institute," *Print Quarterly* 3 (1986), 215–216.

32. Schreiber (1926, 6:43) suggested that *Saint Simon* (S2874) is a copy of a print by Master E. S., but reversed.

33. According to Schreiber (S2848), this print was pulled from a plate owned by a certain Gumpelzheyn in Regensburg in 1780. Schreiber thought that the plate surely was intended for pasteprints. The owner dated the plate 1497 and had several prints pulled. Schreiber made no mention of the pasteprint version in the Bibliothèque Nationale, Paris.

34. The pasteprint in the Staatsbibliothek, Munich, was recorded by Schreiber (S2848) as (and still is) adhered to a handwritten codex from the cloister Schoenthal (Oberpfalz). The codex bears the handwritten inscription, "Ad 15. decemb. anno 87 taufft pro 10 K," which may indicate that either the book or the pasteprint was purchased on 15 December 1487 for ten kreuzer. Georg Leidinger thought this would be a lot of money for a pasteprint and believed the pasteprint was earlier than 1487. *Die Teigdrucke des XV. Jahrhunderts der kgl. Hof- und Staatsbibliothek in München* (Munich, 1908), n. 23. The Munich version is in better condition than the pasteprint in the Bibliothèque Nationale. Schreiber noted a relationship between the latter and the *Mass of Saint Gregory* print. He was not aware, however, that the Munich and Paris pasteprints are identical.

35. Wilhelm Molsdorf, *Beiträge zur Geschichte und Technik des ältesten Bilddrucks* (Strasbourg, 1921), 84.

36. Coombs, Farrell, and Field 1986, 35–39.

37. Only Kistner (1950, 75) suggests, based on the absence of platemarks in the papers, that pasteprints were formed separately then trimmed and adhered to the paper support.

38. Cennini (1933, 109–110) describes the fourteenth-century practice of molding tin foil to decorate caskets, and Thompson (Cennini 1933, n. 2, 109–110), points out that this technique obviated the preparation of the wood surface with a fine coating of gesso. Techniques for stamping tin are also described in a fifteenth-century manuscript by Jehan Le Begue. This manuscript also includes various organic colorants for toning tin. See Merrifield 1967, 160, 162, 163, 165, 220, 240, 304. Another fifteenth-century source, *Liber Illuministarius* from the Benedictine cloister at Tegernsee, includes directions for stamping tin foil identical in detail to those described by Cennini. See Marjolein Broekman-Bokstijn, J.R.J. van Asperen de Boer, Emilie Helena van't Hul-Ehrnreich, and Karin Verduyn-Groen, "The Scientific Examination of the Polychromed Sculpture in the Herlin Altarpiece," *Studies in Conservation* 15 (1970), 389–390, where the instructions are given in translation. Later examples also exist.

39. Cennini (1933, 60–63), describes a technique for using varnish and toning tin to make it appear golden.

40. Bowman 1985, passim.

41. Such staining would be apparent from the front of mounted pasteprints as well. There is also no embossment of the paper support. The paper is somewhat stiffened by the absorption of the ground, and there is slight cockling around the edges of the pasteprint.

42. The metalcut-pasteprint pair were noted by Schreiber 1926, 6:5. The pasteprint is from a small devotional book written between 1471 and 1481 in Tegernsee. The book had contained two other pasteprints, which are lost. According to Schreiber, this pasteprint is part of a series that includes seventeen images, in some cases known in multiples. A related group, described by Schreiber under S2770, is comprised of nine images, several known in multiples as well. Both series are related to another group, whose examples and multiples total thirteen. In all, more than forty-seven pasteprints are related.

43. A separate adhesive layer would be apparent in the cross sections. The yellow fluorescence is not

characteristic of animal glue or other adhesives.

44. I have not arrived at any explanation of when the tin foil would have been decorated. In the manuals, tin was generally toned in one sheet. This process does not seem compatible, however, with the molding process involved in pasteprints. It is very likely that, after embossing, pasteprints were hand decorated. The decoration may have been the work of a different hand. This may explain the drips of varnish apparent in several of the pasteprints in the National Gallery of Art. The application of shellac or another resin applied in liquid form in situ may account for the threads of varnish.

45. Nor is it satisfactory to assume that the object was formed and then adhered to the paper support afterward. If such were the case, it would be very unlikely that the resin layer would be incompletely adhered to the foil. The foil layer would certainly be covered by the resin layer to the very edges and the full image would be intact. Despite the fact that no platemark is evident, observations of surviving pasteprints strongly suggest that the impression was made with the resin and foil in place on the paper support rather than separately formed. Moreover, a faint impression on *Saint John the Baptist* (S2850m) and a barely discernible yellow stain on *Madonna and Child* (S2824c) may indicate the contours of a metalplate.

46. A good example of an area where the resin may have been melted by contact with the metal plate appears at the bottom right corner of *Madonna and Child* (S2826a) in the Salzburg group.

47. See Ernst Philip Goldschmidt, *Gothic and Renaissance Bookbindings*, 2 vols. (Amsterdam, 1967), 1:83–84; Victor Carter, Lotte Hellinga, and Tony Parker, "Printing with Gold in the Fifteenth Century," *British Library Journal* 9 (1983), 1–13.

48. Carter, Hellinga, and Parker 1983, 5–10.

49. The experiments for this study were conducted using the image of the *Pietà* pasteprint (S2822b) in the National Gallery of Art, Washington, greatly enlarged to facilitate execution. The image was carved into a wooden matrix. Prints were pulled from this matrix. A cast was prepared of the matrix using a low-melting alloy of tin, lead, and bismuth. When liquid varnish was applied to the reverse of the molded tin foil or to the paper, the resin did not afford adequate adhesion for the foil, nor was it possible to use the varnish thickly enough on paper to achieve the molded layer that is characteristic of all pasteprints. The more successful experiments with powdered rosin were conducted following the instruction published by Carter, Hellinga, and Parker 1983, 13. The paper, rosin, and foil were placed in contact with the heated cast and weighted in place. The details of the cast were faithfully reproduced in the foil and resin, including the diagonal crack that developed as the cast was heated. No doubt a higher-melting-temperature metal would have been used.

50. In the literature there has been a tendency to link pasteprints with Johannes Gutenberg's invention of movable type because they share the common knowledge of casting technology. Casting was widely used for punches for bookbinding and decoration, however, and bookbinding techniques may be the next fruitful area for further investigation.

51. Panel stamping, a nearly contemporary bookbinding technique, was practiced from approximately 1480 to 1530 in France and somewhat later in Germany. For this technique, metalworkers were employed especially for the purpose of producing large plates used to emboss leather instead of the more laborious work of individual, small punches. See Goldschmidt 1967, 1:54–70.

BIBLIOGRAPHY

Amelung, P. *Der Frühdruck im deutschen Südwesten, 1473–1500.* Stuttgart, 1979.

Bartsch, Friedrich von. *Die Kupferstichsammlung der K. K. Hofbibliothek in Wien.* Vienna, 1854.

Berger, Ernst. *Quellen und Technik der Fresko-, Öl- und Tempera-Malerei des Mittelalters.* 1912. Reprint, Germany, 1973.

Bonnardot, Alfred. *Restauration des anciennes estampes et des livres rares.* Paris, 1858. Reprint, New York, 1967.

Bowman, Cynthia. "Pasteprints: A New Hypothesis about Their Production." *Print Quarterly* 2 (1985), 4–11.

Brachert, Thomas. "Pressbrokat Applikationen, ein Hilfsmittel für die Stilkritik." *Schweizerisches Institut für Kunstwissenschaft, Jahresbericht* (1963), 37–47.

Braunstein, P. "Exposé introductif à Table ronde sur 'La gravure avant Dürer'." *Nouvelles de l'Estampe* (1982), 6–8.

Broekman-Bokstijn, Marjolein, J.R.J. van Asperen de Boer, Emilie Helena van't Hul-Ehrnreich, and Karin Verduyn-Groen. "The Scientific Examination of the Polychromed Sculpture in the Herlin Altarpiece." *Studies in Conservation* 15 (1970), 370–400.

Burch, R. M. *Colour Printing and Colour Printers.* New York, 1910.

Butze, G. "Zwei bemerkenswerte Platten auf einem Einband in Görlitz." In *Festschrift Ernst Kyriss.* Stuttgart, 1961. 281–286.

Campbell, L. "The Art Market in South Netherlands." *Burlington Magazine* 8 (1986), 370–400.

Carter, Victor, Lotte Hellinga, and Tony Parker. "Printing with Gold in the Fifteenth Century." *British Library Journal* 9 (1983), 1–13.

Cennini, Cennino D'A. *Il Libro dell'Arte: A Craftsman's Handbook.* 1437. Translated by Daniel V. Thompson. New Haven, 1933.

Coombs, Elizabeth, Eugene Farrell, and Richard S. Field. *Pasteprints: A Technical and Art Historical Investigation.* Cambridge, Mass., 1986.

Courboin, François. "Quelques enrichissements récents du Cabinet des Estampes." *Revue de l'art ancien et moderne* 31 (1912), 19–28.

Dodgson, Campbell. *Introduction to Early German and Flemish Woodcuts in the British Museum.* Vol. 1. London, 1903.

Field, Richard S. *Fifteenth-Century Woodcuts and Other Relief Prints in the Collection of the Metropolitan Museum of Art.* [exh. cat., Metropolitan Museum of Art] New York, 1977.

———. "A *Passion* for the Art Institute." *Print Quarterly* 3 (1986), 191–216.

Fritz, Johann Michael. *Gestochene Bilder: Gravierungen auf deutschen Goldschmiedearbeiten der Spätgotik.* Cologne, 1966.

Fuchs, R. W. "Die Mainzer Frühdrucke mit Buchholzschnitten, 1480–1500." *Börsenblatt für den Deutschen Buchhandel* (1958), 1129–1164.

Geisberg, Max. *Die Anfänge des Kupferstiches.* Vol. 2. 2d ed. Leipzig, 1923.

———. *Geschichte der deutschen Graphik vor Dürer.* Berlin, 1939.

———. "Holzschnittbildnisse des Kaisers Maximilian." *Jahrbuch der preußischen Kunstsammlungen* 32 (1911), 236–248.

———. "Teigdruck und Metallschnitt." *Monatshefte für Kunstwissenschaft* 5 (1912), 311–320.

Gerhardt, Claus W. "Wie haben Ratdolt und Callierges Ende des 15. Jahrhunderts in Venedig ihre Drucke mit Blattgold hergestellt?" *Gutenberg-Jahrbuch* (1984), 145–150.

Goddard, Stephen H. "Brocade Patterns in the Shop of the Master of Frankfurt: An Accessory to Stylistic Analysis." *Art Bulletin* 67 (1985), 401–417.

Goldschmidt, Ernest Philip. *Gothic and Renaissance Bookbindings*, 2 vols. Amsterdam, 1967.

———. *The Printed Book of the Renaissance.* Cambridge, 1950.

Gusman, Pierre. *La gravure sur bois et d'épargne sur métal.* Paris, 1916.

———. "Un Incunable et son histoire." *Gazette des Beaux-Arts* 7 (1912), 271–278.

Haemmerk, A. *Buntpapier.* Munich, 1977.

Hébert, Michele. *Inventaire des gravures du Nord.* Paris, n.d.

Hecht, Brigitte. "Betrachtungen über Pressbrokate: Rekonstruktionsversuche unter besonderer Berücksichtigung des sogenannten Tegernseer Manuscripts." *Maltechnik-Restauro* 1 (1980), 22–49.

Hirsch, R., "The Decoration of a 1486 Book Wrapper and Its Reappearance in 1531." *Studies in the Renaissance* 6 (1959), 167–174.

Huth, Hans. *Künstler und Werkstatt der Spätgotik.* Augsburg, 1923.

Indestege, L. "Brügger Kaufmannsbücher und ihre Verzierung." In *Festschrift Ernst Kyriss.* Stuttgart, 1961. 261–280.

Kistner, Erwin. "Studien an Teigdrucken aus dem Besitz des Germanischen Nationalmuseums in Nürnberg." In *Festschrift Eugen Stollreither.* Edited by Fritz Redenbacher. Erlangen, 1950. 65–97.

Köster, Kurt. "Gutenbergs Aachener Heiltumsspiegel." In *Das Werk der Bücher: Festschrift für Horst Kliemann.* Freiburg, 1956. 284–301.

———. "Gutenbergs Straßburger Aachenspiegel-Unternehmen." *Gutenberg-Jahrbuch* (1983), 24–44.

———. "Pilgerzeichen-Studien: Neue Beiträge zur Kenntnis eines mittelalterlichen Massenartikels und seiner Überlieferungsformen." In *Bibliotheca Docet: Festschrift Carl Wehmer.* Amsterdam, 1963. 77–100.

———. "Religiöse Medaillen und Wallfahrts-Devotionalien in der flämischen Buchmalerei des 15. und frühen 16. Jahrhunderts." In *Buch und Welt: Festschrift für Gustav Hofmann.* Wiesbaden, 1965. 459–504.

Krys, K. "Notes on a Fifteenth Century Coffret."

Connoisseur (London ed.), September 1957, 62–66.

Lehmann-Haupt, Hellmut. *Gutenberg and the Master of the Playing Cards.* New Haven, 1966.

Lehrs, M. "Die dekorative Verwendung von Holzschnitten im XV. und XVI. Jahrhundert." *Jahrbuch der Kgl. Preußischen Kunstsammlungen* 29 (1908), 183–194.

Leidinger, Georg. *Die Teigdrucke des XV. Jahrhunderts der kgl. Hof- und Staatsbibliothek in München.* Munich, 1908.

———. *Teigdrucke in Salzburger Bibliotheken.* Munich, 1913.

Lemoisne, Paul-André. *Les Xylographes du XIVe et du XVe Siècle au Cabinet des Estampes de la Bibliothèque Nationale.* Paris, 1927.

Lewis, John Frederick. "Teigdrucke." *Proceedings of the Numismatic and Antiquarian Society of Philadelphia for the Years 1902–1903* (1904), 189–194.

Mabbott, Thomas Ollive. "Pasteprints and Sealprints." *Metropolitan Museum Studies* 4, pt. 1 (1932–1933), 55–75.

———. "Seal-prints and a Seal-paste-print." *Bulletin of the New York Public Library* 32 (1928), 511–519.

De Mayerne, Turquet T. *Picturia sculptoria et quae subalternarum artium.* 1620. Reprint, Lyon, 1974.

Merrifield, Mary Philadelphia. *Original Treatises on the Arts of Painting.* 2 vols. London, 1849. Reprint, New York, 1967.

Molsdorf, Wilhelm. *Die Bedeutung Koelns für den Metallschnitt des XV. Jahrhunderts.* Strasbourg, 1909.

———. *Beiträge zur Geschichte und Technik des ältesten Bilddrucks.* Strasbourg, 1921.

Mongan, Elizabeth. "Two Undescribed Fifteenth Century Prints in the Collection of Lessing J. Rosenwald." *Art in America* 31, no. 2 (April 1943), 98–108.

Needham, Paul. *Twelve Centuries of Bookbindings, 400–1600.* New York and London, 1979.

Ognibeni, G., "Brokatapplikationen auf Wachsbasis: Bericht über eine Versuchsreihe am Braunschweigischen Landesmuseum." *Maltechnik-Restauro* 87 (1981), 35–37.

Passavant, Johann D., *Le Peintre-graveur.* Leipzig, 1860–1864.

Ploss, Emil Ernst. *Ein Buch von alten Farben: Technologie der Textilfarben im Mittelalter mit einem Ausblick auf die festen Farben.* Munich, 1962.

Rogers, D. "A Glimpse into Günther Zainer's Workshop at Augsburg, c. 1475," In *Buch und Text im 15. Jahrhundert.* Edited by Lotte Hellinga and Helmar Hartel. Hamburg, 1978.

Ruppel, A., ed. *Gutenberg Festschrift, 1925.* Mainz, 1925.

Schreiber, Wilhelm L. *Die Meister der Metallschneidekunst nebst einem nach Schulen geordneten Katalog ihrer Arbeiten.* 8 vols. Strasbourg, 1926. Volume 6 contains the pasteprint information.

Shestack, Alan. *Master E. S.: Five Hundredth Anniversary Exhibition.* [exh. cat., Philadelphia Museum of Art] Philadelphia, 1967.

Shreier, L. L., ed. *Corrosion.* London, 1976.

Spamer, Adolf. *Das kleine Andachtsbild vom XIV. bis XX. Jahrhundert.* Munich, 1930.

Strasbourg Staatliche Bibliothek. *The Strasburg Manuscript.* Translated by Viola Borradaile and Rosamund Borradaile. London, 1966.

Theophilus. *On Divers Arts.* Translated by John G. Hawthorn and Cyril S. Smith. Chicago, 1963.

Turgoose, S. "The Corrosion of Lead and Tin: Before and After Excavation." In *Lead and Tin Studies in Conservation and Technology.* United Kingdom Institute for Conservation Occasional Papers. London, 1985. 15–26.

Wehmer, Carol. "Gutenbergs Typographie und die Teigdrucke des Monogrammisten d." In *Essays in Honour of Victor Scholderer.* Edited by D. E. Rhodes. Mainz, 1970. 426–484.

Weigel, Theodor Oswald, and August Christian Adolf Zestermann. *Die Anfänge der Druckerkunst in Bild und Schrift an deren frühesten Erzeugnissen in der Weigelschen Sammlung erlandet.* 2 vols. Leipzig, 1865. 331–334.

Weinberger, Martin. *Die Formschnitte des Katharinenklosters zu Nürnberg.* Munich, 1925.

APPENDIX 1

Pasteprints Examined

When available dimensions are noted, height by width in centimeters are followed by approximate height and width in inches. Many of the pasteprints have irregular dimensions due to their fragmented condition.

Bibliothèque Nationale, Paris
S2795 *Crucifixion*
S2811y *Saint Veronica's Veil with Papalarius*
S2820 *Resurrected Christ with Two Angels*
S2821 *Resurrected Christ with Two Angels*
S2845 *Saint George and the Dragon*, identical to S2845a, National Gallery of Art, Washington
S2848b *Mass of Saint Gregory* (fig. 46), 10.6 x 7.2 (4 13/16 x 2 7/8), identical to S2848, in Staatsbibliothek, Munich. A metalcut in the Germanisches Nationalmuseum, Nuremberg, is an identical but reversed image.

British Museum, London
S2776 *Christ Washing the Disciples' Feet*
S2842 *Saint Dorothy*

Germanisches Nationalmuseum, Nuremberg
S2769 *Annunciation*
S2774 *Birth of Christ*
S2774m *Christ in the Temple*

S2775r *Flight into Egypt*
S2777 *Christ Washing the Disciples' Feet*
S2777m *Lord's Supper*
S2778c *Christ at the Mount of Olives*
S2779 *Christ at the Mount of Olives*
S2780 *Arrest*
S2781 *Christ before Pilate*
S2784 *Flagellation*
S2787 *Christ with the Crown of Thorns*
S2801 *Crucifixion*
S2802 *Crucifixion*
S2803 *Descent from the Cross*
S2807 *Lamentation*
S2817r *Christ with the Crown of Thorns*
S2822 *Pietà*
S2844 *Saint George*
S2827 *Madonna in Glory with Four Angels* (fig. 2), 10.4 x 7.5 (4 1/8 x 2 15/16)
S2787m *Christ Mocked*
S2798n *Christ on the Cross with Mary and John*
Pietà
Not Catalogued by Schreiber
Crucifixion

Guildhall Library, London
S2791 *Christ Crucified between Two Thieves* (fig. 3)

Harvard University Art Museums, Cambridge
S2776 *Christ Washing the Disciples' Feet*
S2789 *Christ Disrobed by the Soldiers*
S2851 *Saint Jerome*

Library of Congress, Washington
S2836a *Saint Catherine* (bound in a fifteenth-century German psalter)

Metropolitan Museum of Art, New York
S2839 *Saint Christopher*
S2854b *Saint Margaret*

National Gallery of Art, Washington
S2788, variant *Christ Carrying the Cross* (fig. 4), 10.9 x 7.6 (4 5/16 x 3)
S2811m *Trinity* (fig. 15), 3.9 x 3.1 (1 9/16 x 1 3/16)
S2811z *Sudarium* (fig. 16), 3.9 x 2.9 (1 9/16 x 1 1/8)
S2822b *Pietà* (fig. 14), 3.9 x 3.1 (1 9/16 x 1 1/8). The metalcut in Bibliothèque Nationale, Paris, is the same size.
S2824c *Madonna and Child* (fig. 30), 10 x 7.3 (4 x 2 7/8)
S2825 *Madonna and Child* (fig. 22), 7.5 x 4.5 (2 7/8 x 1 3/4)
S2826a *Madonna and Child* (fig. 11), 3.9 x 3.3 (1 9/16 x 1 5/16)
S2837a *Saint Catherine* (fig. 13), 4 x 3.1 (1 9/16 x 1 1/8)
S2843 *Saint Francis* (fig. 33), 10.3 x 7.4 (4 1/16 x 2 7/8)
S2845a *Saint George and the Dragon* (fig. 5), 9.9 x 7.2 (3 7/8 x 2 13/16), identical to S2845, in the Bibliothèque Nationale, Paris
S2850m *Saint John the Baptist* (fig. 20), 10.5 x 7.5 (4 1/16 x 2 15/16)
S2854d *Saint Margaret* (fig. 12), 4 x 3 (1 9/16 x 1 3/16)
S2856 *Saint Michael* (fig. 34), 10.1 x 7.3 (3 15/16 x 2 7/8)
S2861m *Unknown Saint* (fig. 10), 3.9 x 3 (1 9/16 x 1 3/16)
S2861n *Unknown Saint* (fig. 9), 3.9 x 3.2 (1 9/16 x 1 1/4)
Not Catalogued by Schreiber
Saint Catherine (fig. 35), 5.2 x 4 (2 x 1 9/16)

Staatsbibliothek, Munich
S2775 *Adoration* (fig. 52), 10.8 x 7.5 (4 1/4 x 2 15/16). The metalcut in the Bibliothèque Nationale, Paris (fig. 51), is the same size.
S2778a *Jesus at the Mount of Olives*
S2782 *Flagellation*
S2783 *Flagellation*
S2789m *Christ with Mary and John*
S2794 *Christ on the Cross*
S2797 *Christ on the Cross*
S2806 *Lamentation*
S2807 *Lamentation*
S2808 *Entombment*
S2809 *Descent of the Holy Spirit at Pentecost*
S2810 *Descent of the Holy Spirit at Pentecost*
S2811p *God the Father with the Dead Christ*
S2816 *Man of Sorrows*
S2816m *Man of Sorrows between Mary and John*
S2817 *Man of Sorrows*
S2823 *Madonna and Child* (seated), three examples
S2827a *Madonna in Glory Crowned by Angels*
S2833x *Saint Catherine*
S2834 *Saint Catherine*
S2836 *Saint Catherine*
S2846a *Saint George*
S2848 *Saint Gregory*
S2849 *Saint Helen*
S2852 *Saint Leonard*
S2856m *Saint Nicholas*
S2858 *Saint Sebastian*
S2860b *Saint Wolfgang*
S2862a *Unidentified Saint*
S2862b *Unidentified Saint*
S2862x *Unidentified Person*
S2862y *Unidentified Person*
S2862z *Unidentified Person*

Stadtbibliothek, Nuremberg
S2770 *Annunciation*
S2778 *Jesus at the Mount of Olives*
S2783 *Flagellation*
S2783a *Flagellation*
S2821 *Risen Christ with Two Angels*
S2833a *Saint Barbara*
S2838 *Saint Christopher*
S2854 *Saint Maria Egyptiaca*

APPENDIX 2

National Gallery of Art Scientific Research Department Analysis Report

1943.3.783 (S2824c)
Madonna and Child
German, 15th century

1943.3.786 (S2850m)
Saint John the Baptist
German, 15th century

Pasteprints were produced in the fifteenth and sixteenth centuries mainly in Germany. The method of producing them has been discussed by Coombs, Farrell, and Field.[1] The Mellon Fellow, Sarah Bertalan, is examining pasteprints in the National Gallery's collections. This report addresses some of the technical inquiries made in collaboration with the scientific research department.

Many pasteprints were examined in ultraviolet radiation. The surfaces fluoresced orange and dark purple. The orange fluorescence often suggests the presence of shellac. Two pasteprints were examined closely: *Madonna and Child* and *Saint John the Baptist*. Both were examined using the stereomicroscope at high magnification. Samples were removed for x-ray diffraction studies.[2] Cross sections were removed from both to examine the construction of the pasteprints. The cross section from *Saint John the Baptist* was complete down to and including the paper substrate. The cross sections both have a dark layer of ink as the top layer. The ink layer of the cross section from *Saint John the Baptist* was photographed before the section was mounted. The ink appears to contain colored particles, including small red particles; these are possibly red iron oxide. In both cross sections there is a dark brown layer underneath the ink layer. The brown layer does not contain any visible particulate material. When examined using the Ploemopak illumination system on the Leitz Orthoplan, a xenon gas lamp, and a filter that allows irradiation at c. 500 nm, this brown layer fluoresces orange. Below the brown layer is a thicker layer that is white in the cross section from *Saint John the Baptist* and light brown in the section from *Madonna and Child*. This layer does not fluoresce in visible light. The section from *Saint John the Baptist* has two more layers. The next from the surface is a light brown layer that fluoresces yellow-green when illuminated with c. 500 nm radiation. Close examination of the section from *Madonna and Child* reveals there is a trace of this layer at the bottom of the section. The layer on the bottom of the section from *Saint John* is the paper substrate.

A whitish sample from the bottom layer observable in *Madonna and Child* was examined using the Mettler FP82 hot stage on the Leitz

Table 1. Line Spacings and Intensities of Samples from the Pasteprints and Comparative Standards

Unknown I		*SnO_2, 21–1250 Cassiterite*		*Unknown II*		*NaOH*, 15–895		*Unknown III*		*SnO_2* 21–1250		*SnO* 6–395	
d,Å	I/I_o	d,Å	I/I_o	d,Å	I/I_o	d,Å	I/I_o	d,Å	I/I_o	d,Å	I/I_o	d,Å	I/I_o
3.35	—	3.35	100	3.36	100	—	—	3.36	—	3.35	100	—	—
2.65	—	2.644	80	2.64	50	—	—	2.99	90	—	—	2.99	100
—	—	—	—	*2.50	100	2.50	100	2.68	20	—	—	2.69	35
2.39	—	2.366	6	2.38	10	—	—	2.65	80	2.64	80	—	—
—	—	—	—	*1.78	80	1.77	50	2.93	5	—	—	—	—
1.77	—	1.765	65	1.77	15	—	—	2.41	—	—	—	2.41	14
—	—	1.685	18	1.675	—	—	—	2.38	—	—	—	—	—
—	—	1.593	8	—	—	—	—	1.90	—	—	—	1.90	14
—	—	1.498	14	—	—	—	—	1.80	—	—	—	1.80	25
—	—	—	—	*1.474	20	1.45	14	—	—	—	—	1.60	25
—	—	1.439	18	—	—	—	—	1.783	100	1.765	65	—	—
—	—	1.415	16	—	—	—	—	1.68	—	1.675	18	—	—
—	—	1.322	8	—	—	—	—	1.49	—	1.498	14	1.495	12
—	—	1.215	12	—	—	—	—	—	—	—	—	1.48	12
—	—	—	—	—	—	—	—	1.44	—	1.439	18	—	—
—	—	—	—	—	—	—	—	1.42	—	1.415	16	—	—
—	—	—	—	—	—	—	—	1.34	—	—	—	—	—
—	—	—	—	—	—	—	—	1.32	—	1.322	8	—	—
—	—	—	—	—	—	—	—	1.24	—	1.215	12	—	—

Orthoplan microscope equipped with a x6.5 ultropak objective. The start temperature was 45°C, rate of rise 1°C/minute; the results are summarized below.

Temperature, °C	*Observations*
94.6	movement of sample
127	melting of most of sample
220	charring begins

A second sample had completely melted at 193°C and charred at 220°C.

A sample of the white material from below the ink (unknown I), a sample of white material from on top of the ink (unknown II), and a gray-brown sample (unknown III; the sample was grayish white and topped by a black fragment, possibly ink) from *Saint John* were examined using x-ray powder diffraction (XRD) techniques.[2] The data were collected over eighteen hours on film strip. The white material contained a small proportion of red and blue particles. Line spacings were measured using a calibrated rule and intensities estimated visually and related to the most intense line as a percentage—I/I_0. The results are tabulated below and possible assignments made. The powder diffraction pattern of the material from the surface of the pasteprint had two discrete sets of lines in that one set was rather diffuse and the other set dotted. The sets of lines were inferred to be due to different phases. The dotted lines are asterisked and considered as a separate set when estimating relative intensities. The lines for known species were obtained from JCPDS files.[3]

In ultraviolet light the pasteprints all have areas that fluoresce orange and purple. Evidence of consolidation on one or two pasteprints was shown by white fluorescence. Some pasteprints have red borders that are most likely painted. In one instance the pigment was shown to be red lead (Pb_3O_4).

From the cross sections obtained the two pasteprints examined have a more simple structure than proposed in reference 1. There are five layers. In order from the bottom: (i) the paper substrate, (ii) a layer that fluoresces yellow-green suggesting an oil, resin, or oil-resin mixture, (iii) a white layer which XRD shows to be SnO_2, (iv) a layer that fluoresces orange suggesting shellac,[4] (v) black ink that contains small red particles.

NOTES TO APPENDIX

This report was prepared in September 1988 by Barbara Berrie, acting head of the scientific research department, National Gallery of Art.

1. Elizabeth Coombs, Eugene Farrell, and Richard S. Field, *Pasteprints: A Technical and Art Historical Investigation* (Cambridge, Mass., 1986).

2. The Philips XRG 3100 generator was used equipped with a copper target and a nickel filter to provide monochromatic radiation of 1.540 Å. The anode voltage was 45 kV and the current 25 mA. The sample was mounted onto a glass fiber using silicone grease and run in a Gandolphi camera for 18 hours. When examined under high power, the bottom white layer from *Madonna and Child* could be seen to contain a small proportion of red and blue particles. In transmitted polarized light the red particles were red, spherical, and had high relief.

3. *Powder Diffraction File* JCPDS International Centre for Diffraction Data, Swarthmore, Pa., 1982.

4. Other materials, such as rosin and certain red and yellow organic pigments and dyes also fluoresce orange in ultraviolet light.

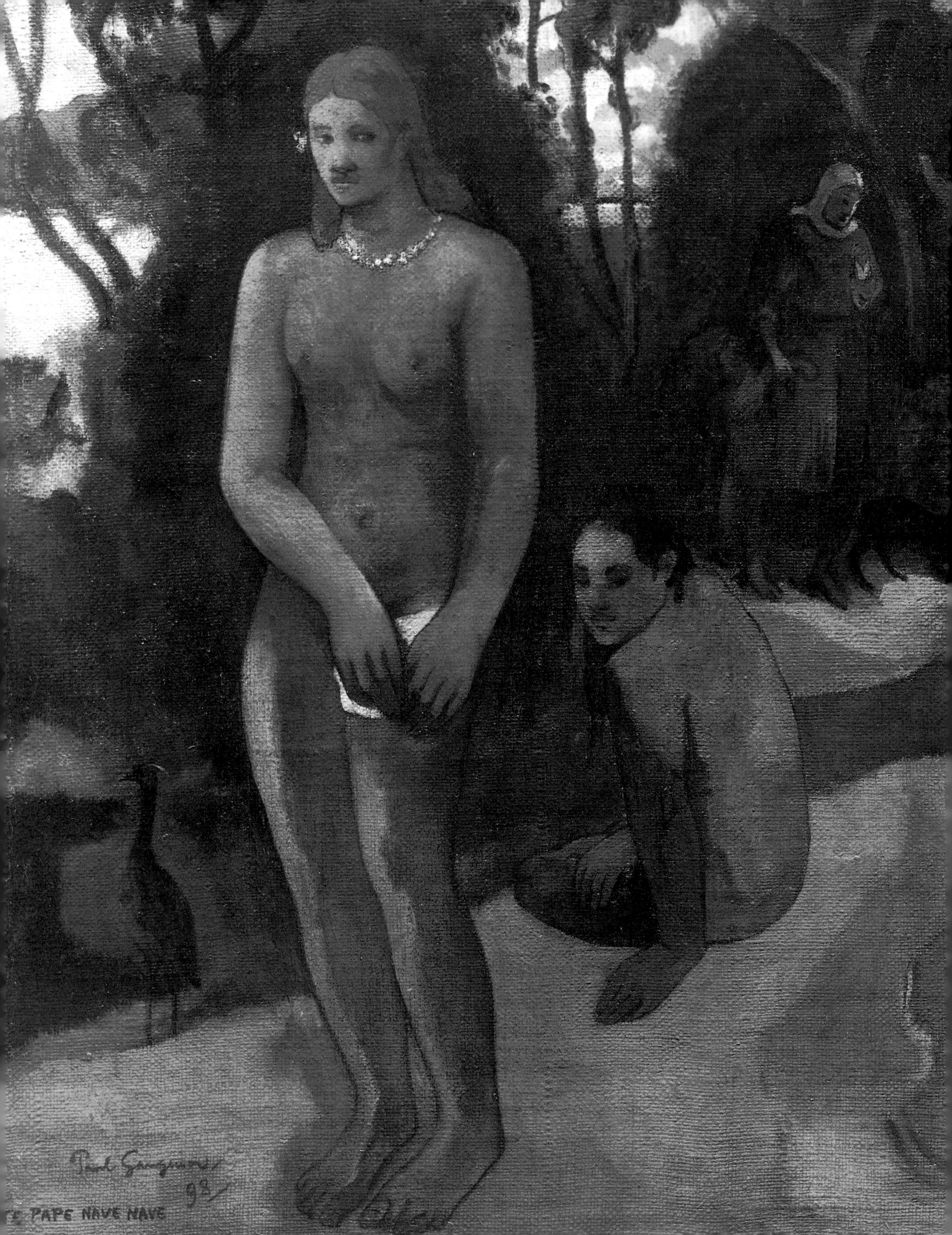
Paul Gauguin
98
PAPE NAVE NAVE

CAROL CHRISTENSEN

The Painting Materials and Technique of Paul Gauguin

Although much has been written about Paul Gauguin the man—about his way of life in the South Seas and the sources of his art—little has been written that considers his art from a technical viewpoint. Nevertheless, a technical study of Gauguin's paintings is particularly interesting, because it allows us not only to examine the degree to which his often remote surroundings influenced his painting technique but also to sort out a number of contradictory impressions we have of him as a painter within these surroundings. Was Gauguin the technical innovator and self-described experimenter[1] whose creative genius blossomed in the isolation of the tropics? Or was he instead the unhappy victim of circumstance whose poverty forced him to paint on native sackcloth?[2] How much, if at all, did his unusual environment influence his technique?

The answers are complex. Gauguin's preference for painting in primitive tropical areas where artists' supplies were limited meant that he had to work in an extremely humid climate, accept the difficulties of shipping his art back to France where it could be exhibited, and endure long periods when he was without art supplies. To some degree all these limitations influenced his painting technique. However, many aspects of his technique generally associated with the South Seas period and assumed to be a result of his special circumstances there were actually first used in Brittany and Arles. Furthermore, there is little in his painting technique, apart from his use of very coarse fabric, that is significantly different from other nonacademic art of his time, so the notion of Gauguin as a technically radical painter is something of a myth,[3] although his role as stylistic innovator is without question.

Gauguin's correspondence is full of information about his materials and technique, but unfortunately he was not always a reliable source. He talked at great length about those aspects of his work that he wanted to share with the public, but about other technical matters he was silent. And because he was a rather shrewd self-promoter, his descriptions of technique occasionally distorted his actual creative process to sell himself to his audience.

For example, Gauguin's assertion that he created his most important work, *Where Are We Going?* (W561) (fig. 1),[4] without preparatory studies in a great burst of activity just before an alleged suicide attempt in 1897,[5] has been disproven by the existence of a preparatory drawing of *Where Are We Going?* (fig. 2), squared for transfer, and several figure studies exhibited in 1988 in *The Art of Paul Gauguin*, National Gallery of Art, Washington. Furthermore, Richard Brettell has convincingly argued that although the painting is dated 1897, Gauguin worked on it extensively during 1898 but insisted on the 1897 date, possibly to link the making of the

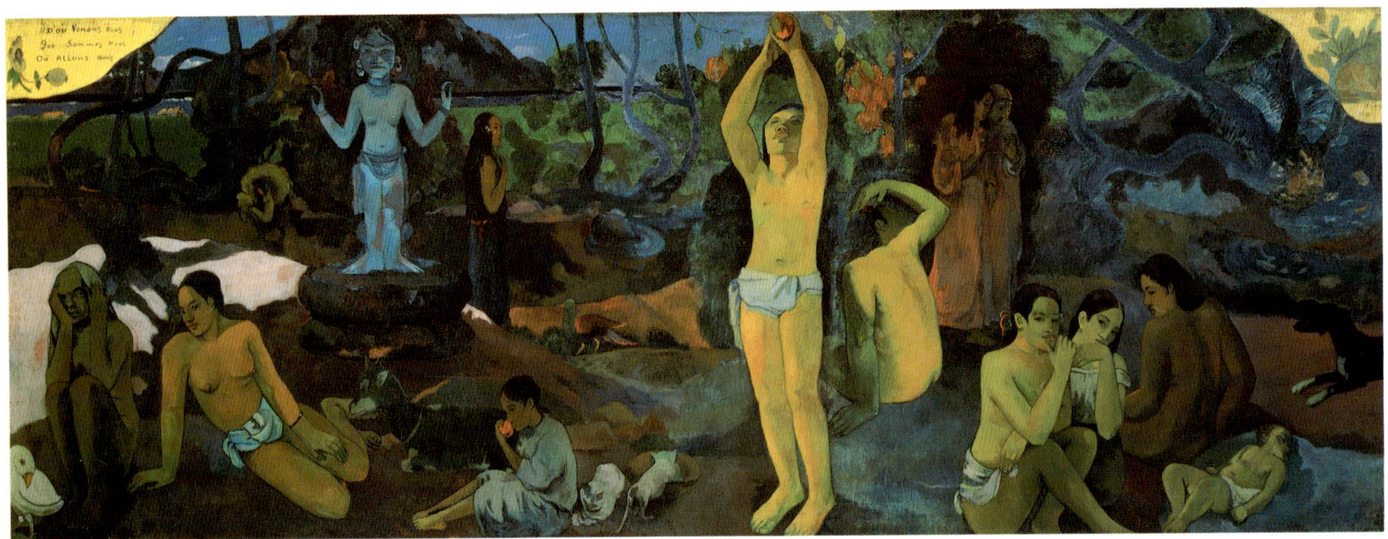

1. Paul Gauguin, *Where Do We Come From? What Are We? Where Are We Going?*, 1897–1898, painting on fabric
Museum of Fine Arts, Boston, Tompkins Collection

painting with his suicide attempt.[6] Brettell's evidence suggests that the painting was very carefully planned—quite the opposite of the impression given by Gauguin himself. This example demonstrates the importance of comparing the physical evidence provided by Gauguin's paintings with his correspondence and other contemporary documents to determine his actual creative process.

The 1988 Gauguin exhibition at the National Gallery of Art, Washington, afforded the opportunity to examine a large body of Gauguin's paintings, and they provided a valuable starting point in a study that eventually included 142 works. Although it was not possible to study all paintings in equal depth, an attempt was made to characterize the type of fabric, priming layer, paint medium, pigments, varnish, stretchers, glazing, framing, and even restoration techniques the artist used. Based on examination of about one-third of his entire work, this study allows the following observations about Gauguin's technique.

During Gauguin's time in the South Seas, such aspects of his style as the thinning of the paint layer, changes in the materials he used to prepare his absorbent grounds, as well as the smaller size and finer weave of the canvases of his very late works were clearly influenced by the hot, humid environment of Tahiti and the Marquesas and by his periodic difficulties in obtaining supplies. However, his use of predominantly coarse canvas, absorbent grounds, and lack of high impasto were developed much earlier, during his time in Brittany and Arles. While he often justified these aspects of his technique as a response to his special environment, in fact he chose to paint the way he did largely for aesthetic reasons and not because of the limitations of his surroundings. (For a brief chronology of Gauguin's life, see app. 1.)

SUPPORTS

Gauguin's choice of coarse fabric for his South Seas paintings is well known, but his use of a wide variety of other fabrics throughout his career is less well documented. Although there is evidence that in the 1890s he came to prefer coarse fabric as a painting sup-

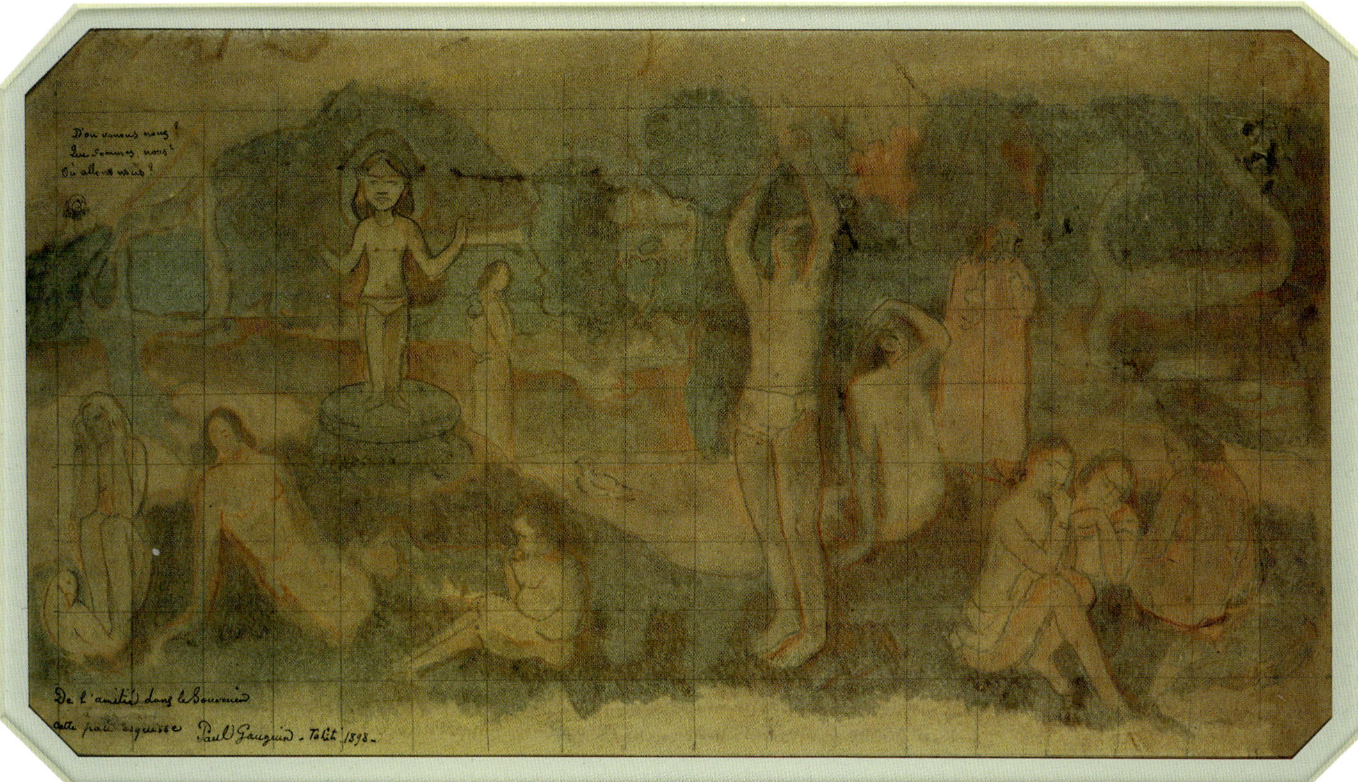

2. Paul Gauguin, squared study for *Where Do We Come From? What Are We? Where Are We Going?*, 1898, brush and blue watercolor and brown crayon pencil over preliminary drawing on tracing paper laid down on wove paper, squared in graphite
Musée National des Arts Africains et Océaniens, Paris

port,[7] he continued to paint on many different types of fabric even during his years in the South Seas. Lack of supplies forced him to paint on one specific type of fabric during his last years in the Marquesas, but in general he was not rigid in his canvas preferences and painted on whatever was available either locally or through shipment from friends.

When he began to paint in the 1870s, Gauguin used the conventional finely woven, commercially primed canvas supports popular with most of the artists of his time, including the impressionists. In his early paintings, the fabric texture is not emphasized, and the priming does not show beneath the thick medium-rich paint layer. During the early 1880s, however, the texture of the fabric support began to play an increasingly important role in the visual impact of Gauguin's paintings; he no longer consistently obscured the texture of his support with a thick layer of paint.

Throughout the 1880s, Gauguin's priming layer became more apparent through the increasingly thin paint layers above it. In this technique he was following a trend of his fellow impressionists, who often painted on fabrics with extremely thin commercially prepared absorbent grounds, which they intentionally left exposed.

During the crucial years of his development (1886–1888), when he was breaking away from impressionism and formulating his own style, Gauguin occasionally painted on unprimed canvas. The roughness of the fabric, the increasing thinness of the priming and paint layers, and the intentionally matte surface created a result in which the support rather than the paint itself provided texture.

It was in Arles, where Gauguin went to live with Vincent van Gogh for the last three months of 1888, that the two artists first experimented with the coarse, burlap-type fabric that has been generally associated with Gauguin's Tahitian paintings. In November 1888, van Gogh wrote to his brother Théo that Gauguin had bought twenty meters of very coarse fabric (*toile très forte*).[8] A week later, in a letter to Emile Bernard, Gauguin described a painting on coarse sackcloth (*grosse toile à sac*), underlining the phrase for emphasis.[9] In late November, he again mentioned the coarse fabric in a letter to his friend Emile Schuffenecker,[10] and in the same week he complained in a letter to Théo van Gogh that the coarse sackcloth was difficult to stretch.[11] The fact that Gauguin mentioned the material so often and complained about the difficulties he experienced with it suggests the fabric was new to him and he was trying to master its use as a painting support. For this reason, it seems probable that Gauguin executed his *Self-portrait Dedicated to Carrière* (W384) (fig. 3), painted on coarse fabric, no earlier than his 1888 Arles visit and not in 1886, as has been recently suggested.[12]

The supports for the Arles paintings vary dramatically. At least four (W304, W305, W239, W311) of the seventeen paintings produced there by Gauguin are on the very coarse (4–8 threads per cm) fabric mentioned by van Gogh in his letters. This same fabric was used as a support by van Gogh when he painted two of his views of the Alyscamps.[13] Interestingly, though, for another version of the same view (W307), Gauguin used a very fine fabric (22–24 threads per cm) with the qualities of handkerchief linen. Another painting by Gauguin from this period, *Farm at Arles* (W308), is painted on a third type of fabric (18 threads per cm). It is clear that, in Arles, Gauguin was experimenting for the first time with a broad range of fabric supports, and the paintings' surface appearances vary considerably because of the differing textures of their fabric supports. For example, in *At the Café* (W305), the support is both very coarse and unprimed, and, as a result, the paint seems to sink into the fabric, creating a nubby, matte surface appearance more characteristic of fresco than conventional easel paintings.

To what degree did Gauguin's choice of fabric influence his painting style at Arles? Examination of a number of his Arles paintings showed that those works painted on coarse canvas usually lack the small, hatched, vertical brushstrokes influenced by the technique of Paul Cézanne that Gauguin used in those Arles paintings executed on more conventional fabric. However, in later paintings, such as *Bonjour M. Gauguin* (W322) from 1890, painted on coarse fabric, the hatched brushstroke is again clearly evident. Therefore, it seems that although Gauguin may have liked the look of the paintings on coarse fabric, the choice of fabric did not specifically lead him to paint in a broader, more smoothly blended style. Rather, his time in Arles was simply a period of experimentation with a variety of combinations of support and brushstroke.

In the two years after he left Arles in December 1888, when he traveled frequently among Paris, Le Pouldu, and Pont-Aven, Gauguin largely abandoned the use of coarse fabric,[14] painting instead on a variety of more finely woven fabrics. The recurrence of at least five different fabrics during Gauguin's travels at this time suggests he probably carried rolls of fabric with him. An exception was his June–November 1890 visit to Le

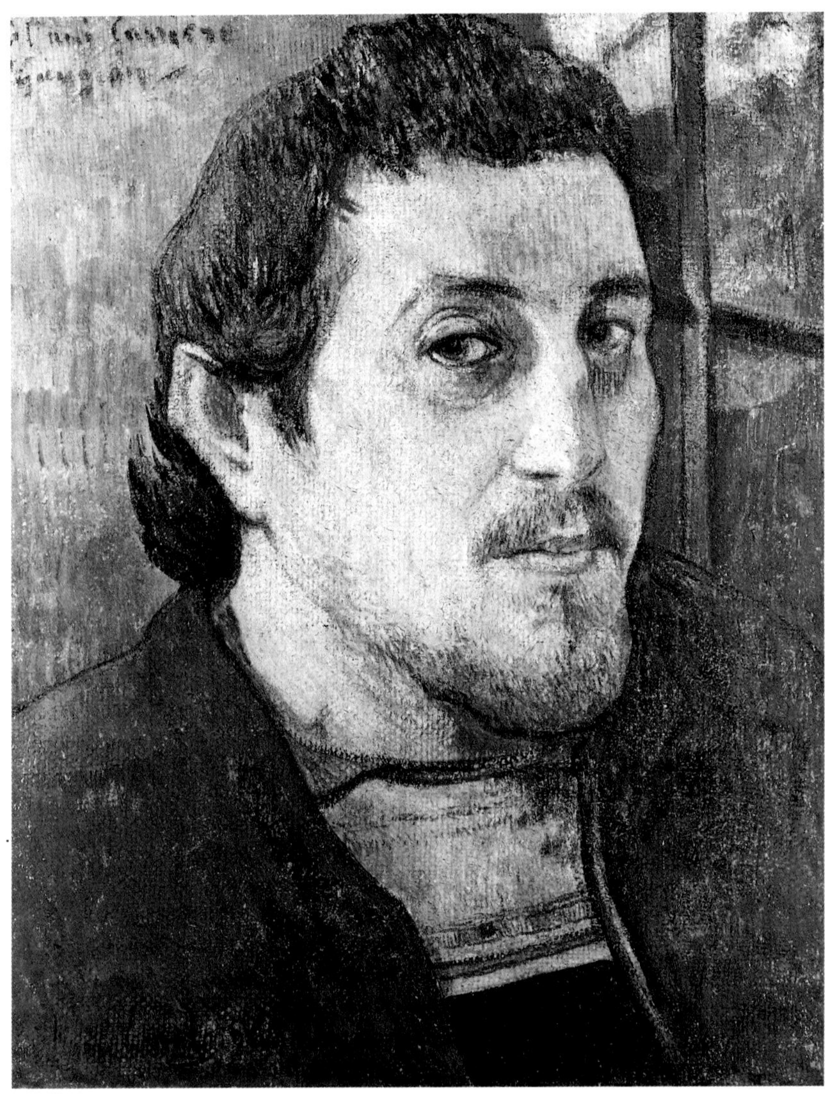

3. Paul Gauguin, *Self-portrait Dedicated to Carrière*, c. 1888, painting on fabric
National Gallery of Art, Washington, Collection of Mr. and Mrs. Paul Mellon

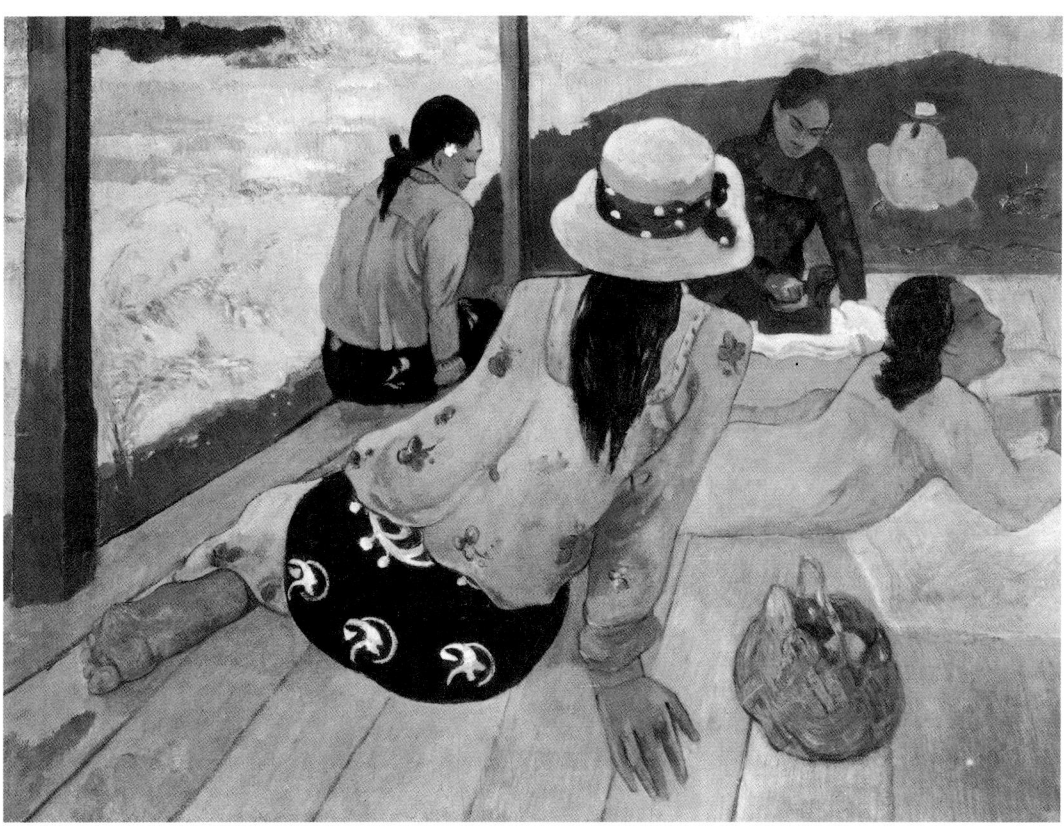

4. Paul Gauguin, *The Siesta*, date uncertain, painting on fabric
Walter H. Annenberg Collection, photograph courtesy Wildenstein & Co., New York

Pouldu, during which he painted primarily on a single type of canvas.[15]

Gauguin may have stopped using coarse fabric during 1889 and 1890 because Schuffenecker wrote to him in December 1888 that, due to this coarse, poor-quality canvas, a shipment of Gauguin's paintings sent to the dealer Théo van Gogh in Paris had arrived "with the paint falling off in chunks; it's very awkward and it makes the pictures impossible to sell at the moment."[16]

Although Gauguin did again use coarse canvas once he had arrived in Tahiti, he continued to paint on conventional artists' canvas periodically throughout the 1890s, and he never complained in his correspondence about having to do so. While he eventually came to prefer coarse fabric when it was available, as we know from his request for it in a letter to Georges-Daniel de Monfreid,[17] his friend and occasional art supplier, we must assume that he did not consider it essential in making a successful painting since he continued to paint on other types of fabric when they were available to him. In fact, according to Lieutenant Jénot, an acquaintance in Tahiti, Gauguin actually brought both coarse and fine fabrics with him from France.[18] It is also noteworthy that, throughout Gauguin's career, there is no correlation between subject matter and fabric choice.

Examination of the fabric supports for Gauguin's entire oeuvre should yield information helpful in dating a few problematic paintings. Examination of 142 of his fabric supports has indicated that, for example, *The Siesta* (W515) (fig. 4), the date of which is uncertain, appears to be on the same fabric used for *Matamoe* (W484) and *Street in Tahiti* (W441), two works painted during his first sojourn in Tahiti. This particular fabric does not resemble any of the five different types on which Gauguin painted after he returned to Paris in 1893 (more than half of these have been examined for this study). It is likely, then, that *The Siesta* was painted in Tahiti rather than Paris, although the most recent catalogue raisonné of Gauguin's paintings suggested the work was done after his return to France.[19]

During his second sojourn in the South Seas, Gauguin received his canvas at first from both de Monfreid and the artist Georges Chaudet, with whom Gauguin had left the unsold paintings from the Hôtel Drouot auction. Judging from Gauguin's correspondence, these supplies generally lasted him about six months, especially when money was included along with the shipment. He wrote de Monfreid in March 1897: "Two months ago I received from Chaudet 1,035 and 1,200 francs, some medicines and painting supplies, canvas and lead white, etc. . . . I am now set for three or four months, which will allow me to work."[20] It is during this time that Gauguin wrote to de Monfreid of his preference for coarse canvas: "If possible, buy me canvas two meters wide (coarse and a bit rough—the nubs don't bother me, they can be cut). . . . If not [available] I need coarse fabric like Puvis de Chavannes [uses], as little prepared as possible, but it's so expensive!"[21]

Why did Gauguin eventually return to using coarse fabric in Tahiti, after abandoning it after he left Arles? By the late 1890s Gauguin had persuaded himself that the flaking paint in his paintings was caused by a faulty priming[22] rather than by the support itself, and for this reason he no longer felt an obligation to avoid the coarse fabric Schuffenecker had warned him about toward the end of his Arles visit.

Despite regular shipments from de Monfreid and others, as well as the availability of fabric from the mail boats, canvas was often hard to obtain from any source, and Gauguin's correspondence during his second Tahitian trip is filled with complaints about a lack of fabric. The shortage seems to have been especially acute between 1897 and 1900. In October 1897, he complained about having had no canvas for the previous few months.[23] By December, he even lacked scraps. He wrote, "I have carefully searched in my supplies for bits of canvas but I find none."[24] By April 1898 he had given up painting to take a government job in Papeete. Although he managed to paint a few pictures during this time, his production was limited until January 1899, when he quit his job. In August of that year he wrote that he was again out of canvas,[25] and the following month he was reduced by lack of fabric to working on previously unfinished paintings.[26] Perhaps these paintings are the ones he meant when he wrote to de Monfreid in January 1900, "Almost simultaneously with this letter you will receive a few paintings which a sailor wishes to transport and which are made up of bits and pieces."[27] The fact that Gauguin appears to have given up painting from late 1899 through 1900 probably has more to do with these shortages of canvas than with any conscious decision to abandon painting.

Bengt Danielsson, who has written extensively about Gauguin's time in the South Seas, theorized that Gauguin turned to the "old solution" of using locally available sackcloth to paint *Where Are We Going?* when he was unable to get canvas from the mail boats.[28] Danielsson's phrasing suggests that Gauguin had been using sackcloth throughout his time in the South Seas. Although an aim of the present study was to distinguish between locally purchased, so-called sackcloth supports and coarse fabric sent from France, these fabrics were not visually dissimilar enough for this examiner to distinguish them without fiber analysis of larger numbers of individual painting fabrics.

In 1900 Gauguin stopped painting on coarse canvas altogether because of an arrangement proposed by the Parisian dealer Ambroise Vollard. According to their March 1900 agreement, Vollard would send Gauguin a monthly stipend and art supplies in return for a steady shipment of paintings and watercolors. As part of the agreement, Vollard insisted that Gauguin's paintings be done on conventional canvas, which he felt would endure the rigors of shipment to France better than sackcloth, and he sent the artist the fabric he preferred. Toward the end of 1899 Vollard wrote to Gauguin: "I am willing to buy everything you do. . . . The pictures must be painted on good canvas, which I could send you, and with good colors, which I could also have sent to you."[29]

It is extraordinary that this arrangement with Vollard continued, since the relationship between the two men was stormy from the beginning. When Vollard wrote to Gauguin that he was sending Ingres watercolor paper and watercolors, he went so far as to stipulate that the sketches should cover the entire paper and also that Gauguin should make him some flower paintings. Gauguin sardonically replied:

> *I am finicky about paper; moreover your requirement that the entire paper must be covered worries me so much that I should never dare to begin work. Now an artist (if you consider me such, and not a mere machine for turning out orders) can only do what he feels, and to the devil with dimensions. . . . You mention flower paintings. I really don't know which ones you mean; although I have done only a few; and that is because (as you have doubtless perceived) I do not copy nature—Today even less than formerly.*[30]

Despite his acerbic tone, Gauguin did make some flower paintings using the supplies he received in June 1900. This canvas caused him to complain bitterly to de Monfreid: "I am baffled by the canvas Vollard sent, accustomed as I am to an absorbent ground. I am master of the technique and much of the freshness of my color is due to this. Now I must learn anew my whole métier."[31] Apparently Vollard had sent him canvas that was unsuitably prepared. Gauguin wrote Vollard in May 1901:

> *I have not yet received the canvas you promised me. The kind you sent before is very difficult to work on and absorbs a great deal of paint. What I need is unsized canvas and a separate parcel of glue for sizing. Or else canvas which you may have simply sized but not prepared with oil; with the glue you send I shall add a second coating mixed with white.*[32]

Gauguin used the unsuitable fabric as the support for a group of still lifes (W602, W603, W606, and W631) painted in 1901. The use of this particular twill fabric in *Still Life with Grapefruits* (W631) (fig. 5) fixes the date for this painting, previously disputed,[33] as not before 1901, since it is painted on the same twill fabric the artist used for all the still lifes painted at this time and Gauguin did not use this particular fabric in the years immediately preceding this series of paintings. He obviously painted these still lifes in response to Vollard's request on the fabric Vollard sent him.

Vollard's choice of cotton-linen twill fabric was somewhat unusual as an artist's canvas at this time; it had only recently been marketed in France and was sold as sketching or student canvas because it was less expensive than pure linen. Its low cost was undoubtedly the reason Vollard selected it. Cotton has also been identified in three other paintings predating Gauguin's association with Vollard (*Mme Alexandre Kohler*, W314, 1887–1889; *Fatata te miti*, W463, 1892; and *Mahana no atua*, W513, 1894), and it is likely that many more examples of cotton supports will be noted as more of Gauguin's paintings undergo fiber analysis.

When Gauguin moved to the Marquesas in September 1901, he became completely dependent on Vollard for fabric and paint since nothing was available locally. De Monfreid no longer sent Gauguin separate shipments once Vollard agreed to act as his dealer, preferring instead to give Vollard supplies, which the dealer was supposed to send out as consolidated shipments. This arrangement resulted in frequent shortages of materials, since Vollard was often negligent about mailing the required canvas and paint. Consequently, Gauguin's letters from this period have an increasingly desperate tone. He had received the twill canvas in June 1900, but in August 1901 he wrote to de Monfreid that he was still waiting for canvas and glue from Vollard.[34] In November he wrote to his friend that he could not paint because he had been waiting more than a year for canvas and white paint from Vollard.[35] Another shipment of fabric finally arrived in March 1902, but the roll of fabric was not very wide, prompting Gauguin to write Vollard, "You will soon have to arrange to send me more canvas, because (figure it out for yourself) one meter of this canvas makes only two pictures."[36] The dimensions of the fabric Gauguin received from Vollard may account for the smaller size of Gauguin's very late paintings. Gauguin knew he had to send Vollard a certain number of paintings per month to receive his stipend, and the larger the paintings, the fewer could be produced with the limited amounts of fabric Gauguin was receiving. This second shipment of fabric must have run out by August 1902, because the following April, Gauguin wrote to Vollard: "It is now more than eight months since you advised me of the shipment of canvases, paper, *totin* glue, and flower seeds. At the present moment my health would permit me to work hard and I have nothing to work with."[37] In fact, the shipment Gauguin referred to never left France, and a month later,

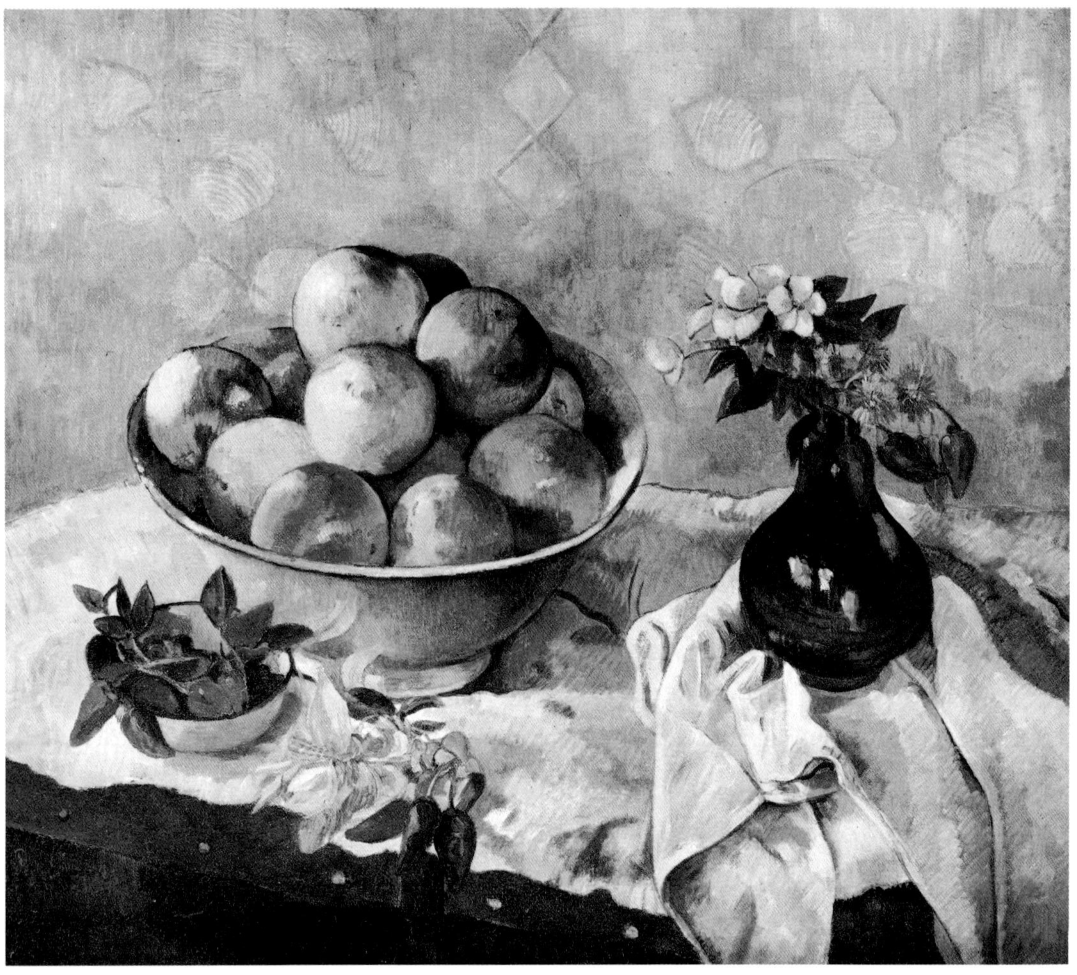

5. Paul Gauguin, *Still Life with Grapefruits*, 1901, painting on fabric
Private collection, Lausanne

still waiting for supplies, depressed and ill, Gauguin died.

That there are fewer paintings from these last years has as much to do with Vollard's slowness in sending supplies as with Gauguin's ill health and involvement in writing projects. As one would expect from the correspondence, examination of the paintings from the years 1901–1903 shows a complete change in fabric support. Vollard did not send the too-absorbent twill fabric a second time, since Gauguin complained so bitterly about it. The next shipment must have contained plain-woven, moderate-weight fabric (10–12 threads per cm), since all of Gauguin's last paintings (1901–1903) seen by this examiner are painted on this fabric except *Riders* (W597), which is painted on herringbone canvas.

Gauguin painted primarily on very thinly primed fabric because he liked the rough surface texture the fabric weave gave his paintings. Occasionally he painted on wood panel, however, and it is noteworthy than in at least two cases (*Self-portrait with Halo*, W323, and *Portrait of Meyer de Haan*, W317), he managed to create a rougher surface by running a coarse comb through the priming before it had completely dried. This combed pattern is clearly evident on the surface of both paintings.

GROUNDS (PRIMING)

Because Gauguin was aware of the critical importance of the priming layer both structurally and aesthetically, his correspondence is full of references to various efforts to find one that would satisfy his requirements. The structural stability of this layer was essential, since his paintings had to be removed from their stretchers for transport to Paris whether from Brittany or Tahiti. The periodic shipment of paintings from Tahiti to France was particularly dangerous, since during the two-month journey by ship the unstretched paintings were extremely vulnerable to physical mishandling and environmentally induced damage.

Gauguin felt that he could achieve the greatest color purity and stability by using an absorbent ground.[38] His use of these grounds was not particularly innovative; he was more likely following a trend of the time. Many nineteenth-century artists' manuals, including those written by Pierre Louis Bouvier, Jean François Léonore Mérimée, Jéhan Georges Vibert, and Frédéric Auguste Antoine Goupil Fesquet recommended using absorbent grounds,[39] which were available commercially at least as early as 1839, when Mérimée wrote that they were a recent innovation introduced by the Paris colorman Monsieur Rey.[40] At the time Gauguin was painting, canvases prepared with absorbent grounds were generally sold unstretched by the meter or in standard sizes on stretchers. They were available in a variety of shades. Ernest Hareux, in his 1870 artists' handbook, lists Rowney Company as producing "artists' canvas prepared in a variety of ways, including pure white, tinted, single-primed, and absorbent grounds."[41]

Absorbent grounds had many advantages; those noted by Bouvier in his 1844 edition include speed of drying, lack of discoloration, good adhesion, and absorption of excess oil in the paint layer to enhance purity and stability of the colors painted on them.[42] Absorbent grounds are evident on many impressionist paintings, where they appear as an extremely thin layer that is almost invisible.

Gauguin's friend and student Paul Sérusier described how to make an absorbent ground in his *ABC de la peinture*: "Take a well-dried wood panel, or a wall without moisture, or a canvas prepared with plaster thinned with Spanish white. The less glue you add, the more absorbent the canvas."[43] The result was a ground that enhanced the purity of the colors with which it was overlaid. Gauguin also favored this type of ground because he could achieve his desired color effects with a relatively small amount of pigment, a real advantage since he lacked the money to use his paint extravagantly.[44] As he wrote to de Monfreid in 1899, "For the last twelve years, as you know, I've been painting on absorbent canvas and I have had to my own taste the desired color effects and color stability."[45]

It took Gauguin some years to work out his system of ground preparation. When he first began to paint, he used the commercially prepared canvases laid with absorbent grounds that were popular with most nineteenth-century artists. Although he wrote as early as 1879 in a letter to Camille Pissarro that he was preparing his canvases himself,[46] visual examination of the paintings from the 1880s suggests that he did not consistently prepare his own canvases until 1887, which would confirm his statement in 1899 that he had been preparing his own canvases for twelve years.[47] While Gauguin primed a number of his paintings himself from the early and mid-1880s, he painted more than half of those examined from the years 1880 to 1886 on commercially primed fabric.[48]

By the time Gauguin moved to the South Seas, he was painting almost exclusively on white priming, typically thin and uneven, that he applied himself. He worked rather carelessly and vigorously with a small trowel or palette knife, and the long, arching scratches these tools made in the wet priming are often visible in a raking light. The priming does not usually extend uniformly to the edges of the picture and, for this reason, the edges of many of his paintings have been overpainted to give them a more "finished" appearance. It was important to Gauguin that the priming not conceal the rough texture of the support, because he relied on the support for surface variations that other artists created by painting in impasto. As he wrote to Emile Bernard during his stay in Arles with van Gogh, "As to pigment, he [van Gogh] appreciates thick paint as Monticelli used it, while I detest any form of tampering by brushwork."[49]

Gauguin's priming was white with very few exceptions,[50] but its composition varied over the years depending on what materials were available to the artist in the often remote areas where he painted. Henri Delavallée, a painter and printmaker who knew

Gauguin in Brittany in 1886, wrote that during the late 1880s Gauguin's priming layer consisted of a mixture of Moudon white (a white chalk or clay powder used both as a pigment and as an abrasive for cleaning tiles and flagstones, also sometimes called Spanish white, and animal skin glue [*colle de peau*]).[51] Sérusier also used this mixture, as was noted in a contemporary review.[52] As Delavallée later commented, it is not surprising that due to the small amount of glue mixed into this absorbent ground, a number of the paintings done at this time turned out to be somewhat friable.[53]

It is possible that, as a remedy for this friability, Gauguin may have for a time added casein to his priming, as was suggested in several artists' manuals of the time. Lieutenant Jénot, who was present at many of Gauguin's canvas preparations during his first Tahitian trip,[54] wrote that the artist made his priming from a mixture of casein, glue, and silver white (*blanc d'argent*), a chalk pigment with small admixtures of lead, alum, or zinc.[55] Gauguin wrote to de Monfreid asking him to send casein during his 1894 trip to Brittany,[56] but since Gauguin also used casein for restoring his own paintings, it is not known whether he used the casein for restoration, preparation of his canvas, or both.

A casein-containing ground[57] would have been less susceptible to water damage, a useful quality in view of Gauguin's practice of washing his paintings to create a matte surface.[58] It would have also made the ground less absorbent, a disadvantage in Gauguin's view. Casein was not identified in any of three paintings specifically analyzed for its presence in the collection of the National Gallery of Art.[59] However, no paintings from Gauguin's first Tahitian sojourn have undergone casein-ground analysis, and it may well be present in paintings of this period. During his second Tahitian sojourn, Gauguin described his preferred priming when he asked de Monfreid to send him "canvas prepared with animal skin glue with a very small amount of Spanish white, not *terre de pipe*, added."[60]

The problems of Gauguin's grounds were a recurrent theme in his correspondence. As early as January 1889 he wrote van Gogh, "The whole *Vintage* [at Arles] has flaked because of the *white* which has separated [from the canvas]."[61] This report does not speak well for the stability of Gauguin's grounds, since the picture had been painted only three months earlier.

Gauguin was not alone in his dissatisfaction with his priming layer. During the 1890s, de Monfreid was also critical of the structural stability of Gauguin's grounds. He was the person to know, since it was his job to make arrangements for restoration of damaged paintings arriving by ship from Tahiti before they could be exhibited and sold in Paris. In a reply to one of his friend's criticisms, Gauguin wrote in 1897:

> *You seriously reproach me with not taking care with* la matière. *Oh yes I do take care as far as the painting goes, but the ground leaves something to be desired. It's true. What do you expect, in my state at the time, nervous and impatient. Then the canvases you're talking about were rolled up by an ignorant naval officer (I was in the hospital), and then left that way for two months, without air, in extreme heat, at enormous risk.*[62]

Judging from a letter written two years later, in 1899, these problems had not been solved. Gauguin attributed the instability in his paintings at the time to the substitution of inferior lead white for the Spanish white (clay white) he preferred to use. He wrote to de Monfreid:

> *I have thought a lot about your observations concerning the ground* [préparation] *of my paintings. It comes from the poor quality of lead white which is sold here coming from America, prepared with tallow. Once it dries, it cracks, not being well enough bound and then the painting cracks. . . . This can be remedied by adding linseed oil, but then to my despair, I'll be working on the painting in an oily paste.*[63]

In fact, Gauguin's preference for absorbent grounds is probably a major factor in the often badly preserved state of his paintings. The more absorbent the ground, the less well bound the layer is and the more likely it is to flake away from the fabric support. It is for precisely this reason that artists abandoned these brittle chalk-glue grounds for oil-bound grounds when flexible canvas began to replace the more rigid wood panel as a painting support in the first part of the sixteenth century. Gauguin exacerbated the problem by rolling his paintings for transport, so that his grounds were even more likely to separate from their supporting canvas. Fortunately, Gauguin applied his ground thinly during his time in the South Seas, so that his paintings were less prone to flaking than a thicker, more traditional priming layer would be.

It was only when he ran out of Spanish white, the white clay pigment presumably available only through friends who sent it to him from France, that Gauguin substituted flake (lead) white or zinc white as the white pigment in his priming. Technical analysis of eight paintings from the 1890s shows that while four are painted on a chalk-glue ground (*Parau na te varua ino*, W458 [see fig. 8]); *Fatata te miti*, W463; *Te pape nave nave*, W568; and the lower ground of *Nevermore*, W558), four others (*Te rerioa*, W557 [see fig. 13]; *Where Are We Going?*, W561 [see fig. 1]; *Portraits of Women*, W610; and *The Invocation*, W635) are painted on lead or lead-zinc white grounds bound with glue.[64]

Shortages of supplies during his time in the South Seas occasionally led Gauguin to experiment with unorthodox materials. According to Jénot, during Gauguin's first Tahitian trip the artist substituted ripe breadfruit for his usual ground, and he used it on small trial paintings and several larger canvases. No paintings with this ground were seen by this examiner, but it is unlikely that they would have survived the high humidity in which they were shipped and almost certain insect attack on account of their edible grounds. Gauguin consoled himself with the thought that this measure was only temporary until he could again restock from the mail boats bringing supplies from France and San Francisco.[65]

A small number of works examined were found to have two grounds, with the upper ground covering another painting that lay beneath. In these cases the lower ground varies, but the upper ground is invariably composed of lead white, whose greater covering power was required to block out a lower design. The practice of painting over a previous image is not unusual in Gauguin's oeuvre and was no doubt the result of poverty. At least six examples are known,[66] and it is assumed that many more would be revealed if more of his paintings were x-rayed.

PAINTING TECHNIQUE

Changes in Gauguin's painting technique are closely bound to his stylistic development. From the impressionist technique of painting *en plein air* (out of doors) or from life in small discrete brushstrokes typical of his early works, Gauguin developed a "simpler" style characterized by broad flat areas of color, less impasto, and increasing abstraction. This stylistic evolution coincided with his shift to generally coarser fabric supports, leaner paint layers, and brighter colors.

The change was also influenced to some degree by the climate in which Gauguin found himself painting once he arrived in Tahiti. Since he worked by applying a layer of smooth paint over an already dry, more thinly painted underlayer, it was essential to work out a system of paint application that would allow each layer to dry as quickly as possible despite the humid climate, so that the succeeding layer could be applied. Thinner, leaner paint applied on an absorbent ground would dry more quickly than heavily impastoed medium-rich paint.

Gauguin argued that using less impasto allowed him to conserve his pigments, which were at various times either too expensive for him to buy or not available locally. In 1899 he wrote to de Monfreid:

> *You say why don't you paint a richer more painterly surface? I don't say no, and I would like to sometimes, but this is less and less possible for me, having to be careful about the amount of color I use; also, I have almost none left in spite of the economy I make with it, and I don't want to ask you for more before knowing when my material existence will be assured. If you can find me someone who will guarantee me 2,400 francs per year for five years, I'll paint in impasto, which requires three times as much time.*[67]

Gauguin's argument is hardly convincing, however, considering that his paintings were not more thickly painted when he had ample paint supplies than when he had practically used up his supplies. His letter to de Monfreid also contradicts his statement, made earlier, in Arles, that he preferred to avoid thick brushwork for aesthetic reasons.[68] It is more likely that his preference for thinner, smooth paint rather than impasto was based on aesthetic preferences together with the demands of the climate and that his reply to

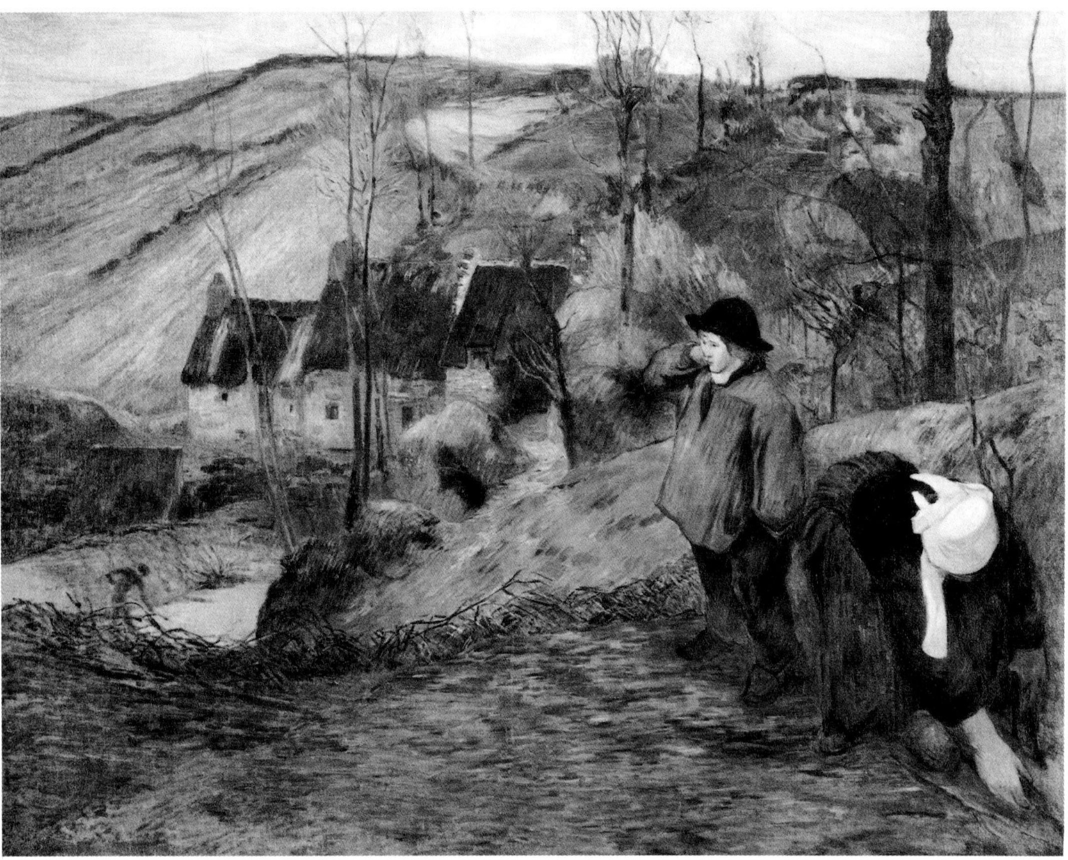

6. Paul Gauguin, *Hilly Landscape with Two Figures* (or, *Landscape of Brittany*), 1888, painting on fabric
National Museum of Western Art, Matsukata Collection, Tokyo

de Monfreid's criticism was an excuse to avoid having to paint more thickly for the market.

Gauguin did not paint exclusively from models or *en plein air* after the early 1880s. While a student of Pissarro, Gauguin occasionally worked in the studio rather than outside, sometimes using small oil sketches as the basis for larger paintings done indoors. Delavallée recalled that in 1886 Gauguin had painted a studio-based landscape, which he said he would finish outdoors.[69]

Later, even paintings that appear to have been done outside, such as the 1888 *Hilly Landscape with Two Figures* (W256) (fig. 6), contain rather large figures that were later painted in on top of the landscape. These figures were selected from earlier drawings that Gauguin called documents, which he used as the starting point for paintings, ceramics, and prints. It is this practice of adding figures later that explains the curious discrepancy in scale between the two figures in this painting.[70] By the late 1880s, Gauguin seems to have been doing little painting from life, relying increasingly on his documents and his memory. We know that when he first arrived in Arles, he began by painting a large composition of black women, which must have been based on sketches he made in Martinique two years earlier.[71] Not long after Gauguin began work on the painting of the women, van Gogh described in a letter to his brother Théo how Gauguin was painting another picture completely from memory.[72] Gauguin's practice of using drawings made some time earlier as the basis for paintings continued after he arrived in Tahiti in 1891, when he wrote de Monfreid, "I am satisfied to inspect what is within me rather than nature, to learn to draw a little, drawing is everything, and then I am accumulating documents for painting in Paris."[73]

This use of documents makes it difficult to discuss Gauguin purely in terms of his paintings, because these documents served equally as a source for the artist's work as a painter, ceramic sculptor, woodcarver, and printmaker. These drawings, which he described as "my letters, my secrets,"[74] would later be combined with elements from the large store of photographs of both Eastern and Western art that he kept with him, so that the finished work of art might contain elements from Borobudur carving, Polynesian Tikis, paintings by Pierre-Cécile Puvis de Chavannes, or prints by Albrecht Dürer.[75] These document figures might appear in a variety of media over a two- or three-year period. The documents were stored in portfolios, photographed, and pasted into notebooks, becoming part of sketchbooks that Gauguin kept for later reference.[76]

Gauguin wrote that before making these documents, he preferred upon arrival in a new place to have a period of several weeks in which to observe life and absorb the local ambience. Somewhat later he would make drawings, and only much later would he begin to paint. He described this procedure upon his arrival in both Arles and in Tahiti.[77] During his time in the South Seas he was also often forced by lack of painting supplies to fall back on making additional documents for later use.

Although Gauguin stressed in his writings that this "incubation period" was necessary before drawing and painting could begin, evidence from his contemporaries suggests that he did not always follow the procedures he espoused. We know from the letters of van Gogh, for example, that Gauguin was painting a picture of washerwomen and a still life within a week of arriving in Arles, although Gauguin had written Théo van Gogh when he first arrived that he would not paint for at least a month.[78]

Why did Gauguin stress this observation period in his writings when he did not always use it? The practice was important to him because it was part of his theory that the image was born in the artist's unconscious some time before the act of putting it down on canvas. When mature, the image would burst forth more or less fully grown from the artist, who gave it form in an act of release akin to a birth.

Gauguin's underlying belief here was that the act of creation was spontaneous and primitive, full of raw emotional power and mystery. This concept of art emerging without the restraint of conscious thought from an idea preformed in the mind of the artist was hardly original; it is similar to certain aspects of neoplatonic thought with which Gauguin was familiar through Paul Sérusier, who had often discussed neoplatonism with students at the Académie Julien before he met Gauguin.[79]

These documents, which made possible the "spontaneous" birth of Gauguin's paintings, took several forms. Quick pencil sketches were the first part of Gauguin's creative process; he made individual figure studies when he wanted to develop a particular pose more fully. During the early part of his career his sketches even contained careful notes on specific pigments to be used in different design elements within the drawings (fig. 7).[80]

The sketches were transferred either by squaring up or, more rarely, in the case of larger designs, by pounced cartoons, as in the main figures for the paintings *Parau na te varua ino* (W458) (fig. 8) and *Te nave nave Fenua* (W455). In the cartoon for *Parau na te varua ino* (fig. 9), the transcription is exact, apart from a lowering of the eyes made visible through infrared vidicon examination (fig. 10), a technique allowing the layer of drawing beneath the paint layer to appear in certain cases on a video monitor when the painting is examined with a camera that has an infrared lens.

After transferring his sketches, Gauguin next roughed in the outlines of the design in thin dark blue underpaint, probably *à l'essence* (explained below). His colors were painted over these lines in some areas, but in many parts of the painting these blue outlines were left visible. Although it has been suggested that Gauguin may have sketched in his underdrawing directly on the unprimed canvas,[81] examination of ten paintings at the National Gallery of Art indicated the brushed underdrawing lay on top of the priming.[82]

The underpaint was often applied in thin washes, with thicker application only in the upper layers. In the 1890s, Gauguin began to scrape thin areas of paint, and palette knife work became more common. He continued to avoid painting in high impasto, however, because of the tropical climate. He wrote de

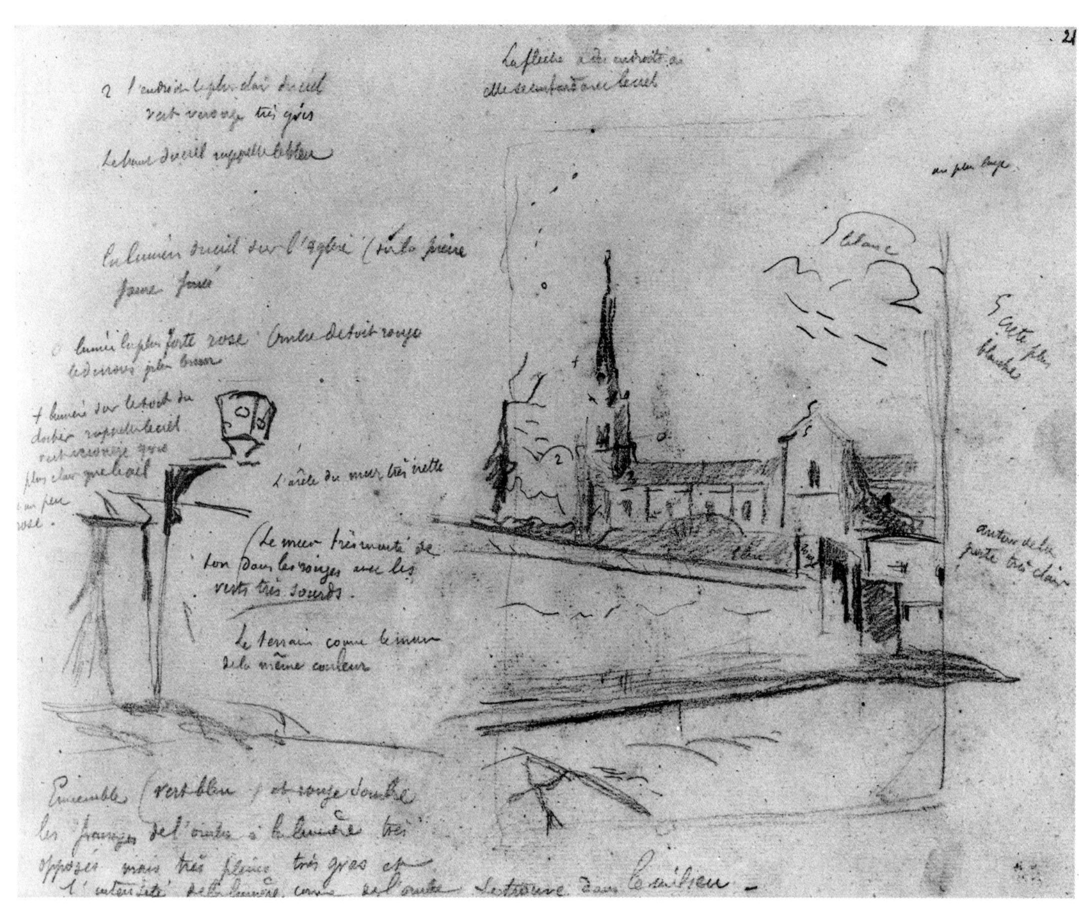

7. Paul Gauguin, "L'église de Vaugirard, seen from rue Carcel," sketch for *Une Nuit à Vaugirard*
Statens Konstmuseer, National Swedish Art Museums, Stockholm

8. Paul Gauguin, *Parau na te varua ino* (Words of the devil), 1892, painting on fabric
National Gallery of Art, Washington, Gift of the W. Averell Harriman Foundation in memory of Marie N. Harriman

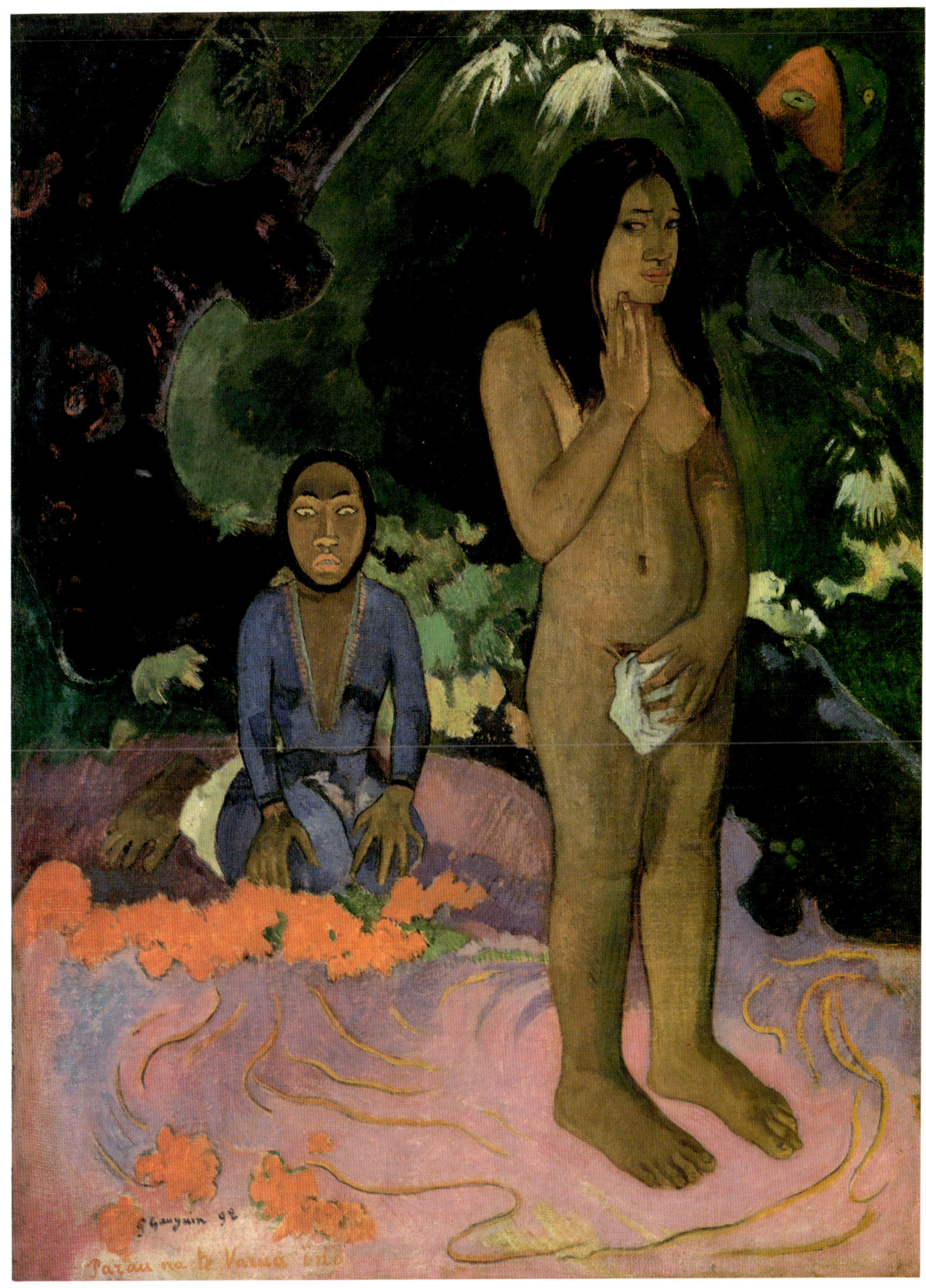
P Gauguin 92
Parau na te Varua ino

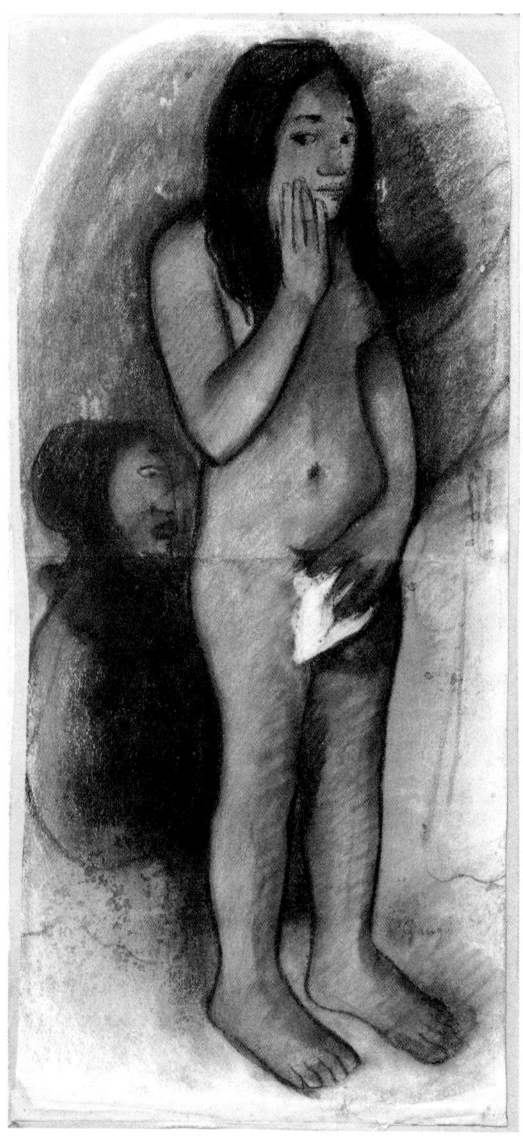

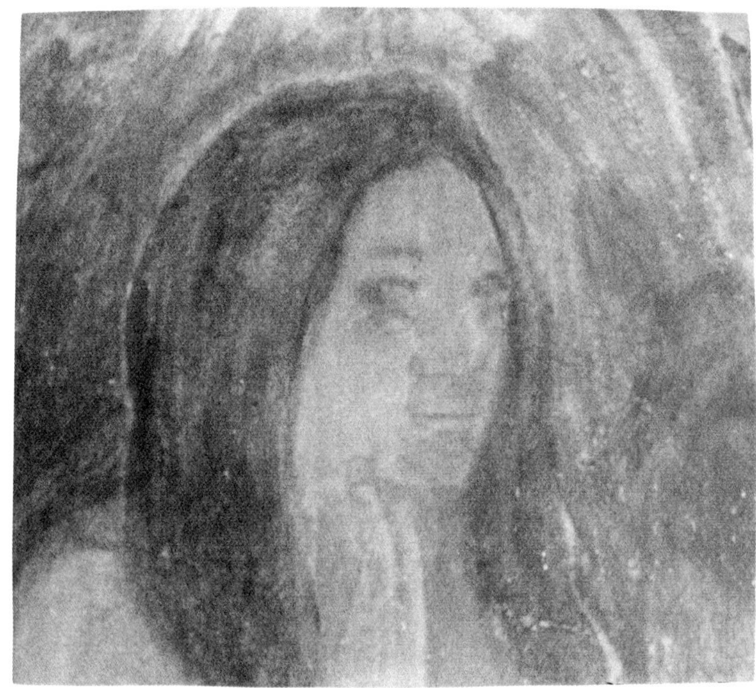

9. Paul Gauguin, cartoon for *Parau na te varua ino* (Words of the devil), 1892, charcoal and pastel selectively stumped and worked with brush and water (or solvent), over preliminary drawing in black chalk; punctured for transfer; on wove paper
Öffentliche Kunstsammlung Basel, Kupferstichkabinett

10. Vidicon, detail of fig. 8.

Monfreid: "Work in high impasto is very dangerous if you go fast; it is especially important in a hot climate to apply the color prudently and daily, to a point where it dries, otherwise you make mud. And then [if I painted in impasto] I would produce only one-third of my present work."[83] In fact, the humid climate also had a disastrous effect on Gauguin's colors in the tube, which often deteriorated while he was waiting for canvas to arrive by ship.[84]

A discussion of changes in Gauguin's painting technique must include the influence of his work in other media. The issue is particularly relevant in Gauguin's case, because he not only worked as a printmaker, woodcarver, and ceramic sculptor but used the same documents as the source for his work in all media. Because of this practice, his work in different media is unusually interrelated not only thematically and stylistically but technically as well. His paintings were not necessarily the end of the creative process but an element of a continuum that might later evolve into a pastel, monotype, or print. Merete Bodelsen has pointed out how this process typically developed: Gauguin began with a drawing, from which he created a painting; next he would use the same motif for a pastel and then translate it into a ceramic sculpture. The sculpture

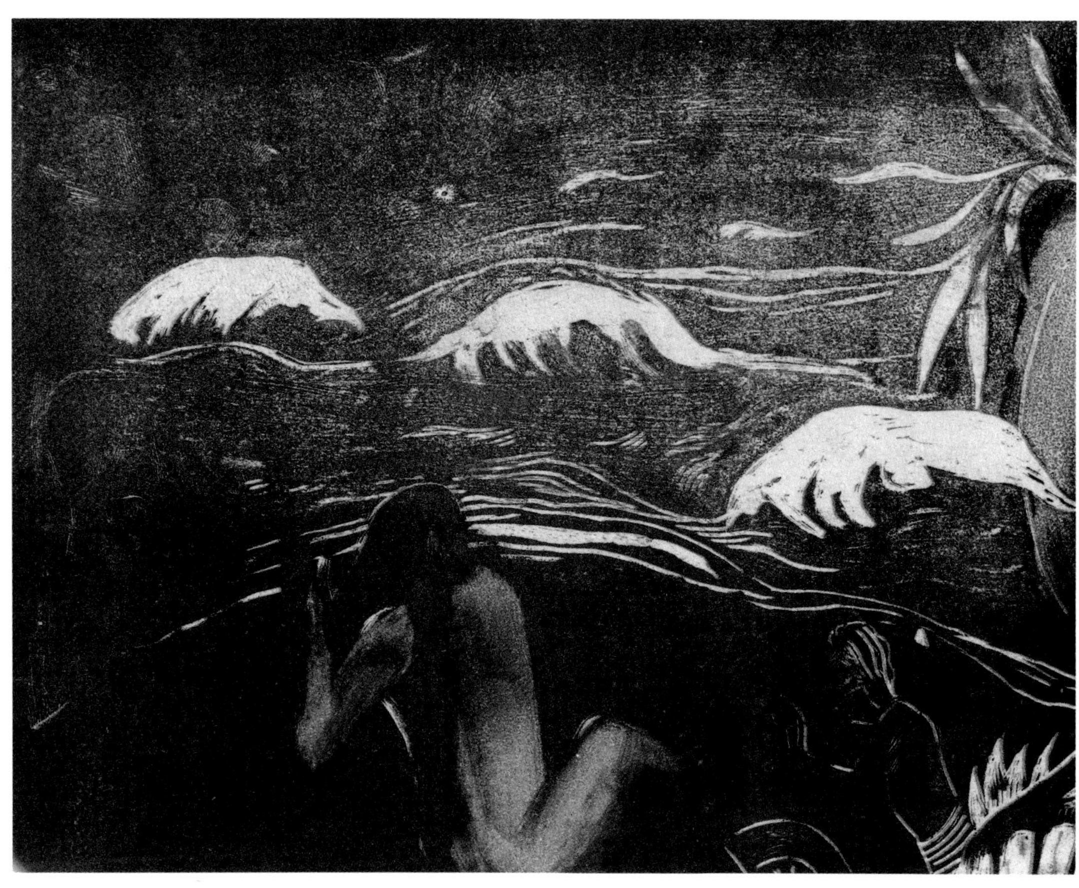

11. Paul Gauguin, *L'Univers est créé*, 1893–1894, woodcut
National Gallery of Art, Washington
Lessing J. Rosenwald Collection

would become part of the background in a portrait or part of a still life and would finally appear in zincographs or woodcuts. The drawing was often reworked for separate exhibition and occasionally even wetted so a counterproof could be made from it.[85]

With this kind of working back and forth among different media, borrowing of techniques from one medium for use in another became inevitable. In a print in the National Gallery of Art (*L'Univers est créé*) (fig. 11), Gauguin pressed twill canvas into the surface of the still wet printed paper to create a rough, fabriclike texture. In paintings, Gauguin sometimes used the butt end of the brush to incise the wet paint, as he did in printmaking or in delineating figures on ceramics. Gauguin's work in ceramics, in which the figures were incised and greatly simplified in terms of color, influenced his use of bold outlines and flat color areas in his paintings beginning in 1887, as Bodelsen has pointed out.[86]

An especially interesting parallel occurs in Gauguin's attempts to create a somewhat ambiguous, mysterious, and "primitive" outline in both prints and paintings. In his prints, he achieved this effect by intentionally printing his woodblock images slightly off register. He achieved much the same effect in his paintings by deliberately leaving visible underdrawn lines and altered contours only partially painted out in the upper paint layers.

Despite Gauguin's claim that he was a rapid and spontaneous painter, it appears that

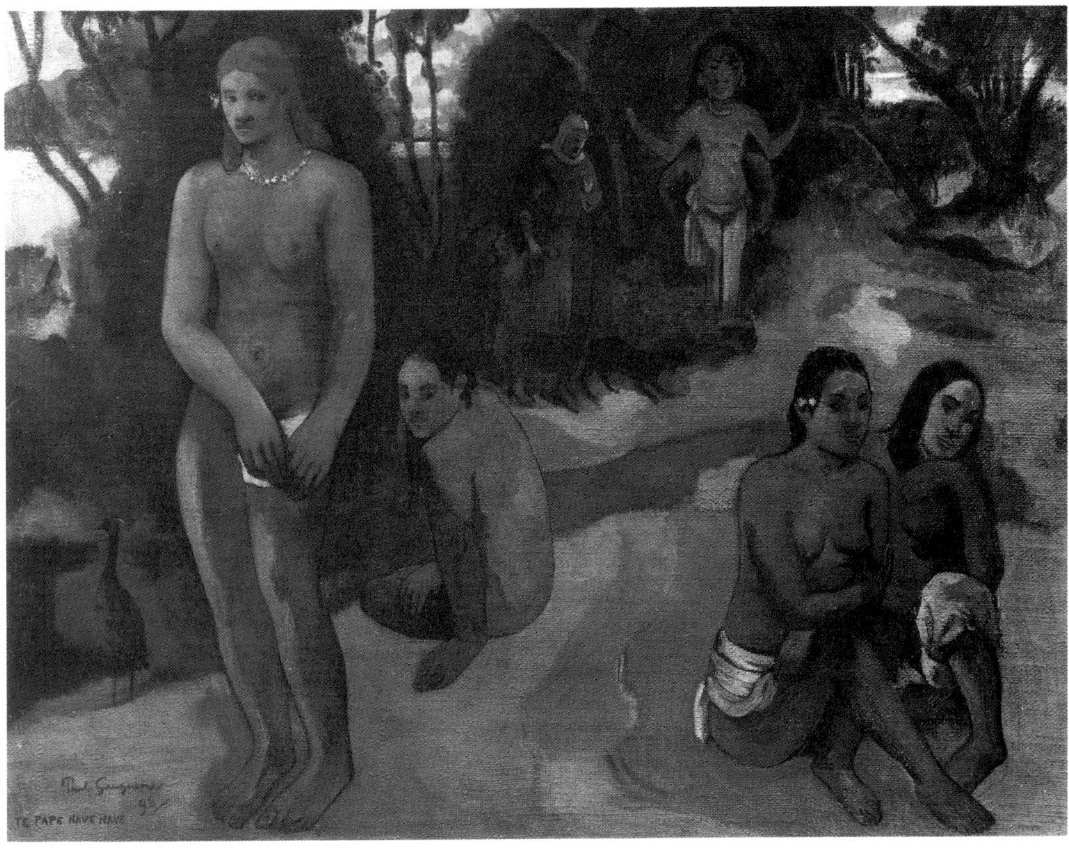

12. Paul Gauguin, *Te pape nave nave* (Delectable waters), 1898, painting on fabric
National Gallery of Art, Washington, Collection of Mr. and Mrs. Paul Mellon

his actual working process was rather labored. For his major paintings, he worked out the composition carefully before painting began. Artist's changes are more often seen in the smaller paintings, because in these he probably felt freer to experiment with figure placement and color changes. For example, the foreground in *Te pape nave nave* (W568) (fig. 12) was originally painted dark blue, as in the right half of *Where Are We Going?* (W561) (see fig. 1), on which it was based. Gauguin changed the foreground color to red, however, perhaps to make it seem less derivative.

Gauguin wrote at the end of his first Tahitian sojourn that he had completed sixty-six paintings in about eighteen months.[87] Because he needed to paint thinly, allowing the lower layers to dry before applying upper layers, he must have worked on several paintings simultaneously to have painted at this rate.

We know exactly how long it took Gauguin to complete at least one painting. *Te rerioa* (W557) (fig. 13) was painted during the ten-day delay of a mail boat's scheduled departure. Gauguin wrote to de Monfreid that he had profited by the delay by painting this additional picture, which was added to the shipment at the last minute.[88]

MEDIUM

Gauguin's matte, smooth paint surface has led to speculation about his medium. Since he wrote nothing specific about it, we must draw our conclusions from a few ambiguous passages in his correspondence, the recollections of people who knew him, and technical analysis of the paintings.

Apart from the artist's requests for specific oil paints, a single reference to Gauguin's medium exists in the published literature: Delavallée recalled that in 1886 Gauguin was painting *à l'essence*.[89] This practice, in which the oil is drained from the paint and then remixed with turpentine, was common

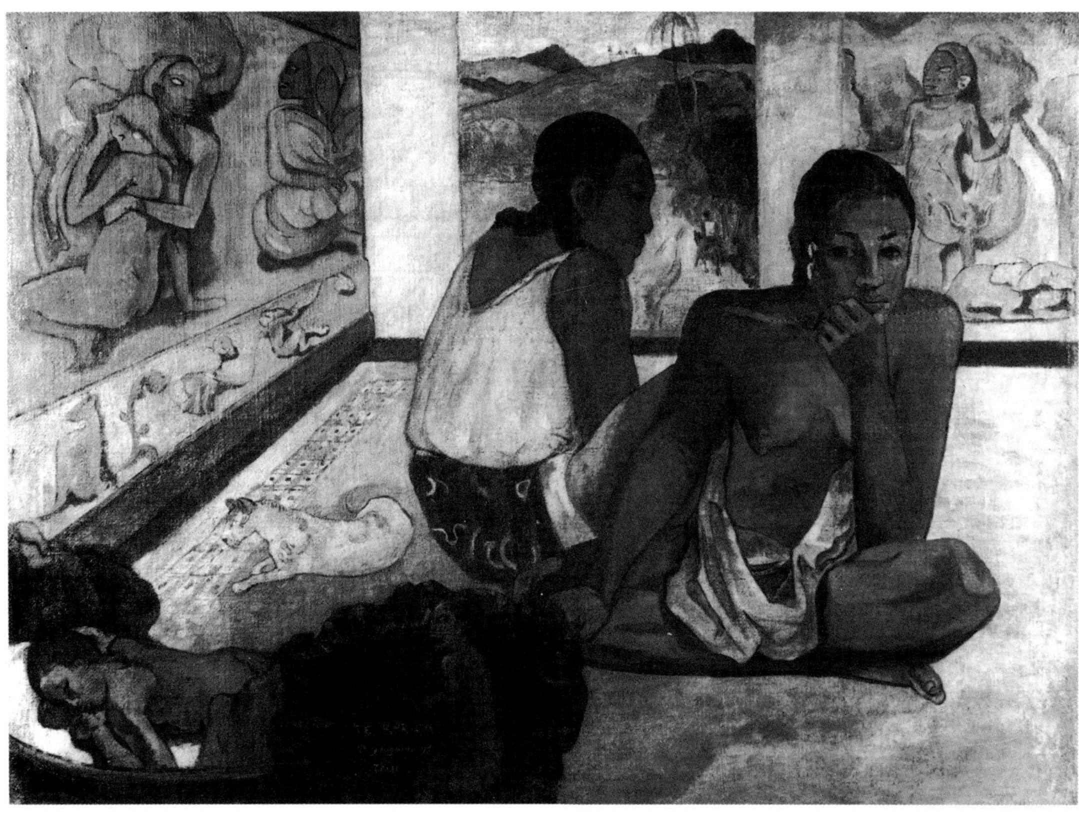

13. Paul Gauguin, *Te rerioa*, 1897, painting on fabric
Courtauld Institute Galleries, Courtauld Collection, London

among artists of the period; Edgar Degas and Henri Toulouse-Lautrec were its best-known practitioners. With the oil drained out of his paints, there was less chance of uneven drying, about which Gauguin complained in 1885.[90] It also would have ensured the matte surface we must assume Gauguin preferred based on his painting technique.

Beyond draining his oil paint and mixing it with turpentine, it has been suggested that Gauguin may have mixed wax into his paint.[91] The reasons for this supposition are: (1) Gauguin's paintings are often very sensitive to solvents; (2) according to Sérusier, van Gogh added wax to his paint,[92] and Gauguin could have learned the practice from him during their time together in Arles; (3) wax would have helped stretch Gauguin's paint supplies and facilitated palette knife application;[93] and (4) Gauguin wrote in 1899 to de Monfreid, "I believe that time, with wax, will greatly improve my paintings" (*Je crois du reste que le temps, avec le cire donnera grandes améliorations à mes toiles*).[94] This passage does not make clear whether the wax was mixed into the paint layer or applied on top of it as a surface coating. In two other letters, however, Gauguin referred to the merits of wax as a protective surface coating and even specifically instructed that it be applied as a surface coating once the paintings had arrived in France.[95] Given these references and because no wax was found in the solvent-sensitive paintings that have undergone medium analysis at the National Gallery of Art,[96] it is prudent to assume that while wax may have been added to some of his paintings, it was not added to most of them.

The sensitivity of some of Gauguin's paintings to solvents is confusing since it is not typical of a specific period or even uniform within a single painting. The most likely explanation for this sensitivity is the leanness of the paint used and the presence of a wax coating on some of the paintings. If, as Gauguin instructed, the paintings had been coated with wax, the wax would surely have migrated into the leaner pigment layers on their absorbent ground, becoming, in the pro-

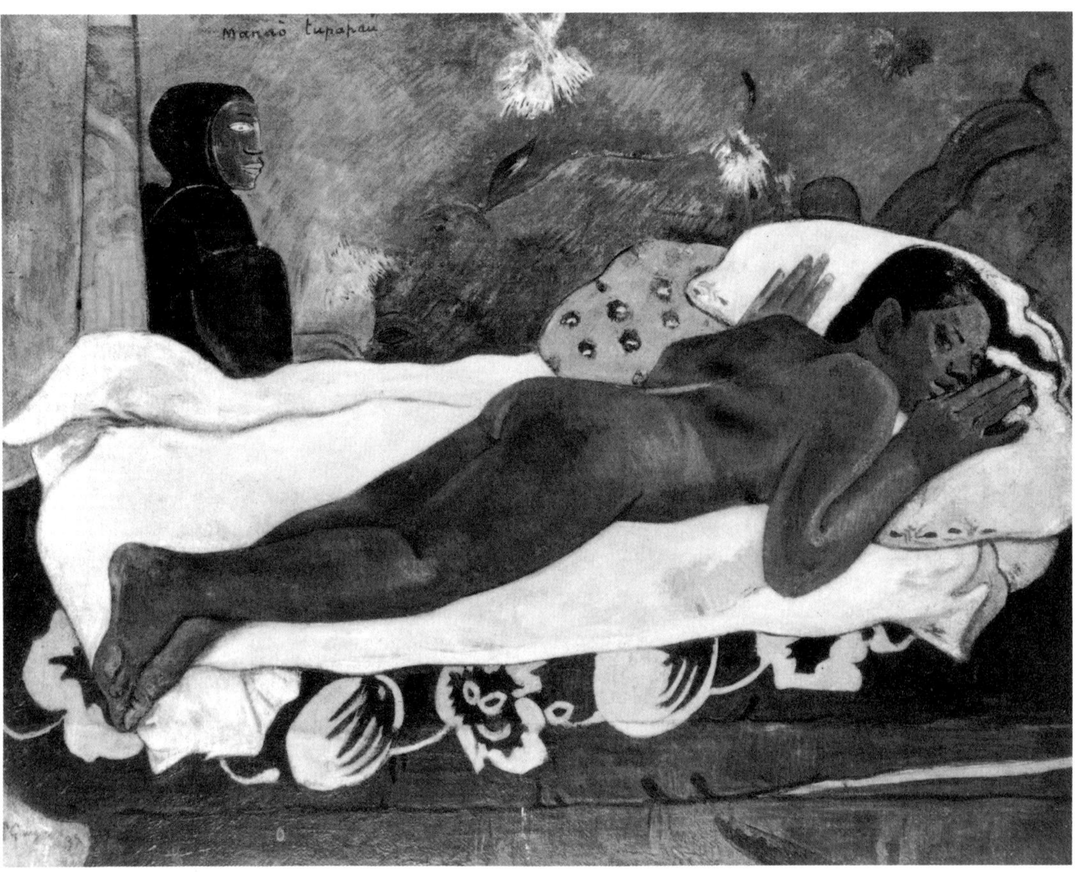

14. Paul Gauguin, *Manau tupapau* (The specter watches over her) (or, *Spirit of the Dead Watching*), 1892, painting on fabric
Albright-Knox Art Gallery, Buffalo, A. Conger Goodyear Collection

cess, a sort of de facto medium for this layer. Paintings that are most soluble are those that most likely were least well bound in oil. Applying a wax coating on top of them would make them especially sensitive to the organic solvents used to remove varnish from pictures.

Gauguin's practices of draining his paints, using an absorbent ground, painting thinly, and adding wax as a surface coating would have produced a matte paint surface. We know Gauguin worried about the possibility of his paintings becoming glossier with time because he expressed dismay that a painting by van Gogh he had known earlier had taken on a medium-rich appearance some years later.[97]

To minimize surface gloss, Gauguin washed his paintings after they had dried. Van Gogh described in a letter to Théo the "degreasing" procedure Gauguin taught him in Arles.[98] The "washing" of the paint probably created a slight blanching that would have increased the matteness of the surface. Gauguin continued the practice in Tahiti, as a letter to de Monfreid indicates. In discussing a shipment of paintings his friend was to receive, Gauguin wrote: "I am worried about the effect of the voyage on the paintings and perhaps repairs will need to be made. Wash them with care and many precautions to avoid picking up the paint and ground layer, and wax them."[99]

Aside from enhancing *Where Are We Going?* (W561) (see fig. 1) with pastel for a photograph, there are no published references indicating Gauguin mixed other materials with his oil paints. The pastel was not meant to be permanent, and, after the photograph was taken, Gauguin partially washed it off; he instructed de Monfreid to wash it upon arrival in France to remove any remaining pastel.[100]

Gauguin preferred to use tube oil paints when they were available. At de Monfreid's suggestion, he tried making a paint medium from castor oil seeds, which were plentiful in Tahiti, but he was not satisfied with the result, complaining that it was too oily.[101]

PIGMENTS

Color was especially important to Gauguin because he believed color could project emotions. He described his painting *Manau tupapau* (W457) (fig. 14) to de Monfreid: "Its beginnings as follows (for you only): Overall harmony; somber sad blue violet and chrome 1—the sheets [on the bed] are chrome 2 because this color suggests the night without explicitly describing it and also serves as a transition between the yellow-orange and the green which completes the musical accord."[102] These references to the symbolic and emotional qualities of color are numerous in Gauguin's writings. Although he was critical of the dogmatic color theories of the neoimpressionists, he experimented with them early in his career and was purported to have possessed obscure tracts on color harmonies.[103]

Gauguin's palette became noticeably brighter after his stay in Arles, but it was not until he began to paint in the aesthetic isolation in the South Seas that he felt free enough to experiment with increasingly pure colors. Yet his palette seemed dull to him. He elaborated when discussing the landscape *Pastorales Tahitiennes* (W470): "It's all made of pure emerald green (*vert véronèse*) and vermilion ditto; but it seems to me to be an old Dutch painting or an old tapestry. Why? I think it is because I haven't seen one of my old paintings or a Beaux Arts picture to take as a point of reference, of comparison."[104]

With this kind of emphasis on pure color; Gauguin needed a large and varied number of bright pigments. His palette included:

Blues—ultramarine, cobalt, Prussian blue, and a powdered pigment known as Charron blue, composed of cobalt blue and barium sulfate, which he had specially ground for him.

Greens—emerald green (*vert véronèse*), viridian (*éméraude*), green earth, and "bottle green" (mentioned in his correspondence but its specific components are not known).

Yellows—cadmium yellow number 2, cadmium citron, yellow ochre, chrome yellow number 1 and number 2.

Whites—lead (flake) white (*céruse*), silver white (*blanc d'argent*, or chalk white with small admixtures of zinc and lead white), Spanish white (*blanc d'Espagne*, or chalk white).

Purples—cobalt violet (*violet foncé*).

Reds—vermilion, red/crimson lake (*lac garance*), carmine, red minium.

Browns—burnt ochre (*ochre ru*).

Gold powders, both red and yellow.

For a list of Gauguin's requests for individual pigments, see appendix 2. Appendix 3 shows results of pigment analysis on the paintings in the National Gallery of Art and several other collections on which pigment analysis was undertaken.

Considering Gauguin's bright palette, it is not surprising that his letters contain no requests for dark earth pigments, such as the umbers and siennas, or for black, and in fact these pigments were not found to be present during pigment analysis.[105] White figures prominently in all his written requests for pigments (he asked for two to three times as much white as other colors), since he used it so often in making tints. Pigment analysis suggests that Gauguin used lead and chalk whites more often than zinc white, perhaps because slow-drying zinc white would be a disadvantage in a humid tropical climate.

Despite his statements about pure color, Gauguin seldom used pigment straight from the tube, apart from ultramarine and Prussian blue, which became for him a substitute for black. The rich vibrancy of these dark blues, with their subtle and mysterious, glowing quality, would have appealed to Gauguin far more than the flatness of black paint.

Gauguin created his vibrant flesh tones by mixing more ochre with less white pigment than is traditionally used. He enhanced his glowing palette by juxtaposing the dark ochre-colored skin of his main figures with very light, bright colors in the middleground and background. These bright colors are often reflected in the highlights of the figures' skin, recalling an effect of reflected tropical light. Gauguin also increased the vibrancy of his palette by juxtaposing complementary

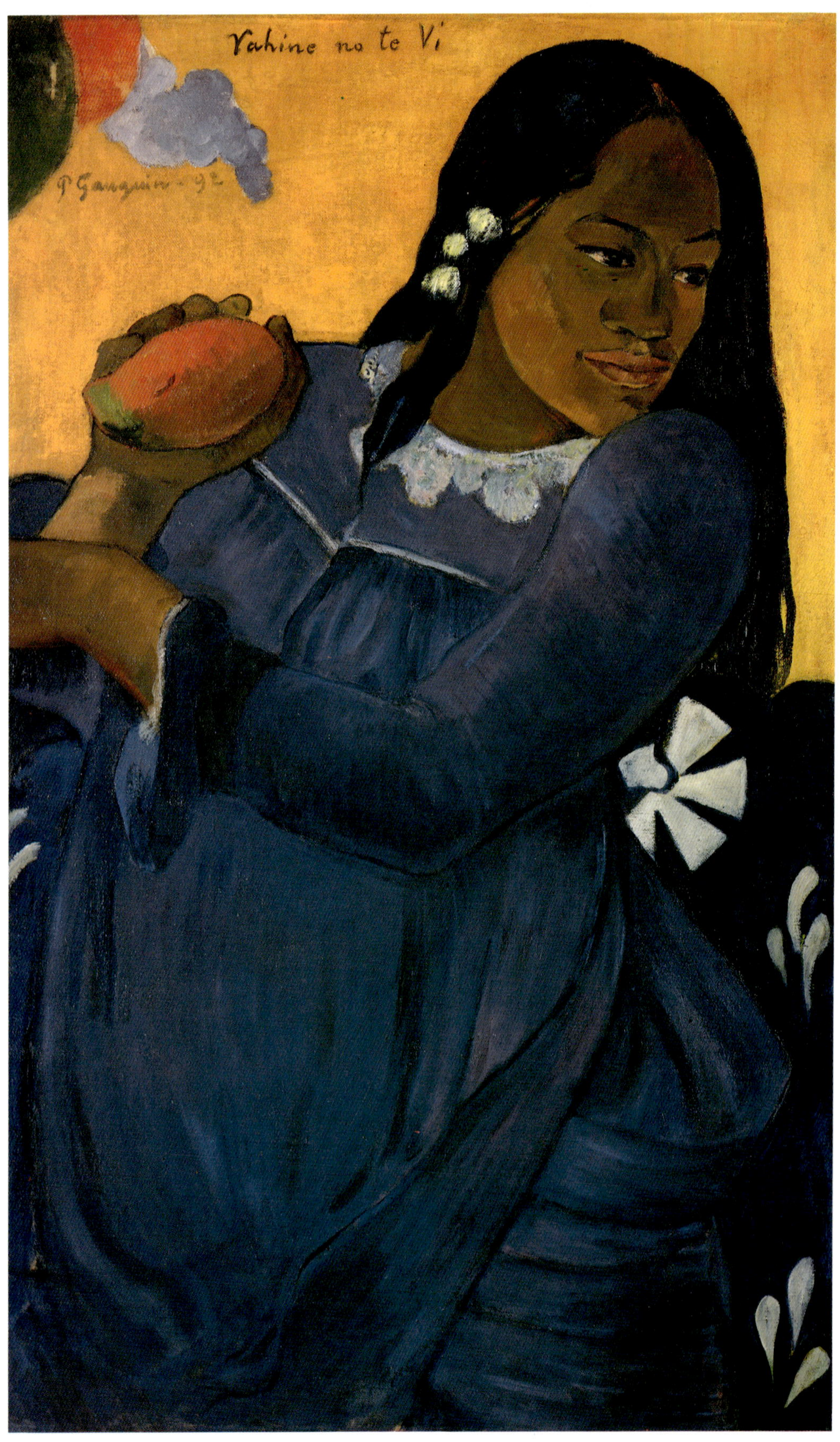

15. Paul Gauguin, *Vahine no te Vi* (Woman of the mango), 1892, painting on fabric
Baltimore Museum of Art, Cone Collection formed by Dr. Claribel Cone and Miss Etta Cone of Baltimore, Maryland

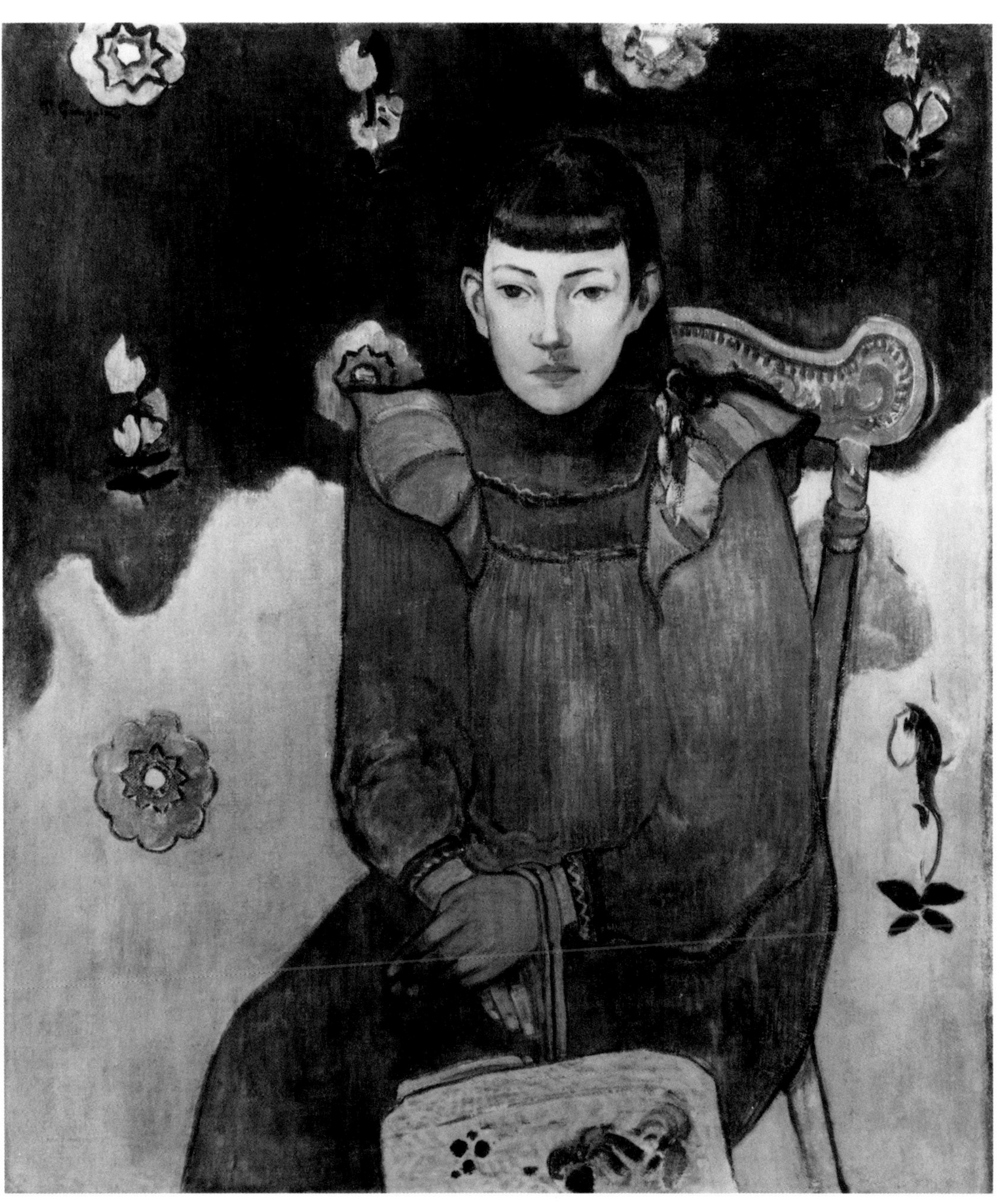

16. Paul Gauguin, *Portrait of Vaïte (Jeanne) Goupil*, 1896, painting on fabric
Ordrupgaard Collection, Copenhagen

colors, as he did in *Vahine no te Vi* (W449) (fig. 15) by placing the purple dress against a yellow background and by laying the upper layer of the purple dress over a pink underpaint.[106]

Although Gauguin generally used pigments that were lightfast, effects of color fading are occasionally evident in his paintings. An example is the background of *Portrait of Vaïte (Jeanne) Goupil* (W535) (fig. 16). Color fading can be seen along the edges, where the painting was once protected by the lip of the frame. There the pink color is more intense, suggesting it has faded in the greater part of the background where the paint was exposed to light. The pigment used here was probably carmine, which is known to be light fugitive.

Despite Gauguin's requests for both yellow and red-gold powders in his letters, no evidence of these pigments was noted during visual examination or elemental pigment analysis of his paintings. Since a number of his contemporaries, including Edgar Degas, used metallic powders in their paintings,[107] it is possible that these powders might be present in paintings not examined for this study. Gauguin certainly used the "gold powder" for both wood carvings and gouache paintings, where it is clearly apparent during even casual visual examination.

Gauguin's choice of pigments did not change significantly during his career; the pigments in his Brittany and South Seas paintings appear to be the same. His paintings became brighter mainly because he mixed less white and complementary colors into his tones after he began painting in the South Seas.

RETOUCHING

After finishing a painting, Gauguin occasionally washed the paint surface, a standard practice among French painters of his time,[108] and then retouched over it. In a letter to Théo, Vincent van Gogh described this practice, as Gauguin had explained it to him.[109] Occasionally retouching was needed when a client preferred a change in a design element. In the case of *Breton Girls Dancing, Pont-Aven* (W251) (fig. 17), the arm of the left figure was altered by Gauguin after it appeared unacceptably prominent when the painting was framed. The change is only barely visible during x-radiographic and infrared examination, although it is well documented in the literature[110] and is faintly evident during normal viewing.

Because Gauguin was known to retouch, a conservator should proceed cautiously when presented with a painting that may seem at first to have been repainted by a restorer. Occasionally the retouches may have been put there by the artist himself, especially for paintings done between 1897 to 1900 when Gauguin was short of canvas and was therefore reduced to reworking old unfinished paintings. Other examples of additions to the original paint layer were necessitated by the distance between where Gauguin painted and where he exhibited. He instructed de Monfreid on at least one occasion to inscribe titles in Tahitian on paintings already sent.[111]

SUPPLIES

Because of his remote location and limited access to artists' supplies, Gauguin relied on friends and dealers as a source of painting materials, so that periodic requests for paints, brushes, canvas, and other supplies appear in his letters.

Paints

Despite his poverty and the lack of paint in some areas where he lived throughout his career, Gauguin never used paint he made himself, though he did once experiment with castor oil-bound pigment. Early in his career he bought his pigments from the Paris colorman Père Tanguy; after his move to the South Seas, he preferred the tube colors prepared by the Le Franc company.

When Gauguin stayed in Brittany for long periods, Schuffenecker and Bernard often sent him supplies from Paris.[112] It is harder to determine what Gauguin acquired locally after he moved to the South Seas. In terms of pigments, we know he bought lead white paint in Tahiti because he complained about it in his letters,[113] but it appears that most other pigments were sent to him by de Monfreid and Vollard or were brought with him in large quantities when he first arrived in a new location.[114] The glue that he used for making his absorbent grounds was not available locally, because he noted in 1899 that it was "impossible to find animal skin glue here."[115]

There are only three orders for pigments in the published correspondence (see app. 2). These requests were made in letters dated 1897, 1900, and 1902.[116] De Monfreid must have sent Gauguin pigments during his first Tahitian trip, as the artist thanked him for them in a letter of 1893.[117] We also know from a letter Gauguin wrote to Emmanuel Bibesco, a prospective patron, that de Monfreid had in Paris a list of all the supplies Gauguin needed for painting,[118] so it is possible that de Monfreid periodically shipped Gauguin supplies without specific requests. It is more likely, however, that other requests by Gauguin for paint materials have simply been lost or have not yet been published.

Several of Gauguin's letters suggest that paint was almost certainly available in Ta-

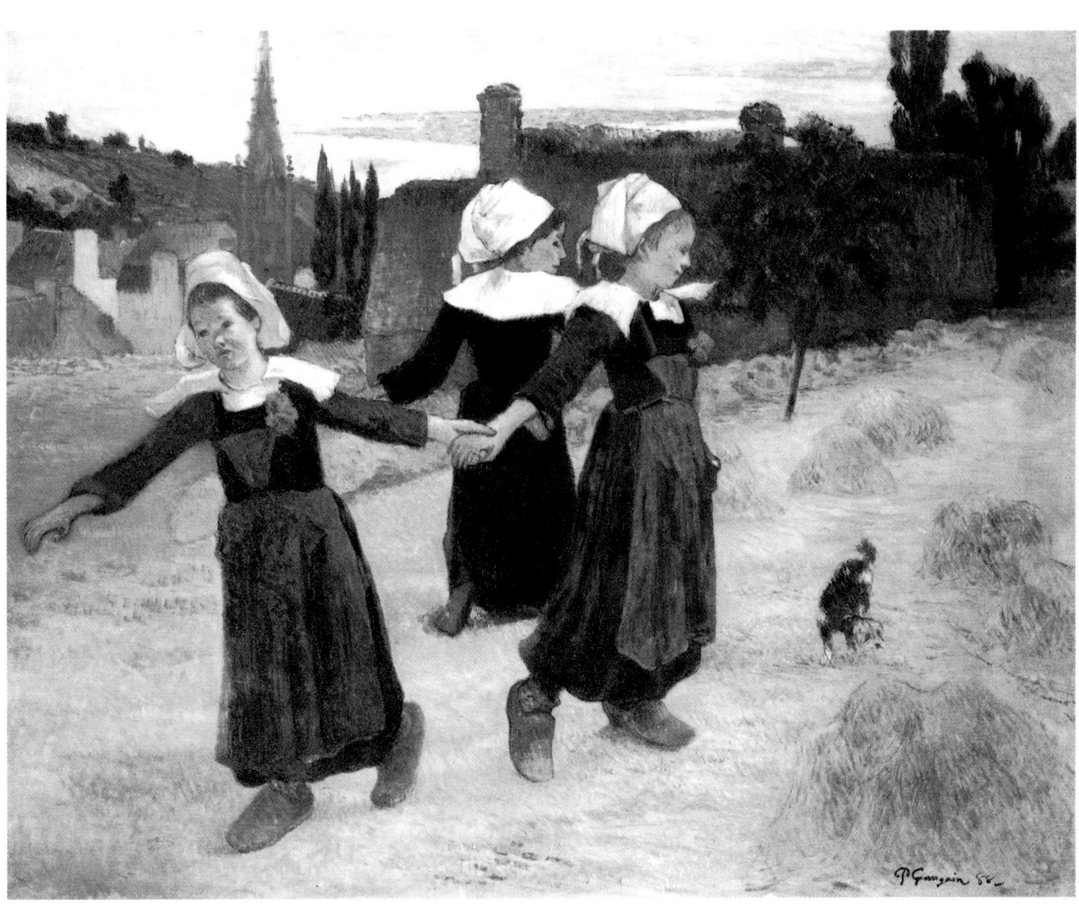

17. Paul Gauguin, *Breton Girls Dancing, Pont-Aven*, 1888, painting on fabric
National Gallery of Art, Washington, Collection of Mr. and Mrs. Paul Mellon

hiti,[119] which by this time was fairly heavily settled with Europeans. Nevertheless, Gauguin probably preferred to have his colors sent from France whenever possible, so he did not have to pay for them himself and could very likely get a wider selection of colors.

Apparently Gauguin preferred Le Franc pigments by the time he moved to the South Seas, as he requested them five times in his letters to Vollard and de Monfreid.[120] In fact he was irritated that Vollard did not send him these particular paints in his 1902 shipment:

Dear M. Vollard—I shall just take a few minutes to write to you again. I have opened your box. Canvas and glue—perfect. Japanese paper—perfect. But the colors!!! It is easy to see that you are not a painter. What do you expect me to do with six tubes of white and of terre verte, which I seldom use? I have only one small tube of carmine left. So you must send me the following [see app. 2]. . . . *I know this means a large outlay, but I can't help it. Now that I am in the mood for work I shall simply devour paints. So buy Le Franc's decorator's colors, they cost only one-third as much, especially as you get a dealer's discount, and they are much better.*[121]

Tools

In 1897, Gauguin ordered brushes from de Monfreid, requesting "50 assorted brushes, and a dozen brushes *en silo*."[122] In January 1900, he requested "a dozen and a half sable brushes for drawing, and twenty brushes of varying sizes."[123] He seems to have preferred sable brushes throughout his career. Delavallée remembered him saying in 1886, "I paint . . . only with sables. In this way, the color keeps its intensity. When you use ordinary brushes, two neighboring colors mix. With sables you obtain colors in juxtaposition."[124]

Gauguin requested palette knives in August 1901,[125] and palette knife work is particularly prominent in the work of his second

Tahitian sojourn. He had used a palette knife as early as his stay in Arles[126] and probably brought a supply of them with him from France, since he used them both for laying on his grounds and for paint application.

Stretchers

Throughout his career, Gauguin stretched his canvases on keyed wooden stretchers of standard sizes, later removing the paintings and rolling them up for transport after they had dried. Writing to Théo van Gogh from Arles in 1888, Gauguin described how to re-stretch his paintings for exhibition: "I've just sent a roll of canvases. . . . This sackcloth may be difficult to stretch. The way to do it is to stretch them as much as possible and dampen them everywhere, and not key out the stretcher until later when the paintings are dry and limp from expansion."[127] In Tahiti four years later, Gauguin wrote to de Monfreid in a similar vein:

> *You will receive a package of paintings. . . . Ask if the exhibition will pay the cost of shipping; if so, then send them mounted on keyed stretchers. If not, a roll. . . . In order to stretch them well, dampen the fabric slightly on the reverse, and then stretch. Put the nails in the same holes, otherwise there will be pulls in the canvas.*[128]

It is difficult to describe Gauguin's typical stretcher, since few have been documented. Two possibly original stretchers were noted on *The Invocation* (W635) and on *Haystacks* (Courtauld Institute, London).[129] In both cases, the stretchers were rather thin five-member pine specimens, with butt joins.

FRAMES

Most of Gauguin's paintings are not framed today as the artist originally intended. From the early 1880s, Gauguin exhibited his paintings in simple white or stained wood frames. A review of the 1882 impressionist exhibition noted, "M. Paul Gauguin exhibits . . . in white frames."[130] In a letter to Camille Pissarro written from Rouen in 1884, Gauguin blamed the rejection of a painting from an exhibition there on his use of white frames.[131] After Gauguin joined van Gogh in Arles, Vincent described in a letter to Théo how he and Gauguin made frames from "simple wooden strips nailed to the stretcher and painted. . . . Do you know that it is Gauguin who invented the white frame?"[132] Théo van Gogh, who arranged a one-person show for Gauguin in November 1888, noted in a letter to the artist that he had displayed "all of the paintings of size 30 . . . in frames either white or of natural wood."[133]

White-framed paintings appear in the background of many still lifes and portraits Gauguin painted between 1885 and 1893, although the paintings so framed are not by Gauguin himself but by other painters whose works he collected. Contemporary accounts indicate, however, that he used white frames for his own paintings in the 1893 Durand-Ruel exhibition. When these paintings did not sell, he repainted the frames yellow.[134] One of these yellow frames, on *Manau tupapau* (W457) (see fig. 14), is visible in the background of Gauguin's 1893–1894 *Self-portrait with Hat* (W506) (fig. 18). These yellow frames were probably also used for his 1894 exhibitions.

After his return to Tahiti in 1895, Gauguin continued to use simple wood frames, both stained and painted. Although it has been suggested that Gauguin abandoned white frames after 1893,[135] he continued to prefer them for certain pictures such as *Where Are We Going?* (see fig. 1). Gauguin sent de Monfreid the following instructions for framing this painting once it arrived in Paris: "The big picture needs a frame, but as cheap as possible. A simple band of wood 0.10 [cm] thick painted with whitewash—an apparent mural."[136] Because he was leaving Paris for a time, de Monfreid left this painting and others from the shipment with Georges Chaudet, who wrote to Gauguin with assurances that he had followed the artist's framing instructions: "I had the large painting framed in a white wooden frame. I had the other paintings framed in the old frames which I had repainted."[137] These "old frames" were probably the yellow ones framing the unsold paintings from the 1895 Hôtel Drouot auction. Gauguin also expressed his preference for a simple wooden frame in a letter to a prospective collector dated 1896.[138]

Gauguin's paintings may often have been glazed. In 1882, he wrote Pissarro two letters thanking him for taking a frame for a painting Gauguin had recently done to a shop

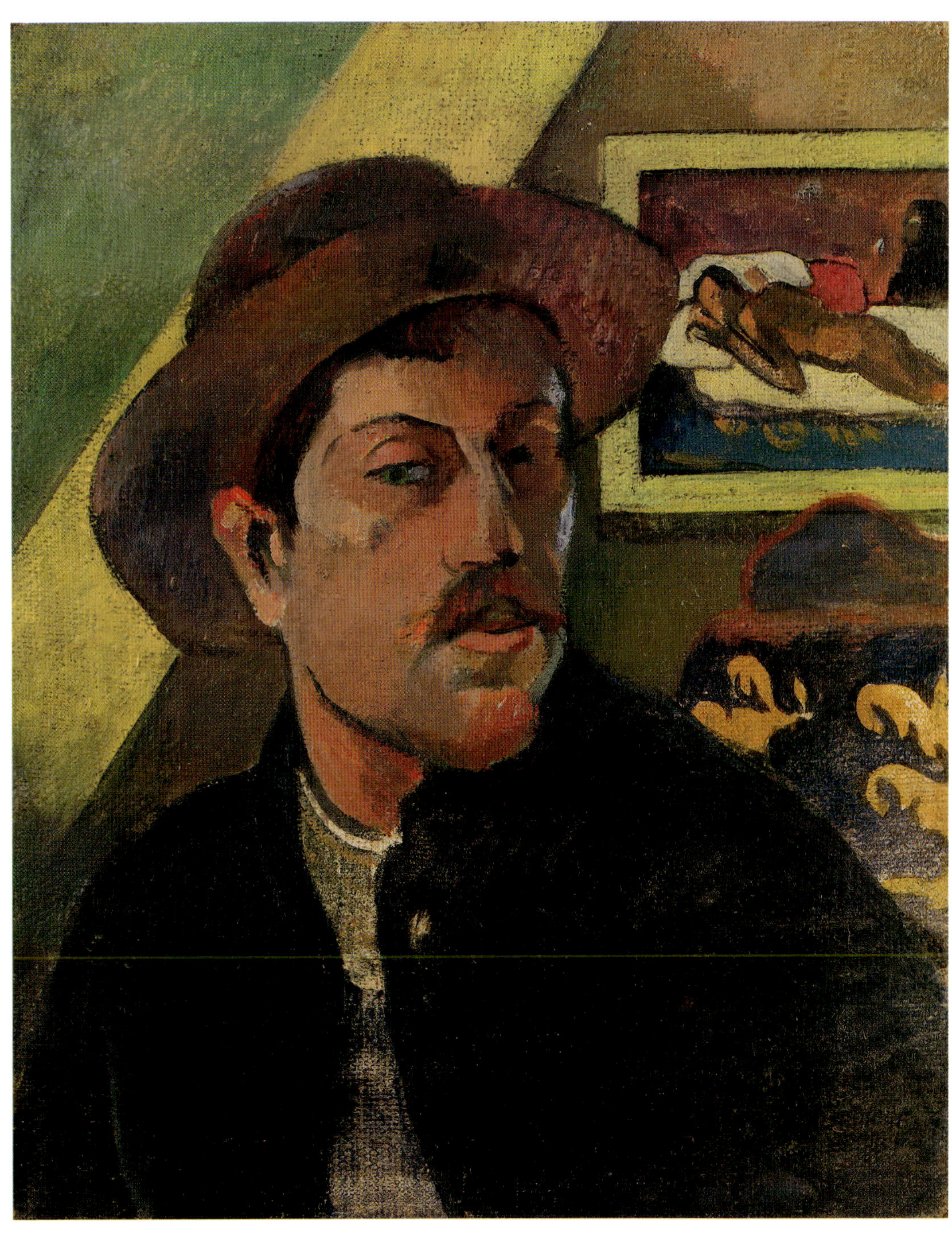

18. Paul Gauguin, *Self-portrait with Hat*, 1893–1894, painting on fabric
Musée d'Orsay, Paris

where glass could be easily fitted for it.[139] Late in his career, Gauguin still appears to have endorsed glazing his paintings; his 1896 letter to the prospective collector instructed him to place a recently done panel painting in a frame under glass "which sets it off and keeps its freshness by protecting it from the changes that are always caused by the atmosphere of one's room" (fig. 19).[140]

Gauguin was not alone in the practice of glazing his paintings. A review of an 1891 exhibition of Nabi painters notes that Gauguin's protégé, Maurice Denis, was also showing his paintings behind glass.[141] The glazing of paintings by Gauguin and his circle is particularly important since the paintings were either left unvarnished or coated with only a thin layer of wax, rather than the thick glossy varnish typical of the academic artists' procedures of the time, and they are therefore particularly vulnerable to grime and vandalism if left unglazed.

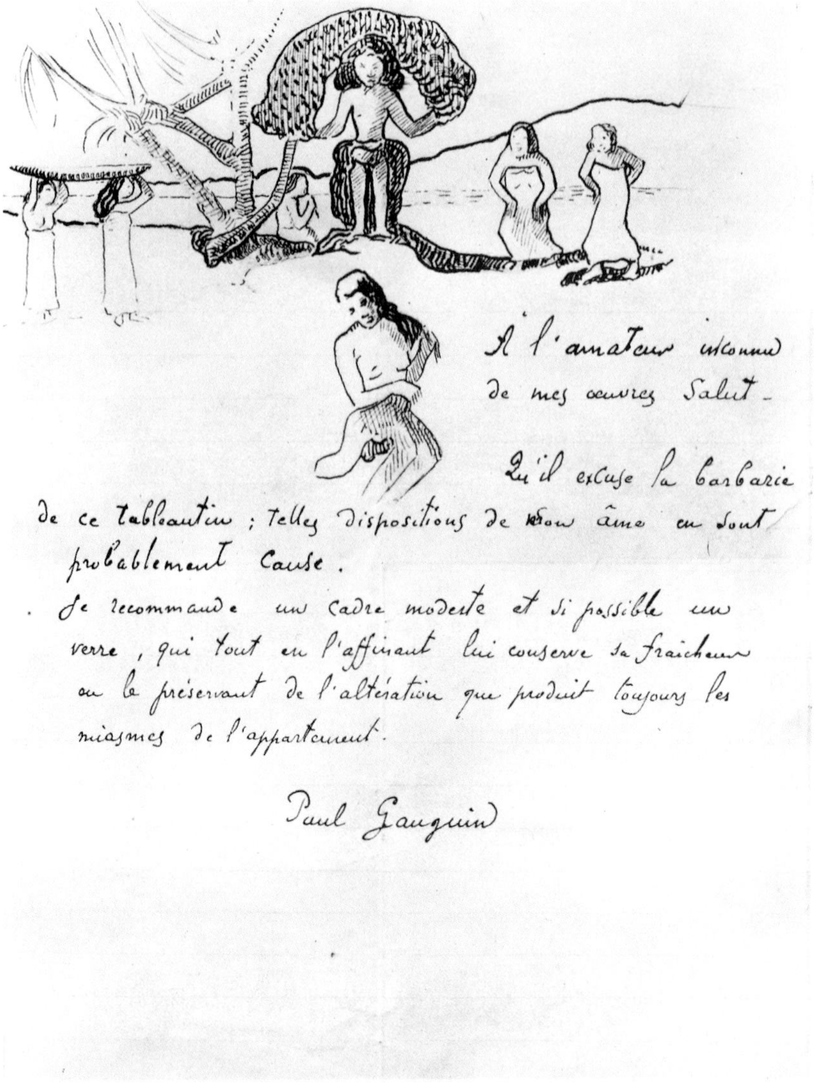
A l'amateur inconnu de mes œuvres Salut.
Qu'il excuse la barbarie de ce tableautin; telles dispositions de mon âme en sont probablement cause.
Je recommande un cadre modeste et si possible un verre, qui tout en l'affinant lui conserve sa fraîcheur en le préservant de l'altération que produit toujours les miasmes de l'appartement.
Paul Gauguin

19. Letter from Paul Gauguin to unknown collector, 1896
Mr. and Mrs. Alex M. Lewyt, New York

RESTORATION

Gauguin frequently restored his own paintings, as well as those in his collection by other artists.[142] After returning from Tahiti, he wrote to his wife in September 1893, "I have . . . many paintings to repair and retouch for my exhibition."[143] It is not difficult to see why this would be necessary. During his time in the South Seas, his paintings suffered severe damage, partly because Gauguin removed them from their stretchers to reuse the stretchers for works in progress. In this state they were especially vulnerable to damp environmental conditions, as is clear from the account of C. Le Moine, who inventoried Gauguin's studio after his death: "Our disappointment was great . . . to discover only six or seven sketches painted on packing cloth, mostly without frames or stretchers, mostly flaking, cracked, incapable of being conveniently wrapped or of surviving the voyage [to France]."[144] Gauguin tried to pack his paintings carefully, but occasionally he was sick and others packed for him, causing further damage. A letter to de Monfreid in 1899 contains a typical comment: "I know nothing about the bad condition of my last paintings: it must be that the transport badly damaged them."[145]

The most common problem in Gauguin's paintings was a damaged ground that required consolidation. This problem is hardly surprising, since he used a ground that was more suitable to panel paintings than paintings on fabric. As a result of the flaking ground, he often felt it was necessary to reconsolidate his damaged paintings.

Gauguin described his method of reattachment twice, first in 1889 to Vincent van Gogh:

It is very easy to do and may be very good for your canvases which need retouching. You stick newspapers on your canvas with flour paste. Once dry, you place your canvas on a smooth board and press it down hard with a very hot iron. All your flakes of color remain, but they will have flattened and you will have a very beautiful *surface. Afterward, you wet your covering of paper well and lift off all the paper.*[146]

This technique was certainly used to repair *The Yellow Christ* (W327) (fig. 20). The print from the newspaper facing described in Gauguin's letter to van Gogh has transferred onto the paint surface itself, where it is still faintly visible throughout the upper third of the painting.

Writing to de Monfreid eight years later, Gauguin described a similar procedure, but with several significant modifications:

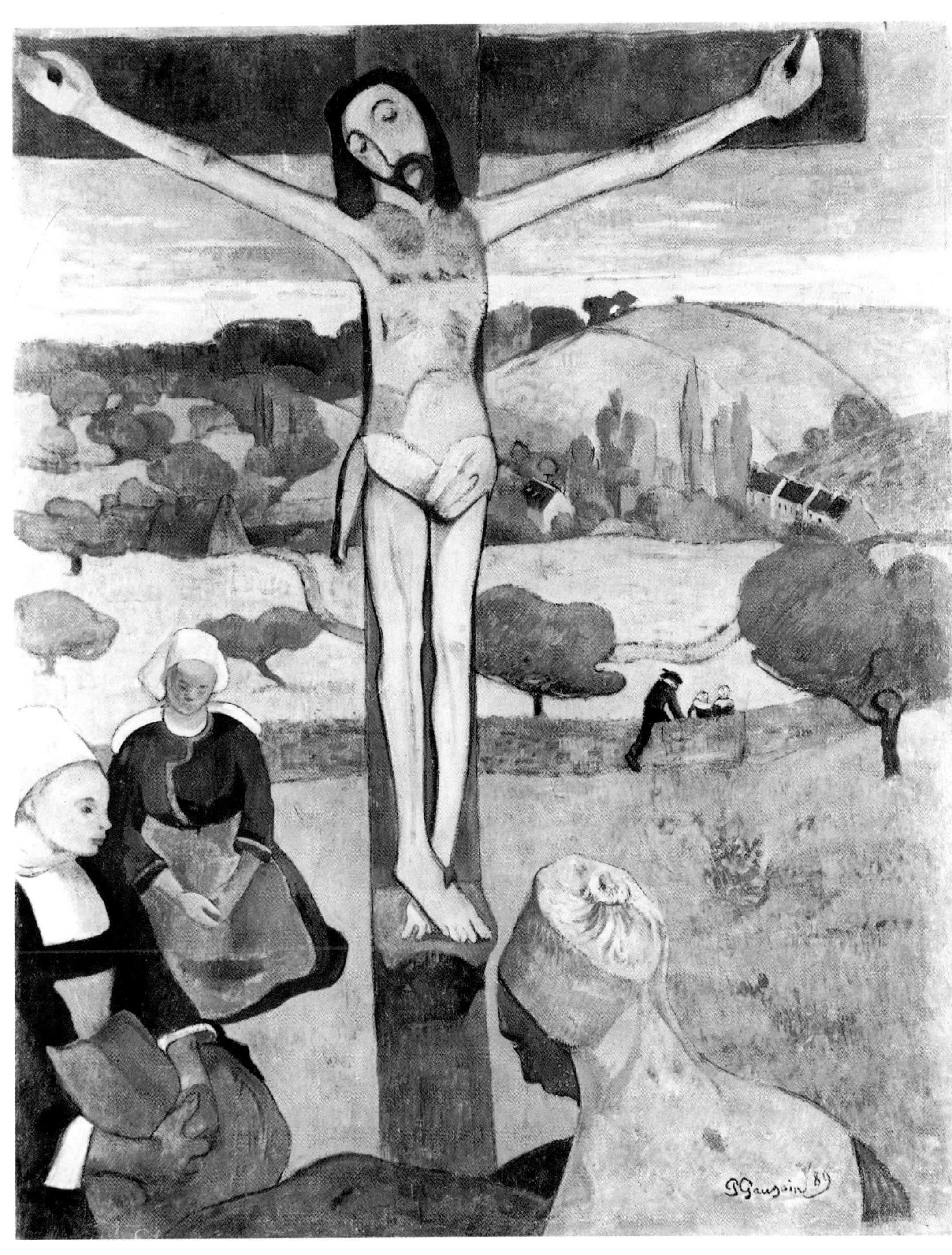

20. Paul Gauguin, *The Yellow Christ*, 1889, painting on fabric
Albright-Knox Art Gallery, Buffalo, General Purchase Funds

You make a facing by coating a bit of paper with flour paste and placing it on the side of the painting which is painted; you turn it over stretched out on a plank of wood and you apply a light coat of almost cold glue; work it in well with a knife and try to force it through the fabric and up into the Spanish white [ground]. Once dry, you pass a warm iron over it with as much pressure as possible. When afterward the painting is well supported on a stretcher, the paper comes up easily enough with a damp finger—how much work I give you—in this manner I repaired a van Gogh which was flaking everywhere. If some cracks remain, what does it matter.[147]

In his later description, Gauguin specified using a warm rather than a very hot iron; excessive heat could melt the paint surface, as he may have discovered through bad experience. He also recommended stretching the painting "out on a board" during the application of the paste to the picture's reverse; this step would minimize possible shrinkage of the fabric during the drying of the paste.

These changes and a number of others noted by Vojtech Jirat-Wasiutynski and H. Travers Newton in their technical study of the restoration by Gauguin of van Gogh's *Self-portrait Dedicated to Paul Gauguin*,[148] suggest the artist had learned by experience how to more gently repair his paintings. In both passages, however, Gauguin insisted on using great pressure, so that the paint was very flat after treatment. He even described this flatness as "*very beautiful*,"[149] underscoring his own preference for smooth paint with no impasto, which may have been acceptable for his own paintings but was surely unfortunate for the highly impastoed painting of van Gogh that Gauguin restored.

For the retouching phase of his restoration process, Gauguin preferred to use casein-bound pigments, as he explained in a letter to Arsene Alexandre:

The colors [in the painting] are bound to the support by a binder, which may be composed of either glue or oil. When they are old and therefore starved of oil, the perfectly dry color is a layer which is hard but porous. It goes without saying that all of the new oil [in the restoration] is little by little absorbed by the dry color bordering the damaged area. From this come these brushstrokes which yellow more each day. Make an experiment on a porous block of dry color, for example Spanish white. Once undertaken, it will be obvious that oil is the enemy—Here is an alternative method—One must fill the holes with casein-bound paint, which alone is not attacked by humidity, not even being soluble in a prolonged bath of ammonia. It is not possible to match the neighboring color, but it is easy to finish by glazing with a glaze of oil paint degreased with volatile spirits such as benzine or mineral spirits. The porous body disappears and a solid layer remains.[150]

Gauguin was accurate in his assessment of the failings of oil as a retouching medium. His choice of casein as a substitute was especially good for the restoration of his own paintings, since this medium, made from milk and lime, dries with a very matte surface and therefore could adequately reproduce the matteness of Gauguin's paint surface. It also dries quickly, so that the restoration procedure would not be too time consuming. Finally, as Gauguin wrote, it is totally impervious to water and it does not discolor.

SURFACE COATING

Because of his efforts to create a matte paint surface (draining his oil paints, painting on an absorbent ground, and washing his paintings to degrease them), Gauguin was adamant that his paintings not be varnished with the glossy natural resin varnishes common during his time. He occasionally recommended that his paintings be protected with a piece of glass when framed, but more often he made reference to using wax as a protective surface coating. He wrote to de Monfreid in 1901, "While I am thinking about it, have you well instructed Vollard on the maintenance of my paintings using wax? because I am always worried that they will be ruined with this dirty disgusting varnish which picture dealers use, and which is so common."[151]

Although there is no published description of precisely how Gauguin applied this wax coating, it is most likely that he dissolved the wax in warm mineral spirits and brushed on the solution. The mineral spirits would quickly evaporate, leaving a thin layer of wax behind. The surface created by this method would be matte, although it could be buffed with a soft cloth to create a more satiny sheen. The wax coating was never applied by Gauguin before his paintings left the South Seas because he was never sure in what state they would arrive in France. It was obviously more sensible to apply the wax coating after damaged areas had been reconsolidated and repaired in France.

In 1895 Gauguin described for Alexandre why he preferred wax as a surface coating:

Varnish of extra quality *is nothing more than a conduit of resin. No matter how bleached it is, it always returns to its origin which is yellow; furthermore it has in its nature the weakness of suppressing air on the painting without having the ability to stop acids from decomposing the colors. Resin is a good conductor of* everything. *You know as I do that the unvarnished Rembrandts have remained fresh and gray as they were on their first day. To what can we attribute this difference, if not to varnish. — White wax has none of these disadvantages, we have proof in ancient paintings made with wax. My neighbor tried wax as a surface coating, and he has obtained the same result. Wax prevents on paintings, as on wood, every type of crack and deterioration.*[152]

For these reasons, Gauguin concluded that his paintings, "once restretched and waxed, risk less."[153] A wax surface coating, probably original, has been noted on several paintings by Gauguin, among them *Mahana no atua* (W513), *Nevermore* (W558), *Te rerioa* (W557) (see fig. 13), and *Ia orana Maria* (W428),[154] but, sadly, one finds many more paintings covered with the same inappropriately glossy "dirty disgusting varnish which picture dealers use" so despised by the artist.

CONCLUSION

This study is by no means complete, since it is based on examination of only one-third of Gauguin's work, and most of these examinations were not carried out with the aid of sophisticated technical analysis. There is also still much to be learned from several forthcoming volumes of previously unpublished correspondence currently being edited by Victor Merlhès. However, the information gathered to date has been useful in understanding how Gauguin mastered certain technical processes to achieve a desired visual effect in his paintings as well as in learning how he adjusted certain materials and aspects of his technique in response to his environment.

It appears that Gauguin was always ready to experiment, from his first attempts at preparing his own grounds while a student of Pissarro in the late 1870s. This experimentation continued in the 1880s, as he tried painting on unprimed canvas, framed his paintings with unconventional painted frames, and eventually began to work on coarse fabric in Arles. In the 1890s, his decision to wax rather than varnish his paintings, his Tahitian attempt to make a paint medium from castor oil seeds, and, if Jénot is to be believed, his use of a breadfruit priming for trial paintings suggest that he was still prepared to improvise with unconventional materials when necessary.

It is also clear, however, that most of Gauguin's technical experiments with paintings were carried out long before he traveled to the South Seas. He established his painting technique, which consisted of painting with lean paint on coarse fabric primed with an absorbent ground, during the late 1880s in Brittany and Arles, and he did not radically alter it in the South Seas. It cannot be argued that Gauguin changed his painting technique significantly in response to his tropical environment. As we have seen, he used the humid climate of his surroundings as an excuse for painting less richly, mainly in an attempt to avoid having to paint for the market. The fact that there are no dramatic differences in materials and technique between his Arles and late South Seas paintings supports this conclusion.

His environment and periodic lack of supplies did force Gauguin to adjust his painting technique in several smaller ways. These alterations included varying the size and texture of his fabric supports, substituting preferred priming materials when they were not available, and layering individual paint layers more thinly. In his last years, when he was living in the Marquesas and was totally dependent on Vollard for supplies, Gauguin was most clearly a victim of circumstance, as can be seen in the smaller size of his paintings and in his forced use of the conventional artist's canvas sent to him by Vollard.

Even when he was most limited by his environment, however, Gauguin refused to compromise in those technical issues where change would have meant an undesirable aesthetic effect. For example, although he knew his priming would be less likely to flake if he added linseed oil to it, he refused to do so because the ground would then lose its absorbency and consequently the paint would appear oilier (that is, richer in binding medium), a result that would not produce the matte surface he preferred.

Gauguin's rather fussy insistence on using Le Franc pigments exclusively is another example of his unwillingness to compromise despite his isolation. Although it is difficult to ascertain what range of artist's supplies were available in Tahiti during the 1890s, the fact that Gauguin mentioned that lead white pigment coming from America was locally available[155] suggests he was probably able to buy other paints there as well, but he seems to have used only those pigments manufactured by Le Franc and sent to him by his friends.

Moreover, despite the weaknesses of his painting technique, Gauguin refused to alter it even in the face of criticism by his friends and periodic reports of structural instability that made the paintings unsalable. His disregard for good technique when it collided with his desired aesthetic effect is most clearly shown in his 1899 remark to de Monfreid: "Questions of paint thickness, of care in execution and even of the priming of the canvas . . . *one can always fix it later, right?*"[156]

As for Gauguin's occasional tendency to distort the details of his life and his creative process to present himself as more of an innovator in technique than he really was, this is hardly surprising in view of his personality. More than most artists of his time, Gauguin tried to live out his artistic vision; and this commitment explains why he is so endlessly fascinating as a man as well as an artist. He was in a sense creating himself along with his art, and therefore he may have felt freer than more conventional artists to alter facts when it suited him. One must remember, too, that there was no witness to contradict his inventions.

It may be that Gauguin's close identification with his art was responsible for several ways in which he was truly technically innovative. The most noteworthy is the thematic interrelatedness of his work in so many different media. The process in which a document became a large-scale drawing, then a painting; his practice of reworking his preparatory drawings into pastels and watercolors; his use of figures from paintings in his ceramic sculptures, which would then later appear in prints, monotypes, or other paintings—these practices are unique to Gauguin. It was perhaps the only natural way of making art to someone whose artistic impulse was so strong that it led him to make not only paintings but also his house, his shoes, and his eating utensils. Also technically innovative was the way Gauguin borrowed techniques and materials from one medium for use in another, so that the boundaries between the visual effects of painting, woodcarving, drawing, watercolor, and printmaking became blurred in a way which presaged the art of the twentieth century.

As always in a study of this type, one is left at the end with as many questions as one has answered. Examination of the remaining two-thirds of Gauguin's fabric supports is essential to establish clear patterns in the artist's use of canvas. Ultimately this information can perhaps aid in dating a number of problematic paintings, such as the group of Breton snow scenes that have been assigned dates as divergent as 1894 and after 1902.

Pigment analysis should make clear precisely which pigments Gauguin used on a larger number of paintings than it was possible to analyze in the course of this study. It might be useful in determining attribution of paintings such as the 1903 *Invocation* (W635), which contains a manganese pigment not identified in the other paintings studied by this examiner. It may also help to determine with absolute certainty whether Gauguin varied his pigments at different stages in his career and whether he added metallic powder to his pigments, as did some of his contemporaries.

Medium analysis may explain the curious gouachelike appearance of a number of paintings such as *Ta matete* (W476), and it may confirm or refute this examiner's hypothesis about the general absence of wax in the artist's paint. Publication of Gauguin's correspondence from 1888 until his death in 1903 will perhaps ascertain more clearly what range of materials was available to the artist in Tahiti. Fiber analysis should eventually distinguish the native "sackcloth" from the coarse fabric Gauguin brought with him from Europe. The role within the artist's oeuvre of a number of large paintings on paper needs to be more clearly explored. It is possible that some of these are reworked cartoons. Finally, Gauguin's motivation in making several close variations of the same subject, as in *I raro te oviri* (W431 and W432), *Tahitian Women* and *Parau Api* (W434 and W466), *Te Fare Maorie* (W436 and W437), *Te Raau Rahi* (W436 and W437), and *Maternity* (W581 and W582), should be investigated.

Late in his life and in his typical caustic fashion, Gauguin wrote somewhat prophetically of the future of his art: "The artist dies; the heirs fall upon his work; everything is divided up; copyrights, auctions, and all the rest of it. There he is, completely stripped. With this in mind, I strip myself beforehand. That is a comfort."[157] His loss has been our gain. As more and more of his paintings enter museum collections, there will be greater opportunity to study his paintings and to answer those questions about his painting technique that still remain.

NOTES

This research would not have been possible without the generous sharing of information by the following conservators, art historians, and scientists: Albert Albano of the Museum of Modern Art; Inge Fiedler of the Art Institute of Chicago; Richard Field of the Yale University Art Gallery; Patricia Garland of the Wadsworth Atheneum; Tim Green of the Tate Gallery; Gloria Groome of the Art Institute of Chicago; Paul Haner of the Worcester Museum; Gisela Helmkampf of the Metropolitan Museum of Art; Bruce Miller of the Cleveland Museum of Art; David Miller of the Indianapolis Museum of Art; Kathryn Olivier of the Harvard University Art Museums; Mary Sebera of the Baltimore Museum of Art; and Bridget Smith of the Museum of Fine Arts, Boston. In addition I would like to acknowledge Charlotte Hale of the Metropolitan Museum of Art, whose unpublished 1982 project at the Courtauld Institute, University of London, was a valuable starting point for this research.

At the National Gallery of Art, Ross Merrill, David Bull, and Sarah Fisher of the conservation division supported my research efforts. Andrew Krieger, registrar's department, collected data about paintings by Paul Gauguin in the former Soviet Union. Conservation scientists Barbara Berrie, Susana Halpine, Suzanne Lomax, Michael Palmer, and Deborah Rendahl provided the analyses upon which much of this paper is based.

Carolyn Villers of the Courtauld Institute, London, as well as Charles Moffett and Arthur Wheelock, National Gallery of Art, kindly read drafts of this research and made many useful suggestions for its improvement. Mervin Richard spent many hours retrieving this paper from computer neverland when it was thought irretrievably lost. Finally, I would like to thank Marla Prather, research associate in the department of modern painting, for generously sharing with me over a period of several years her knowledge of Gauguin and for uncomplainingly reading numerous versions of this text.

Unless otherwise indicated, all translations are mine and all italics are by the authors quoted.

1. John Rewald, ed., *Gauguin: Letters to Ambroise Vollard and André Fontainas* (San Francisco, 1943), 31.

2. Bengt Danielsson, *Gauguin in the South Seas* (New York, 1966), 212.

3. It is noteworthy that although Gauguin's painting technique may not be extremely experimental, his printmaking techniques were. A possible reason was that Gauguin focused on painting more fully earlier in his career, when he was surrounded by a European tradition. By contrast, much of his experimenting with printmaking took place in the tropics, where European workshop techniques would have had less influence.

4. Georges Wildenstein, *Gauguin*, ed. Raymond Cogniat and Daniel Wildenstein (Paris, 1964). References to paintings will include Wildenstein's catalogue number.

5. Paul Gauguin to Charles Morice, July 1901, *Lettres de Gauguin à sa femme et à ses amis*, ed. Maurice

Malingue (Paris, 1946), no. 174; Gauguin to Georges-Daniel de Monfreid, February 1898, *Lettres de Paul Gauguin à Georges-Daniel de Monfreid*, ed. Annie Joly-Segalen, rev. ed. (Paris, 1950), no. 40.

6. Richard Brettell, Françoise Cachin, Claire Frèches-Thory, and Charles F. Stuckey, with assistance from Peter Zegers, *The Art of Paul Gauguin* [exh. cat., National Gallery of Art] (Washington, 1988), 417.

7. Gauguin to de Monfreid, January 1900, Joly-Segalen 1950, no. 60.

8. Vincent van Gogh to Théo van Gogh, [5?] November 1888, *Verzamelde Brieven van Vincent van Gogh*, 3 vols. (Amsterdam, 1953) (hereafter van Gogh 1953), no. 559.

9. Gauguin to Emile Bernard, n.d. [c. 2d week November 1888], *Correspondance de Paul Gauguin*, ed. Victor Merlhès (Paris, 1984), no. 179.

10. Gauguin to Emile Schuffenecker, [23?] November 1888, Merlhès 1984, no. 184.

11. Gauguin to Théo van Gogh, 22 November 1888, Merlhès 1984, no. 183.

12. Françoise Cachin, "#29: Self-Portrait for Carrière," in Brettell et al. 1988, 75–76.

13. Ronald Pickvance, *Van Gogh in Arles* [exh. cat., Metropolitan Museum of Art] (New York, 1984), 115–117.

14. Of thirty-five paintings from 1889 and 1890 examined (representing 50 percent of the paintings done in these years), only one (Prague version *Bonjour M. Gauguin*, W322) is painted on coarse fabric.

15. Nine of eighteen paintings from this visit were examined; all were painted on a moderate-weight linen canvas with 10–12 threads per cm.

16. Schuffenecker to Gauguin, 11 December 1888, Merlhès 1984, no. CI.

17. Gauguin to de Monfreid, January 1900, Joly-Segalen 1950, no. 60.

18. Lieutenant Jénot, "Le premier séjour de Gauguin à Tahiti d'après le manuscrit Jénot (1891–1893)," *Gazette des Beaux-Arts*, 6 sér., vol. 47 (January–April 1956), 120.

19. Wildenstein 1964, entry for W515.

20. Gauguin to de Monfreid, 12 March 1897, Joly-Segalen 1950, no. 30.

21. Gauguin to de Monfreid, January 1900, Joly-Segalen 1950, no. 60.

22. Gauguin to de Monfreid, 14 July 1897, April 1899, October 1900, Joly-Segalen 1950, nos. 34, 53, 68.

23. Gauguin to de Monfreid, October 1897, Joly-Segalen 1950, no. 37.

24. Gauguin to de Monfreid, December 1897, Joly-Segalen 1950, no. 39.

25. Gauguin to de Monfreid, August 1899, Joly-Segalen 1950, no. 57.

26. Gauguin to de Monfreid, September 1899, Joly-Segalen 1950, no. 58.

27. Gauguin to de Monfreid, January 1900, Joly-Segalen 1950, no. 61.

28. Danielsson 1966, 212.

29. Ambroise Vollard to Gauguin, late 1899, Rewald 1943, 31.

30. Gauguin to Vollard, January 1900, Rewald 1943, 31–32.

31. Gauguin to de Monfreid, October 1900, Joly-Segalen 1950, no. 68.

32. Gauguin to Vollard, May 1901, Rewald 1943, 47.

33. Richard Brettell, "#255: Still-Life with Grapefruits," in Brettell et al. 1988, 458.

34. Gauguin to de Monfreid, August 1901, Joly-Segalen 1950, no. 77.

35. Gauguin to de Monfreid, November 1901, Joly-Segalen 1950, no. 78.

36. Gauguin to Vollard, March 1902, Rewald 1943, 52.

37. Gauguin to Vollard, April 1903, Rewald 1943, 63–64.

38. Gauguin to de Monfreid, October 1900, April 1901, Joly-Segalen 1950, nos. 58, 73.

39. Pierre Louis Bouvier, *Manuel des jeunes artistes et amateurs en peinture*, 3d ed. (Paris, 1844), 535; Jean François Léonore Mérimée, *The Art of Painting in Oil and in Fresco* (1830), 3d ed., trans. William Benjamin Sarsfield Taylor (London, 1839), 221; Jéhan Georges Vibert, *The Science of Painting*, 8th ed., trans. by the author (London, 1892), 97, 102–103, 108–109; Frédéric Auguste Antoine Goupil Fesquet, *Peinture à l'huile* (Paris, 1900), 23–24.

40. These early "absorbent grounds" appear to have been composed of a thin layer of oil laid on several lower layers of distemper-bound priming. See Mérimée 1839, 221, n. 1.

41. Ernest Hareux, "Materials for Oil Painting," *Practical Manual of Painting in Oil Colours*, 3d ed., trans. H. B. Hayes (London, 1870), 23.

42. Bouvier 1844, 535–536.

43. Paul Sérusier, *ABC de la peinture suivi d'une correspondance inédite* (Paris, 1950), 31.

44. Gauguin to de Monfreid, April 1901, Joly-Segalen 1950, no. 73.

45. Gauguin to de Monfreid, September 1899, Joly-Segalen 1950, no. 58.

46. Gauguin to Camille Pissarro, 26 September 1879, Merlhès 1984, no. 11.

47. Gauguin to de Monfreid, September 1899, Joly-Segalen 1950, no. 58.

48. This conclusion was obvious from examination of the tacking margins. Artist-applied priming did not extend onto tacking margins or in many cases even to the edges of the painting. In contrast, the priming of commercially prepared canvas extended onto tacking margins, since it was applied before the painting was cut and stretched onto its auxiliary support.

49. Gauguin to Bernard, n.d. [3d or 4th week November 1888], Merlhès 1984, no. 182.

50. Two exceptions known to this examiner are *The Three Puppies* (W293) and *Portrait of Aline Chazal*,

the Artist's Mother (W385), both of which have a dark red ground.

51. Pierre François Tingry, *The Painter and Varnisher's Guide* (London, 1804), 286–289; Charles Chassé, *Gauguin et son temps* (Paris, 1955), 44.

52. "Quelques peintres idéistes," *Le Chat noir*, 19 September 1891, quoted in Félix Fenéon, *Oeuvres plus que complètes* (Geneva, 1970), 201.

53. Chassé 1955, 44.

54. Jénot 1956, 120.

55. Rosemond D. Harley, *Artists' Pigments, c. 1600–1835* (London, 1970), 154.

56. Gauguin to de Monfreid, 20 September 1894, Joly-Segalen 1950, no. 18.

57. Casein grounds were not unusual in the late nineteenth century. Vibert (1846–1904), described the preparation of a casein ground:

Grind zinc white in water in the proportion of 100 grammes of water to 100 grammes of zinc and mix this zinc white with 200 grammes of caseine paste already prepared. . . . The canvas should be stretched on a frame and freed from grease with benzine. When it has evaporated, give with a swallow-tail brush, a first coating of paste and white. Let this dry at a mild temperature. . . . Give a second layer.

Vibert 1892, 186–187.

58. Vincent to Théo van Gogh, n.d. [c. 20 November 1888], van Gogh 1953, no. 563.

59. High-performance liquid chromatography (HPLC) was used to search for the presence of casein in the ground layer in *Mme Alexandre Kohler* (W314), *Brittany Landscape* (1888, National Gallery of Art, Washington), and *The Invocation* (W635).

60. Gauguin to de Monfreid, January 1900, Joly-Segalen 1950, no. 60.

61. Gauguin to Vincent van Gogh, 9 January 1889, *Paul Gauguin: 45 Lettres à Vincent, Théo et Jo van Gogh*, ed. Douglas Cooper (The Hague and Lausanne, 1983), no. GAC 34.

62. Gauguin to de Monfreid, 14 July 1897, Joly-Segalen 1950, no. 34.

63. Gauguin to de Monfreid, April 1899, Joly-Segalen 1950, no. 53.

64. Composition of the grounds of *Nevermore* (W558) and *Te rerioa* (W557) was reported in Courtauld Institute examination reports done between 1981 and 1982 by Charlotte Hale. Composition of the ground of *Portraits of Women* (W610) is based on examination of its x-radiographs.

65. Jénot 1956, 120.

66. *Still Life with Fan* (W377), *Aita* (W508), *Ia Orana Maria* (W428), *Nevermore* (W558), *Carrières du Chou, Près de Pontoise* (W71), and *Brittany Landscape* (National Gallery of Art, Washington).

67. Gauguin to de Monfreid, May 1899, Joly-Segalen 1950, no. 54.

68. Gauguin to Bernard, n.d. [3d–4th week November 1888], Merlhès 1984, no. 182.

69. Chassé 1955, 44–45.

70. Françoise Cachin, "#42: Hilly Landscape with Two Figures," in Brettell et al. 1988, 92.

71. Vincent van Gogh to Théo van Gogh, 27 October 1888, Merlhès 1984, no. LXXXVIII.

72. Vincent van Gogh to Théo van Gogh, [5?] November 1888, van Gogh 1953, no. 559.

73. Gauguin to de Monfreid, 7 November 1891, Joly-Segalen 1950, no. 2.

74. Gauguin, *Avant et après*, January–February 1903, quoted in Ronald Pickvance, *The Drawings of Paul Gauguin* (London and New York, 1970), 5.

75. Identification of the stylistic sources for Gauguin's work is beyond the scope of this paper, but it has been well-documented in the literature. See Bernard Dorival, "Sources of the Art of Gauguin from Java, Egypt, and Ancient Greece," *Burlington Magazine* 93, no. 577 (April 1951), 118–122; William M. Kane, "Gauguin's *Le Cheval Blanc*: Sources and Syncretic Meanings," *Burlington Magazine* 108, no. 760 (July 1966), 352–362.

76. Raymond Cogniat and John Rewald, *Paul Gauguin: A Sketchbook* (Paris and New York, 1962); Bernard Dorival, *Carnet de Tahiti* (Paris, 1954); René Huyghe, *Le Carnet de Paul Gauguin* (Paris, 1952).

77. Gauguin to Théo van Gogh, 27 October 1888, Merlhès 1984, no. 175; Gauguin to de Monfreid, 7 November 1891, Joly-Segalen 1950, no. 2.

78 .Vincent van Gogh to Théo van Gogh, 27 October 1888, Merlhès 1984, no. LXXXVIII; Gauguin to Théo van Gogh, 27 October 1888, Merlhès 1984, no. 175.

79. Ziva Amishai-Maisels, *Gauguin's Religious Themes* (New York and London, 1985), 400–401.

80. An example is the preparatory drawing for *Une Nuit à Vaugirard* (Statens Konstmuseer, The National Swedish Art Museums, Stockholm), illustrated in Merlhès 1984, 17, with transcription of notes on 346.

81. H. Travers Newton and Vojtech Jirat-Wasiutynski, "Reconstruction of Gauguin's Aesthetic from the Evidence of His Paintings," paper presented to College Art Association, New York, 16 February 1990.

82. This examination used stereo-binocular microscope and cross-sectional paint samples.

83. Gauguin to de Monfreid, 22 February 1899, Joly-Segalen 1950, no. 51.

84. Gauguin to de Monfreid, October 1897, Joly-Segalen 1950, no. 37.

85. Merete Bodelsen, "Gauguin's Bathing Girl," *Burlington Magazine* 101, no. 674 (May 1959), 186–188; Peter Zegers, quoted in Brettell et al. 1988, 84.

86. Merete Bodelsen, *Gauguin's Ceramics: A Study in the Development of His Art* (London, 1964), 50–52.

87. Gauguin to de Monfreid, [April–May?] 1893, Joly-Segalen 1950, no. 13.

88. Gauguin to de Monfreid, 12 March 1897, Joly-Segalen 1950, no. 30.

89. Chassé 1955, 43–47.

90. Gauguin to Camille Pissarro, late May 1885, Merlhès 1984, no. 79.

91. Anthea Callen, *Techniques of the Impressionists*

(London, 1982), 162–163; Charlotte Hale, "A Study of Paul Gauguin's Correspondence Relating to His Painting Materials and Techniques, with Specific Reference to His Works in the Courtauld Collection" (unpublished project, Courtauld Institute, University of London, 1982), 24.

92. Sérusier 1950. Van Gogh's addition of wax has been confirmed by medium analysis undertaken at the National Gallery, London.

93. Hale 1982, 25.

94. Gauguin to de Monfreid, 22 February 1899, Joly-Segalen 1950, no. 51.

95. Gauguin to de Monfreid, 8 December 1892, 25 February 1901, Joly-Segalen 1950, nos. 8, 72.

96. Analysis undertaken by the scientific research department at the National Gallery of Art, Washington, using gas chromatography and high-performance liquid chromatography, indicated the pigments in Gauguin's *Self-portrait with Halo* (W323), *Te pape nave nave* (W568), and *Brittany Landscape* (National Gallery of Art, Washington) were bound only with oil. No traces of wax were present.

97. Gauguin to de Monfreid, May 1899, Joly-Segalen 1950, no. 54.

98. Vincent van Gogh to Théo van Gogh, n.d. [c. 20 November 1888], van Gogh 1953, no. 563.

99. Gauguin to de Monfreid, 8 December 1892, Joly-Segalen 1950, no. 8.

100. Gauguin to de Monfreid, 18 June 1898, July 1898, Joly-Segalen 1950, nos. 44, 45.

101. Gauguin to de Monfreid, September 1899, Joly-Segalen 1950, no. 58.

102. Gauguin to de Monfreid, 8 December 1892, Joly-Segalen 1950, no. 8.

103. Gustave Kahn, "Au temps du pointillisme," *Mercure de France* 171 (April–May 1924), 16; Isabelle Cahn, "Chronology, June 1848–June 1886," in Brettell et al. 1988, 9.

104. Gauguin to de Monfreid, late December 1892, Joly-Segalen 1950, no. 9.

105. This analysis was based on energy-dispersive x-ray fluorescence spectroscopy (EDX) and microscopy of crushed samples.

106. Mary Sebera, examination report, 1987, Baltimore Museum of Art.

107. Carolyn Villers, personal communication, September 1990.

108. Frédéric Auguste Antoine Goupil Fesquet and P. Steck, *Traité méthodique et raisonné de la peinture à l'huile*, rev. ed. (Paris, 1904), 63.

109. Vincent van Gogh to Théo van Gogh, n.d. [c. 20 November 1888], van Gogh 1953, no. 563.

110. Vincent van Gogh to Théo van Gogh, n.d. [c. 20 November 1888], van Gogh 1953, no. 563; Gauguin to Théo van Gogh, n.d. [c. 22 November 1888], Merlhès 1984, no. 183.

111. Gauguin to de Monfreid, 8 December 1892, Joly-Segalen 1950, no. 8. The titles are *Te Faaturuma* (W440), *Te raau rahi* (W439), *Te fare maori* (W436), and *I raro te oviri* (W432).

112. Gauguin to Bernard, n.d. [Arles, 1888], Malingue 1946, no. 78; Gauguin to Schuffenecker, n.d. [Pont-Aven, June 1890], Malingue 1946, no. 104; Gauguin to Bernard, n.d. [Arles, 3d–4th week November 1888], Merlhès 1984, no. 182.

113. Gauguin to de Monfreid, April 1899, Joly-Segalen 1950, no. 53.

114. Jénot 1956, 120.

115. Gauguin to de Monfreid, September 1899, Joly-Segalen 1950, no. 58.

116. Gauguin to de Monfreid, January 1887, January 1900, Joly-Segalen 1950, nos. 28, 60; Gauguin to Vollard, March 1902, Rewald 1943, 60–61.

117. Gauguin to de Monfreid, [April/May?] 1893, Joly-Segalen 1950, no. 13.

118. Gauguin to Emmanuel Bibesco, n.d. [July 1900], Malingue 1946, no. 173.

119. Gauguin to de Monfreid, late December 1892, Joly-Segalen 1950, no. 9; Gauguin to de Monfreid, August 1892, Malingue 1946, no. 132.

120. Gauguin to de Monfreid, June 1892, January 1900, August 1900, October 1900, Joly-Segalen 1950, nos. 5, 60, 66, 68; Gauguin to Vollard, March 1902, Rewald 1943, 50–51.

121. Gauguin to Vollard, March 1902, Rewald 1943, 51–52.

122. Gauguin to de Monfreid, January 1897, Joly-Segalen 1950, no. 28.

123. Gauguin to de Monfreid, 27 January 1900, Joly-Segalen 1950, no. 61.

124. Chassé 1955, 43–44.

125. Gauguin to de Monfreid, August 1901, Joly-Segalen 1950, no. 77.

126. Vincent van Gogh to Théo van Gogh, n.d. [c. 20 November 1888], van Gogh 1953, no. 563.

127. Gauguin to Théo van Gogh, n.d. [c. 22 November 1888], Merlhès 1984, no. 183.

128. Gauguin to de Monfreid, 8 December 1892, Joly-Segalen 1950, no. 8.

129. Hale 1982, 28.

130. "Impressionisme," *Le Voltaire*, 3 March 1882, Merlhès 1984, 366.

131. Gauguin to Camille Pissarro, late July 1884, Merlhès 1984, no. 50.

132. Vincent van Gogh to Théo van Gogh, n.d. [9–12 November 1888], van Gogh 1953, no. 561. Van Gogh's assertion that Gauguin invented the white frame may not be correct; the quotation is included only to show that Gauguin was using white frames during his time in Arles.

133. Théo van Gogh to Gauguin, November 1888, in Merete Bodelsen, "An Unpublished Letter by Théo van Gogh," *Burlington Magazine* 99, no. 651 (June 1957), 200.

134. Istvan Genthon, *Rippl-Ronai: The Hungarian "Nabi"* (Budapest, 1958), 21.

135. Richard Brettell, "#16: Still Life with Vase of Japanese Peonies and Mandolin," in Brettell et al. 1988, 41.

136. Gauguin to de Monfreid, July 1898, Joly-Segalen 1950, no. 45.

137. Georges Chaudet to Gauguin, 15 January 1899, Jean Loize Archive, Papeete, Tahiti. I am indebted to Gloria Groome of the European paintings department at the Art Institute of Chicago for this reference.

138. Note at the bottom of a drawing illustrated in Pickvance 1970, pl. 83.

139. Gauguin to Pissarro, late July 1882, 2 August 1882, Merlhès 1984, nos. 25, 27.

140. Note at the bottom of a drawing illustrated in Pickvance 1970, pl. 83.

141. "Quelques peintres idéistes," quoted in Fenéon 1970, 200.

142. Vojtech Jirat-Wasiutynski, H. Travers Newton, Eugene Farrell, and Richard Newman, *Vincent van Gogh's Self-portrait Dedicated to Paul Gauguin: An Historical and Technical Study* (Cambridge, Mass., 1984).

143. Gauguin to Mette-Sophie Gauguin, n.d. [c. September 1893], Malingue 1946, no. 142; see also Gauguin to Théo van Gogh, [19–20] December 1888, Merlhès 1984, no. 192.

144. C. Le Moine, quoted in Jean de Rotonchomp [Louis Brouillon], *Paul Gauguin* (Weimar, 1906), 196–197.

145. Gauguin to de Monfreid, 22 February 1899, Joly-Segalen 1950, no. 51.

146. Gauguin to Vincent van Gogh, 9 January 1889, Cooper 1983, no. GAC 34.

147. Gauguin to de Monfreid, 14 July 1897, Joly-Segalen 1950, no. 34.

148. Jirat-Wasiutynski et al. 1984, 17–20.

149. Gauguin to Vincent van Gogh, 9 January 1889, Cooper 1983, no. GAC 34.

150. Gauguin to Arsene Alexandre, n.d. [10 February 1895], Malingue 1946, no. 155.

151. Gauguin to de Monfreid, 25 February 1901, Joly-Segalen 1950, no. 72.

152. Gauguin to Alexandre, n.d. [10 February 1895], Malingue 1946, no. 155.

153. Gauguin to de Monfreid, 14 July 1897, Joly-Segalen 1950, no. 34.

154. Louis Pomerantz, n.d., conservation report, conservation department, Art Institute of Chicago; Hale 1982, 38; Gisela Helmkampf, painting conservator at the Metropolitan Museum of Art, personal communication, 1987.

155. Gauguin to de Monfreid, April 1899, Joly-Segalen 1950, no. 53.

156. Gauguin to de Monfreid, May 1899, Joly-Segalen 1950, no. 54.

157. Paul Gauguin, journal, January–February 1903, in *Paul Gauguin's Intimate Journals*, trans. Van Wyck Brooks (Bloomington, Ind., 1958), 246.

BIBLIOGRAPHY

Letters

Cooper, Douglas, ed. *Paul Gauguin: 45 Lettres à Vincent, Théo et Jo van Gogh.* The Hague and Lausanne, 1983.

Joly-Segalen, Annie, ed. *Lettres de Paul Gauguin à Georges-Daniel de Monfreid.* Rev. ed., Paris, 1950.

Lettres de Paul Gauguin à Emile Bernard, 1888–1891. Geneva, 1954.

Malingue, Maurice, ed. *Lettres de Gauguin à sa femme et à ses amis.* Paris, 1946. Rev. ed., Paris, 1949.

Merlhès, Victor, ed. *Correspondance de Paul Gauguin.* Paris, 1984.

Oeuvres écrites de Gauguin et Van Gogh. [exh. cat., Institut Néerlandais] Paris, 1975.

Rewald, John, ed. *Paul Gauguin: Letters to Ambroise Vollard and André Fontainas.* San Francisco, 1943.

Sérusier, Paul. *ABC de la peinture suivi d'une correspondance inédite.* Paris, 1950.

Gauguin's Writings and Sketchbooks

Gauguin, Paul. *The Intimate Journals of Paul Gauguin.* Translated by Van Wyck Brooks. Bloomington, Ind., 1958.

Cogniat, Raymond, and John Rewald. *Paul Gauguin: A Sketchbook.* New York, 1962.

Danielsson, Bengt, and Patrick O'Reilly. *Gauguin Journaliste à Tahiti et ses articles des "Guêpes."* Paris, 1966.

Dorival, Bernard. *Carnet de Tahiti.* Paris, 1952.

Huyghe, René. *Le Carnet de Paul Gauguin.* Paris, 1952.

Writings about Gauguin

Amishai-Maisels, Ziva. *Gauguin's Religious Themes.* New York and London, 1985.

Artur, Gilles. "Notice historique du Musée Gauguin de Tahiti suivie des quelques lettres inédites de Paul Gauguin." *Journal de la Société des Océanistes* 38, nos. 74–75 (1982), 7–17.

Bodelsen, Merete. "Gauguin's Bathing Girl." *Burlington Magazine* 101, no. 674 (May 1959), 186–190.

———. *Gauguin's Ceramics: A Study in the Development of His Art.* London, 1964.

———. "An Unpublished Letter by Théo van Gogh." *Burlington Magazine* 99, no. 651 (June 1957), 199–202.

———. "The Wildenstein-Cogniat Gauguin Catalogue," *Burlington Magazine* 108, no. 754 (January 1966), 27–38.

Brettell, Richard, Françoise Cachin, Claire Frèches-Thory, and Charles F. Stuckey, with assistance from Peter Zegers. *The Art of Paul Gauguin.* [exh. cat., National Gallery of Art] Washington, 1988.

Cachin, Françoise. *Gauguin.* Paris, 1968.

Callen, Anthea. *Techniques of the Impressionists.* London, 1982.

Chassé, Charles. *Gauguin et le groupe de Pont-Aven.* Paris, 1921.

———. *Gauguin et son temps.* Paris, 1955.

Danielsson, Bengt. *Gauguin in the South Seas.* New York, 1966.

Dorival, Bernard. "Sources of the Art of Gauguin from Java, Egypt, and Ancient Greece." *Burlington Magazine* 93, no. 577 (April 1951), 118–122.

Fenéon, Félix. *Oeuvres plus que complètes.* Geneva, 1970.

Field, Richard S. *Paul Gauguin: The Paintings of the First Trip to Tahiti.* New York, 1977.

Genthon, Istvan. *Rippl-Ronai: The Hungarian "Nabi."* Budapest, 1958.

van Gogh, Vincent. *Verzamelde Brieven van Vincent van Gogh.* 3 vols. Amsterdam, 1953.

Hale, Charlotte. "A Study of Paul Gauguin's Correspondence Relating to His Painting Materials and Techniques, with Specific Reference to His Works in the Courtauld Collection." Unpublished project, Courtauld Institute, University of London, London, 1982.

Jénot, Lieutenant. "Le premier séjour de Gauguin à Tahiti d'après le manuscrit Jénot (1891–1893)." *Gazette des Beaux-Arts,* 6 sér., vol. 47 (January–April 1956), 115–126.

Jirat-Wasiutynski, Vojtech, H. Travers Newton, Eugene Farrell, and Richard Newman. *Vincent van Gogh's Self-portrait Dedicated to Paul Gauguin: An Historical and Technical Study.* Cambridge, Mass., 1984.

Kahn, Gustave. "Au temps du pointillisme." *Mercure de France* 171 (April–May 1924), 16.

Kane, William M. "Gauguin's *Le Cheval blanc*: Sources and Syncretic Meanings." *Burlington Magazine* 108, no. 760 (July 1966), 352–362.

Morice, Charles. "Quelques opinions sur Paul Gauguin." *Mercure de France* 48, no. 167 (November 1903), 415.

Natanson, Thadée. "Expositions: Oeuvres récentes de Paul Gauguin." *La Revue blanche* 5, no. 26 (December 1893), 418–422.

Pickvance, Ronald. *The Drawings of Paul Gauguin.* London and New York, 1970.

———. *Van Gogh in Arles.* [exh. cat., Metropolitan Museum of Art] New York, 1984.

Rewald, John. *The History of Impressionism.* 3d ed. New York, 1961.

———. *Post-Impressionism from Van Gogh to Gauguin.* New York, 1956.

de Rotonchomp, Jean [Louis Brouillon]. *Paul Gauguin.* Weimar, 1906.

Varnedoe, Kirk. "Gauguin." In *Primitivism in 20th Century Art.* [exh. cat., Museum of Modern Art] New York, 1984, 179–210.

Wildenstein, Georges. *Gauguin.* Edited by Raymond Cogniat and Daniel Wildenstein. Paris, 1964.

Technical References and Artists' Handbooks

Bomford, David, Jo Kirby, John Leighton, and Ashok Roy. *Art in the Making: Impressionism.* [exh. cat., National Gallery] London, 1990.

Bouvier, Pierre Louis. *Manuel des jeunes artistes et amateurs en peinture.* 3d ed. Paris, 1844.

de Carbonnel, Katrina Vanderlip. "A Study of French Painting Canvases." *Journal of the American Institute for Conservation* 20 (1981), 3–20.

Goupil Fesquet, Frédéric Auguste Antoine. *Peinture à l'huile.* Paris, 1900.

———, and P. Steck. *Traité méthodique et raisonné de la peinture à l'huile.* Rev. ed. Paris, 1904.

Hareux, Ernest. *Practical Manual for Painting in Oil Colours.* 3d ed. Translated by H. B. Hayes. London, 1870.

Harley, Rosemond D. *Artists' Pigments c. 1600–1835.* London, 1970.

Mérimée, Jean François Léonore. *The Art of Painting in Oil and Fresco.* 1830. 3d ed. Translated by William Benjamin Sarsfield Taylor. London, 1839.

Tingry, Pierre François. *The Painter and Varnisher's Guide.* London, 1804.

Vibert, Jéhan Georges. *The Science of Painting.* 8th ed. Translated by the author. London, 1892.

APPENDIX 1

A Brief Chronology of Gauguin's Life

1848 Born in Paris. Father Clovis Gauguin, a journalist; mother Aline Chazal, of Peruvian extraction.

1849 Gauguin family moves to Peru; father dies during journey.

1854 Paul and family return to Europe.

1865–1868 Employed in the merchant marine, traveling between Le Havre and Rio de Janeiro.

1868–1871 Serves in French navy.

1872 Enters stockbrokerage firm of Bertin, Paris.

1873 Marries a Dane, Mette-Sophie Gad. Working at Académie Colarossi. Begins to paint.

c. 1875 Begins to buy impressionist pictures. Meets Camille Pissarro.

1876 One of his paintings accepted at the Salon.

1877 Friendship with the impressionists. Begins to sculpt.

1880 Exhibits in Fifth Impressionist Exhibition.

1881 Exhibits in Sixth Impressionist Exhibition. Paints with Pissarro, Paul Cézanne, and Armand Guillaumin. Paul Durand-Ruel, a Paris dealer, buys three of his paintings.

1882 Exhibits in Seventh Impressionist Exhibition.

1883 *January*: resigns from Bertin (works part-time until end of year).
October: moves to Rouen with his family.

1884 *November*: moves to Denmark with his family.

1885 *June*: returns to Paris with his oldest son Clovis.
July–October: living in Dieppe.

1886 Exhibits in Eighth (last) Impressionist Exhibition. Begins to work with ceramics.
June–November: in Pont-Aven, Brittany. Meets Emile Bernard. Exhibits in Nantes.

1887 Wife takes Clovis back to Denmark.
April–October: in Panama and Martinique with Charles Laval.
November: returns to Paris.

1888 *January–October*: in Pont-Aven.
Winter: one-person exhibition at Boussod and Valadon, Paris, due to efforts of Théo van Gogh.
October–Christmas: with Vincent van Gogh in Arles.

1889 *January–March*: in Paris.
February: exhibits with Les XX in Brussels.
April: exhibits with impressionists and synthesists at Café Volpini.
February–April/July–September: moving between Pont-Aven and Le Pouldu.
October–December: at Le Pouldu with Paul Sérusier and Meyer de Haan.
October: exhibits in Copenhagen in group show.

1890 *February*: returns to Paris.
June–November: in Pont-Aven and Le Pouldu.
November: returns to Paris.

1891 *February*: first sale of his works at Hôtel Drouot.
April: leaves for Tahiti (arrives in June).

1892 Ill, begins to write *Cahier pour Aline*.

1893 *March*: participates in two group exhibitions in Copenhagen.
June: returns to Paris (arrives August); receives inheritance from uncle.
November: one-person exhibition at Durand-Ruel, Paris; writing *Noa Noa*.

1894 *January*: in Brussels for group show at La Libre Synthétique.
April–November: at Le Pouldu and Pont-Aven.
December: returns to Paris.

1895 *February*: second sale at Hôtel Drouot.
July: leaves for Tahiti (arrives September). Settles in Papeete.

1896 *April–August*: seriously ill.
November: one-person show at Galerie Vollard.

1897 *April*: receives news of the death of his daughter Aline. Correspondence with wife ceases. Financially destitute.
October: ill.
December: alleged suicide attempt.

1898 Living in poverty.
March: takes job as draftsman for Public Works Department.
March–August: not painting.
September: in hospital.
December: Vollard buys nine pictures.

1899	*January*: receives money from Georges-Daniel de Monfreid. Quits job. Contributes articles to Papeete satirical journal *Les Guêpes*. Starts his own periodical *Le Sourire*.
1900	Vollard offers to buy twenty-five paintings per year for 300 francs monthly. *April*: relative security. *December*: in hospital for two months.
1901	*September*: leaves Tahiti for the Marquesas, where he settles at Atuana (Hivaoa).
1902	*Winter*: seriously ill. Writing *Avant et après*. Writes *L'Esprit modernes et le catholicisme*.
1903	*March*: sentenced to three months in prison and a fine for championing natives against local authorities. *May 8*: death.

APPENDIX 2

Gauguin's Requests for Pigments in His Correspondence

Paul Gauguin to Georges-Daniel de Monfreid, January 1897, *Lettres de Paul Gauguin à Georges-Daniel de Monfreid*, ed. Annie Joly-Segalen, rev. ed. (Paris, 1950), no. 28

Number of Tubes	*Pigment*
10	ultramarine
5	cobalt
15	*carminée*
5	*garance ordinaire*
20	white
5	*ochre ru* (burnt ochre)
10	yellow ochre
5	*eméraude* (viridian)
3	vermilion
2	cadmium yellow
3	cadmium citron
	gold powder, both red and yellow

Gauguin to de Monfreid, January 1900, Joly-Segalen 1950, no. 60

Number of Tubes	*Pigment*
25	white
10	ultramarine
5	Prussian blue
5	cobalt
5	chrome yellow
10	yellow ochre
5	*ochre ru* (burnt ochre)
3	cadmium deep
3	cadmium number 2
4	*vert eméraude* (viridian)
20	*vert véronèse* (emerald green)
5	terre verte
5	vermilion
3	*garance*
5	carmine lake
5	minium
5	*Charron bleu* (wheel-wright's blue)

This order was to be repeated two or three times over, according to the letter, so it is probably the most typical pigment selection for Gauguin.

Gauguin to Ambroise Vollard, March 1902, *Gauguin: Letters to Ambroise Vollard and André Fontainas*, ed. John Rewald (San Francisco, 1943), 60–61.

Number of Tubes	*Pigment*
2	light vermilion
10	emerald green
5	yellow ochre
2	*ochre ru* (burnt ochre)
2	red ochre
20	white
1.5 liter large tube of powdered color	*Charron bleu*

APPENDIX 3

Pigment Analysis of Paintings by Gauguin

Color	*Pigments noted in appendix 2*	*A*	*B*	*C*	*D*	*E*	*F*	*G*	*H*	*I*	*J*	*K*	*L*	*M*	*N*	*O*	*P*
Whites	lead white	X	X	X	X	X	X	X	X	X	X	X	X	X	X	X	X
	Spanish white (*blanc d'Espagne*)	X	X	X	X		X	X	X	X	X			X	X		
	silver white (chalk + zinc)	X	X	X		X		X	X		X	X	X			X	X
Yellows	cadmium citron cadmium yellow, number 2 cadmium deep		X			X		X	X	X				X	X	X	X
	chrome yellow, number 1 chrome yellow, number 2				X	X	X	X	X		X	X	X				X
	Naples yellow*			X													
	yellow ochre	Ps		Ps	X		X	X		X	X	X	X	X	Ps	X	
Reds	vermilion	X	X	X	X	X	X	X	X	X	X	X	X	X	X	X	X
	carmine (*lac garance*)		X								X						X
	red minium				X												
	ochre (*ru*)	X	X		Ps			X							Ps	X	
Blues	Prussian blue *Charron bleu* (Prussian blue + barium white extender)	Ps	Ps	Ps	X	X	X		X	X	X	Ps	X	X	X	X	X
	ultramarine		X	Ps	Ps			X	X	X	X	Ps				X	
	cobalt blue	X	X	X		X				X	X	X			X	X	
Greens	emerald green (*véronèse*)	X	X	X	X	X	X	X	X	X	X	X	X	X	X	X	X
	viridian (*eméraude*)		X		X						X	X		X	X	X	
	verdigris*				X			X									
	terre verte																
Purple	cobalt violet (*violet foncé*)																
	manganese purple*																X

Note: Analysis was based on energy-dispersive x-ray fluorescence spectroscopy (EDX) and observation of pigment morphology of paint samples. Unless indicated otherwise, paintings are in the National Gallery of Art, Washington.

Key:
- * does not appear in correspondence but detected in pigment analysis
- † not catalogued
- X noted
- Ps possible
- ‡ analysis performed by Charlotte Hale
- A *Mme Kohler* (W314), 1887
- B *Brittany Landscape*, 1888†
- C *Breton Girls Dancing, Pont-Aven* (W251), 1888
- D *Self-portrait Dedicated to Carrrière* (W354), 1888–1889
- E *Self-portrait with Halo* (W323), 1889
- F *Haystacks* (Courtauld Institute), 1890‡, †
- G *Landscape at Le Pouldu* (W398), 1890
- H *Haystacks in Brittany* (W397), 1890
- I *Fatata te Miti* (W463), 1892
- J *Parau na te varua ino* (W458), 1892
- K *Where Are We Going?* (Museum of Fine Arts, Boston) (W561), 1897–1898
- L *Te rerioa* (Courtauld Institute) (W557), 1897‡
- M *Nevermore* (Courtauld Institute) (W558), 1897‡
- N *Te pape nave nave* (W568), 1898
- O *The Bathers* (W572/67), 1897
- P *The Invocation* (W635)

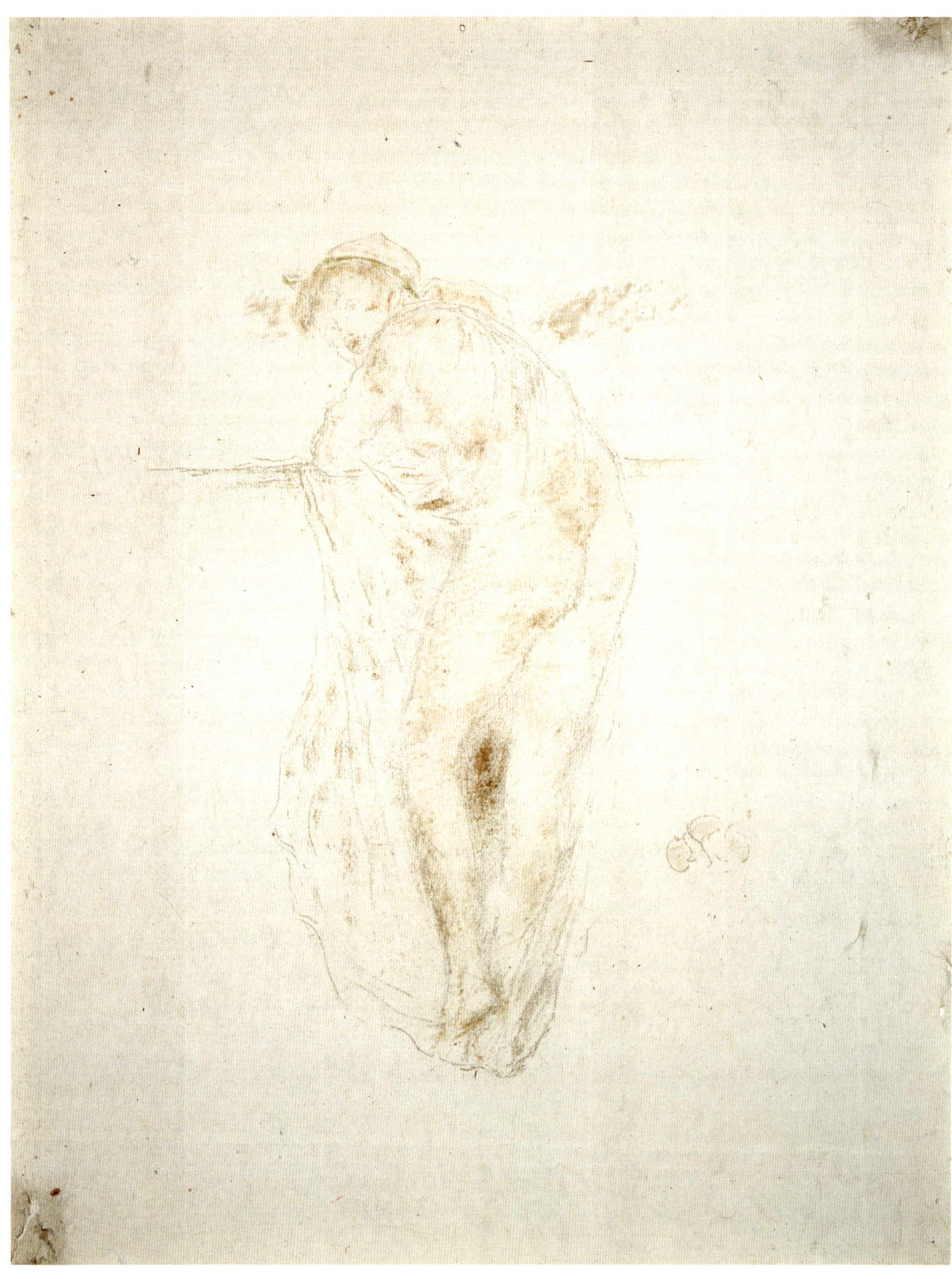

ANTOINETTE DWAN

A Method for Examining and Classifying Japanese Papers Used by Artists in the Late Nineteenth Century

The Prints of James Abbott McNeill Whistler

After centuries of isolation, Japan rapidly built trading relationships with North America and Europe following the commercial treaty negotiated by the American Commodore Matthew C. Perry in 1854. With the exchange of ideas that accompanied the new trade, Japanese art and culture soon had a remarkable impact on European artists, who adopted both Japanese styles and Japanese materials.[1] Printmakers, in particular, were delighted with the qualities of Japanese papers and eagerly used them as soon as they became available. James Abbott McNeill Whistler, studying art in Paris in the 1850s, was soon influenced by the Japanese prints that made their way to that city and sought out Japanese papers for his own prints and etchings.

This investigation concerns more than two hundred prints by Whistler in the collections of the National Gallery of Art, Washington; the Freer Gallery of Art, Smithsonian Institution, Washington; and the Baltimore Museum of Art. Using information gleaned from an 1885 Japanese export document, translated for the author, Japanese papers are classified and described using authentic Japanese paper names instead of colloquial but inaccurate terms such as China paper, India paper, rice paper, japon, or vellum. Beta-radiographs helped to identify and develop categories for the Japanese papers used by Whistler, and the method is described in full so that it might be applied to other artists using Japanese paper in the late nineteenth century.

1. James Abbott McNeill Whistler, *Nude Model, Backview*, lithograph on *gampi* paper viewed with transmitted light
National Gallery of Art, Washington
Lessing J. Rosenwald Collection

QUALITIES OF JAPANESE PAPERS

During the nineteenth century, printmakers experimented liberally with a wide variety of materials while exploring artistic possibilities. Often an artist would simply vary the inking or print the image on a different paper to suggest another mood. Newly introduced Japanese papers, often called "oriental," quickly became popular for developing a range of images. Whistler and his contemporaries embraced these papers both for their unique color and for their receptivity to ink.

One type of Japanese paper, made from *gampi* fibers, the most expensive of the imported papers, introduced a new quality of transparency that gave prints a spatial ambiguity (fig. 1). Images appeared to float, and the silky luster of the paper caught the light of an image in a new way. Whistler's drypoint portraits on *gampi* paper are beautifully rich impressions. Wood engravers also preferred *gampi* paper because it produced the finest printed detail and line.

For printing lithographs, Whistler, as well as Pierre Bonnard, Henri Fantin-Latour, Edouard Manet, Edouard Vuillard, and others, preferred very white and opaque Japanese papers called *hōsho* and *gasenshi*, or thicker, lustrous vellums named *torinoko* and *kyoku-shi*, often referred to as "japon." Paul Gauguin used a thin, sheer *tengujō* as a veil in some of his woodblock prints, such as *Te Auta* and *Soyez Amoureuse Vous Serez*

Heureuses (National Gallery of Art, Washington).[2] He first printed a block in black on a support paper, then adhered thin Japanese paper so that the original black showed through as gray. He then recut and reprinted the block over the two sheets that produced a rich impression, strong in impact yet veiled by the thin *tengujō*.

Nineteenth-century printing manuals evidence concern for the aesthetic qualities of papers, and several ranked paper by availability. At the beginning of the century there was little choice. Writing in 1822, William Savage explained:

The best paper for receiving an impression from types or an engraving is India paper, which comes from China; that which comes as the linings of tea chests [cha-gami] *is equal in quality to any, but many object to its colour; a thicker and whiter sort comes as wrappers for silk; both pieces may be selected for proofs, or if sufficiently large for octavo and frequently for quarto. A perfect paper of large sized sheets is imported direct, in chests of two thousand sheets . . . .*

The next best paper for printing, is French Plate paper; after that English Plate paper, and the worst of all, is our (English) hard sized paper, made of common materials, and bleached with acid to make it look white, but which destroys its texture.[3]

A century later, Ernest S. Lumsden cited poor-quality papers as the reason that artists such as Whistler scavenged for old papers from books on which to print their impressions.

The finding of suitable paper upon which to print is one of the most urgent and difficult problems with which the modern etcher has to deal. Till the 19th century—about 1820—when the adulteration which ended in making cheap paper by machinery began, a good quality article could be had for the very ordering. Now it is a very different matter, as very few firms make really reliable paper at all, and still fewer make one which combines those qualities necessary for the printing from an intaglio plate. This regrettable state of affairs—simply a matter of supply and demand—has caused artists to fall back upon the use of old paper. In itself it is a risky proceeding; but most consider it the lesser of two evils, preferring paper which will take an impression well and having the colour which only comes from age, to a stronger production more easily obtainable and freer from blemishes, yet which will not print so sympathetically.[4]

Yet the lack of suitable European printing papers was only one of several reasons why Japanese papers were preferred. In 1880, Maxime Lalanne gave further guidance on selecting printing papers:

India paper promotes purity of line; but as its surface is dull, it furnishes somewhat dry and dim proofs. Japanese paper, of a warm yellowish tint, silky and transparent is excellent, especially for plates which need more of mystery than of brilliancy, for heavy and deep tones, and for concentration of effect. Japanese paper absorbs the ink, and it is necessary, therefore, to bring up the plate strongly and to wipe it with the rag.[5]

Along with these qualities Lumsden pointed to additional advantages of Japanese papers:

Being absorbent . . . so yielding is the fibre, and so clinging, that it picks up more ink from both surface and line than any paper, with the possible exception of good quality European makes, which are almost impossible to find. It is far easier to obtain "all there is" from a plate with Japanese paper than with any ordinary rag paper.

In nearly all modern Western papers the pigment employed is too crudely yellow. For beauty of colour one has to rely upon Japan.[6]

These qualities explain why Japanese papers were so eagerly sought after by Western artists such as Whistler. The most desirable types of paper for printing during the nineteenth century were "old" papers, Japanese papers, and "India" paper, which is actually a Japanese (or Chinese) paper called *gasenshi*.

THE EXPORT OF JAPANESE PAPERS TO THE WEST

Even after the Tokugawa shogunate broke off trade with Europe in the 1630s, the Dutch were allowed to maintain a small trading post in Nagasaki. In 1643–1644, the Dutch East India Company imported two shipments of Japanese paper (approximately three thousand sheets), which are probably the source of the Japanese papers used by Rembrandt for his prints. Two centuries later the Parisian master printer Auguste Delâtre (1822–1907) was undoubtedly aware of the unique effects Rembrandt had been able to achieve with Japanese papers. It is possible that Delâtre was the first to reintroduce them to artists when he printed Whistler's etchings on Japanese papers as early as 1858 and 1859. Just four years after Commodore Perry "opened" Japan, there were three British-controlled ports. Civil turmoil, however, made it unlikely that papers were exported from Japan in large quantities until after 1867, when Tokugawa control was finally broken and Japan's new Meiji government set about reorganizing the country.

Japanese papers were exhibited at the world fairs in London in 1862, Paris in 1867, Vienna in 1873, and Philadelphia in 1876. In 1868, Philip Gilbert Hamerton described their reception and his frustrated efforts to obtain sheets.

> *The best paper in the world for printing etchings is the Japanese, but there has hitherto been a great difficulty about getting it. . . . In 1866, M. Delâtre gave me a few sheets of Japanese paper, which were all he was able to procure in Paris, and on inquiry in London I could not get any larger quantity.*
>
> *When the Exhibition of 1867 was opened, one of the first things I attended to was the Japanese department, which I visited every day, in hope of seeing some of this precious paper unpacked. At last, I beheld a small cartload of it, of the most various and beautiful qualities, some far stouter and better than any I had yet met with. Being unhappily, ignorant of Japanese, I tried to negotiate for the purchase of this, in English and French, with Japanese exhibitors who spoke more or less of these languages, and I received a promise of sale at a reasonable price. Afterwards this promise was evaded on various pretexts, and neither myself, nor a friend who pursued the matter after I left Paris, was ever able to procure a single ream of the paper, it had been bought in the mass, along with various other merchandise, by some merchant, whose name I have not ascertained. This is the only instance, so far as I know, of Japanese paper having been seen in any quantity, and publicly offered for sale in Europe. It is possible that, as a result of the Paris Exhibition, some Parisian dealer in Oriental curiosities may think it worthwhile to invest in Japanese paper; but until then, there is, I fear, little chance of a supply sufficient even for etchers. The most striking quality of Japanese paper is its exceedingly beautiful tone.*[7]

In 1871 the British requested, and received, a shipment of samples of Japanese papers from Sir Harry Parkes, its minister in Edo (today Tokyo).[8] Yet that same year lists in Hamerton's *Etcher's Handbook* did not include any Japanese papers for sale.[9] By the end of the decade, however, Japanese papers were available in Paris and London shops that specialized in oriental goods. These shops included, in Paris, Decelle's L'Empire Chinoise on Rue Vivienne, which opened after 1850; E. Desayne's, which opened in 1862, and Samuel Bing's Oriental Import Shop on 22 Rue de Provence, which opened in 1888.[10] In London there was Farmer and Roger's Oriental Warehouse on Regent Street, which opened in 1863.[11]

In 1885 the records department of the Japanese Ministry of Finance compiled existing documents on the exportation of paper since 1868, the year of the Meiji Restoration and the earliest recorded date for the exportation of Japanese papers directly to the West.[12] In 1868 these papers, described only as book papers or "lower class" papers, went only to Italy. Beginning in 1873 there was an increase in the amount and types of papers exported, and they went to the United States and a number of European countries. Specific types of paper were named, including *gampi*, *gasenshi*, and *senka-shi*, all of which became popular with Whistler and European artists. Between 1868 and 1878 the availability of Japanese papers in Europe was limited. The last catalogue entry shows, however, a substantial increase in paper exportation to sixteen European countries between 1879 and 1883.

Increased demand led to the formation of import companies such as the Japan Paper Company established in New York in 1901 and now known as Andrews/Nelson/Whitehead.[13] The trade went both ways, of course. In 1872, a modern European-type of paper mill was established in Tokyo with the help of two Englishmen, Thomas Waters and John Rogers.[14] Between 1878 and 1894, wood pulp began to supplement or replace traditional fibers, and by 1896 Japan was producing newsprint.

CLASSIFICATIONS OF JAPANESE PAPERS

The following discussion outlines a systematic means for evaluating nineteenth-century Japanese papers found in Whistler's prints. Describing Whistler's papers using this method eliminates inconsistencies from one examiner to another working in different collections and the confusion associated with inaccurate terms such as China, India, rice, japon, or vellum.

Descriptions of Japanese papers used in Western artwork have tended to employ the terms traditionally used for European papers—watermarks, chain and laid lines or wove markings, color, texture, thickness, fiber content, sizings, and dimensions. Yet many of these characteristics, such as watermarks, surface texture, and sizing are not significant in Japanese papers. Historians of Japanese paper typically refer to papers by the name and locality (such as Tosa or Mino) of the papermaker, the dimensions, the paper's intended use, or the fiber from which it is made.[15] Because the origin of many nineteenth-century Japanese papers is unknown and identifying features were lost when sheets were trimmed for use, another method of describing these papers must be developed.

Most characteristics helpful in identifying Japanese papers can be categorized as primary or secondary. Primary characteristics, including mold or pulp characteristics and fiber type, impart inherent characteristics to the sheet. For instance, a sheet made from *gampi* fiber will have a silky and lustrous polish regardless of thickness or degree of pulp preparation. Secondary characteristics, such as thickness, color, and texture, result from a primary characteristic or from general papermaking procedures. (Interestingly, texture is not usually remarked upon in Japanese papers, as they are mainly smooth, due to the fiber, or rough because a dampened sheet has been brushed out to dry.) Primary and secondary characteristics of Japanese papers are described below and illustrated with beta-radiographs from prints by Whistler (figs. 2–44).[16]

Confusion about specific Japanese papers also arises out of the traditional names these papers have been given. Definite characteristics were associated with these traditional names, but as technology in Japanese papermaking changed, so did the characteristics of the resulting sheets even though the traditional name was retained. Consequently, modern samples with traditional names may not have been made with traditional materials or methods and may not look and feel anything like the nineteenth-century examples under discussion. Traditional papers either used by Whistler or mentioned in the 1885 export document include *yoshino-gami*, *tengujō*, *gampi*, "lower class," *senka-shi*, book paper, *gasenshi*, *cha-gami*, *kyoku-shi*, *hōsho*, *torinoko*, and *aburagami*. Each is described below, following the descriptions of paper characteristics. For a clarification of terms used throughout these descriptions, see appendix 1.

Primary Characteristics

Pulp Characteristics

Japanese papermaking is extremely labor intensive. The degree to which the fibers are cooked, the amount of extraneous matter removed from the pulp, how much the pulp is beaten and washed, and the degree of homogeneity of the final pulp determine the quality of the paper.

Two primary characteristics relate to the pulp: quality of the pulp and distribution of the pulp on the mold. High-quality pulp consists of evenly separated fibers of about the same length; it produces a uniform sheet (see *Amsterdam, from the Tolhuis*, K91, fig. 10). Medium- to low-quality pulp has a more random mixture of fiber lengths and contains fiber knots and fiber or plant particles that look like debris and in Japanese are termed *chiri* (in English, "lumps and shives") (see *Fumette's Bent Head*, K57, fig. 6).

An even sheet is formed from a uniform distribution of the pulp on the surface of the *su*—the removable screen placed on top of the mold to catch the fibers suspended in the bath (see *Zaandam*, K416, fig. 17). An "uneven" sheet has an inconsistent distribution of pulp with thicker and thinner areas when viewed by transmitted light (see *F. R. Leyland*, K102, fig. 8). Although there are variations, high-quality papers generally have both a clean and consistent preparation of the fibers and an even distribution of pulp, while lower-quality sheets often show various fiber lengths, much extraneous plant material, and an uneven pulp distribution.

Mold Characteristics

Japanese papermaking molds are constructed differently from European molds. They are made of lightweight wood with the deckle—a frame holding the *su*—hinged on one side. After the fibers are deposited on the *su*, the deckle is opened. The *su* is removed and lowered, paper side down, across a pile of previously stacked sheets. The *su* is then drawn away, leaving the new sheet of paper on top of the pile. Then the *su* is replaced on the mold, and another sheet of paper is made. The impression seen on Japanese papers that results from the materials and construction of the *su* can be confused with European markings.

Su characteristics that are evident in a sheet are similar to the European chain-line intervals and laid-line frequency, although the molds from which they are derived are of completely different construction and materials. Laid patterns can be made by bamboo, reed, or grass strips across the *su*. (Compare the width of laid lines in *Street at Saverne*, K19, figs. 33–34, to see the wider reed impression.) Chain lines are made with thread that sews the strips of the *su* together. Chinese or Korean papers generally have a much closer chain-line interval than Japanese papers. However, Japanese papers imitating traditional Chinese papers, such as the calligraphy papers called *gasenshi*, mimic the foreign *su* (see, e.g., *The Unsafe Tenement*, K17, fig. 38; *Study*, W77, fig. 35; *The Duet, No. 2*, W65, fig. 36). Often very thin papers show the markings of a *sha*, a fabric covering attached to the *su* that eliminates chain and laid impressions and prevents the fine fibers from falling through while the paper is being made. The impression of a *sha* can resemble that made by a European wove mold (see *Drouet*, K55, fig. 24). Papers made with a *sha* are generally very high quality and very expensive. Wove moldlike markings can also be made by couching or drying paper against fabric, as with *kyoku-shi* papers.

Sheet dimensions, determined by the mold, are very important for identification, as some papers are made only in particular sizes. Unfortunately, the paper found in prints has often been trimmed.

Fiber Type

The three traditional Japanese papermaking fibers are *kōzo*, *gampi*, and *mitsumata*. Each has distinctive properties. Fiber type is a primary characteristic when *gampi* (see *Little Wapping*, K73, fig. 26; *The Rag Gatherers*, K23, fig. 23) or *mitsumata* (see *Rue Furstenburg*, W59, fig. 29) is used. *Gampi* is silky, transparent, and very expensive compared to other Japanese fibers. *Mitsumata* is crisp and translucent and, depending on how it is processed, has a pink-brown tone. Most papers were made with *kōzo*, and their characteristics are less distinctive. This single plant fiber yields a wide variety of effects depending on locality, season of harvest, and method of processing. In addition to these fundamental fibers, some papers contain supplementary fibers such as grasses (rice or wheat straw), bamboo, or hemp. These and additives to the pulp, such as clays, talc, white chalk, or starches, may change the character of the fibers.

Formation aids are used during Japanese papermaking to keep the pulp disbursed, but these are not the same as Western sizing agents. In fact, Japanese sheets are generally not sized by the papermaker and are therefore very absorbent, similar to Western unsized, or "waterleaf" sheets.

Secondary Characteristics

Thickness

Compared to Western papers, most Japanese papers are thin and have been routinely described that way without reference to differences among them. Thin sheets require special pulp preparation and great skill by the papermaker. Heavier sheets require more material, considerably more fiber preparation time, and more time at the vat per sheet.

A remarkably transparent *gampi* sheet (as seen, for example, in *The Rag Gatherers*, K23, fig. 23), is .01 millimeter thick. Medium-thick papers range from .03 to .06 millimeter (see the etchings, *Steps, Amsterdam*, K403, fig. 14, and *Pierrot*, K407, fig. 15, both on paper made of *kōzo* fiber). Many lithographs are on thicker paper, from .09 millimeter (see *Draped Figure, Seated*, W46, fig. 43, on paper made of *gampi* fiber) to .15 millimeter (see *The Little Balcony*, W50, fig. 44, also *gampi*). These thicker Japanese papers are comparable to Western medium-thick papers. (Although the thickness is the property that is measured, thin papers are conventionally called "lightweight" and thick papers "heavyweight.")

Texture

The texture of a sheet is often the result of a primary characteristic, such as the fiber type (e.g., *gampi*), or the addition of fillers, such as talc in *hōsho* papers. Texture is also the result of general papermaking practices. While most oriental papers show the stroke of the drying brush on one side of the sheet, papers dried on sheet metal driers are usually much smoother than those dried on wooden boards. The latter sometimes show the wood grain imprint of the drying surface. In the descriptions of papers by name, texture will be described only if it is a primary characteristic, as it is with the vellum papers and high-quality *gampi* papers.

Color

Color in Japanese papers is usually a secondary characteristic. Unless the pulp is specifically dyed or intentionally loaded with colored earth pigments, color is only a byproduct of primary papermaking characteristics. For example, white talc filler is added to *hōsho* for absorbency and opacity. The source, locality, and species of the fiber, the degree to which the fiber has been cleaned, the number of washings, the amount of time it is cooked, the method of drying, and the use of bleaching agents, even the time of year the paper is made—all influence the final color and tone. High-quality *gampi* papers have been cleaned and refined to the extent that they appear light in color. (But very white *gampi* sheets are often made from a mixture of chemically bleached *kōzo* and *gampi* fibers—certainly a nontraditional technique.) Many factors affect the color of Japanese paper, and the color of the final sheet can vary significantly but randomly.

In addition, aging of the papers combined with exposure to light or poor-quality matting materials during the life of a print can greatly affect the color, either lightening or darkening the fiber. Sizing applied prior to printing can also affect the color, and it can change with age. Thin Japanese papers may be transparent, so the color of the mat board on which the print is mounted can greatly influence the perceived color.

Selecting a white paper or a toned paper is a fundamental artistic choice. In general, a white paper creates more contrast with the print's color range than can be produced on a toned paper. White paper can also produce more contrast, drama, and tension with deeper spatial relationships. A toned paper creates a unifying effect but shallower space and less contrast between the line and paper tones. Toned papers also present a softer, more diffuse image with a narrower color range. To document the artist's paper selection for cataloguing purposes, the main color categories are described only as white tones or brown tones in the section that follows. White tones include cream colors and describe papers bleached, processed, loaded with white fillers, or exposed to light to the extent that all the natural color of the plant fibers has been removed. Brown tones refer to all the nuances of the natural brown color of the plant fibers regardless of the degree the color may have been modified during processing.

NAMED PAPERS

The 1885 export document records that several specific papers were shipped to Europe and the United States. These are described below and illustrated with a beta-radiograph of the paper, when possible. A few of the papers described are also mentioned in the nineteenth-century printing manuals quoted in the opening pages of this essay. During the nineteenth century there were more than two hundred thousand papermakers in Japan, working in small shops, each with its own methods and products. Consequently there is wide variation within any class of paper that needs to be considered when viewing the beta-radiographs and trying to fit a paper into a particular group. Examples of variations possible within one type of paper can be seen in the several beta-radiographs of *gasenshi* and also in the book papers. For a correlation of papers used in Whistler's etchings and lithographs, see appendix 2.

Yoshino-gami

Yoshino-gami is a very thin, high-quality, white-toned, *kōzo* paper available in several thicknesses (fig. 45). A white clay or pigment filler contributes to its dimensional stability. It is unsized. It is frequently seen in nineteenth-century books as an interleaf to protect images.[17] Today it is used by traditional scroll mounters as an internal, cushioning first lining.

Tengujō

Tengujō is a very high-quality, tissue-thin, white-toned, *kōzo* paper, without any fillers (fig. 46). It is unsized. Extreme care is required in pulp preparation and great skill in its formation. Currently, it is made by only one papermaker in Japan, Shoji Hamada of Kōchi. Layers of pulp are deposited on the screen in both directions, a technique that makes the paper dimensionally stable, with little or no grain. Considering its thinness, it is very strong and coherent. It can be seen laminated to another sheet in Whistler's *Limehouse* (W4) and in two Paul Gauguin prints at the National Gallery of Art, *Te Auta* and *Soyez Amoureuse Vous Serez Heureuses*. Because of its thinness and its attachment to another paper, this paper is difficult to see and can easily be overlooked.

Gampi-Fibered Papers

Except when used in the thick vellum papers, *gampi* fibers are usually easy to recognize in papers (see figs. 1, 23–26). *Gampi* papers are silky, lustrous, and transparent. They are usually very thin and brown toned and may have a *sha* marking rather than chain and laid patterns from the mold. As with other papers, they are unsized. During the nineteenth century they were approximately four times more expensive than other imported Japanese papers.[18] Early in the twentieth century, *gampi* was imported as "copying paper" for tracings.[19] *Gampi*-fibered papers have very strong expansion and contraction characteristics and, if improperly mounted, can buckle and distort dramatically. Because of their thinness, they tear and wrinkle easily, and repairs are often seen. Several articles have been written on the conservation treatment of *gampi* papers.[20]

Lower-Class Paper

"Lower-class paper" is the direct translation from the export document. These papers are thin to mediumweight, low-quality, brown-toned, *kōzo* papers considered acceptable for export purposes. This type of paper was one of the first to be exported to Europe, as early as 1868. It may have been made by prisoners on the island of Hokkaidō, who were known to make paper for export to other countries. Many "lower class" papers are found in Whistler's early etchings, such as *Rotherhithe* (K66, fig. 7).

Senka-shi

Senka-shi is a medium- to heavyweight, brown-toned, *kōzo* fiber paper that is unsized (fig. 33). It was traditionally made with a double screen that folded to make a single "sandwich" type of paper which was very strong. It evolved into a crisp but lighter-weight paper used for books, still thicker and rougher than other book papers. It is made in various qualities.

Book Paper

"Book paper," a direct translation from the export document, is a *kōzo* paper with a brown tone, of medium weight, and unsized (figs. 47–48). It is thinner than the *senka-shi* paper also used for books. It was shipped to Europe as early as 1868 and is seen in prints from that time. Nineteenth-century Japanese books were made with various qualities of *kōzo* paper. Beta-radiographs from Whistler etchings from the early 1870s are shown in figures 2–8.

Gasenshi

Gasenshi is often found in several thicknesses; the lighter weight was used for *chine collé*, and heavier versions were popular for lithography (figs. 49–50). *Gasenshi*, translated as "imitation Chinese calligraphy paper" is probably the "India paper, which comes from China" described by William Savage in 1822.[21] The Japanese also made convincing *gasenshi*, however, with similar materials on a mold imitating a Chinese mold, and it is sometimes difficult to determine whether a sheet of *gasenshi* was fabricated in Japan or China. The 1885 export document reveals that Japan actually exported *gasenshi* to China in 1873 and 1874.

Gasenshi papers are traditionally made with *mitsumata* and bamboo fibers that are both short and weak. The absorbent quality is due to the fibers and to the addition of *wara*, or rice straw fiber, digested to a powder consistency. *Wara* is prepared by cutting rice stalks, boiling them in strong caustic solution, and then pounding them until they are pulpy. *Wara* is a very absorbent material, and it fills the pores of the paper and adds a luster.

It is likely that it is this *wara* that moves by redeposition in the paper during conservation treatments and produces white tide lines. Use of starch enzymes during conservation treatments affect the filler. It is very easy to skin (abrade) these papers because of their weak fibers and lack of sizing, and special precautions are needed during treatments.[22]

Gasenshi papers are available in a range of qualities, from coarse papers with many shives to very refined and clean papers. Coarse "practice papers" are often brown and full of shives. Better-quality papers are gray to white in color and, due to the *wara* filler, have a chalky feel, which is also responsible for their absorbency. They are unsized. They have comparatively narrow chain-line intervals (1.5–2.0 cm compared to 3.0–4.0 cm of other Japanese papers). *Gasenshi* generally has distinct brush marks on one side as a result of the drying process.

When *gasenshi* papers are printed with either etchings or lithographs, the plate area becomes compact and takes on a glossy, burnished quality compared to the unprinted area. Because of the paper's weak fibers and absorbent nature, it can be difficult to retain these burnished and matte areas during aqueous conservation treatments. Retaining the depth of an intaglio impression is also difficult.

A European imitation of *gasenshi*, called "Oxford India" or "Bible Paper," was made in England in 1875;[23] this could be the imitation India paper referred to in nineteenth-century printing manuals.

Cha-gami

Cha-gami (paper for wrapping tea) is a *mitsumata* paper that was used to wrap boxes for storage or transportation of tea. Although it was mentioned by William Savage, it has not been observed as used for artwork.

Japanese Vellums

Several traditional vellums[24]—*kyoku-shi, hōsho*, and *torinoko*—are described below. At the end of the nineteenth and beginning of the twentieth century, the original composition of these papers was altered, and they were made specifically for export purposes to the West.

Kyoku-shi

Kyoku-shi is translated as "bureau paper." It was a popular vellum paper that is generally called "japon" (figs. 28–32). It was originally made in 1874 by the Meiji government's Printing Bureau of the Ministry of Finance as security paper for bank notes and other important legal documents. *Kyoku-shi* is most often made with *mitsumata* fiber, although it is also made with *kōzo* fiber; it was considered an excellent security paper since any changes or alterations could easily be detected in its smooth, calendered surface. *Kyoku-shi* was exhibited at the World Exhibition in Paris in 1878 and, starting in 1885, was exported by the Mitsui Bussan Company.[25] *Kyoku-shi* was made "Western style," that is, couched between fabric; it looks very much like a Western wove paper.

Kyoku-shi can be calendered on one or both sides of the sheet or uncalendered.[26] The calendered and uncalendered sheets are very different in appearance. The calendered version has a mottled quality when viewed through transmitted light and shiny, dense interrupted areas when viewed in raking light. The *mitsumata* fibers give it a characteristic luster and a warm yellow tone. It was an extremely popular paper for printmaking. Used for both etchings and lithographs, it can be found in almost all nineteenth-century artists' prints. Many of Gauguin's woodcut prints are on *kyoku-shi* paper.

Of several Whistler prints on *kyoku-shi* paper analyzed, fiber microscopy confirmed that *Rue Furstenburg* (W59, fig. 29) and *Figure Study* (W76, fig. 31) were made of *mitsumata* fiber and one, *The Red House, Paimpol* (W100, fig. 32), contained both *mitsumata* and softwood fibers, consistent with later export papers. For comparison, analysis was made of eight exported Japanese vellum papers sold in 1910 by the Japan Paper Company in New York and bearing its watermark. For a sample of *kyoku-shi* from the Shidzuoka mill, see figure 51. Five contained the traditional Japanese papermaking fibers *kōzo* and *mitsumata*, and three contained 5–15 percent wood pulp fibers. The incorporation of wood pulp fiber can be used to date late or posthumous Whistler impressions.

The *kyoku-shi* later produced for export purposes was made with a variety of fibers

Table 1
Fiber Analysis of Eight Exported Japanese Vellum Papers, Sold 1910

Paper Type	*Fiber*
Imperial Japanese Handmade Paper (*kyoku-shi*)	
#3 weight, #2 weight Insatsu mill	*mitsumata* fiber
Japanese Handmade Paper (*kyoku-shi*)	
#3 weight, #2 weight	*mitsumata* fiber
Shidzuoka mill	85% *mitsumata*, 15% wood pulp
#1 weight, Shidzuoka mill	
interleaving, Shidzuoka mill	95% *mitsumata*, 5% wood pulp
Torinoko	55% *kōzo*, 45% *mitsumata*
Mokuroku	90% *mitsumata*, 10% wood pulp

added to *mitsumata*, including wood pulp. These papers appear more calendered, smoother, without the dense fibrous areas of 100 percent *mitsumata* papers, and with a browner tone. They are easily confused with European "japon simili" papers, which were developed later. It appears that "japon" papers from the nineteenth century were in fact made in Japan and that not until the early twentieth century were European "japon" vellum papers able to imitate Japanese vellums. During the early twentieth century, "vellums" were made in several European countries. In France, two mills made imitation Japanese papers. One, located at 76 Rue de Rennes, Paris, produced a paper called "Dujardin" with four watermarks: a stylized chrysanthemum flower design running along one edge, "japon dujardin Paris," "ORIENT," and "Normandy vellum." Another, Ville Sur Saulx mill, produced a paper watermarked "normandy vellum france." The Van Gelder mill in Amsterdam advertised its papers as "simili japon papers for lithography and collotype printing." They have either the Van Gelder design as a watermark or "simili japon." L. S. Dixon and Company of Liverpool and London made a handmade book paper and a Bible paper watermarked "simili."[27] Strathmore also produced a paper with the watermark "Strathmore" and "Japon."

Conservation treatments on *kyoku-shi* are complex. *Kyoku-shi* is difficult to dry clean since the fibers are very easily abraded. Aqueous treatments can swell the calendered surface and thus also swell the intaglio impression. These papers were prized by artists, and impressions on "japon" should not receive secondary consideration.

Hōsho

Hōsho is a traditional Japanese wood block printing paper and a popular nineteenth-century lithography paper that can be easily identified (figs. 39–42). It is a highly refined *kōzo* paper that is generally very clean, and its chain lines are readily visible. Talc filler in the pulp emphasizes the contrast between the opacity of the sheet and the translucency of the chain lines. The talc fills the pores of the paper, making the surface very smooth, opaque, white, and very absorbent for printing. *Hōsho* is sometimes sized with animal glue and can appear slightly yellower than the stark white unsized sheets.

The layers of each original dipping of *hōsho* can easily delaminate. Several nineteenth-century manuals suggest that, if there is a printing mistake, the paper can be split and the clean side used for printing.[28] Although the talc helps the paper remain dimensionally stable, there is no sizing to protect the talc, and that makes dry cleaning treatments difficult. Unsized sheets can be easily skinned while removing attachments such as hinges or old mends.

Torinoko

Torinoko paper was traditionally a very high-quality *gampi* paper (figs. 43–44). Because it was made very thick, it is opaque but retains the polished surface qualities and crisp printing characteristics of *gampi*. Many of Whistler's lithographs are printed on this paper. During its evolution, *torinoko* was made with other fiber combinations; first with *gampi* and *mitsumata*, then with *kōzo* fibers, and finally with wood pulp fibers. The color changes depend on the principal fiber: *gampi torinoko* has a brown tone, *mitsumata torinoko* has a pink-to-white tone, and wood pulp and *kōzo* combinations make a brown tone. It is generally a high-quality paper, and the chain and laid lines are difficult to distinguish. It can easily be mistaken for a Western paper. In the early twentieth century, the Japan Paper Company distributed several different types that were made in Japan with its company watermark.

CONCLUSION

The information about Japanese papers presented here is intended to provide a reliable technical reference for future researchers rather than to draw conclusions. While it is tempting to speculate on the technical and aesthetic reasons for Whistler's choice of particular papers for specific impressions, these will be understood only when more is known about Whistler's technical printing decisions and his relationship with his various printers.

Some observations, however, can be tentatively proposed. As a substantial number of Whistler's etchings and lithographs were executed on Japanese papers, it is certain that he had a definite preference for their color and printing properties. There are also patterns in his use of Japanese papers, some based on availability and others clearly related to aesthetic properties. For instance, his very sensitive portraits of Drouet (K55), Becquet (K52), and Maude (K114), and the etching *Weary* (K92) were printed on the highest quality, transparent, and extremely delicate *gampi* tissue. Other etchings from the same period are almost exclusively on a low-quality book paper, probably the only Japanese paper readily available at the time. Undoubtedly Whistler overlooked the defects in favor of the warm brown tone, transparency, and printing qualities. Yet, because he valued the portraits highly, he chose scarce and expensive *gampi* paper for these special impressions.

Generally, however, Whistler's use of Japanese papers closely relates to their availability. As more varieties were imported, he was quick to incorporate them into his oeuvre. By the time he did his *Amsterdam* series, late in his career, he could be quite selective in his use of Japanese papers. When he did select Japanese papers, he seemed satisfied with the color, wiping the plate cleanly and not leaving residual plate tone as he did on similar impressions pulled on Western papers. It is possible that Whistler's use of plate tone on Western papers was intended, at least in part, to correct their color or tonal range.

With very few exceptions, the Japanese papers Whistler selected for his lithographs were very different from those he used for his etchings. The differences form stark contrasts: the lithographs are on opaque white papers while the etchings are on transparent brown papers. Since there was a large variety of Japanese papers commercially available when Whistler was making lithographs, his selection seems to have been based on aesthetic or technical considerations rather than availability. While final conclusions about the reasons for his choices cannot be reached until more information is available, the documentation of the characteristics of Japanese papers he did use offers some insight.

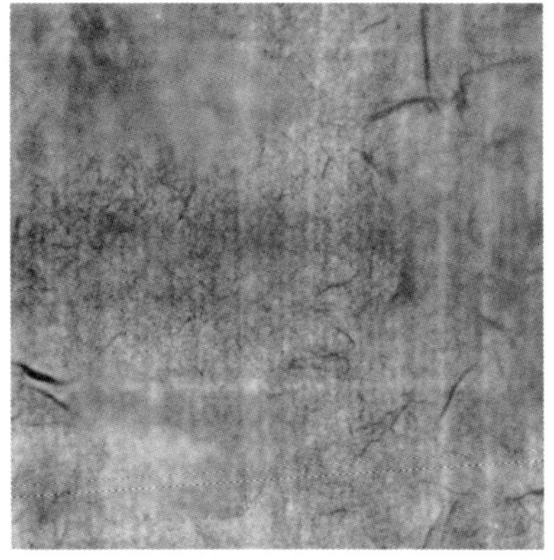

2. *Soupe à Trois Sous*
low-quality *kōzo*
1943.3.8431

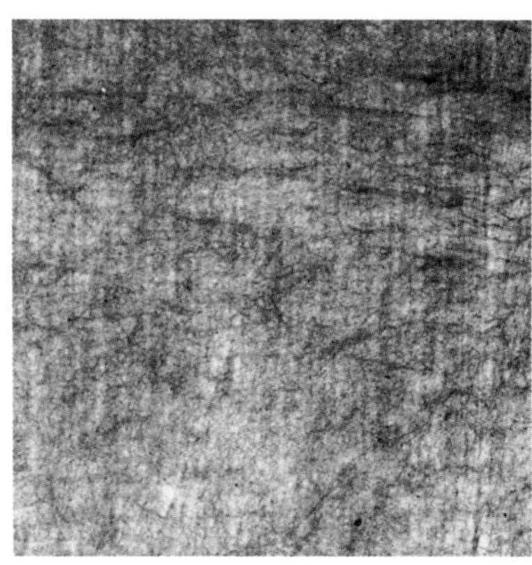

3. *Becquet*
low-quality *kōzo*
1943.3.8435

4. *Astruc, A Literary Man*
low-quality *kōzo*
1943.3.8436

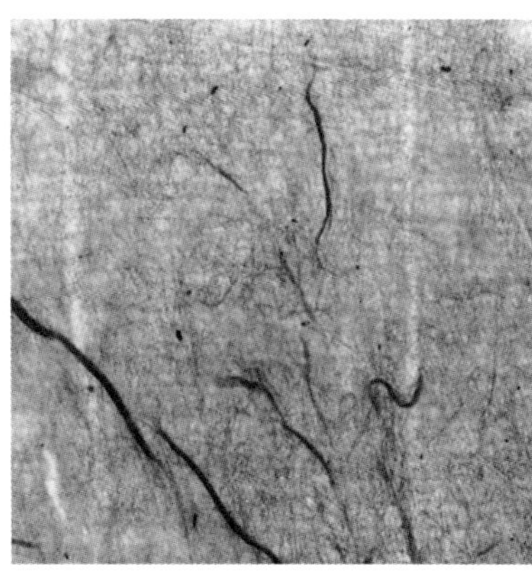

5. *Fumette, Standing*
low-quality *kōzo*
1949.5.531

6. *Fumette's Bent Head*
low-quality *kōzo*
1949.5.532

7. *Rotherhithe*
low-quality *kōzo*
1943.3.8442

All works by James Abbott McNeill Whistler are in the collection of the National Gallery of Art, Washington. Accession numbers distinguish multiple impressions of the same print. See also appendix 2.

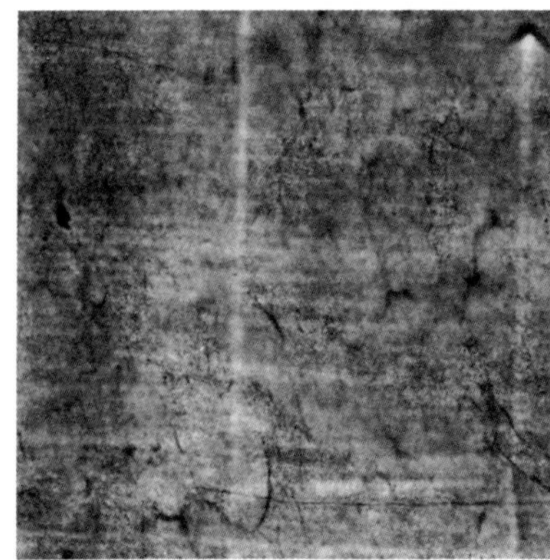

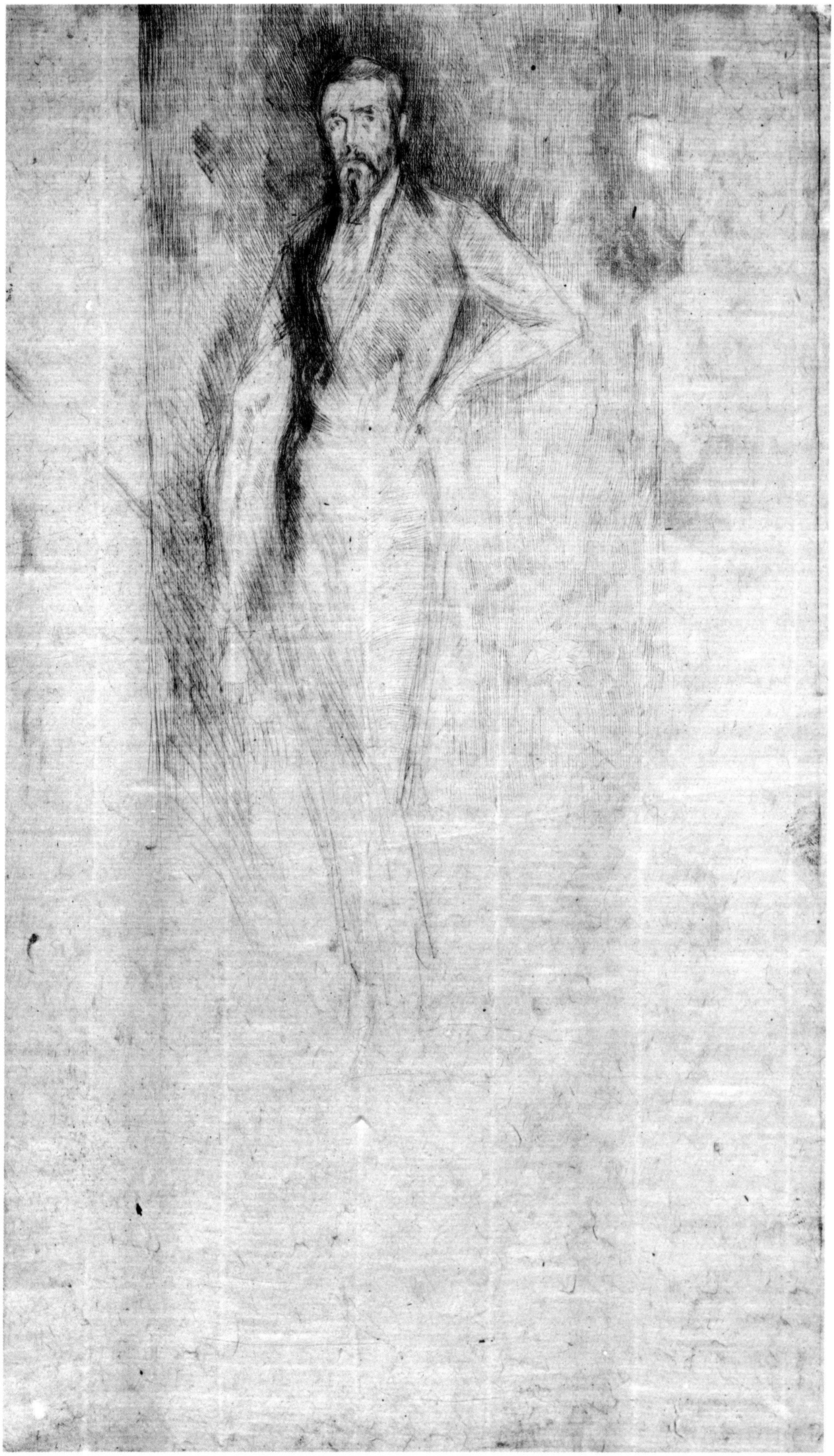

8. *F. R. Leyland* (i/ii)
low-quality *kōzo*
1949.5.538

9. Fig. 8, viewed with transmitted light

10. *Amsterdam, from the Tolhuis*
high-quality *kōzo*
1943.3.8457

11. *Fanny Leyland*
high-quality *kōzo*
1943.3.8466

12. *Free Trade Wharf*
high-quality *kōzo*
1943.3.8496

13. *Fishing-Boats, Hastings*
high-quality *kōzo*
1943.3.8491

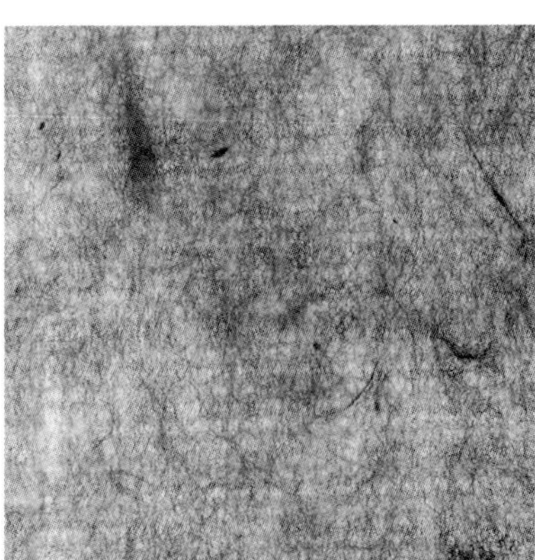

14. *Steps, Amsterdam*
senka-shi kōzo
1943.3.8639

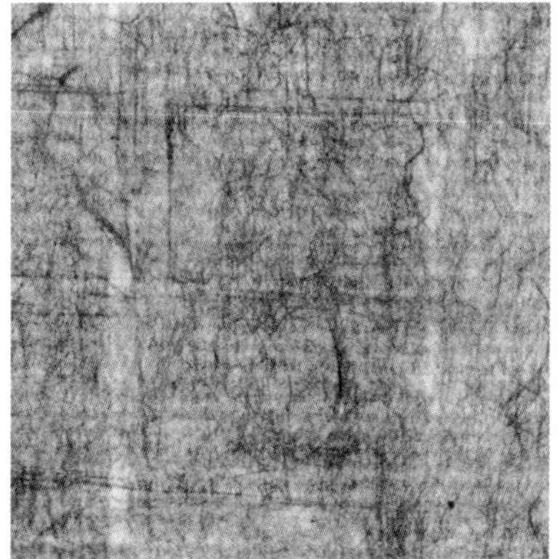

15. *Pierrot*
senka-shi kōzo
1943.3.8643

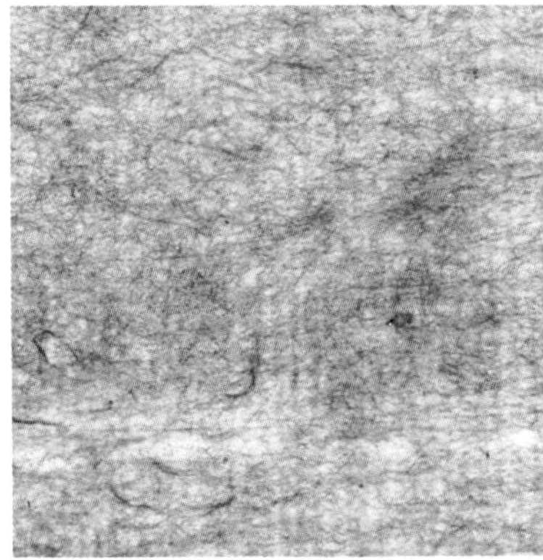

16. *Little Drawbridge, Amsterdam*
senka-shi kōzo
1943.3.8647

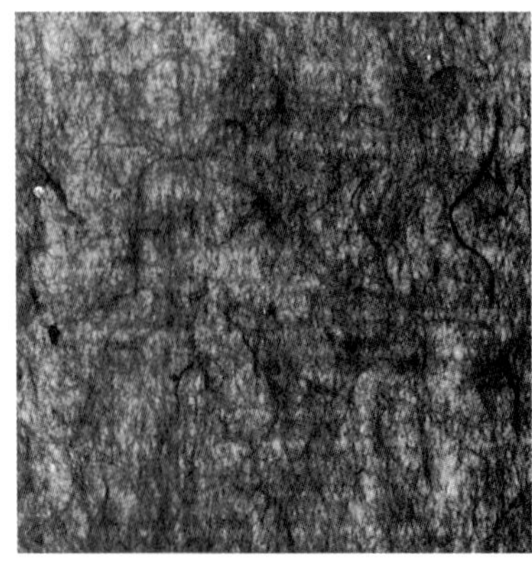

17. *Zaandam*
senka-shi kōzo
1943.3.8649

18. *The Velvet Dress*
senka-shi kōzo
1943.3.8464

19. *Florence Leyland*
senka-shi kōzo
1943.3.1729

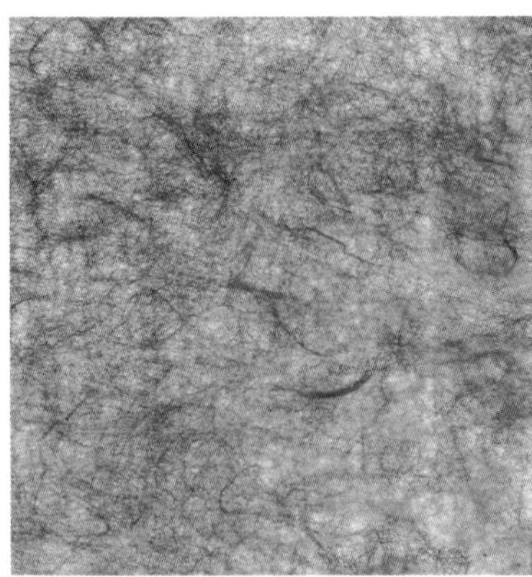

20. *The Garden*
senka-shi kōzo
1943.3.8697

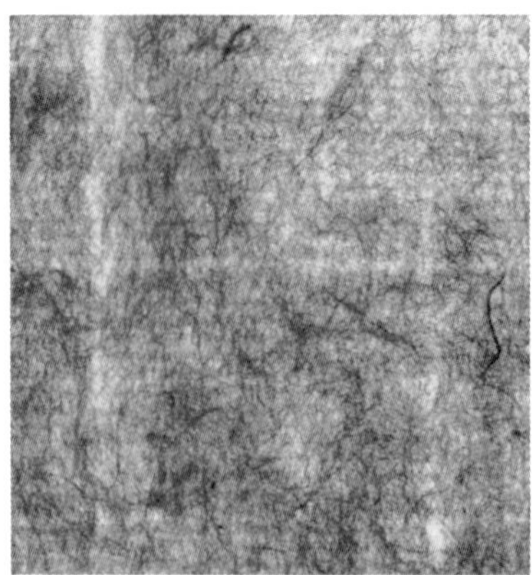

21. *Draped Figure Standing*
senka-shi kōzo
1947.10.2

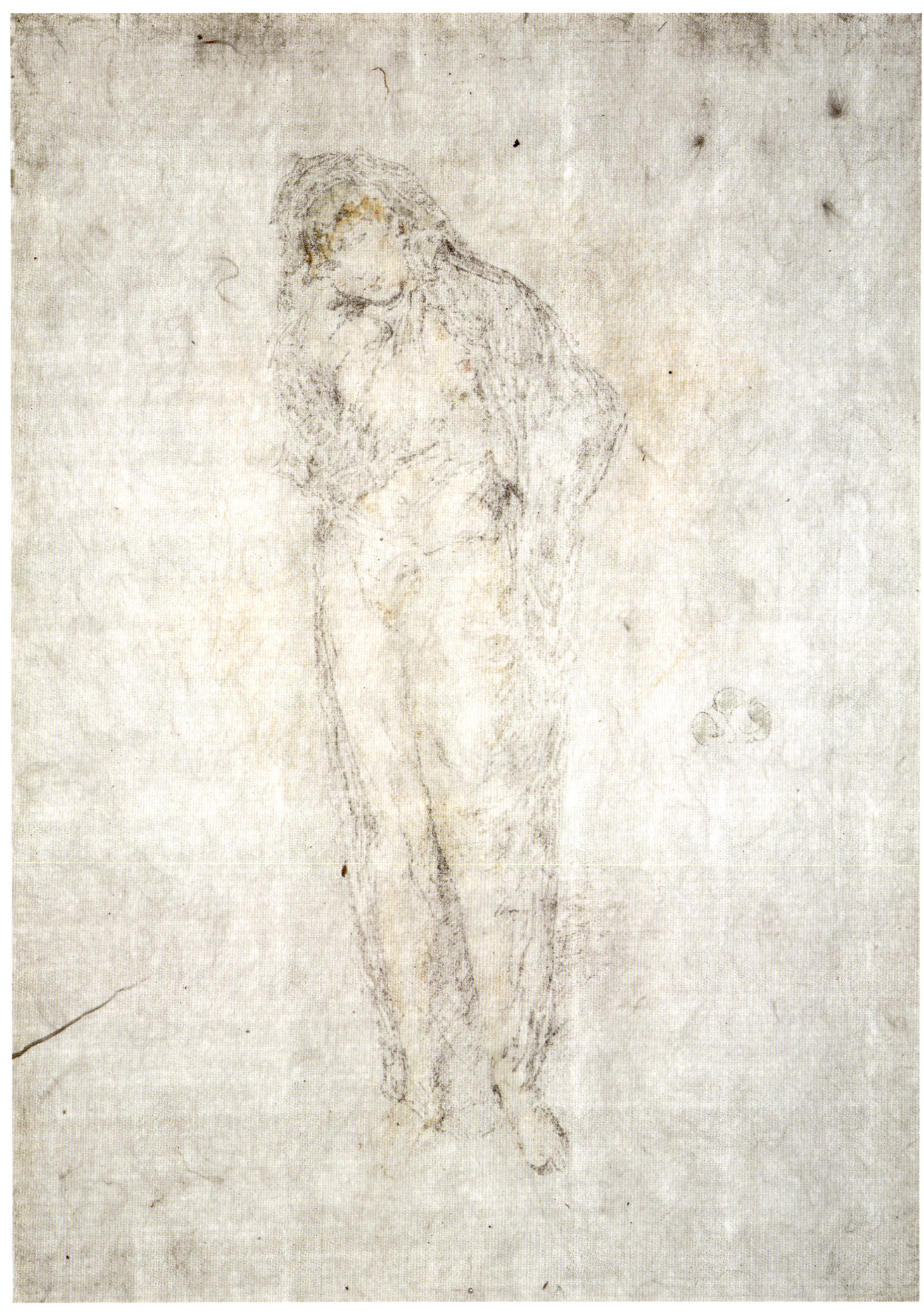

22. Fig. 21, viewed with transmitted light

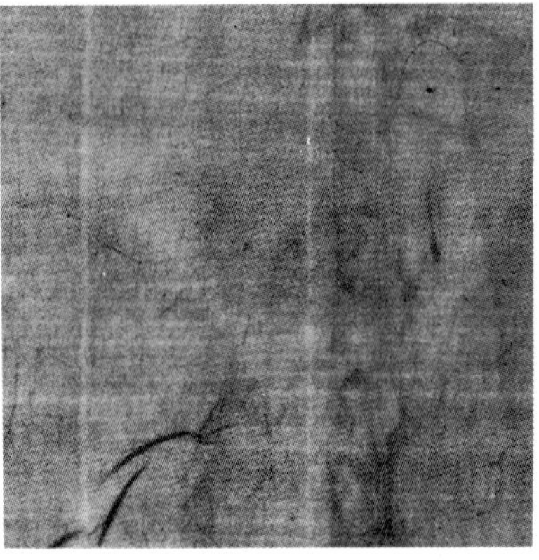

23. *The Rag Gatherers*
thin, transparent *gampi*
1951.13.22

24. *Drouet*
thin, transparent *gampi*
1943.3.8659

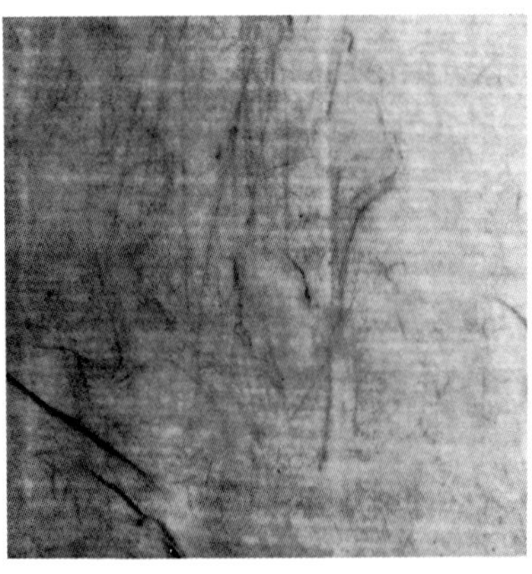

25. *The Forge*
thin, transparent *gampi*
1943.3.8444

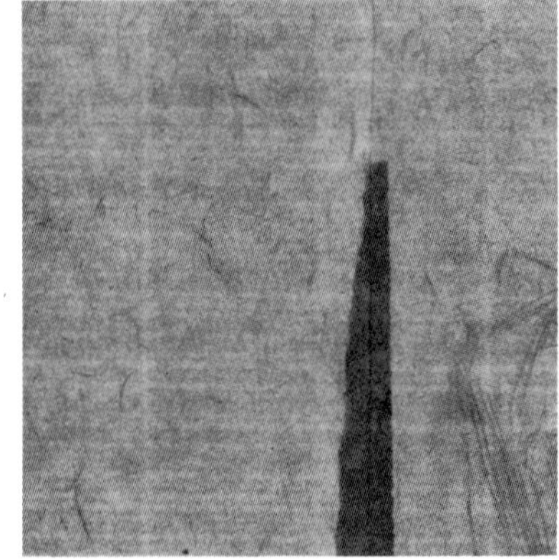

26. *Little Wapping*
thin, transparent *gampi*
1943.3.8446

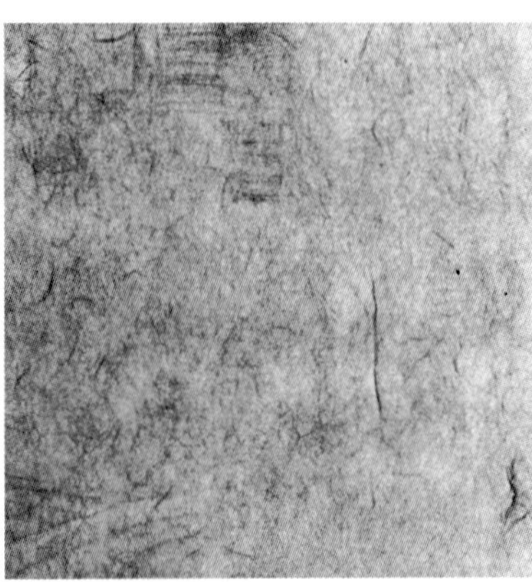

27. *The "Adam and Eve," Old Chelsea*
medium, opaque *gampi*
1943.3.8508

28. *Greenwich Park*
kyoku-shi mitsumata
1949.5.528

29. *Rue Furstenburg*
kyoku-shi mitsumata
1943.3.8719

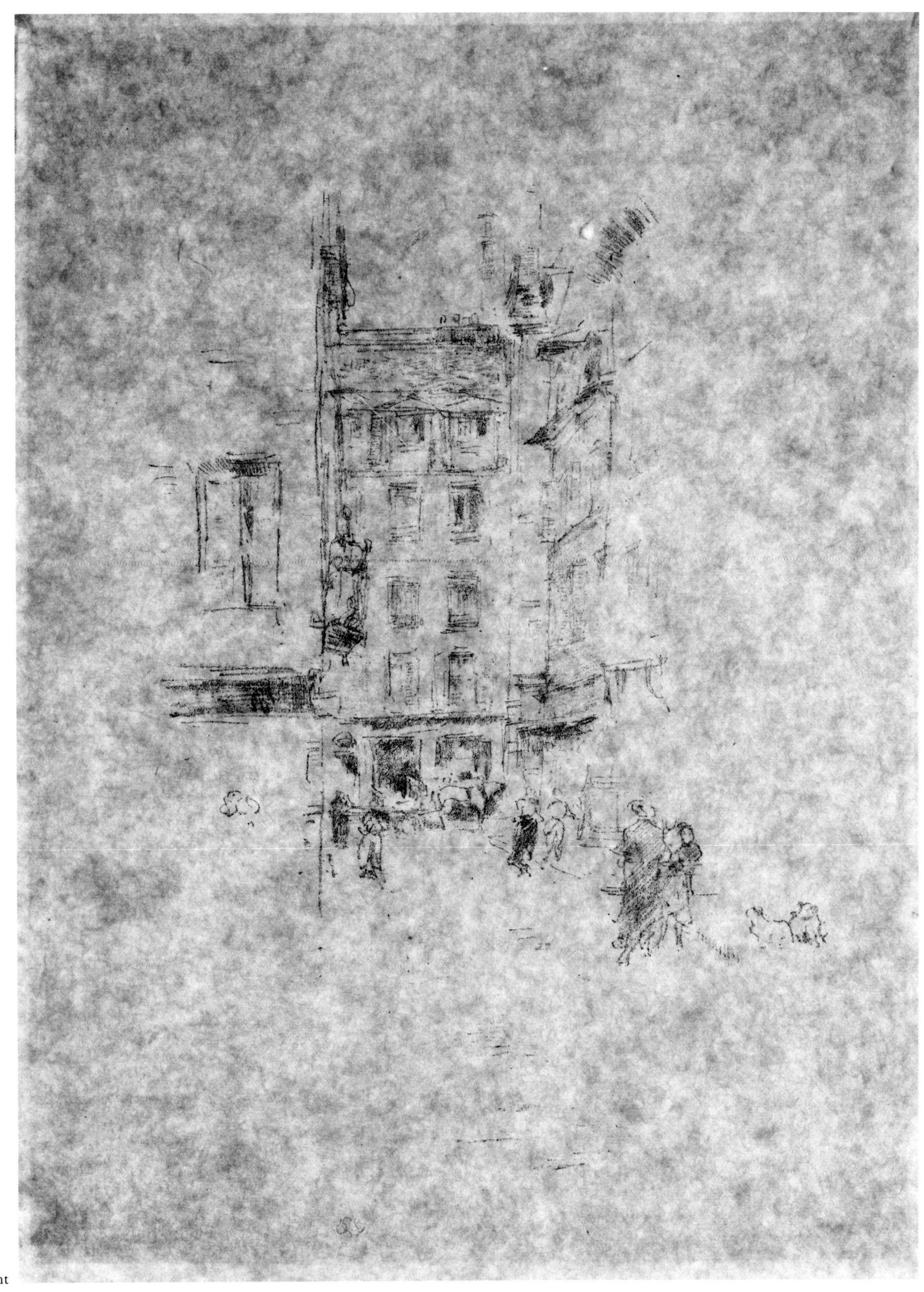

30. Fig. 29, viewed with transmitted light

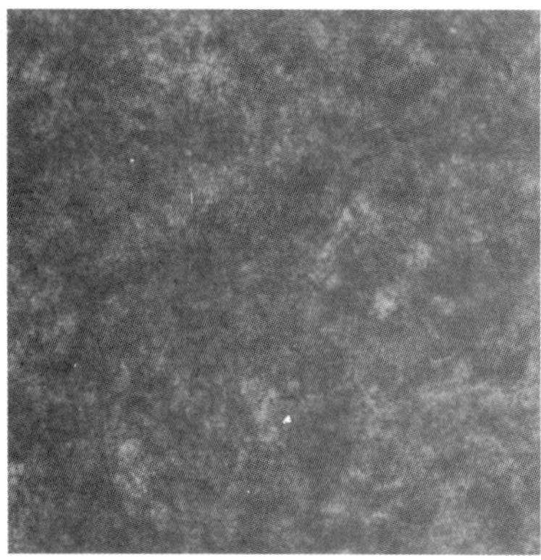

31. *Figure Study*
kyoku-shi mitsumata
1946.21.369

32. *The Red House, Paimpol*
kyoku-shi mitsumata and softwood pulp
1943.3.8757

33. *Street at Saverne*
senka-shi
1943.3.8407

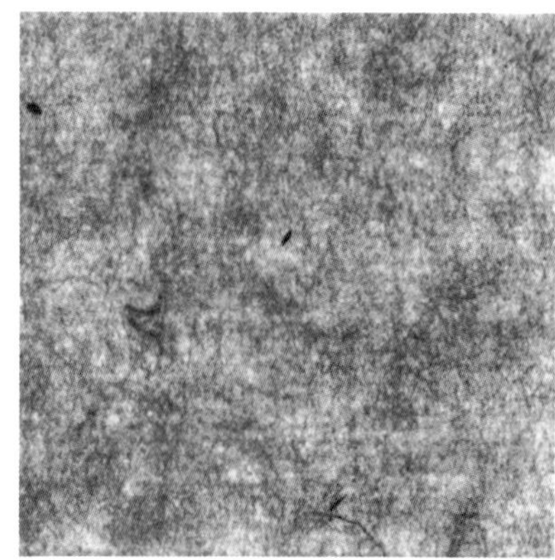

34. *Street at Saverne*
not determined
1943.3.8405

35. *Study*
gasenshi
1946.17.1

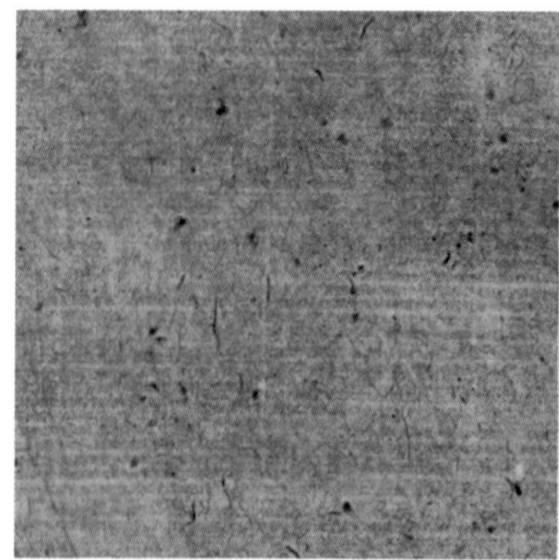

36. *The Duet, No. 2*
gasenshi
1943.3.8725

37. *The Medici Collar*
gasenshi
1943.3.8798

38. *The Unsafe Tenement*
low-quality *gasenshi*
1943.3.8403

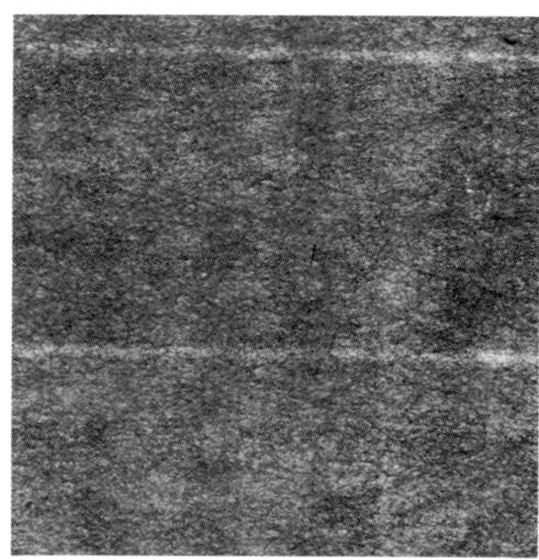

39. *The Tyresmith*
hōsho kōzo
1943.3.8687

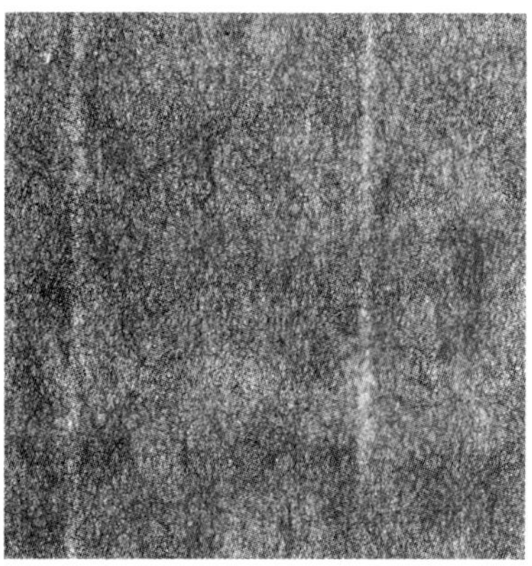

40. *The Fair*
hōsho kōzo
1943.3.8750

41. *The Manager's Window, Gaiety Theatre*
hōsho kōzo
1943.3.3128

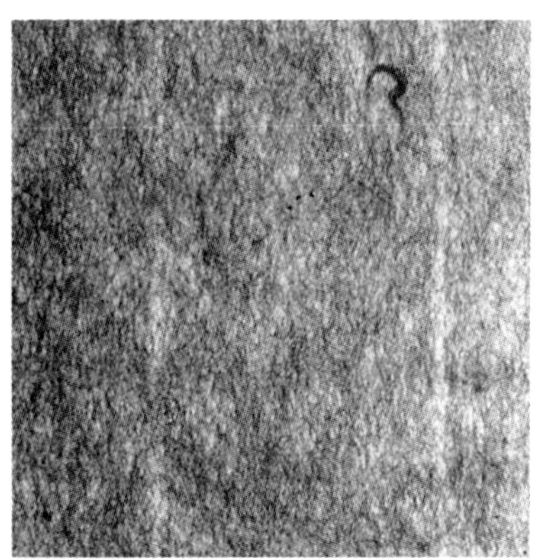

42. *Sketch—Grande Rue Dieppe*
hōsho kōzo
1943.3.8792

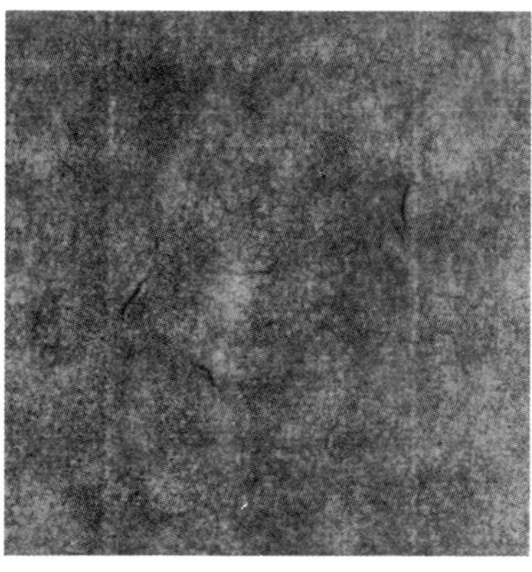

43. *Draped Figure, Seated*
torinoko gampi
1943.3.8706

44. *The Little Balcony*
torinoko gampi
1943.3.8710

45. *Yoshino-gami* sample

46. *Tengujō* sample

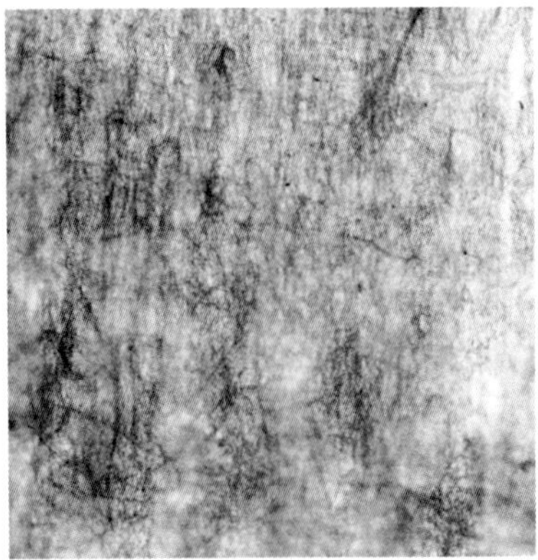

47. Nineteenth-century Japanese "book paper"

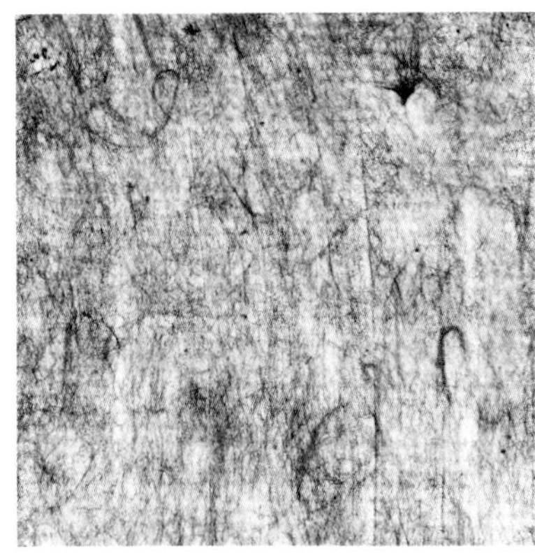

48. Nineteenth-century Japanese "book paper"

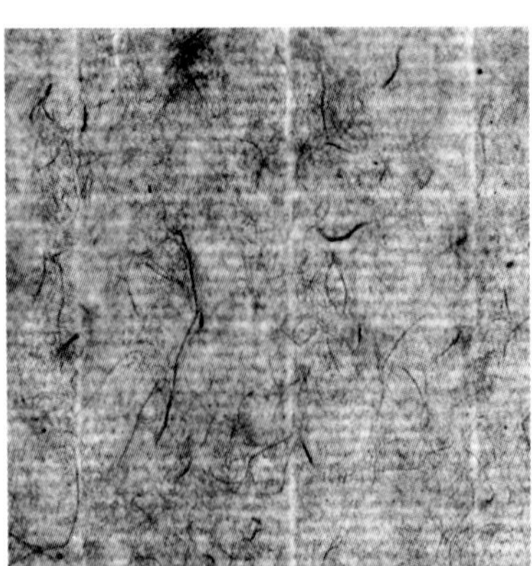

49. *Gasenshi* sample

50. *Gasenshi* sample

51. *Kyoku-shi* sample, from the Shidzuoka mill, Japan Paper Company, 1910

NOTES

I would like to thank the Mellon Foundation for funding my position at the National Gallery of Art, conservation division. Additional funding for this project was provided by the Asian Cultural Council. Ruth Fine, curator, department of modern prints and drawings, National Gallery of Art, encouraged the project and made many valuable contributions to it. Shelley Fletcher, head of paper conservation, and Nancy Ash, then senior paper conservator, provided time for this research as well as many useful suggestions. Michael Palmer, conservation scientist, scientific research department of the National Gallery, identified the fibers in Whistler's *The Red House, Paimpol*. John Krill, senior paper conservator, Henry Francis du Pont Winterthur Museum, provided many references and made substantial editorial contributions. Judith Walsh, senior paper conservator, National Gallery of Art, also contributed to several sections of this article. Timothy Barrett, director of Papermaking Facilities, University of Iowa, School of Art and Art History, helped by reviewing the sections on Japanese paper characteristics. Akinori Okawa, Kōchi Prefectural Pulp and Paper Laboratory, identified the fibers in the export papers. Philip Meredith provided samples of nineteenth-century Japanese papers. Many people in Japan assisted my research and understanding of Japanese papers; of particular help were Masakuni Aoki, Hiraku Kido, Yoshinari Kobayashi, Yoko Kuzume, Hisao Miyajima, Toshio Miyazawa, and Asao Shimura.

1. Several exhibitions and publications have focused on the Japanese influence on art. See, e.g., *Rembrandt: Experimental Etcher* [exh. cat., Museum of Fine Arts, Boston] (Boston, 1969), 180, for discussion of Japanese papers used by Rembrandt; Gabriel P. Weisberg et al., *Japonisme: Japanese Influence on French Art, 1854–1910* [exh. cat., Cleveland Museum of Art] (London, 1975); Robert H. Getscher, *The Stamp of Whistler* [exh. cat., Allen Memorial Art Museum, Oberlin College] (Oberlin, 1977), 4, for discussion of the mid-nineteenth-century etching revival; Society for the Study of Japonism, ed., *Japonism in Art: An International Symposium* (n.d.).

2. Andrew Robison, *Paper in Prints* [exh. cat., National Gallery of Art] (Washington, 1977), 24.

3. William Savage, *Practical Hints on Decorative Printing* (London, 1822), 31.

4. Ernest S. Lumsden, *The Art of Etching* (New York, 1924), 137.

5. Maxime Lalanne, *A Treatise on Etching* (London, 1880), 60.

6. Lumsden 1924, 137.

7. Philip Gilbert Hamerton, *Etching and Etchers* (London, 1868), 345.

8. Harry S. Parkes, "Reports on the Manufacture of Paper in Japan Presented to Both Houses of Parliament by Command of Her Majesty" (London, 1871), in *Mr. Gladstone's Washi, A Survey of Reports on the Manufacture of Paper in Japan: The Parkes Report of 1871*, ed. Hans Schmoller (Newtown, Pa., 1984).

9. Philip Gilbert Hamerton, *Etcher's Handbook* (London, 1871).

10. Weisberg 1975, 3, 4.

11. Clay Lancaster, *Japanese Influence in America* (New York, 1963), 25.

12. In 1885 the records department of the Japanese Ministry of Finance compiled existing documents on the exportation of paper since 1868. Paper was classified by type, and entries include the years of exportation, exporting harbors, destinations, prices, and amounts. As the data were gathered from a variety of entries, the format differs from one to another. Taken as a whole, the document provides significant information on the kind and extent of Japanese paper exportation during the late nineteenth century.

This document, now in the Oji Paper Museum, Tokyo, was translated by Masokuni Aoki, museum director, and Toshio Miyazawa, museum manager. The entries include information on *cha-gami*, "paper for wrapping tea"; "lower class of paper"; "paper for books"; and other papers including *tengujō*, *aburagami*, *gasenshi*, and *senka-shi*. Italy is the only European country identified as receiving paper shipments in 1868. Beginning in 1873 there was an increase in the amount and type of papers exported, and shipments were sent to England, France, Germany, British East India, Austria, and the United States.

A copy of the translated document is on file in the paper conservation department at the National Gallery of Art, Washington.

13. John Krill, "Harrison G. Elliott: Creator of Handmade Papers," *Quarterly Journal of the Library of Congress* 35 (1978), 4–26.

14. P. D. Perkins, *The Paper Industry and Printing in Japan* (Tokyo, n.d.).

15. For a complete explanation of Western papermaking terms, see Dard Hunter, *Papermaking: History and Technique of an Ancient Craft* (New York, 1978). For Japanese papermaking, see Timothy Barrett, *Japanese Papermaking: Traditions, Tools, and Technique* (New York, 1983). See also app. 1.

16. Nancy Ash, "Recording Watermarks by Beta-Radiography and Other Means," *AIC Postprints*, 10th Annual Meeting of the American Institute for Conservation, Book and Paper Group (Washington, 1982), 7–13.

Beta-radiography is a nondestructive method of recording paper characteristics such as fiber dispersion, watermarks, and chain and laid lines. Its detailed one-to-one image is the most accurate method of imaging paper characteristics. A radiograph is made with a beta-plate—a carbon-14 source embedded in a thin sheet of plastic. The plate emits electrons in the form of extremely low-energy beta particles that can measure the differences of density within a sheet of paper. A beta-radiograph is made by placing the appropriate photographic film under the print and the beta-plate on top of the print and exposing the film for a period of time depending on the thickness of the paper.

Evaluating beta-radiographs takes some practice. The image is similar to that seen when viewing a print by transmitted light such as seen through a light box. Wrinkles, mends, tears, and even parts of the image must be distinguished from the paper structure. Beta-radiographs shown are actual size, one-quarter of the plate printed. Figures 9, 22, and 30 also show the Whistler print photographed with transmitted light.

Whistler's prints and etchings are identified by numbers assigned in Edward Guthrie Kennedy, *The Etched Work of Whistler: Illustrated by Reproduction in Collotype of Different States of the Plates—Compiled, Arranged, and Described*, 6 vols. (New York, 1910); his lithographs are identified by numbers assigned in Thomas R. Way, *The Lithographs by Whistler, Illustrated by Reproduction in Photogravure and Lithography, Arranged According to the Catalogue by Thomas R. Way, with Additional Subjects Not before Recorded* (New York, 1914). When possible, states are noted.

17. John Krill, Henry Francis du Pont Winterthur Museum, personal communication, April 1988.

18. Parkes 1984.

19. R. T. Stevens, *The Art of Paper Making in Japan* (New York, 1909).

20. Shelley Fletcher and Judith Walsh, "The Treatment of Three Prints by Whistler on Fine Japanese Paper," *Journal of the American Institute for Conservation* 18 (1979), 118–128; Catherine Nicholson, "The Conservation of Three Whistler Prints on Japanese Paper," in *The Conservation of Far Eastern Art*, ed. H. Mabuchi and Perry Smith (London, 1988), 39–44.

After aqueous treatments, I have had success drying *gampi* papers between two pieces of smooth Gore-tex touching the artifact, with blotters and felts on either side. The smooth surface of the Gore-tex allows the smooth *gampi* surface to be retained while moisture is removed from the sheet. The light weight and light restraint of the Gore-tex and felts help retain the impression of the print.

21. Savage 1822, 31.

22. Special precautions include providing protective framing and limiting handling of *gasenshi* impressions altogether because they are especially vulnerable and current treatment options compromise impression qualities. When conservation treatments are necessary, especially aqueous treatment, propyl alcohol or butyl alcohol can be successfully used as a resist to isolate areas of the impression that do not require treatment. These alcohols temporarily bond with the cellulose and repel water, while noncoated areas receive the water and cleanse the paper where necessary. Propyl alcohol is soluble in water, and butyl alcohol is soluble in 8 percent or less concentrations. By varying the number of applications of the alcohol resist between baths or varying the duration of immersion, the alcohols can provide an effective temporary resist that is eventually, and in a controlled manner, replaced with atmospheric moisture.

This approach has the advantages of "local" treatments in that the paper and impression qualities of nondamaged areas are not affected by overall treatment. Due to the vulnerability of the paper and reactions of the *wara* filler, use of the suction table or other standard local treatment options are not recommended. Because the *wara* filler is rice starch, starch enzymes cannot be used during treatment.

23. E. J. Labarre, *Dictionary and Encyclopaedia of Paper and Paper-Making* (Amsterdam, 1952), 37, 178.

24. "Vellum" originally referred to a form of parchment or animal skin. It later was used by Europeans to describe papers, such as these "Japanese vellums," that are dense with a very smooth, often calendered surface.

25. Shigo (Paper Industry Times), *Paper Merchandise Encyclopaedia: All Paper Guide* (Tokyo, 1983).

26. Pulp and Paper Technical Association, *Pulp and Paper Encyclopaedia* (Tokyo, 1973).

27. Harrison Elliot Paper Collection sample books, Rare Book Room, Library of Congress, Washington.

28. Lumsden 1924, 143.

APPENDIX 1

Terms Used in Describing Japanese and European Papers

The following explanations amplify the discussion in the text and describe standards for classifying Japanese papers. Terms and spellings vary considerably for Japanese paper making; the source followed here is Sukey Hughes, *Washi: The World of Japanese Paper* (Tokyo, 1978), 171–195.

Pulp Characteristics

High-quality: fibers are of a consistent length overall, and no shives, lumps, or debris are present in the sheet.

Medium- and low-quality: fibers are of various lengths and/or shives, lumps, or debris are present in the sheet.

Even distribution: the sheet is uniform when viewed through transmitted light.

Uneven distribution: the sheet is not uniform, and thicker and thinner areas can be seen when viewed through transmitted light.

Mold Characteristics

Chain-line intervals: centimeters between chain lines.

Laid-line frequency: number of laid lines per centimeter.

Sha texture: present or not.

Other: random occurrences; for example, irregularities in the laid lines.

Fiber

Gampi
Kōzo
Mitsumata
Supplementary fibers such as grasses (straw), bamboo, or hemp

Thickness

Thin papers or light weight: .01–.03 millimeter

Medium papers or medium weight: .03–.06 millimeter

Thick papers or heavy weight: .06 millimeter and thicker

Color

Brown tones
White tones

APPENDIX 2

Correlation of Papers in Whistler's Etchings and Lithographs

Within the collection at the National Gallery of Art, Washington (NGA), the separate categories of Japanese papers found in Whistler's prints were identified. Using worksheets (see sample at the end of this appendix) and following the methodology described in the text, each paper was examined. A description of each category is suggested as a possible catalogue entry for use in a revised catalogue raisonné of Whistler's prints. A similar examination was completed for prints from collections at the Freer Gallery of Art, Smithsonian Institution, Washington (FGA), and the Baltimore Museum of Art (BMA). These museums are designated in the following lists by acronyms. Etchings are identified by numbers assigned in Edward Guthrie Kennedy, *The Etched Work of Whistler: Illustrated by Reproduction in Collotype of Different States of the Plates—Compiled, Arranged, and Described*, 6 vols. (New York, 1910). Lithographs are identified by numbers assigned in Thomas R. Way, *The Lithographs by Whistler, Illustrated by Reproduction in Photogravure and Lithography, Arranged According to the Catalogue by Thomas R. Way, with Additional Subjects Not before Recorded* (New York, 1914). When possible, states are noted in parentheses.

Thin, low-quality, brown-tone Japanese *kōzo* paper

The etchings on this paper are similar and characteristic for prints from *Greenwich Pensioner* (K34) through *The Little Pool* (K74). These papers form a distinct group that includes the following characteristics: poor pulp preparation, poor distribution, many lengths of fibers with additional plant pieces, and often irregularities in the mold. The papers were very loose and thinly made. The thinness of the sheets makes them somewhat transparent. It is likely that these were the only Japanese papers available at the time these early prints were made. These papers could be the "lower class" or "book papers" mentioned in the 1885 export document.

Etchings

Greenwich Pensioner, K34 (FGA 95.7; 98.259)
Thames Warehouses, K38 (FGA 98.264)
Old Westminster Bridge, K39 (FGA 98.265)
Limehouse, K40 (BMA L1933.53.12325)
Black Lion Wharf, K42 (FGA 98.271)
The Pool, K43 (FGA 98.273, 98.274)
The Pool, K43 (BMA L1933.53.12326)
Thames Police, K44 (BMA L1933.35.1654)
Thames Police, K44 (FGA 98.275)
Longshoremen, K45 (FGA 90.5; 98.276)

The Lime-Burner, K46 (FGA 90.3)
Billingsgate, K47 (FGA 08.189; 98.278)
A Wharf, K48 (FGA 98.269)
Soupe à Trois Sous, K49 (FGA 98.250)
Soupe à Trois Sous, K49 (i/i) (NGA 1943.3.8431), fig. 2
Bibi Lalouette, K51 (FGA 90.2; 98.254; 98.255)
Becquet, K52 (iii) (NGA 1943.3.8435), fig. 3
Astruc, A Literary Man, K53 (FGA 98.285)
Astruc, A Literary Man, K53 (ii) (NGA 1943.3.8436), fig. 4
Portrait of Whistler, K54 (FGA 98.288)
Fumette, Standing, K56 (i) (NGA 1949.5.531), fig. 5
Fumette, Standing, K56 (FGA 98.286)
Fumette's Bent Head, K57 (i) (NGA 1949.5.532), fig. 6
Fumette's Bent Head, K57 (FGA 98.287)
Finette, K58 (FGA 98.291; 98.294)
Venus, K59 (FGA 98.2950)
Arthur Haden, K61 (FGA 98.282; 92.1)
Annie Haden, K62 (FGA 98.297; 98.296)
Mr. Mann, K63 (FGA 98.298)
Axenfeld, K64 (FGA 98.30.2)
Rotherhithe, K66 (iii) (NGA 1943.3.8442), fig. 7
Rotherhithe, K66 (FGA 98.265)
Rotherhithe, K66 (BMA L1933.35.7637)
The Miser, K69 (BMA L1933.53.9095)
The Little Pool, K74 (FGA 98.319; 90.6)
F. R. Leyland, K102 (i/ii) (NGA 1949.5.538), fig. 8

Thin, high-quality, brown-tone Japanese *kōzo* paper

Kōzo fiber in these papers has been carefully prepared so that all the fibers are of a consistent length without any impurities in the pulp. The paper was carefully made to produce sheets with even distribution of pulp.

Etchings

The Pool, K43 (BMA L1933.53.12319)
Drouet, K55 (BMA 75.29.20)
The Storm, K81 (FGA 91.8)
Amsterdam, from the Tolhuis, (i) K91 (NGA 1943.3.8457), fig. 10
Amsterdam, from the Tolhuis, K91 (FGA 98.328)
The Model Resting, K100 (FGA 98.333)
The Velvet Dress, K105 (89.25)
Fanny Leyland, K108 (i) (NGA 1943.3.8466), fig. 11
Seated Girl, K118 (FGA 98.348)
Free Trade Wharf, K163 (undetermined state) (NGA 1943.3.8496), fig. 12
Free Trade Wharf, K163 (BMA L1933.53.11676)
Fishing-Boats, Hastings, K158 (ii) (NGA 1943.3.8491), fig. 13

Medium-thick, medium-quality, brown-tone (*senka-shi*) Japanese *kōzo* paper

The *kōzo* paper was made with several fiber lengths and overall uneven distribution. The papers are very crisp and less absorbent than other Japanese papers. They form a distinct group typical of Whistler's late etchings, the *Amsterdam* series. Earlier etchings may have been reprinted at this later date. It is significant that Japanese papers were not used for a substantial period in Whistler's career and that their use was more selective in later etchings. On these brown-tone Japanese papers, Whistler did not need to leave a plate tone of ink, and the impressions are cleanly wiped.

Etchings

Steps, Amsterdam, K403 (iii) (NGA 1943.3.8639), fig. 14
Long House—Dyer's—Amsterdam, K406 (FGA 06.118)
Pierrot, K407 (v) (NGA 1943.3.8643), fig. 15
Little Drawbridge, Amsterdam, (ii) K412 (NGA 1943.3.8647), fig. 16
Atelier de Bijouterie, K433 (FGA 06.131)
Rue Vauvilliers, K439 (FGA 03.96)
Zaandam, K416 (ii) (NGA 1943.3.8649), fig. 17
Zaandam, K416 (FGA 06.120)
The Velvet Dress, K105 (iv) (NGA 1943.3.8464), fig. 18
The Velvet Dress, K105 (BMA 32.179)
Florence Leyland, K110 (iii) (NGA 1943.3.1729), fig. 19
Florence Leyland, K110 (FGA 98.340; 98.341)
Maude, Standing, K114 (FGA 98.345)
Price's Candle-Works, K154 (FGA 91.14)
Melon-Shop, Houndsditch, K293 (FGA 92.14)

Lithographs

The Winged Hat, W25 (FGA 95.6)
The Garden, W38 (NGA 1943.3.8697), fig. 20
Draped Figure Standing, W155 (NGA 1947.10.2), fig. 21

Medium-thick, high-quality, brown-tone Japanese *kōzo* paper

The *kōzo* fiber was carefully prepared and evenly distributed. Both the inking and the paper are very distinct, and these entries warrant further investigation as a group. It is possible that they were printed (reprinted?) at the same time.

Etchings

Sketch of Ships, K151 (FGA 98.361)
Nude Figure Reclining, K343 (FGA 00.49)
Boulevard Poissonière, K423 (FGA 05.1)
Balustrade, Luxembourg Gardens, K427 (FGA 06.123)
Café Corazza, Palais Royal, K436 (FGA 03.95)

Lithographs

Dancing Girl, W30 (FGA 06.154)
The Cap, W158 (FGA 05.13)

Thin, transparent, brown-tone Japanese *gampi* paper
These impressions are on various qualities of *gampi* paper. However, the transparency, ability of the shiny surface to reflect light, and exceptional absorbency take precedence over quality. *Gampi* papers were approximately four times more expensive than other Japanese papers.

Etchings
The Rag Gatherers, K23 (v) (NGA 1951.13.22), fig. 23
Billingsgate, K47 (BMA 1932.17.3)
Becquet, K52 (FGA 92.32)
Drouet, K55 (FGA 98.290)
Drouet, K55 (NGA 1943.3.8659), fig. 24
The Forge, K68 (iii) (NGA 1943.3.8444), fig. 25
The Forge, K68 (BMA L1933.53.11663)
Millbank, K71 (BMA L1933.53.11686)
Millbank, K71 (FGA 94.38)
Little Wapping, K73 (i) (NGA 1943.3.8446), fig. 26
Little Wapping, K73 (FGA 98.317)
The Little Pool, K74 (BMA 32.17.8)
Weary, K92 (iia; ii) (NGA 1943.3.8458; 1947.10.5)
Weary, K92 (FGA 98.329; 05.164; 89.28)

Lithographs
Gatti's, W34 (FGA 06.158)
Mother and Child #4, W135 (FGA 06.197)
La Danseuse, A Study of the Nude, W148 (NGA 1945.5.1332)
La Danseuse, A Study of the Nude, W148 (BMA L1933.53.8315)
Nude Model Standing, W154 (BMA L1933.53.8324)
Draped Figure Standing, W155 (FGA 06.201)
Nude Model, Back View, W165 (FGA 04.165)
Nude Model, Back View, W165 (NGA 1946.21.372)

Medium-thick, high-quality, brown-tone Japanese *gampi* paper
These *gampi* papers were made thicker so that they are opaque rather than transparent. They have a polished surface and an absorbent quality.

Etchings
The Unsafe Tenement, K17 (BMA 74.42.15)
The Forge, K68 (BMA 32.17.7)
The Forge, K68 (FGA 94.23)
The "Adam and Eve," Old Chelsea, K175 (ii/ii) (NGA 1943.3.8508), fig. 27
The "Adam and Eve," Old Chelsea, K175 (FGA 93.92)

Medium-thick, high-quality, brown-tone vellum (*kyoku-shi*, or "japon") Japanese *mitsumata* paper
Mitsumata fiber was carefully prepared and evenly dispersed on "Western-style" molds. *Kyoku-shi* has a smooth surface, is often calendered, and has a very absorbent quality.

Etchings
Reading by Lamplight, K32 (FGA 98.247)
Greenwich Park, K35 (ii) (NGA 1949.5.528), fig. 28
Landscape with the Horse, K36 (FGA 98.280)
Bibi Valentin, K50 (FGA 98.251)
The Little Mast, K185 (FGA 98.380)
The Little Lagoon, K186 (FGA 05.180)
The Doorway, K188 (BMA 46.112.5964)
Two Doorways, K193 (FGA 98.390)
The Mast, K195 (FGA 98.394)

Lithographs
Rue Furstenburg, W59 (NGA 1943.3.8719), fig. 29
Figure Study, W76 (NGA 1946.21.369), fig. 31
Yellow House, Lannion, W101 (NGA 1947.10.4)
Study—Mr. Thomas Way, No. 1, W107 (NGA 1943.3.8764)
Kensington Gardens, W109 (NGA 1943.3.8766)
The Russian Schube, W112 (NGA 1943.3.8769)
Draped Figure Standing, W155 (BMA L1933.53.8317)
Unfinished Sketch of Lady Haden, W143 (formerly NGA B10,855, deaccessioned)
Draped Figure, Standing, W155 (NGA 1946.21.365)

Medium-thick, medium-quality, brown-tone vellum (export-quality *kyoku-shi*) *mitsumata* and softwood pulp paper
The Red House, Paimpol, W100 (NGA 1947.10.3; 1943.3.8757), fig. 32

Medium-thick, white-tone, vellum (*gasenshi*, or "China" or "India") Japanese paper
Mitsumata and bamboo fibers with rice starch filler make this paper extremely smooth, absorbent, and opaque. Various qualities are represented below.

Lithographs
The Sisters, W71 (FGA 03.82)
A Portrait, Miss Howells, W75 (FGA 03.83)
Study, W77 (NGA 1946.17.1), fig. 35
The Duet, No. 2, W65 (NGA 1943.3.8725), fig. 36
Yellow House, Lannion, W101 (NGA 1943.3.8758)
Count Robert de Moutesquiou, W137 (NGA 1943.3.8786; 1943.3.8787; 1943.3.8788)
Count Robert de Moutesquiou #2, W138 (FGA 03.215)
Count Robert de Moutesquiou #3, W139 (FGA 04.71)
Dancer, W148 (FGA 98.413)
The Shoe Maker, W151 (NGA 1943.3.8797)
The Medici Collar, W153 (NGA 1943.3.8798), fig. 37

Medium-thick, high-quality, white-tone, vellum (*hōsho*) Japanese *kōzo* paper
Kōzo fiber was carefully prepared, with even,

clean distribution on the mold. Talc filler makes the sheets white, opaque, and absorbent.

Lithographs
Study, W3 (FGA 06.135)
The Tyresmith, W27 (NGA 1943.3.8687), fig. 39
The Fair, W92 (NGA 1943.3.8750), fig. 40
The Manager's Window, Gaiety Theatre, W114 (NGA 1943.3.3128), fig. 41
By the Balcony, W124 (FGA 05.212)
Mother and Child #4, W135 (NGA 1946.21.371)
Sketch—Grand Rue Dieppe, W146 (NGA 1943.3.8792), fig. 42
Sketch—Grand Rue Dieppe, W146 (NGA 1943.3.8793)

Thick, high-quality, white-tone, vellum (*torinoko*) Japanese *gampi* paper
Gampi fiber, possibly with supplementary fibers, was formed to produce a thick, opaque sheet that is absorbent, with a polished surface.

Lithographs
Draped Figure, Seated, W46 (NGA 1943.3.8706), fig. 43
The Little Balcony, W50 (NGA 1943.3.8710), fig. 44
The Little Balcony, W50 (FGA 06.166)
Little Draped Figure Leaning, W51 (FGA 06.167)
Long Gallery, Louvre, W52 (NGA 1943.3.8712)
The Whitesmiths—Impasse des Carmélites, W53 (NGA 1943.3.8713)
The Whitesmiths—Impasse des Carmélites, W53 (FGA 06.169)
Tête-à-Tête in the Garden, W54 (NGA 1943.3.8714)
Le Belle Jardinière, W63 (NGA 1943.3.8723)
La Belle Dame Endormie, W69 (NGA 1943.3.8729)
La Fruitière de la Rue de Grenelle, W70 (NGA 1943.3.8730)
The Garden Porch, W140 (NGA 1943.3.8789)
The Man with a Sickle, W141 (FGA 04.159)
Afternoon Tea, W147 (NGA 1943.3.8794)
Afternoon Tea, W147 (FGA 04.69)
Nude Model Standing, W154 (FGA 07.173)

Miscellaneous
These papers do not fit into a category and were unique examples in the collections surveyed.

Etchings
Street at Saverne, K19 (iii/v) (NGA 1943.3.8407), fig. 33 (probably *senka-shi kōzo*)
Street at Saverne, K19 (NGA 1943.3.8405), fig. 34, not determined
The Unsafe Tenement, K17 (NGA 1943.3.8403), fig. 38, a brown-tone low-quality *gasenshi*
The Kitchen, K24 (FGA 98.238), medium quality, many shives, brown tone
Annie Haden, K62 (FGA 92.5), medium quality, thick, white tone

Lithographs
Study, W1 (FGA 05.205), thick, white-tone *kōzo*
Confidences in the Garden, W60 (FGA 06.177), high quality, medium thick, white tone

Thin, Japanese paper attached overall to Western plate paper
These papers are difficult to identify since they are attached overall to Western plate paper.

Lithographs
Gaiety Stage Door, W10 (FGA 88.24)
Old Battersea Bridge, W12 (FGA 88.28)
Reading, W13 (FGA 88.30)
The Fan, W14 (FGA 04.68)
A Portrait, Miss Howells, W75 (FGA 12.2)
Back of the Gaiety Theatre, W81 (FGA 05.211)
The Limehouse, W4 (FGA 06.135), thin *tengujō*

WORKSHEET FOR JAPANESE PAPERS

Print Title:
Accession Number:
Catalogue Raisonné Number:
number and state:
beta-radiograph:

Pulp Characteristics
pulp quality and description (high, medium, low)
pulp distribution (even, uneven)

Mold Characteristics
chain-line intervals
laid-line frequency
watermark
presence of unusual markings (*sha*, wove appearance)
interpretation

Fiber Type
Western fibers: bast, cotton, pulp
oriental fibers: *kōzo*, *mitsumata*, *gampi*
supplementary fibers: bamboo, hemp, grasses, wood pulp
fillers: talc, starch, other
sizing: strong, weak

Thickness
thin (.01 mm)
medium (.03–.06 mm)
thick (.06–.15 mm)

Color
white tones
brown tones

Texture (if appropriate)

Specific Paper Name (if appropriate, for example, *gasenshi*, *hōsho*, *kyoku-shi*, *senka-shi*, *torinoko*)

Summary (catalogue entry)

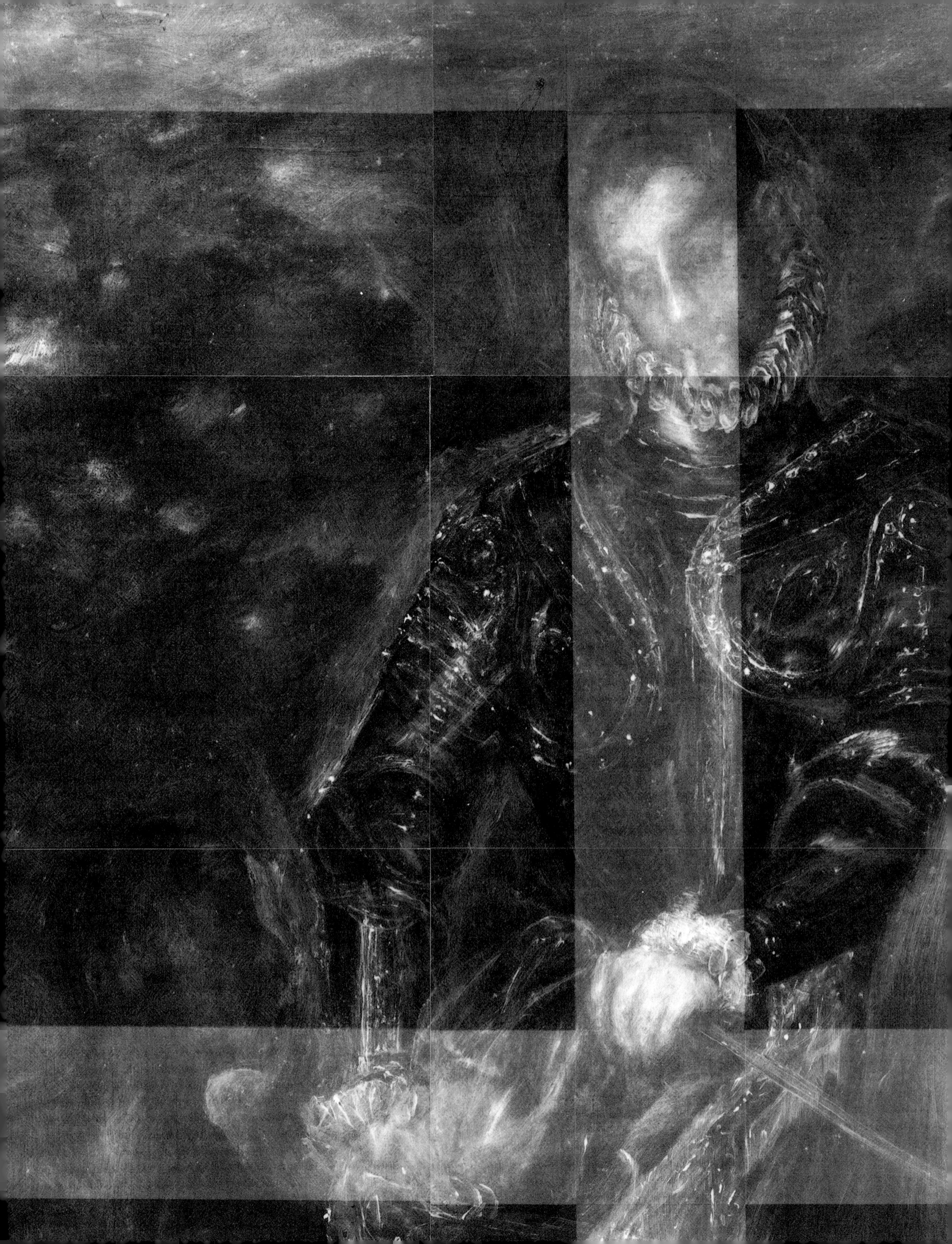

SUSANNA P. GRISWOLD

Two Paintings by El Greco: Saint Martin and the Beggar

Analysis and Comparison

El Greco (1541–1614), "the Greek," was born in Crete, but it was in Spain, between the years 1577 and 1614, that he became a major artistic force. He was a prolific painter and, in conjunction with his workshop, produced multiple versions of his more successful paintings. Today it is not unusual to find three or even five smaller versions of an altarpiece in existence.

Little is known about El Greco's creative process of painting. We do know that, at least late in his career, he generally sketched his compositions with a brush and black paint onto a red *imprimatura* that lies on top of the traditional white ground. We also know that he made color sketches for his compositions, apparently in preparation for execution of the final version. Such sketches, which are often completed paintings, are known as *modellos*. In contrast, copies of completed paintings are known as *ricordos*. Visual analysis alone is often insufficient to distinguish a *modello* from a *ricordo*, as both are generally finished paintings. Moreover, little is known about El Greco's participation in the execution of *ricordo* paintings by his workshop.

This essay originated as an investigation into the chronological relationship of two paintings in the collection of the National Gallery of Art, Washington. Both were attributed to El Greco and are entitled *Saint Martin and the Beggar* (figs. 1–2).[1] Their chronological relationship was soon established: the smaller version showed clear evidence of being a *ricordo* (and not a *modello*) of the larger altarpiece.

The identification of the smaller version of *Saint Martin and the Beggar* as a *ricordo* raised the further question of whether it was painted by El Greco or by his workshop. This issue has been addressed by scholars by means of connoisseurship. However, those scholars who have dealt with this question do not agree as to the authorship of the *ricordo*.[2] This essay serves to add detailed information about the technical differences and similarities between the two versions to facilitate the establishment of authorship. It is based on a comparative study of the two paintings that includes the supports, ground layers, paint films, painting techniques, and signatures, with consideration of other paintings by El Greco in the collection of the National Gallery of Art. Additional consideration is given to a smaller version of the altarpiece of *Saint Ildefonso* (fig. 3), which bears a similar relationship (*modello* or *ricordo*) to the larger altarpiece painted for the Hospital of Charity in Illescas, Spain (fig. 4).

The larger of the two versions of *Saint Martin and the Beggar* was painted for the left side of the altar of the Chapel of San José in Toledo.[3] For the other side of the altar, El Greco painted *Madonna and Child with Saint Martina and Saint Agnes* (fig. 5). The main altarpieces, *Saint Joseph and the Infant Christ* and *Coronation of the Virgin*, are still

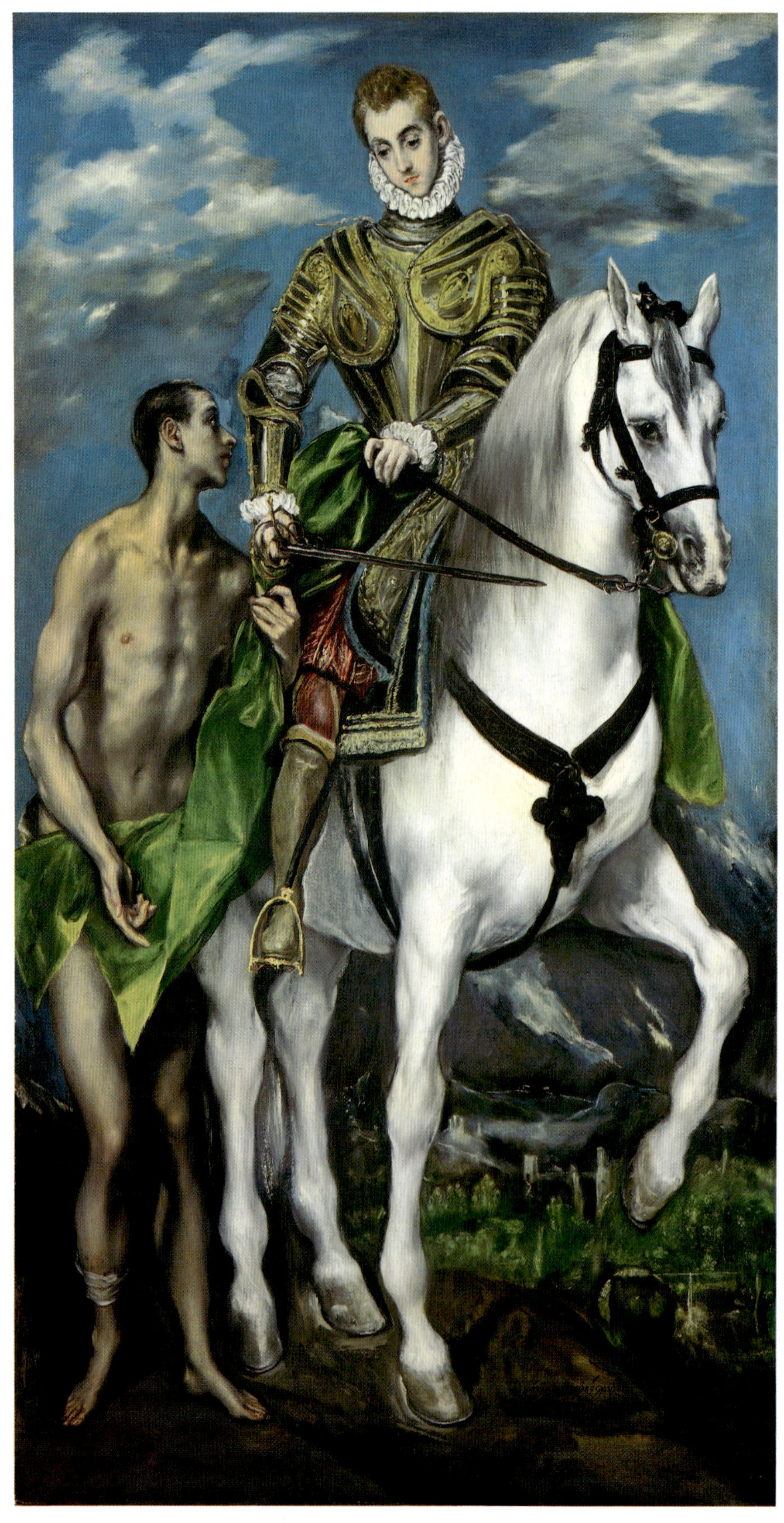

1. El Greco, *Saint Martin and the Beggar* (altarpiece), 1597–1599, oil on fabric
National Gallery of Art, Washington, Widener Collection

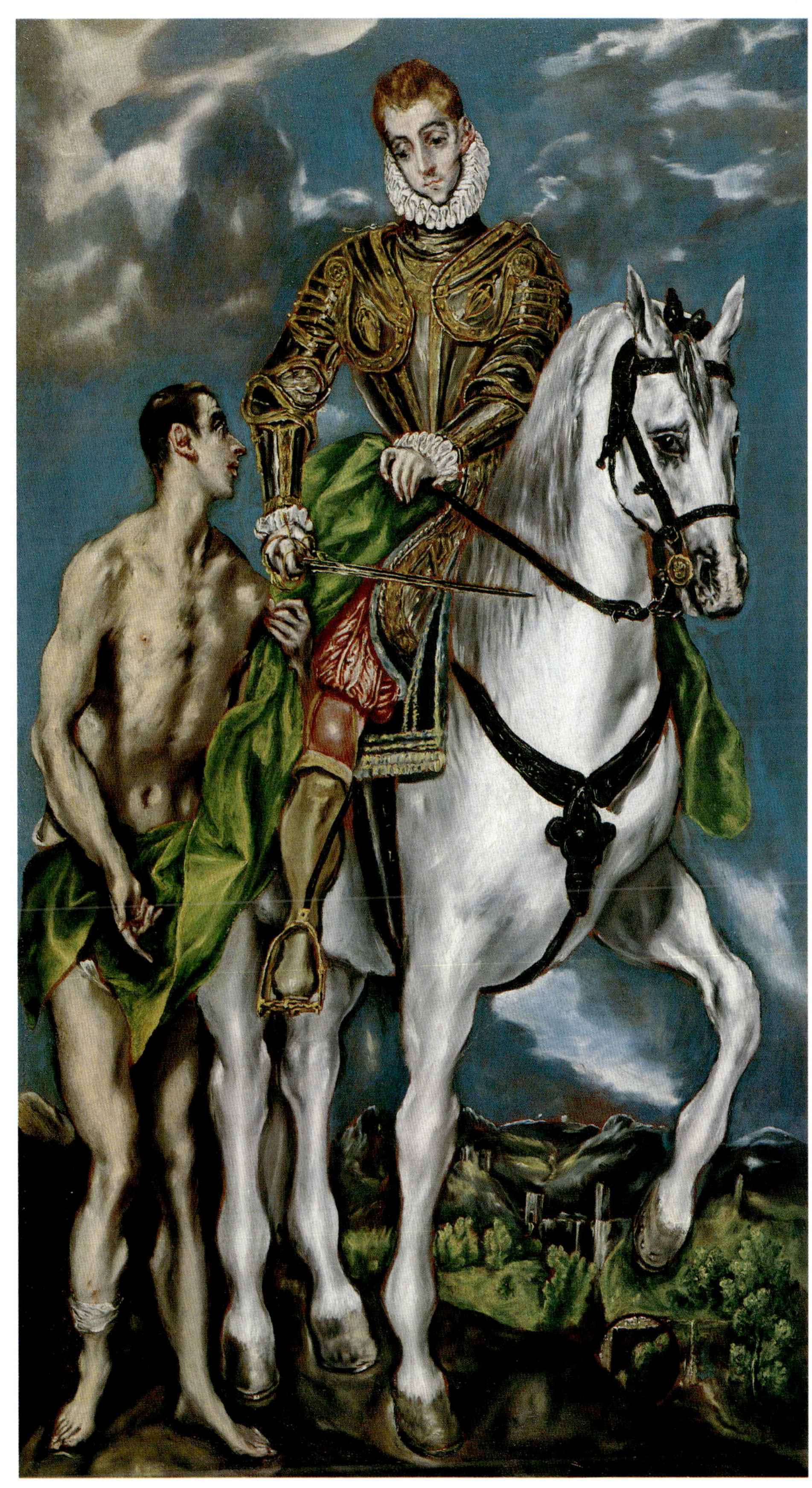

2. El Greco workshop, *Saint Martin and the Beggar* (smaller version), 1600/1605?, oil on fabric, after cleaning
National Gallery of Art, Washington, Andrew W. Mellon Collection

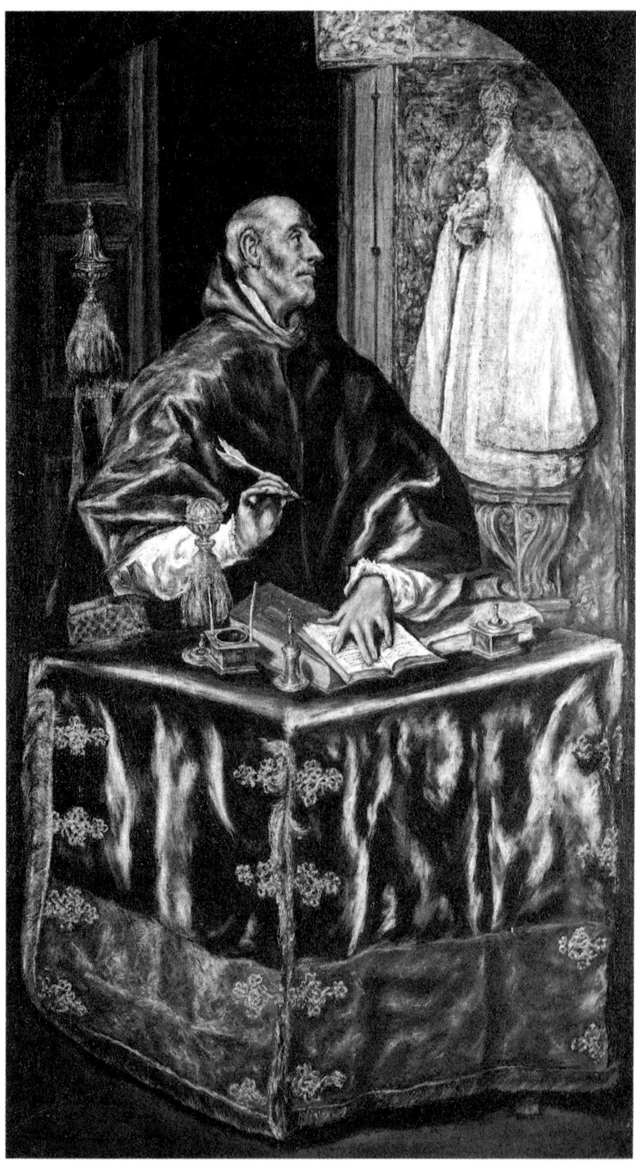

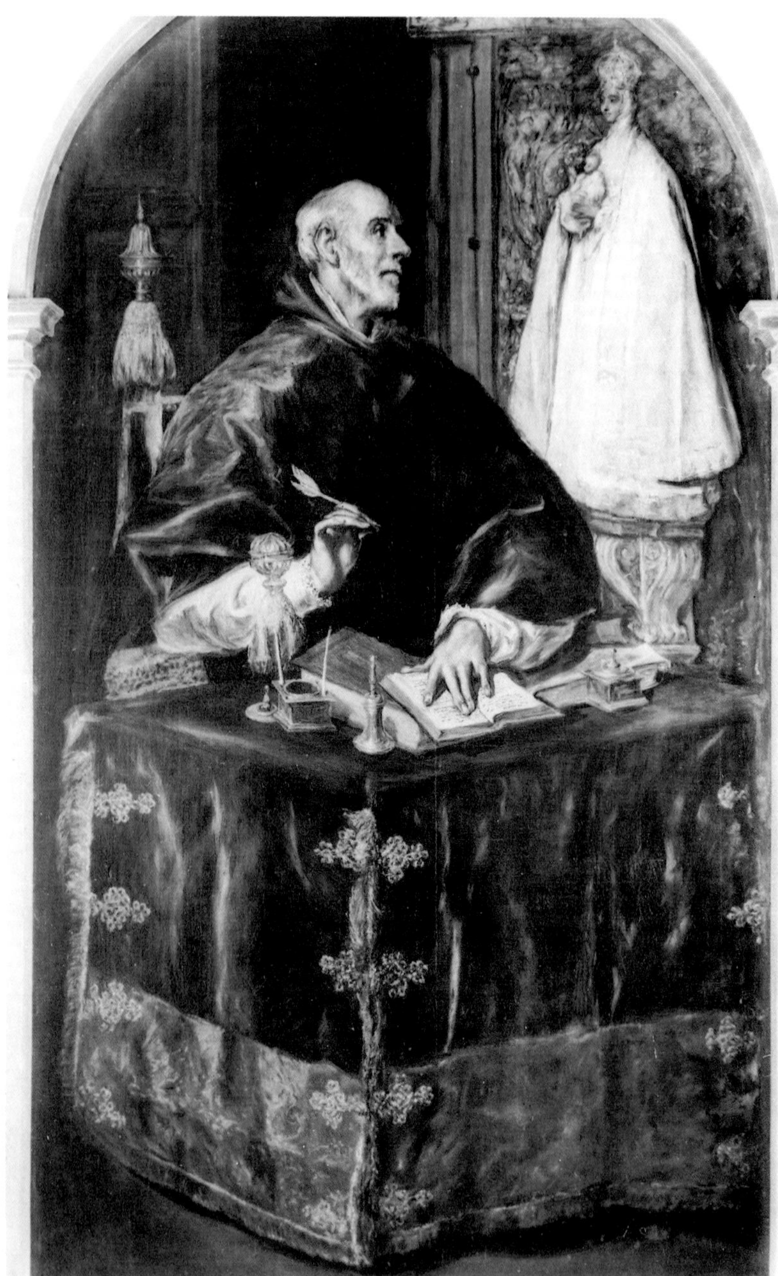

3. El Greco, *Saint Ildefonso* (smaller version), 1600/1605?, oil on fabric
National Gallery of Art, Washington, Andrew W. Mellon Collection

4. El Greco, *Saint Ildefonso* (altarpiece), 1600?, oil on fabric
Hospital of Charity, Illescas, Spain

in situ, but the chapel is privately owned and not open to the public.

The National Gallery's smaller version of *Saint Martin and the Beggar* is one of four, possibly five, existing paintings of this theme executed on the same smaller scale (figs. 6–9).[4] No records have survived explaining the purpose for which any of the smaller versions were created. Presumably some were commissioned by provincial parishes in the countryside around Toledo, while one might have remained in El Greco's possession as an example of the artist's craft.[5]

How can a *modello* be distinguished from a *ricordo*? Changes made during the drawing and painting states—an expression of the artist's creative process—are the most obvious indication of a *modello*. In contrast, as a *ricordo* copies the surface of another painting, compositional changes are absent.

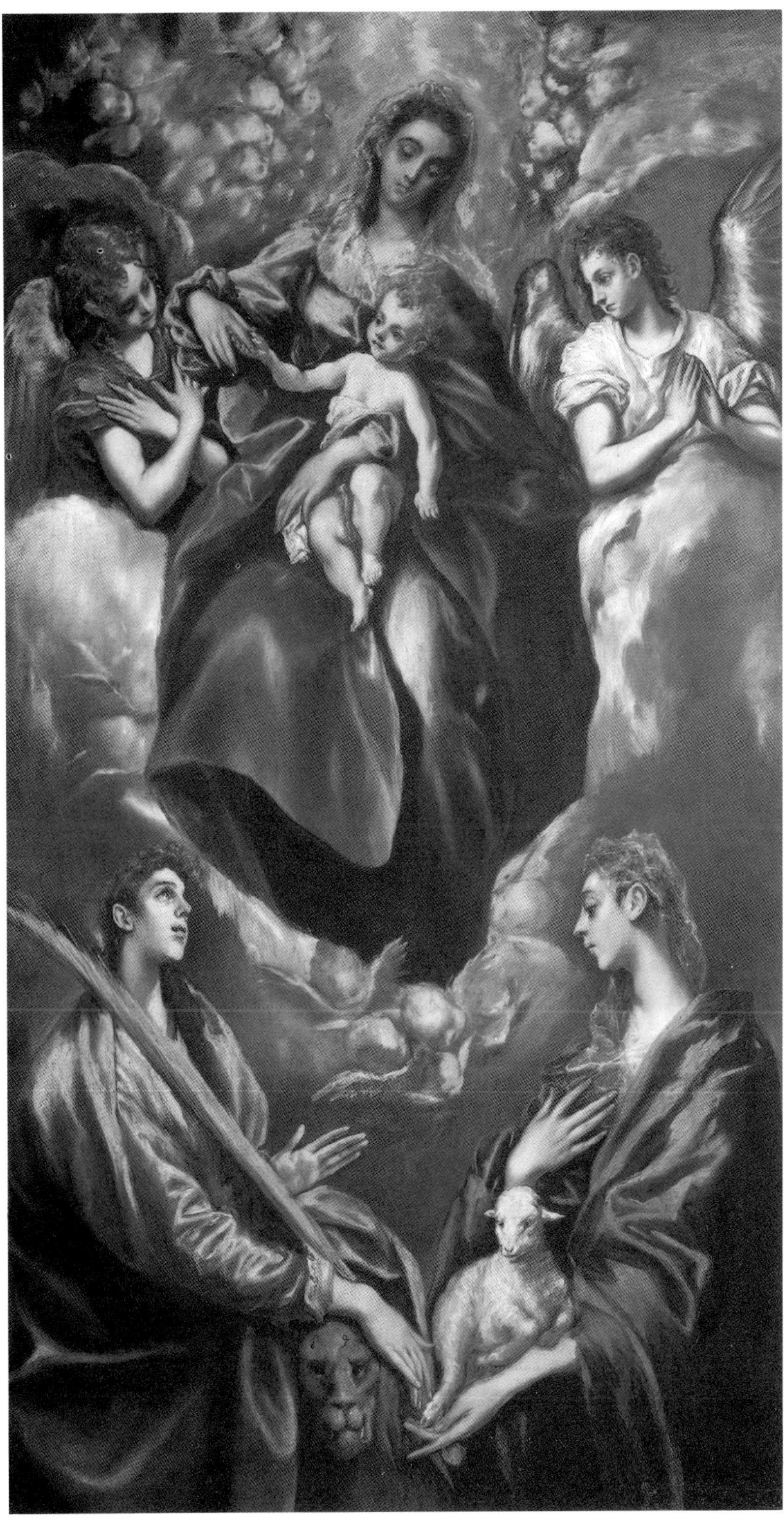

5. El Greco, *Madonna and Child with Saint Martina and Saint Agnes* (altarpiece), 1597–1599, oil on fabric
National Gallery of Art, Washington, Chester Dale Collection

X-radiography, infrared photography and reflectography, microscopic examination of the surface, and cross-section analysis were used in this study to reveal the layering of the paint film and its support structure.

El Greco's practice of producing smaller versions of his altarpieces was recorded by Francesco Pacheco[6] and is often discussed in the secondary literature. The question of *modello* versus *ricordo* arises with each high-quality version. Knowledge of the artist's materials and techniques of translating an idea to canvas helps answer this question, and several scholars have examined the technical aspects of individual paintings by El Greco.[7] Only the following information is known, however, about his creative process.

An inventory of El Greco's possessions in 1614, shortly after his death, recorded 150 drawings.[8] Only a few have survived. The only safely attributed drawing, *Saint John the Evangelist* (National Library, Madrid), is executed in black and white chalk and is squared with black chalk to prepare it for transfer to a larger scale.[9] The 1614 inventory also lists thirty *trazas*, presumably tracings of some sort. Perhaps these tracings were the means by which compositions were transferred onto canvas.

Several early paintings exhibit a type of masterful underdrawing that defines the outer and inner contours of the figures with both precise and free marks. *El Espolio* (Upton House, National Trust), *Holy Family* (Prado), and *Pietà* (Philadelphia Museum of Art) are small in size, have the same skillful underdrawing that shows no signs of a copying hand, and—above all—exhibit changes made during the painting process. These characteristics strongly suggest that these paintings were created as *modellos*.[10] The three paintings share another attribute: the support consists only of a white ground layer.

From study of El Greco's unfinished paintings, including *Saint Jerome* (fig. 10) and the last Apostle series (Museo del Greco, Toledo), it has been determined that at least during his later years, but probably during most of his career, the artist sketched his compositions with a brush and black paint onto a red *imprimatura*, which always seems to lie on top of a traditional white ground. This sketching is not detectable using infrared reflectography because of the low con-

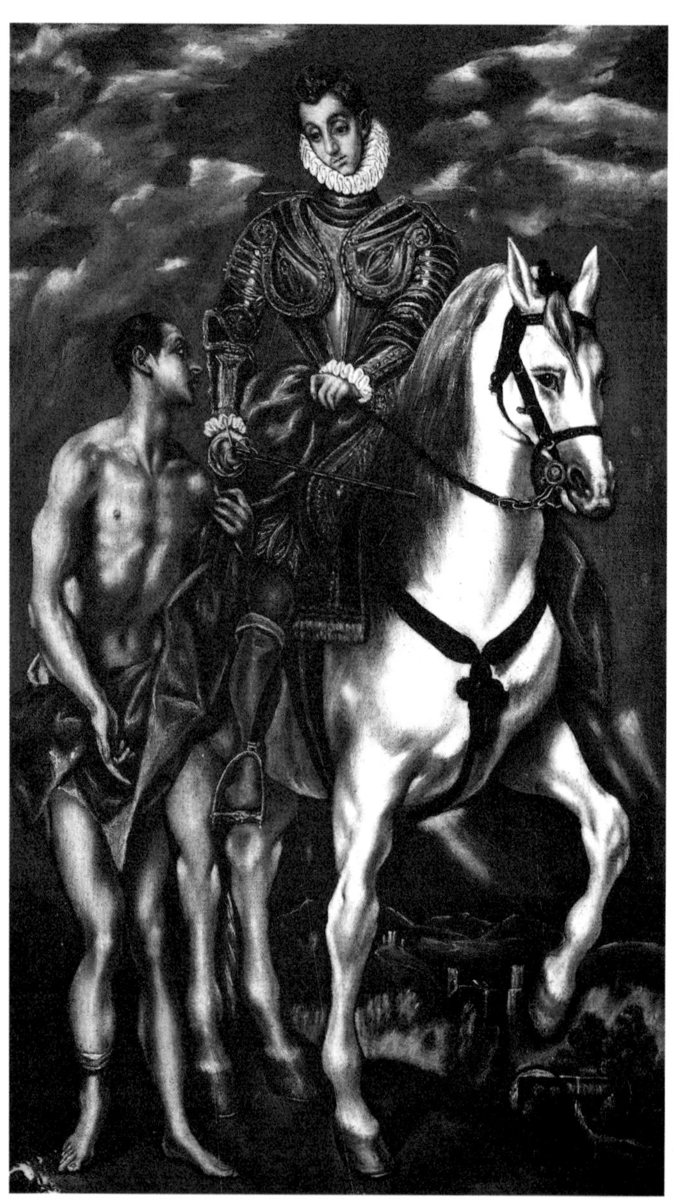

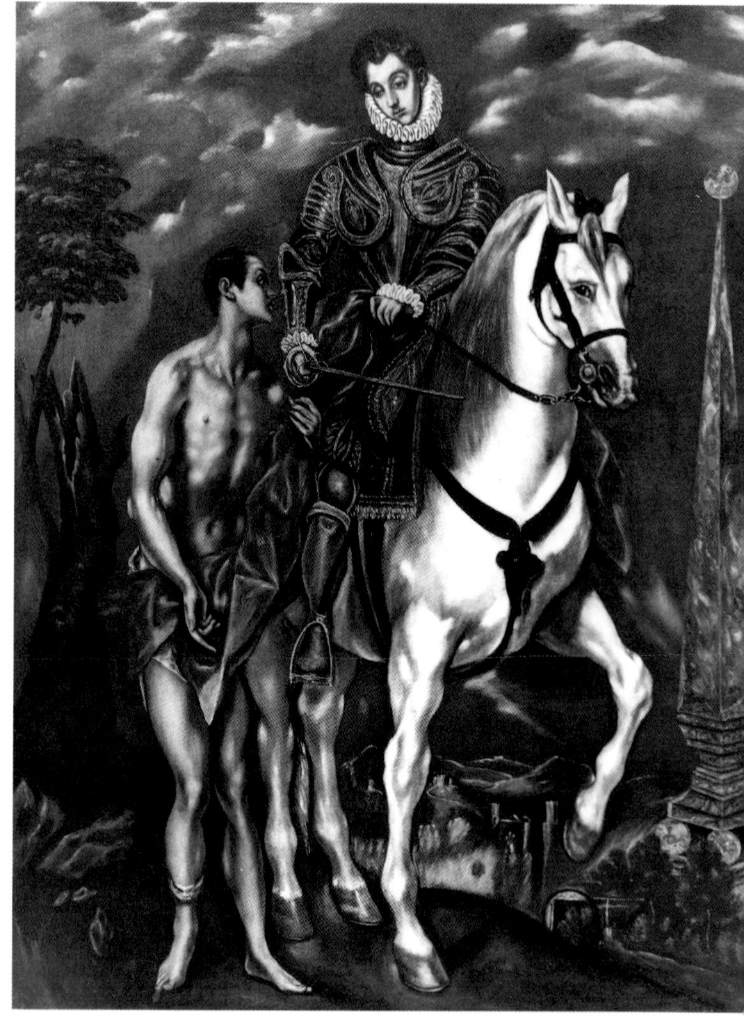

6. El Greco workshop (Jorge Manuel Theotocópuli), *Saint Martin and the Beggar*, 1615–1620, oil on fabric
Contini-Bonacossi Collection, Florence

7. El Greco workshop (Jorge Manuel Theotocópuli), *Saint Martin Dividing His Cloak with the Beggar*, 1615/1620?, oil on fabric
John and Mable Ringling Museum of Art, Sarasota

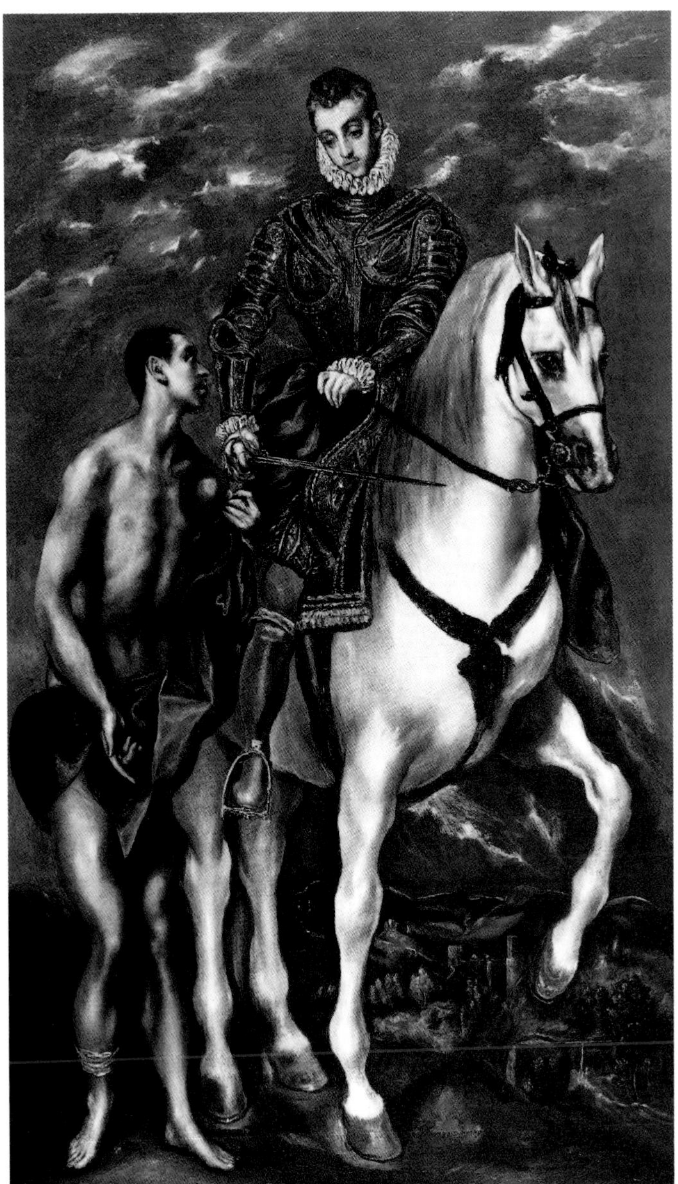

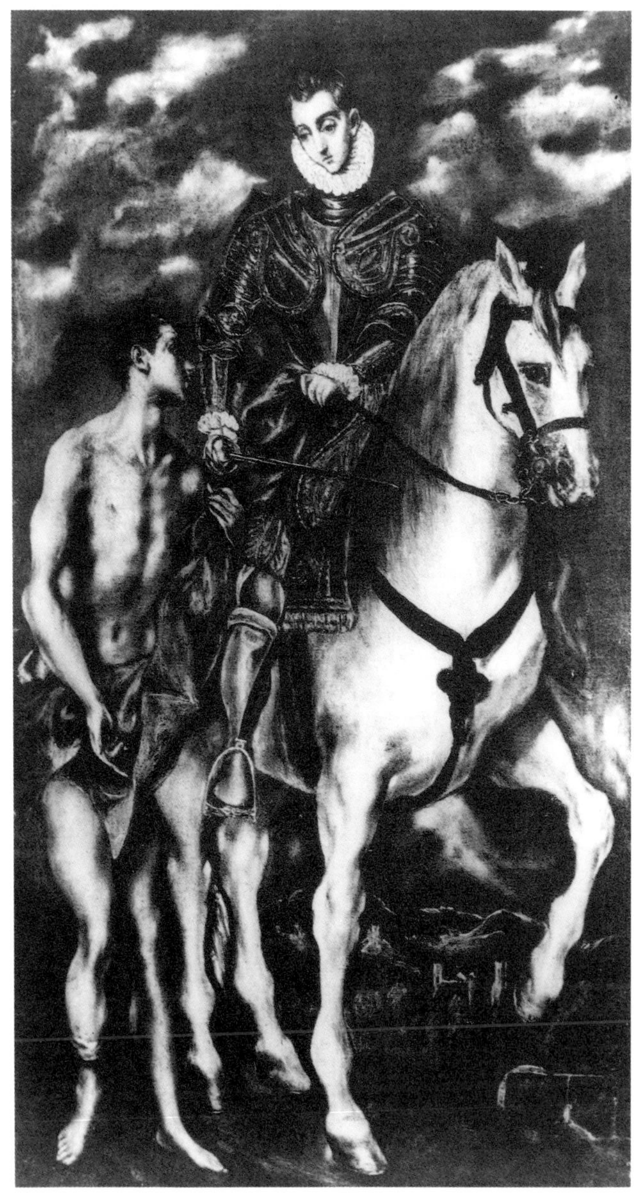

8. [Here attributed to workshop of] El Greco, *Saint Martin and the Beggar*, 1600/1605?, oil on fabric
Art Institute of Chicago, Gift of Mr. and Mrs. Chauncey McCormick

9. El Greco workshop, *Saint Martin and the Beggar*, 1610/1614?, oil on fabric, present location unknown, formerly in the Royal Palace, Bucharest
Photograph Ampliaciones MAS

trast between the black drawing and the red *imprimatura.*[11]

Among El Greco's contemporaries, Tintoretto and other Venetian artists are known to have sketched compositions with a brush and black and/or white paint onto a dark-colored *imprimatura.*[12] Both El Greco and Tintoretto are also reported to have used clay models to establish the figurative elements,[13] strengthening the suggestion of a close link between the two painters. Tintoretto and El Greco were associated with the circle around Titian, and El Greco's technique of painting should be studied with his contemporaries in mind.

As a great number of compositional changes can be observed in all the larger-scale paintings by El Greco owned by the National Gallery of Art, it seems that the artist did not work out all compositions on paper or in preparatory oil sketches. These findings correspond with unpublished studies carried out during the past few years on paintings by El Greco owned by the Prado Museum, Madrid, by Maria del Carmen Garrido, head of the museum's technical department.

Valuable insight into an artist's working technique can also be gained through close examination of the support and the paint films themselves. Such studies are especially useful for comparing two paintings by the same artist. For this study we analyzed the support (fabric fiber, fabric weave, stretcher), the composition of the ground layers and paint films (pigments, media, sequence of layers), the painting techniques, and the signatures as revealed through x-radiography and stereo-microscopical examination. The results are reported below.

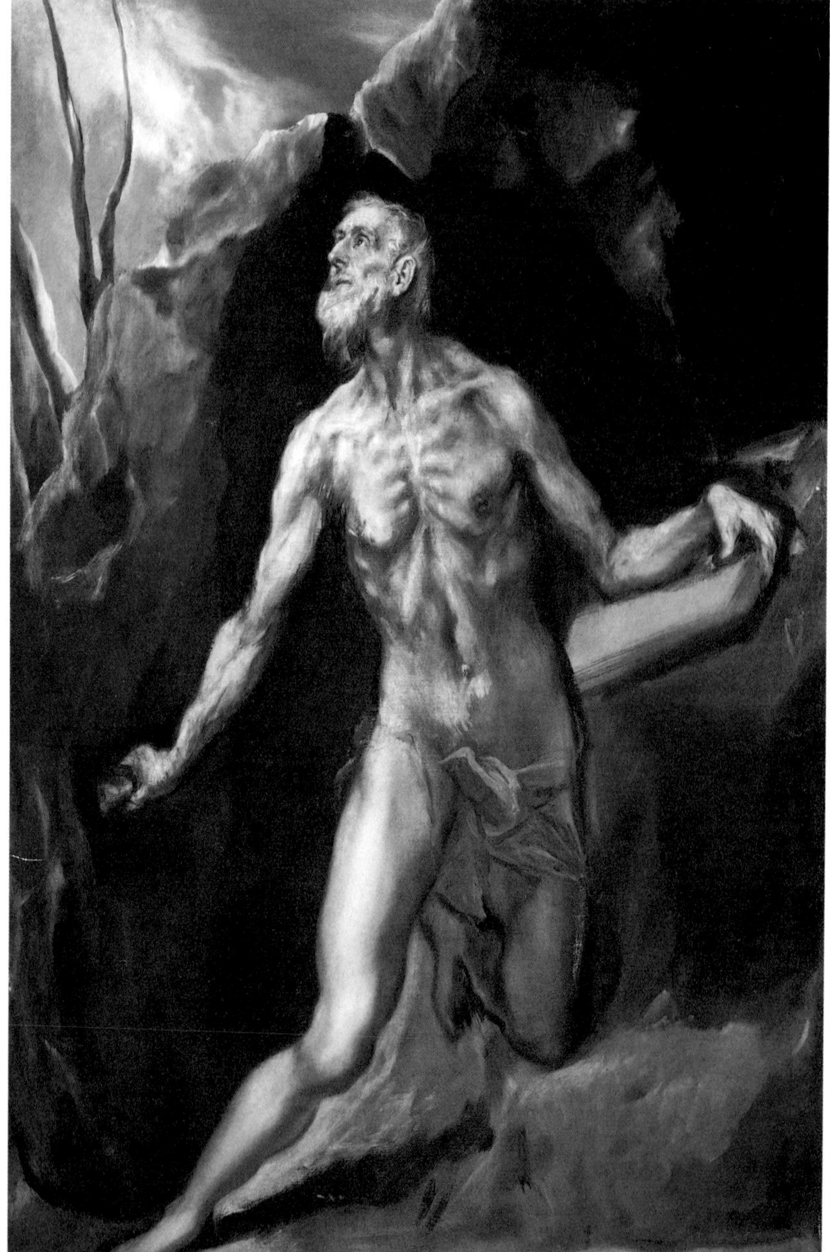

10. El Greco, *Saint Jerome*, 1610/1614?, oil on fabric
National Gallery of Art, Washington, Chester Dale Collection

SUPPORT

Primary Support

The fabric support of El Greco's *Saint Martin and the Beggar*, both altarpiece and smaller version, were analyzed, as well as his altarpiece, *Madonna and Child with Saint Martina and Saint Agnes.*

Both altarpieces are painted on fabrics with an unusual compound twill weave in irregular diamond-shaped pattern. The texture of the fabric, which is cut from one piece, is clearly visible on the surface of each painting (fig. 11). The tacking edges of both paintings have been removed and the reverse of the supports lined to secondary fabrics so that the fabric weave can only be studied as it is reflected in the x-radiographic image and in the configuration of the painted surface. No complete diagram of the weave could be reconstructed, but in a study on the treatment and reinstallation of El Greco's *Burial of the*

11. Detail, fig. 5, showing painted surface with canvas pattern

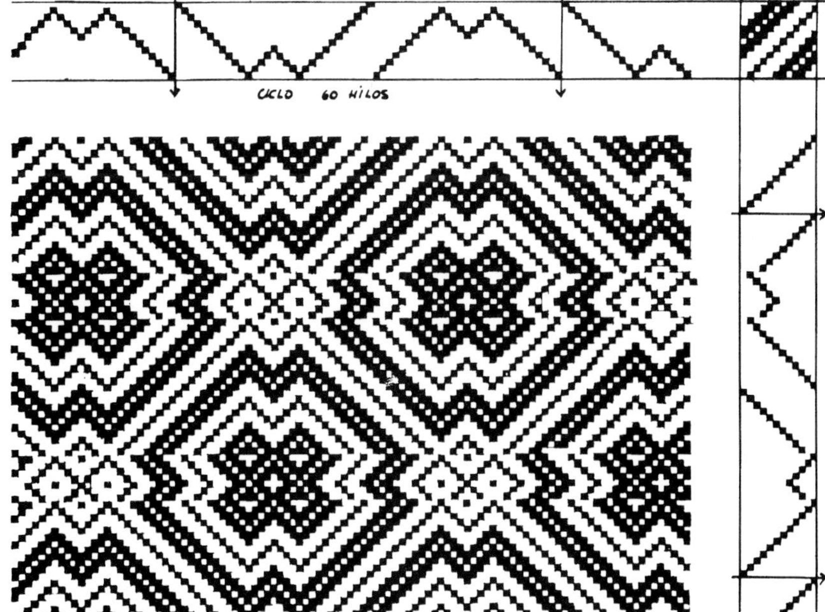

12. Diagram of weave of canvas, El Greco, *Burial of the Conde de Orgaz*, 1586–1588, Santo Tomé, Toledo
From María Socorro de los Ríos y Rojas, "Análisis del tejido de dos muestras procedentes de la tela y el forro del cuadro del Greco *Entierro del Conde de Orgaz* conservado en la Iglesia de Santo Tomé de Toledo," in *Informes y trabajos del Instituto de Restauración de Obras de Arte* 13 (Madrid, 1977), 93

Conde de Orgaz (Santo Tomé, Toledo), the Instituto de Restauración de Obras de Arte, Madrid, has recorded the weave for the fabric of that painting (fig. 12), which is very similar to, if not the same as, the weave used for the two fabrics under discussion.[14]

El Greco painted a great number of his larger altarpieces on the same or very similar types of fabrics,[15] known in Spain as *Mantelillo veneziano* and *Rosetta de Barga.* Other artists did not generally use this type of fabric, although Titian's *Vendramin Family* (National Gallery, London) is painted on a strikingly similar fabric.[16] The name, *Mantelillo veneziano,* may refer to the Venetian origin of the fabric.

Identification of a fiber from the fabric of the altarpiece of *Saint Martin and the Beggar* using polarized light microscopy has established it as linen. The fiber's positive sign of elongation and the presence of nodes and cross markers, as well as its high birefringence, indicate that it is made from flax fibers.[17] Fabrics used for painting were most commonly made of linen in the sixteenth and seventeenth centuries.

The smaller version of *Saint Martin and the Beggar* is painted on a fine, plain-weave fabric cut from one piece. The painting's original tacking edges are extant but presently flattened out and incorporated in the enlargement of all four sides. Fiber analysis was not carried out as no sample could be extracted. Most of the smaller paintings by El Greco and copies done by his workshop are painted on fine-to-medium weight, plain-weave fabric.

El Greco usually used fabric rather than wood as a primary support for his paintings.[18] Having apprenticed in Venice for ten years,[19] he was undoubtedly familiar with the advantages of fabric over the traditional wooden support. Contemporaneous treatises and letters testify to the changing usage of support materials. Venetian artists in particular changed from panel to fabric early in the sixteenth century.[20]

El Greco's use of coarse, open-weave, or twill-weave fabrics also has much in common with the Venetians. Such fabrics were regularly used for painting supports by Tintoretto, Veronese, Titian, and other Venetian artists who exploited the textural fabric varieties to a greater degree than any other school, and scholars have suggested that these heavily patterned fabrics were chosen by artists for their textural quality and the effect they created on the surface of paintings.[21] Undoubtedly practical reasons, such as availability or strength of fabric, were also factors influencing their selection. Neither Giorgio Vasari in Italy, however, nor any of the seventeenth-century Spanish treatises on painting give advice on the choice of fabric types, and no surviving letters, contracts, or other records testify to the motivations of the artists. Some later Spanish artists, such as Diego Velázquez, continued to be interested in the textural variety of their supports, whereas others did not.[22]

Secondary Support

In 1942 conservators at M. Knoedler and Company in New York lined the two altarpieces from San José. According to the conservation report, the two paintings were stretched over a "heavy frame with a solid backing" when they arrived at the studio. This construction was undoubtedly original, as El Greco used the same type of support for the altarpieces of Santo Domingo el Antiguo. Of the nine paintings that adorned the original altar at the church, *Saint John the Evangelist, Saint John the Baptist,* and *Resurrection of Christ* are still in situ. Each is mounted on a strainer and pine panels. The fabric is glued only to the sides and face of the strainer; the remainder rests against the pine backing.[23]

A logical improvement over a simple strainer, this kind of support served not only as a moisture barrier but also prevented damage from impact on the back. Although this hybrid between a solid panel support and a fabric support was quite common during the sixteenth and seventeenth centuries,[24] it was gradually replaced by mortise and tenon stretchers of today and is now rarely encountered.

No records have survived testifying to the type of original secondary support of the smaller version of *Saint Martin and the Beggar.* At present, the painting is mounted on a recent mortise and tenon stretcher.

GROUND AND PAINT LAYERS

Ground

A thin-to-moderately thick white ground was found on the two paintings under examination as well as on *Madonna and Child with Saint Martina and Saint Agnes* and *Saint Ildefonso.* X-ray diffraction powder analysis and microscopy on the grounds of the two versions of *Saint Martin and the Beggar* indicated that both consist of a mixture of gypsum (calcium sulfate in the unburnt, dihydrate form, $CaSO_4.2H_2O$) and lead white ($2PbCO_3.Pb(OH)_2$), with calcium sulfate predominating. The use of this type of gypsum for the preparation layer was a standard practice in Venice, although calcium sulfate in both the anhydrite and dihydrite form was more common in other areas of Italy.[25] To date, no comprehensive research on Spanish grounds has been carried out.[26]

A sample of the ground revealed the medium to be glue based, as suggested by its sensitivity to water. As a confirmation, the ground of one cross section, taken from the smaller version of *Saint Martin and the Beg-*

gar, was stained using amido black 3. The result indicated a proteinaceous medium. All samples of the ground exhibited a yellow-to-brown color when observed under the polarized light microscope. Cross sections of grounds that are bound with glue often look brown when viewed with transmitted light, as old glue is quite yellow. The ground applied to the panel support of El Greco's *Espolio*, however, has been found to be still in a pure white condition, suggesting that perhaps a staining by absorption of layers lying below the ground could also be responsible for the yellow-to-brown color.[27] No difference could be determined in terms of composition, thickness, or application of the respective grounds of the two versions of *Saint Martin and the Beggar.*

When artists changed from wood to fabric supports, they no longer needed a thick and smooth white ground. Thinner preparations could be used, and later more flexible materials became popular so that the canvas could be rolled up and transported.[28] El Greco prepared most of his canvases with both a white ground and an oil-based, relatively thick red *imprimatura* over it. Some of his early works painted on the traditional wooden support were prepared with a white ground alone.

Imprimatura

Analysis of the *imprimaturas* of the two versions of *Saint Martin and the Beggar*, *Madonna and Child with Saint Martina and Saint Agnes*, and *Saint Ildefonso* revealed that all were composed of the same pigments—iron oxides, red lake, carbon black(s), and lead white—in varying quantities that produced corresponding differences in tonality. These variations suggest that the paint for the *imprimatura* was individually prepared from the same general formula.[29] A single layer of *imprimatura* on the larger version of *Saint Martin and the Beggar* was detected by means of a scanning electron microscopy (SEM) micrograph (see detail of cross section G).

The *imprimatura* is always applied with a brush to achieve an even and smooth appearance. Frequently, however, a thinning out of the ground and the *imprimatura* can be observed toward the edges of the painting. The two altarpieces from San José, but not the smaller version of *Saint Martin and the Beggar*, show a thinner application of the preparation layers along all four edges compared to the central field of the fabric, perhaps reflecting an effort to economize on materials.

Pigments

Analysis of pigments helps to evaluate the time frame in which a painting was painted. For the purpose of comparing two paintings, an analysis of the palette can establish incongruities and advance an understanding of the artist's technique.

For the two versions of *Saint Martin and the Beggar* it was not possible to sample the paint film in exactly the same locations. X-ray fluorescence spectroscopy (XRF) and polarized light microscopy show, however, that the palette used for both versions is virtually the same.[30] One minor exception is the use of red lead for a highlight on the stirrup of the smaller version; the presence of red lead was not confirmed in the larger version. These findings and other pigment studies of paintings by El Greco suggest his palette was fairly consistent and quite restrained.[31]

METHODS OF PAINTING: A COMPARISON

A comparison of the x-radiograph mosaic of the two paintings of *Saint Martin and the Beggar* strongly suggests their different intents and premises. Direct comparison is facilitated by the similarity of palette. Lead white and lead-tin yellow are the two most highly x-ray absorptive pigments within these paint films. They appear white or gray of different gradations on the x-radiograph and create clear images of the horse, Saint Martin, and the green cloak. The beggar and the landscape are painted with a lesser amount of x-ray opaque pigment, exhibiting an image that is not of very high contrast.

Most striking on first sight is the forceful modeling of the horse of the larger version. Closer examination of the chest of the horse reveals that during the early process of painting, the neck strap with martingale was originally placed slightly higher than its final position (figs. 13–14). This change was made when the white paint was still wet, as some

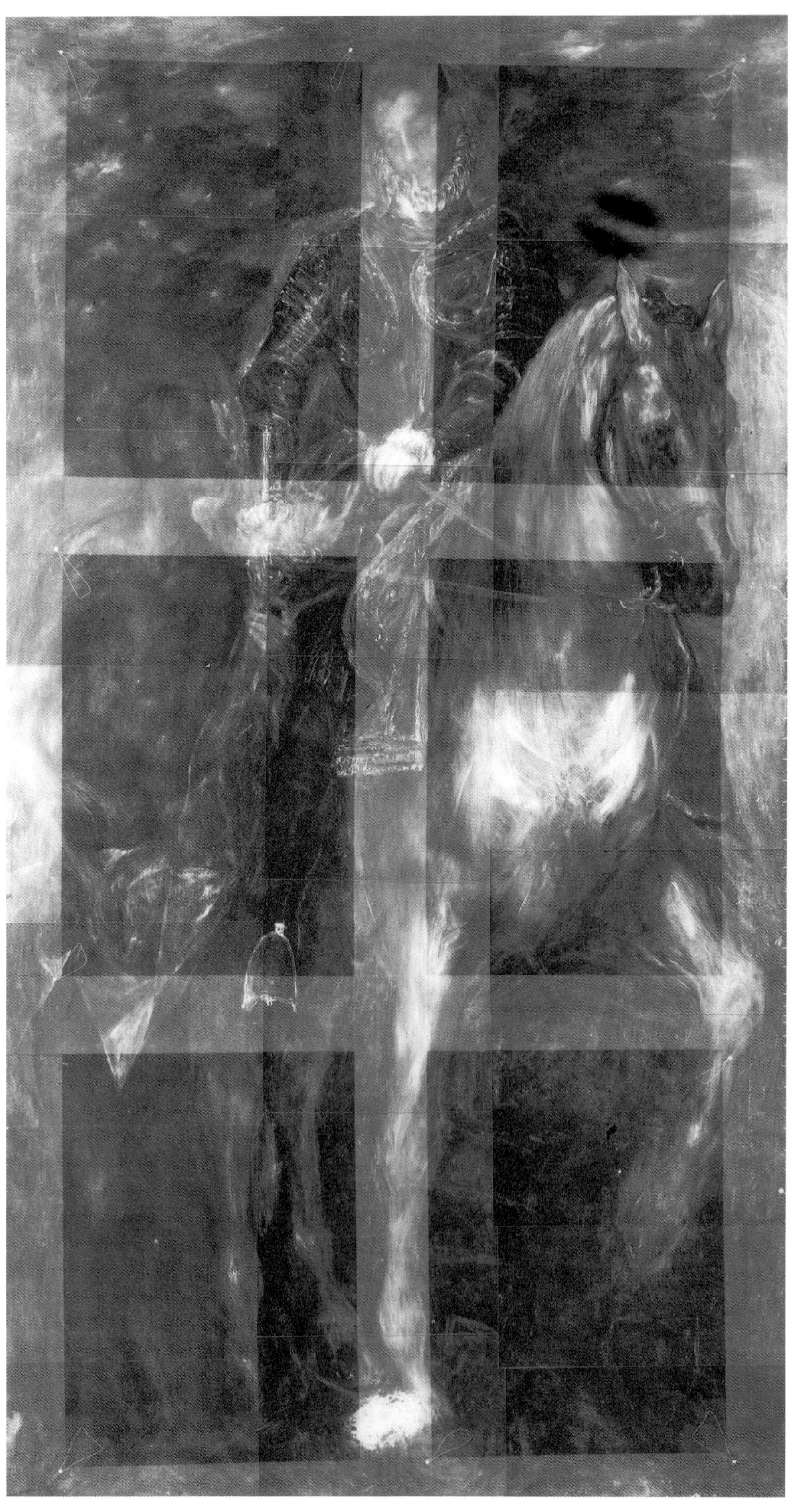

13. X-ray mosaic, fig. 1 (40kW, 50mA, 3s)

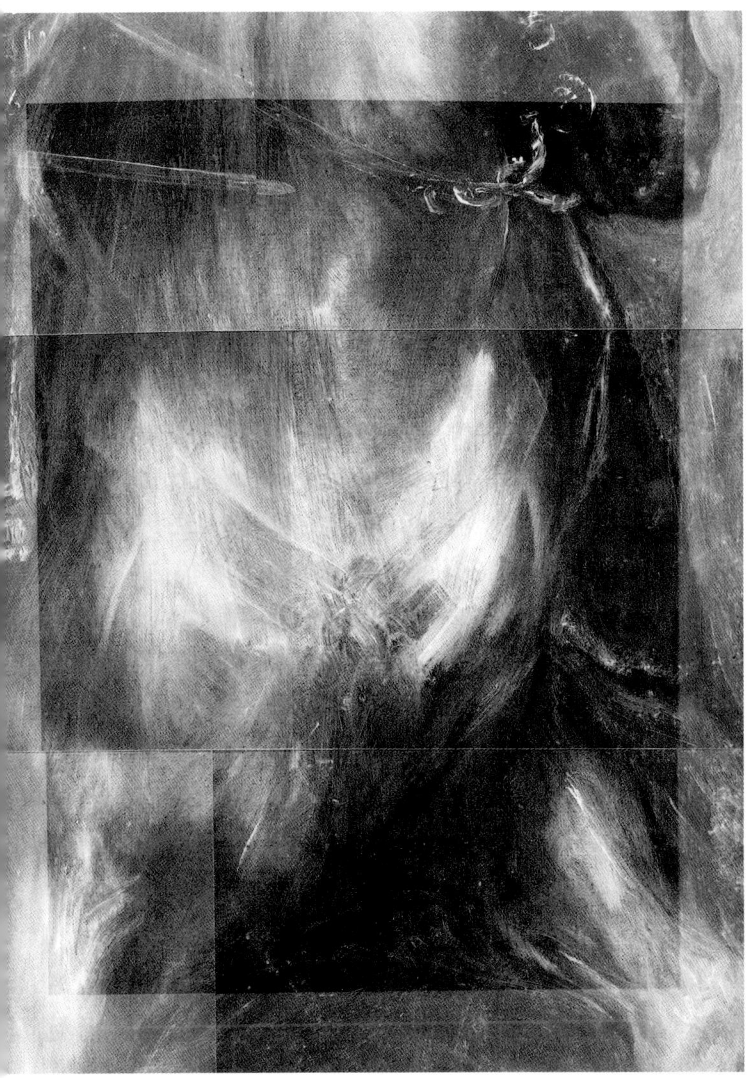

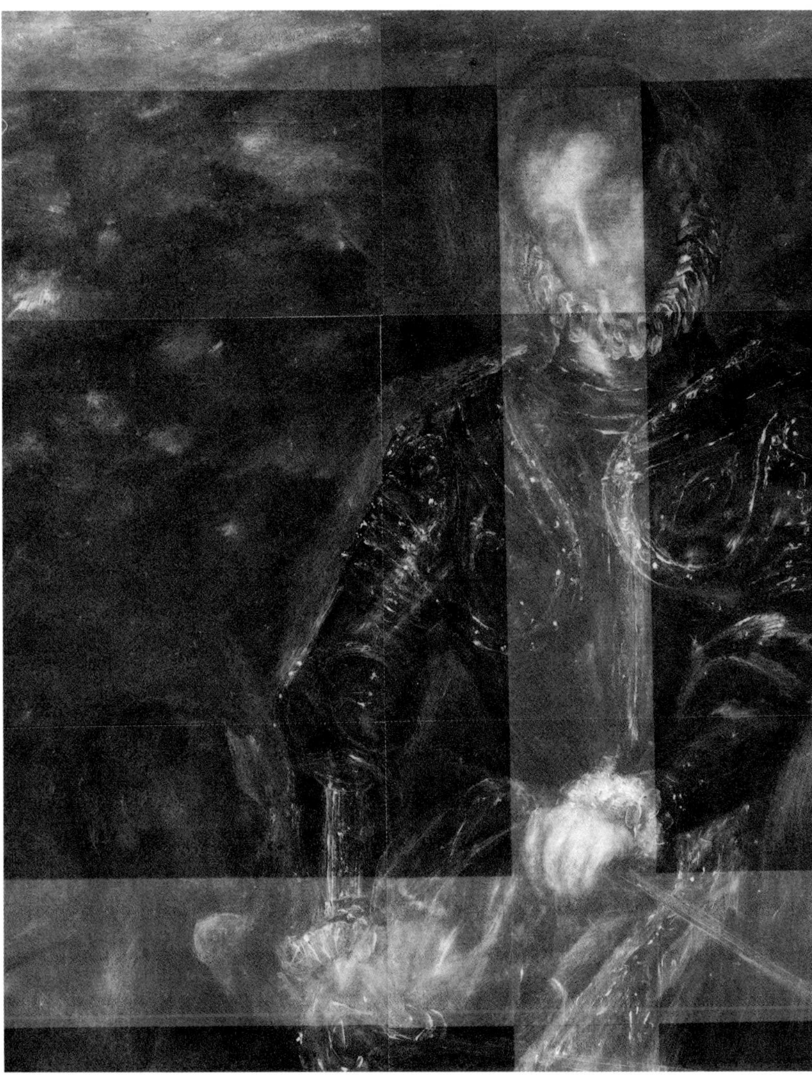

14. Detail, fig. 13

15. Detail, fig. 13

lead white from the chest was carried up by the brush to the point where the neck strap disappears underneath the saddlecloth. The painting of the neck strap in its final position was carried out soon thereafter, as the wet lead white was pushed aside, forming a ridge, when the brush carrying the black paint passed over.

Another change in the larger version is strongly suggested by a heavy buildup of a very dense material, probably lead white, along the outline of Saint Martin's right shoulder (fig. 15). The x-radiograph also reveals that the raised position of Saint Martin's left-hand index finger was painted after having been initially sketched in a lower position. In contrast, changes or adjustments, often an integral part of the creative painting process, are completely absent from the x-radiograph mosaic of the smaller version (fig. 16). In fact, the artist who carried out the smaller version repeated the final position of the horse's saddle gear shown in the larger version, first sketching in the neck strap with martingale, the rein, and the sword directly on the red *imprimatura* and continuing with the white and gray modulations of the horse. It can be assumed that the artist had the large altarpiece or a similar version in front of him as a model for this painting.

The painting process for the two versions

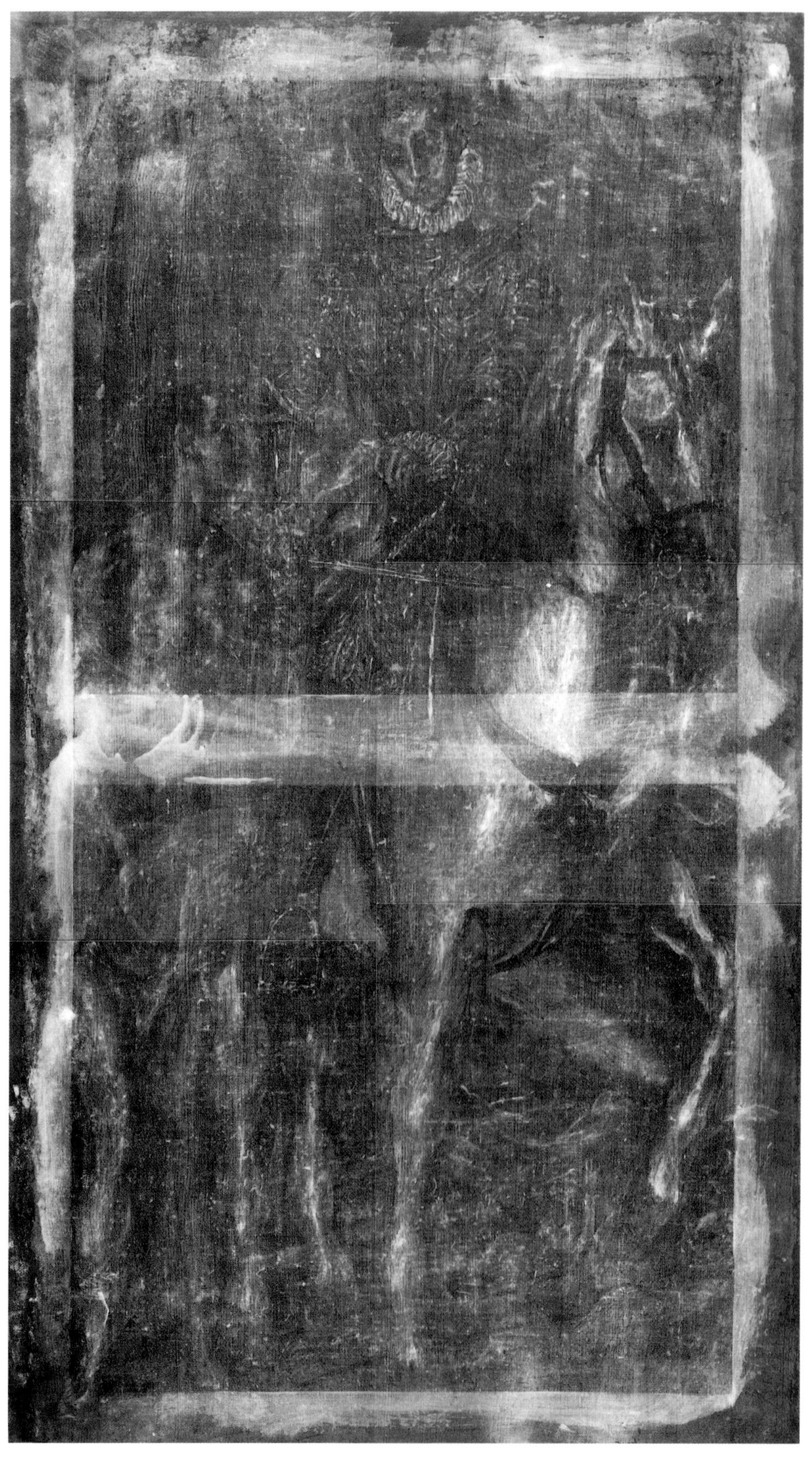

16. X-ray mosaic, fig. 2 (35kV, 50mA, 3s)

17. Photomicrograph, fig. 2, showing remnants of the signature

of *Saint Martin and the Beggar* can also be studied by comparing cross sections (see app.). Cross section E was taken next to a loss on the larger version of *Saint Martin and the Beggar,* from the connecting metal piece of the rein and the bit under the horse's lower jaw. This element of the horse's bridle overlies the green cloth and the blue sky behind it. The cross section includes nine, perhaps ten layers, suggesting that the artist first outlined a figurative element such as the horse or the horse's bridle with gray paint over the red *imprimatura* and then sketched in the sky. On top of that layer followed the painting of the green cloth and the two layers defining this specific part of the horse's bridle. In contrast, cross section F, taken from the same area on the smaller version, reveals just two layers—a white layer and a gray layer—lying on top of the *imprimatura.* These two layers mimic the surface of the same area of the larger version without having gone through the compositional painting process. The cross sections taken from the larger version of *Saint Martin and the Beggar* were generally composed with a more complex layering. Black or gray layers on top of the red *imprimatura,* or close to that layer, suggest preliminary sketching with gray or black paint in several places (cross sections A, E, and G). In contrast, the cross sections taken from the smaller version have a simple layering of colors applied to achieve the same results shown on the surface of the larger version.

SIGNATURE

The remnants of the signature of the smaller version of *Saint Martin and the Beggar* are too few to suggest conclusions (fig. 17). The individual letters are placed at the bottom edge of the left-hand corner and are very small. A signature with exceptionally small letters is characteristic of El Greco's works of the last decade of the sixteenth century, the decade during which the San José altarpiece was painted. However, El Greco's signatures varied in style and location on a painting throughout his life. *Saint Joseph and the Infant Christ,* the painting that still adorns the main altar of the Chapel of San José, carries a signature with the same small letters. Some paintings attributed to El Greco's workshop also have this miniature type of signature. The altarpiece of *Saint Martin and the Beggar* carries a larger signature in cursive Greek letters. The painting created for the other side of the side altar of San José, *Madonna and Child with Saint Martina and Saint Agnes,* shows the artist's initials.

AUTHORSHIP

Technical evidence has established the chronological relationship of the altarpiece and the smaller version of *Saint Martin and the Beggar* in the collection of the National Gallery of Art. Technical evidence does not provide us with an answer regarding authorship of the smaller version, however. Factors such as workshop practices of the time[32] and the relationship of other small versions of other subjects with their respective larger altarpieces need to be considered and compared. Consideration here of *Saint Ildefonso* (see fig. 3) is fruitful. This *Saint Ildefonso* was also painted as either a *modello* or a *ricordo* of the larger altarpiece (see fig. 4). X-radiographs of the smaller version do not reveal any changes of composition, suggesting that the painting, like the smaller version of *Saint Martin and the Beggar*, is a *ricordo*. But the two *ricordo* paintings are very different in execution. The small version of *Saint Martin and the Beggar* has a tightness and lack of energy that are in sharp contrast to the painterly freedom and sophistication of *Saint Ildefonso*. The "dressing-out" of the artist's brush, for example, often seen on authenticated paintings by El Greco, is visible along both vertical edges of *Saint Ildefonso* but not on the smaller version of *Saint Martin and the Beggar*. This discrepancy in execution suggests that the two paintings are by different hands. However, it is reasonable to assume that El Greco, like other artists such as Titian, touched up *ricordo* paintings copied by his workshop. The extent of these touch-ups would likely have varied according to the purpose of the *ricordo* painting and the degree of success in execution by the workshop. As the smaller version of *Saint Martin and the Beggar* in the collection of the National Gallery of Art, even though tight in execution, is the most successful version of the smaller *ricordo* paintings of this theme, El Greco may well have participated in the final stages of painting.

CONCLUSION

Evidence resulting from this study at the National Gallery of Art establishes that the smaller version of *Saint Martin and the Beggar* is a copy of an already existing image. The x-radiograph of the larger version reveals the dynamic force with which this painting was created, an energy also translated onto the surface of the painting. The smaller version lacks that energy. The difference is confirmed by the technical analysis. The changes made during the execution of the larger altarpiece and the lack of such changes in the smaller version demonstrate that the smaller version was not created as a *modello* for the altarpiece but is instead a copy, or a *ricordo*, of the altarpiece. The much greater complexity of the paint layers of the altarpiece of *Saint Martin and the Beggar*, compared with a simple layering of colors of the smaller version, supports this conclusion. Indeed, it appears that none of the smaller versions still in existence was created as a *modello*, as the design of the larger altarpiece is closely repeated in each version. It is yet to be determined whether any preparatory works were created for this composition, as most of El Greco's works of art on paper have vanished.

NOTES

Pigment, medium, and fiber analyses were carried out by Barbara Berrie, then acting head of the scientific research department of the National Gallery of Art, Washington. The research was made possible by the support of the Mellon Foundation and the National Gallery of Art.

I wish to thank the members of the painting conservation department for their generous assistance and Ashok Roy, National Gallery, London, for helpful comments on the manuscript.

1. The larger format *Saint Martin and the Beggar* (National Gallery of Art, Washington, Widener Collection) is an altarpiece painted for the lateral altar (left side) of the Chapel of San José in Toledo. Inscribed at the lower right in Greek cursive letters:

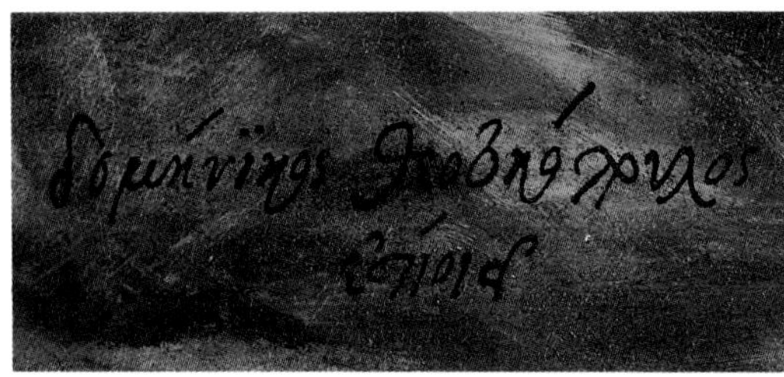

translated as "Doménikos Theotokópoulos made it." The original contract for the painting is not extant but is cited in a subsequent agreement for payment of 1599. It is generally assumed that it was painted between 1597 and 1599. Today's measurements: height 1.935 m, width 1.030 m.

The smaller format *Saint Martin and the Beggar* (National Gallery of Art, Washington, Andrew W. Mellon Collection) is one of four, possibly five, existing smaller versions of the same subject (see n. 4). Conservation treatment in 1987 uncovered remnants of a signature in Greek cursive letters in the lower left-hand corner (see fig. 17). Various dates have been assigned to the painting: 1600–1605 by Harold Edwin Wethey, *El Greco and His School*, 2 vols. (Princeton, 1962), 2:247; 1604–1614 by Manuel B. Cossío, *El Greco* (Barcelona, 1972), 386; 1604–1612 by August L. Mayer, *Dominico Theotocópuli El Greco* (Munich, 1926), 48. Today's measurements: height 1.043 m, width 0.603 m. Original measurements: height 0.995 m, width 0.550 m. The painting is hung with the nonoriginal areas covered by a period frame, thus permitting the viewer to see the painting with the original dimensions.

2. Wethey 1962, 2:247; Cossío 1972, 386; Mayer 1926, 48.

3. Wethey 1962, 2:11–13.

4. Wethey 1962, 2:246–248. The other three versions are in the Contini-Bonacossi Collection, Florence; John and Mable Ringling Museum of Art, Sarasota; and Art Institute of Chicago. The fifth version, location presently unknown, was formerly housed in the Royal Castle, Bucharest.

5. The inventory taken in 1614 after El Greco's death listed "un S. Martin" still in the possession of the artist. Many other paintings in the inventory appear to have been smaller versions of the artist's commissioned altarpieces (see n. 6). Francisco de Borja de San Román y Fernández, *El Greco en Toledo* (Madrid, 1910), 193. A second inventory taken in 1621, listing the possessions of El Greco's son, Jorge Manuel, included two paintings of *Saint Martin and the Beggar*. Francisco de Borja de San Román y Fernández, "De la vida de El Greco," *Archivo español de arte y arqueologia* 3 (1927), 301, 303.

6. Francesco Pacheco wrote in his treatise, *The Art of Painting* (1649), "In the year 1611, Domenico Greco showed me a cupboard of clay models by his hand which he used in his works; I also saw something else exceeding all admiration—the originals of all he had painted in his life, painted in oil on small canvases and kept in a room that he instructed his son to show me. What will the presumptuous and lazy say to this? How is it that they do not drop dead, hearing of such examples? Seeing such diligence among the giants, etc." *Artists' Techniques in Golden Age Spain: Six Treatises in Translation*, ed. and trans. Zahira Veliz (Cambridge, 1986), 40.

7. Hubertus Falkner von Sonnenburg, "Zur Maltechnik Grecos," *Münchner Jahrbuch* (Munich, 1958–1959), 243–255; von Sonnenburg and Frank Preusser, "El Grecos *Entkleidung Christi* (Espolio) in der Alten Pinakothek," *Maltechnik-Restauro* 82, no. 3 (July 1976), 142–156; Elisabeth C. G. Packard, "A Problem in Technical Research: The Walters *St. Francis*—A Contribution to El Greco Studies," *Journal of the Walters Art Gallery* 23 (1960), 49–71; Instituto de Restauración de obras de Arte, "El Entierro del *Conde de Orgaz*: Nueva Instalacion Estudio cientifico y tratamiento," in *Ministerio de Cultura, Direccion General del Patrimonio Artistico, Archivos y Museos* (Madrid, 1977); Maria del Carmen Garrido and José Maria Cabrera, "Estudio tecnico comparativo de dos Sagradas Familias del Greco," *Boletin del Museo del Prado* 3, no. 8 (May–August 1982), 93–101; Maria del Carmen Garrido, "Estudio tecnico de cuatro Anunciaciones de El Greco," *Boletin del Museo del Prado* 8, no. 23 (May–August 1987), 85–109; Ann Massing, "The Examination and Restoration of El Greco's *El Espolio*," in *The Bulletin of the Hamilton Kerr Institute: The First Ten Years* (Cambridge, 1988), 1:76–82.

8. San Román y Fernández 1910, 195.

9. This drawing is a preparatory drawing for the figure of Saint John the Evangelist in the altarpiece of Santo Domingo el Antiguo in Toledo. Diego Angulo and Alfonso E. Pérez Sánchez, *A Corpus of Spanish Drawings, 1400–1600* (London, 1975), 43–45, 159.

10. *El Espolio:* Massing 1988, 76–82; *Holy Family:* Maria del Carmen Garrido, "Un dessin sous-jacent du Greco comme critère d'attribution des dessins isolés du même auteur," in *Dessin sous-jacent et autres techniques graphiques*, ed. Roger van Schoute and Dominique Hollanders-Favart (Louvain-la-Neuve, 1985), 182–187; *Pièta:* unpublished infrared reflectograms at the Philadelphia Museum of Art, 1981.

11. Infrared reflectography of unfinished areas of El Greco's *Saint Jerome* (National Gallery of Art, Washington, Chester Dale Collection) confirmed this find-

ing, as early outlines of black paint, lying directly on the *imprimatura*, could be studied without overlying paint layers.

12. Hubertus Falkner von Sonnenburg, "Beobachtungen zur Arbeitsweise Tintorettos," *Maltechnik-Restauro* 3 (1974), 133–143; Joyce Plesters, "Tintoretto's Painting in the National Gallery of Art," *National Gallery Technical Bulletin* (London) 4 (1980), 32–49; Joyce Plesters and Lorenzo Lazzarini, "Preliminary Observations on the Technique and Materials of Tintoretto," in *Conservation of Pictorial Art*, ed. Norman Brommelle and Perry Smith (London, 1976), 7–26. Plesters and Lazzarini examined ten grounds of canvases by Tintoretto. Two canvases had dark brown grounds lying directly on the canvas, two canvases had a dark brown or blackish upper layer of ground lying on a thin white ground, and six canvases had only a thin white ground layer.

13. Von Sonnenburg 1974, 135; El Greco's use of clay and wax models was observed by Pacheco. Veliz 1986, 40. The inventory of 1614 lists twenty models in clay and wax. San Román y Fernández 1910, 195.

14. María Socorro Mantilla de los Ríos y de Rojas, "Análisis del tejido de dos muestras procedentes de la tela y el forro del cuadro del Greco *Entierro del Conde de Orgaz* conservado en la Iglesia de Santo Tomé de Toledo," in *Informes y trabajos del Instituto de Restauración de Obras de Arte* 13 (Madrid, 1977), 93.

15. Besides the published examples of this type or similar types of fabric (e.g., Garrido 1987, 106; Mantilla de los Ríos y de Rojas 1977, 91–98), many of El Greco's canvases evidence this characteristic texture. Among them are *Madonna of Charity, Nativity*, and *Coronation of the Virgin* (all Hospital of Charity, Illescas), *San Bernardino di Siena* (Casa del Greco, Toledo), and *Espolio* (Cathedral, Toledo).

16. Based on photographic records provided by the conservation staff of the National Gallery, London.

17. Martha Goodway, "Fiber Identification in Practice," *Journal of the American Institute for Conservation* 26, no. 1 (1987), 27–44.

18. Of El Greco's generally accepted body of works (Wethey 1962), only eleven paintings are on wood. After the late 1570s he no longer used wooden supports at all. All of the wooden supports he used are small, ranging from .17 x .24 m to .66 x .84 m.

19. It is generally accepted that El Greco spent ten years in Venice, from about 1559/1560 to 1570; then he traveled to Rome. A letter from Giulio Clovio has survived, introducing "un giovane Candiotto" (from the city of Candia, Crete), "discepolo di Titiano" to S. Cardinale Farnese. Wethey 1962, 1:3–19; José Camón Aznar, *Dominico Greco*, 2 vols. (Madrid, 1950), 1:95; Ellis K. Waterhouse, "El Greco's Italian Period," *Art Studies* 8 (1930), 61–88.

20. According to Giorgio Vasari, painting on fabric was already common practice in Venice in the fifteenth century. He wrote in his biography on Jacopo Bellini:

All those and many others were painted by Jacopo [Bellini] with the aid of his sons, and the last scene was done on canvas, as has nearly always been the custom in Venice, where they very rarely make use, as they do elsewhere, of panels of wood made from the tree known to many people as poplar and to some as silver poplar. . . . But in Venice they do not make panels, and when they occasionally do so they use only wood from the fir, of which that city has an abundance, because of that river Adige which brings a great quantity of it from German soil. . . . So then it is much the custom in Venice to paint on canvas, either because it does not split or become worm-eaten, or because they can make pictures whatever size they wish, or again for the convenience, as said elsewhere, of being able to send paintings where ever they want, with little bother or expense.

Lives of the Artists (1568), trans. George Bull, 2 vols. (London, 1987), 2:59. The reasons for choosing fabric rather than panel seem to have been very much the same for the Paduan artist Andrea Mantegna. In 1477 he wrote to his patron, the marquis of Mantua:

I do not understand since your excellency wants them so quickly in what manner they are to be done. In a drawing only or in color. On a panel or on canvas and what size. If your lordship wants to ship them far away they should be done on thin canvas so they can be wrapped around a little pole.

Italian Art, 1400–1500: Sources and Documents, comp. and trans. Creighton E. Gilbert (Englewood Cliffs, N.J., 1980), 12. Also in Spain, Pacheco, father-in-law of Diego Rodriguez de Silva Velázquez, advocated the use of canvas for primary supports. He wrote in 1638: "The invention of oil painting was very useful because of the risk of panels splitting, and because of the light weight of canvas and the convenience of being able to carry a painting to distant places." *Art of Painting*, Veliz 1986, 68.

21. Garrido 1987, 100; Madeleine Hours-Miédan, *A la découverte de la peinture par les méthodes physique* (Paris, 1957), 23.

22. Hubertus Falkner von Sonnenburg, "Zur Maltechnik Murillos," *Maltechnik-Restauro* 88, no. 3 (July 1980), 60.

23. Zahira Veliz, "Three Unlined Paintings by El Greco," paper presented at the American Institute for Conservation, Vancouver, 20–24 May 1987, excerpt in *AIC Preprints*, 15th Annual Meeting (Washington, 1987), 215–216.

24. According to Pacheco (Veliz 1986, 68), it was common practice in Spain to protect large canvases from humidity by stretching and nailing them over thick panels, "where they last many years."

25. Rutherford J. Gettens and M. E. Mrose, "Calcium Sulphate Minerals in the Grounds of Italian Paintings," *Studies in Conservation* 1, no. 4 (1954), 182–183. Recent x-ray diffraction powder analysis of white grounds carried out at the National Gallery, London, has confirmed these results.

26. F. Ewald-Schuebeck has studied the varying luminosities created by combinations of white ground layer with transparent and opaque *imprimaturas*. "Estudios sobre la Tecnica de los Pintores Espanoles y especialmente sobre los cuadros de Murillo," *Archivo Espanol de Arte* 149 (1965), 43–57.

27. Massing 1988, 1:80.

28. Giorgio Vasari wrote:

Unless these canvases intended for oil painting are to remain stationary, they are not covered by gesso which would interfere with the flexibility, seeing that the gesso would crack if they would roll up. A paste however is made of flour and walnut oil with two or three macinate *of white lead put into it, and after the canvas has been covered from one side to the other with three or four coats of smooth size, this paste is spread on by means of a knife, and all the holes come to be filled up by the hand of the artist. That done, he gives it one or two more coats of size and then the composition or priming.*

Vasari on Technique, trans. Louisa S. Maclehose, ed. G. Baldwin Brown (New York, 1960), 236.

29. Analytical reports are on file in the scientific research and painting conservation departments of the National Gallery of Art, Washington.

30. Lead white, carbon black pigments (type was not identified), azurite, iron oxide(s), red lake, copper resinate or verdigris, and lead-tin yellow. Red lead was used for a highlight of the stirrup of the smaller version.

31. Garrido and Cabrera 1982; Garrido 1987.

32. El Greco is known to have had assistants while working in Toledo: Francisco Preboste, an Italian by birth, followed El Greco to Spain; Jorge Manuel, El Greco's son; and Luis Tristán, El Greco's pupil and assistant during the first decade of the sixteenth century. No documents relating the workshop practices have come down to us, however. San Román y Fernández 1910, 142, 155–156, 160; San Román y Fernández 1927, 161–164, 276–277.

Cross sections A–H

Photomicrographs were taken of paint cross sections of paintings by El Greco in the National Gallery of Art, Washington. All samples were prepared and photographed by Barbara Berrie, then acting head of the scientific research department, National Gallery of Art. The cross sections were photographed by reflected light at 220 × magnification.

*The white ground layers of the photographic reproductions of cross sections A-H exhibit differences in transparency and color. This is due solely to the photographic process and not to differences of composition of the ground.

**Examination of the green layers in plain and in polarized transmitted light revealed the presence of birefringent particles of verdigris mixed in an isotropic green medium, suggesting verdigris and copper resinate. The birefringent particles could be unreacted verdigris in the oleo-resinous medium.

***The type of black pigment has not been identified.

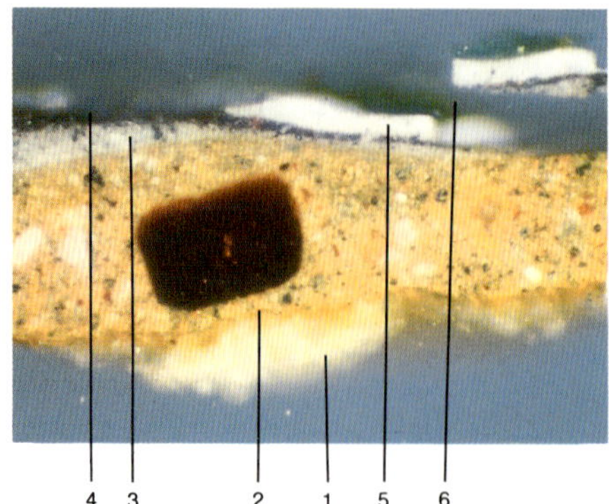

Cross section A: *Saint Martin and the Beggar* (altarpiece), green drapery next to the horse's abdomen

1. *White ground (trace)
2. *Imprimatura:* iron oxides, lead white, ***carbon black(s), red lake
3. Light gray layer: lead white, carbon black(s)
4. Pinkish dark gray layer: carbon black(s), some lead white, red lake
5. White layer: lead white, some carbon black(s)
6. **Green layer; verdigris and/or copper resinate, some lead-tin yellow

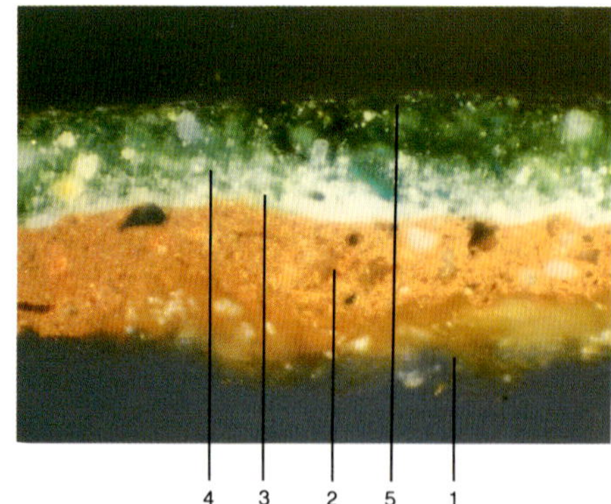

Cross section B: *Saint Martin and the Beggar* (smaller version), green drapery next to the horse's abdomen

1. *White ground (trace): browned with glue?
2. *Imprimatura:* iron oxides, lead white, ***carbon black(s), red lake
3. White layer: lead white
4. **Green layer: verdigris and/or copper resinate, lead white, some lead-tin yellow

   (3 and 4 are painted wet in wet)
5. Dark green layer; verdigris and/or copper resinate, traces of lead-tin yellow

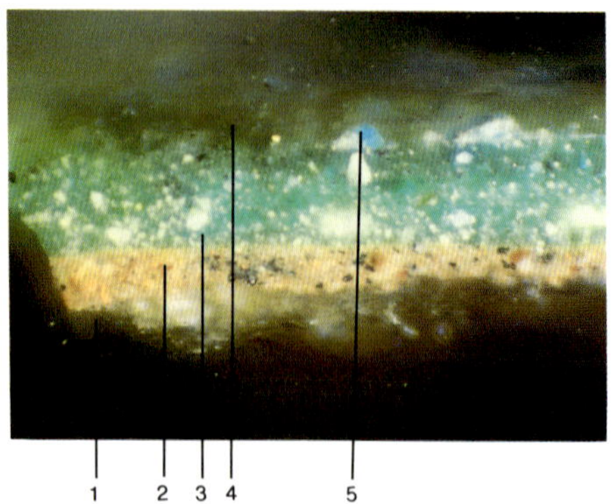

Cross section C: *Saint Martin and the Beggar* (altarpiece), mottled green landscape

1. *White ground (trace): browned with glue?
2. *Imprimatura:* iron oxides, lead white, ***carbon black(s), red lake
3. **Green layer: verdigris and/or copper resinate, lead white, some lead-tin yellow
4. Dark green layer: verdigris and/or copper resinate, some lead white, some carbon black(s)
5. Light blue "swirl": azurite, lead white

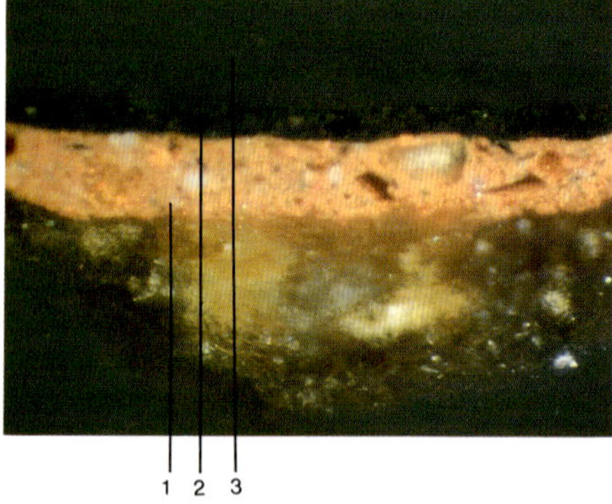

Cross section D: *Saint Martin and the Beggar* (smaller version), brown foreground

1. *White ground: browned with glue?
2. *Imprimatura:* iron oxides, lead white, ***carbon black(s), red lake
3. Dark brown layer: carbon black(s), umber

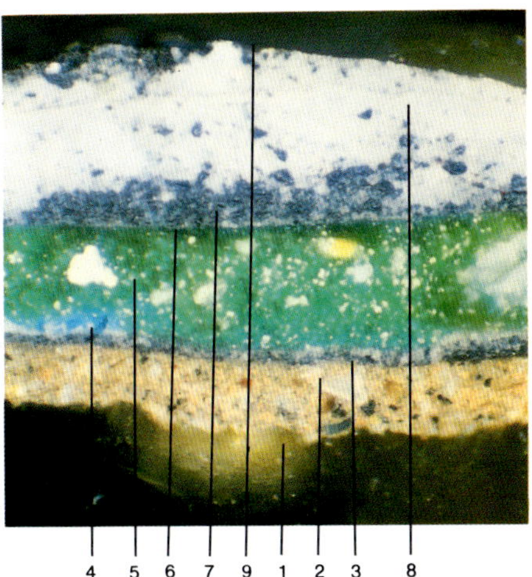

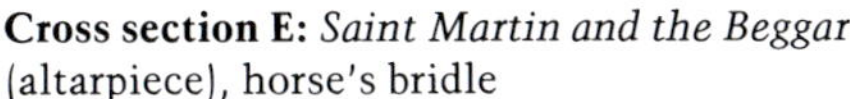

Cross section E: *Saint Martin and the Beggar* (altarpiece), horse's bridle
1. *White ground (trace): browned with glue?
2. *Imprimatura:* iron oxides, lead white, ***carbon black(s), red lake
3. Dark gray layer: carbon black(s), lead white
4. Light blue layer: azurite, lead white
5. **Green layer: verdigris and/or copper resinate, lead white, lead-tin yellow, and an iron oxide particle
6. Dark green layer: verdigris and/or copper resinate
7. Disrupted black layer: carbon black(s)
8. White layer: lead white, carbon black(s), and a particle of azurite
9. White layer: lead white, carbon black(s)
10. Gray layer: carbon black(s), lead white

9 and 10 may be one layer

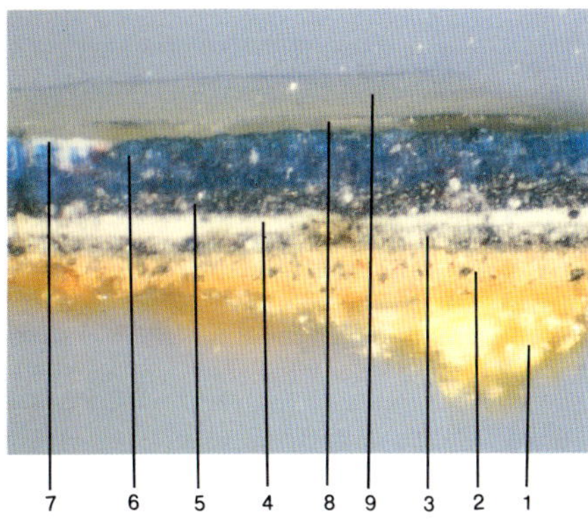

Cross section G: *Saint Martin and the Beggar* (altarpiece), blue saddle cloth
1. *White ground (trace): browned with glue?
2. *Imprimatura:* iron oxides, lead white, ***carbon black(s), red lake
3. Gray layer: lead white, carbon black(s)
4. White layer: lead white with just a few carbon black particles
5. Dark, pinkish gray layer: carbon black(s), lead white, red lake
6. Purplish blue layer: azurite, lead white, red lake
7. White/blue layer: lead white, azurite

8 and 9. Discolored varnish layers (absent from cross section A, C, and E)

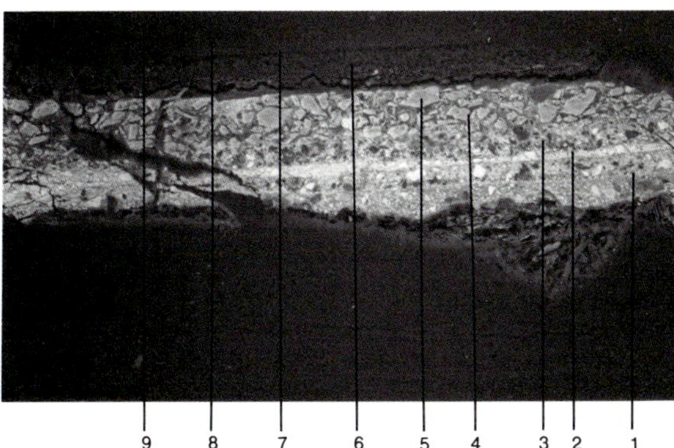

Detail of cross section G: *Saint Martin and the Beggar* (altarpiece), blue saddle cloth. SEM micrograph of cross section (Photograph courtesy of Melanie Feather)
1. *White ground (trace): browned with glue?
2. *Imprimatura:* iron oxides, lead white, ***carbon black(s), red lake
3. Gray layer: lead white, carbon black(s)
4. White layer: lead white with just a few carbon black particles
5. Dark, pinkish gray layer: carbon black(s), lead white, red lake
6. Purplish blue layer: azurite, lead white, red lake
7. White blue/ layer: lead white, azurite
8. and 9. Discolored varnish layers

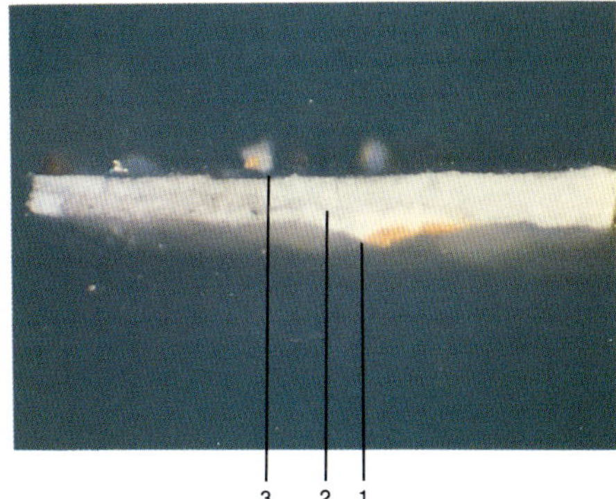

Cross section F: *Saint Martin and the Beggar* (smaller version), horse's bridle
White ground is absent from this cross section.
1. *Imprimatura* (trace)
2. White layer: lead white
3. Gray layer: lead white, ***carbon black(s)

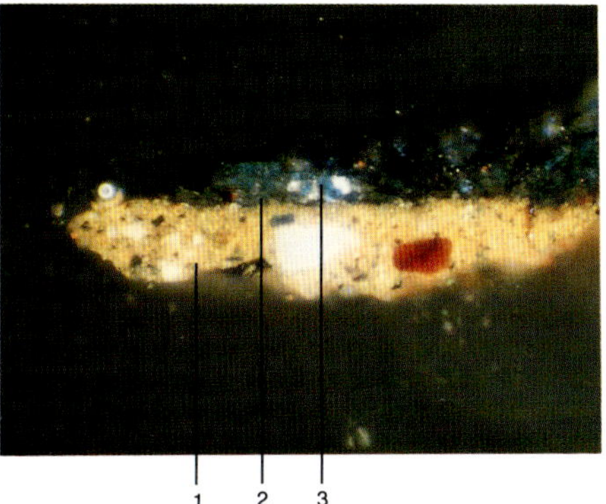

Cross section H: *Madonna and Child with Saint Martina and Saint Agnes,* dark blue drapery of Madonna (see also figs. 5 and 11).
White ground is absent from this cross section.
1. *Imprimatura:* iron oxides, lead white, ***carbon black(s), red lake
2. Blue layer (underlayer): azurite, some lead white
3. Dark blue glaze: ultramarine

APPENDIX
ANALYSIS OF PAINT LAYERS

Green Cloth, *Saint Martin and the Beggar* (both versions)

The green cloth that Saint Martin is dividing to share with the beggar was sampled on both paintings next to the horse's abdomen (cross sections A and B). The layering of the two samples differed significantly. The larger version exhibited six layers. Starting from the bottom, they are: (1) traces of a white ground layer, (2) followed by the *imprimatura*, (3) a light gray layer, (4) a pinkish dark gray layer (early outlinings of the composition), (5) a white layer (horse's abdomen), and (6) a green layer, consisting of verdigris and/or copper resinate (green cloth).[1]

In contrast, the layering of the smaller version (cross section B) shows only one intermediary layer, which is white. Above the white layer (horse's abdomen) are two thick green layers (green cloth). Below lie the *imprimatura* and traces of a white ground layer.

Landscape, *Saint Martin and the Beggar* (altarpiece)

Cross section C was taken from the landscape of the larger version. Here the green layer consists of two distinct layers. They are, starting from the bottom: (3) a layer of verdigris light in color and/or copper resinate, lead white, and some lead-tin yellow; and (4) a darker layer of verdigris and/or copper resinate, some lead white, and a few carbon black(s). A few azurite and lead white pigments on top of the green layer (5) stem from a swirl of blue paint of the sky that was pulled over the green layer.

No opportune location was found for sampling the landscape of the smaller version of *Saint Martin and the Beggar.*

Brown Foreground, *Saint Martin and the Beggar* (smaller version)

The brown foreground of the smaller version is made from umber and black pigments, applied in one thin layer (cross section D). The *imprimatura* and the ground are the only two other layers.

X-ray fluorescence spectroscopy and a scraping of the brown foreground taken from the larger version suggests the same composition of the paint layer.

Horse's Bridle, *Saint Martin and the Beggar* (both versions)

A sample was taken from the larger version of the connecting part between the rein and the bit of the horse's bridle, where a sizable loss on the larger version provided an opportune place (cross section E). Again, a complex layering was found. Starting from the bottom, the layers are: (1) a trace of white ground, (2) followed by the *imprimatura*, (3) a dark gray layer (early outlining of the composition), (4) a light blue layer (a swirl of sky), (5 and 6) a thick green layer and a thin, dark green layer (green cloth), (7) a disrupted black layer (more outlining of the composition?), (8) a thick white layer (horse's neck), (9) another white layer, and (10) a gray layer (horse's bridle) that may be the same layer as (9).

Cross section F taken at the same location on the smaller version exhibits only one white layer (horse's abdomen), lying directly on the *imprimatura* and a thinner gray layer on top of the white layer (horse's bridle).

Blue Saddle Cloth, *Saint Martin and the Beggar* (altarpiece)

Taken from a highlight of the blue saddle cloth of the altarpiece, cross section G exhibits the following sequence of layers. Starting from the bottom, they are: (1) a layer of white ground, (2) followed by the *imprimatura*, (3) a gray layer (early outlining of the composition), (4) a white layer (horse's body), (5) a dark, pinkish gray layer (sketching of saddle cloth), (6) a purplish blue layer (saddle cloth), and (7) a white/blue layer (highlight on saddle cloth). No opportune location was found for sampling the blue saddle cloth of the smaller version.

The admixture of red lake to azurite to give the blue a more purplish hue can be observed in the works of Italian artists from the early Venetian masters onward, such as Cima da Conegliano.[2] It has also been encountered in blue paint films of other paintings by El Greco, such as in the dark folds of the blue robe of *Saint Ildefonso.*[3]

The Use of Ultramarine, *Madonna and Child with Saint Martina and Saint Agnes*

For this study azurite and ultramarine were analyzed in the altarpieces of *Saint Martin and the Beggar* and *Madonna and Child with Saint Martina and Saint Agnes.* A varied approach was found in the blues of the *Madonna and Child with Saint Martina and Saint Agnes.* Cross section H, taken from a dark fold of the Madonna's blue mantle, reveals that the blue color was built up with a first layer made from azurite and some lead white and a second layer of ultramarine applied as a glaze, a technique well known in Italy as well as in northern Europe.[4] These two blue layers lie on the *imprimatura*. The white ground is absent from this cross section.

It was thought that the use of ultramarine was rare in Spain during El Greco's period,[5] as

Francesco Pacheco referred to "ultramarine which is neither used in Spain nor have the painters enough wealth to use it."[6] But this assumption seems to be inaccurate, at least for the more well-to-do artists, since ultramarine has not only been found in several of Diego Velázquez' paintings,[7] but has recently been discovered in several of the works of El Greco as well.[8] El Greco's use of the precious blue pigment is also documented. The prior of El Escorial was ordered in a royal decree to satisfy El Greco's request for ultramarine for use in his painting *Saint Maurice* (Escorial, Chapter House).[9] Unfortunately, we do not know from which source the prior imported the costly pigment.

NOTES TO APPENDIX

1. Examination of the green layer in plain and in polarized transmitted light revealed the presence of birefringent particles of verdigris mixed in an isotropic green medium, suggesting the use of verdigris and copper resinate. The birefringent particles could be unreacted verdigris in the oleo-resinous medium.

2. See, for example, the study of the work of the Venetian artist Cima da Conegliano by Jill Dunkerton and Ashok Roy, "The Technique and Restoration of Cima's 'The Incredulity of S. Thomas'," *National Gallery Technical Bulletin* (London) 10 (1986), 14.

3. El Greco, *Saint Ildefonso* (smaller version), scientific research department report, 29 September 1987, conservation file, National Gallery of Art, Washington.

4. Of the many published examples, two references are given: Joyce Plesters, "Tintoretto's Paintings in the National Gallery of Art," *National Gallery Technical Bulletin* (London) 4 (1980), 32–47; David Bomford, Ashok Roy, and Alistair Smith, "The Techniques of Dieric Bouts: Two Paintings Contrasted," *National Gallery Technical Bulletin* (London) 10 (1986), 39–57.

5. Joyce Plesters, "Ultramarine Blue, Natural and Artificial," *Studies in Conservation* 11, no. 2 (May 1966), 64–65.

6. Francesco Pacheco, *The Art of Painting* (1649) in *Artists' Techniques in Golden Age Spain: Six Treatises in Translation*, ed. and trans. Zahira Veliz (Cambridge, 1986), 75, see also n. 76. Later in his discourse on blue pigments, Pacheco qualified his earlier statement, writing that he did not approve of glazing blue unless it is with ultramarine.

7. Enriqueta Harris and Herbert Lank, "The Cleaning of Velázquez' Portrait of Camillo Massimi," *Burlington Magazine* 125 (July 1983), 410–415; Manuela Mena Marqués, "La restauración de *Las Meninas* de Velázquez," *Boletin del Museo del Prado* 5, no. 14 (May–August 1984), 87–109; Maria del Carmen Garrido and M. T. Davila y Rocio Davila, "*Las Hilanderas*: Estudio tecnico y restauración," *Boletin del Museo del Prado* 7, no. 21 (September-December 1986), 145–166.

8. Maria del Carmen Garrido, "Estudio tecnico de cuatro Anunciaciones de El Greco," *Boletin del Museo del Prado* 8, no. 23 (May–August 1987), 104–105.

9. This much-cited document was first published in Eugenio Llaguno y Amirola, *Noticias de los Arquitectos y Arquitectura de España desde su restauración*, 4 vols. (Madrid, 1829), 3:349, doc. 26.

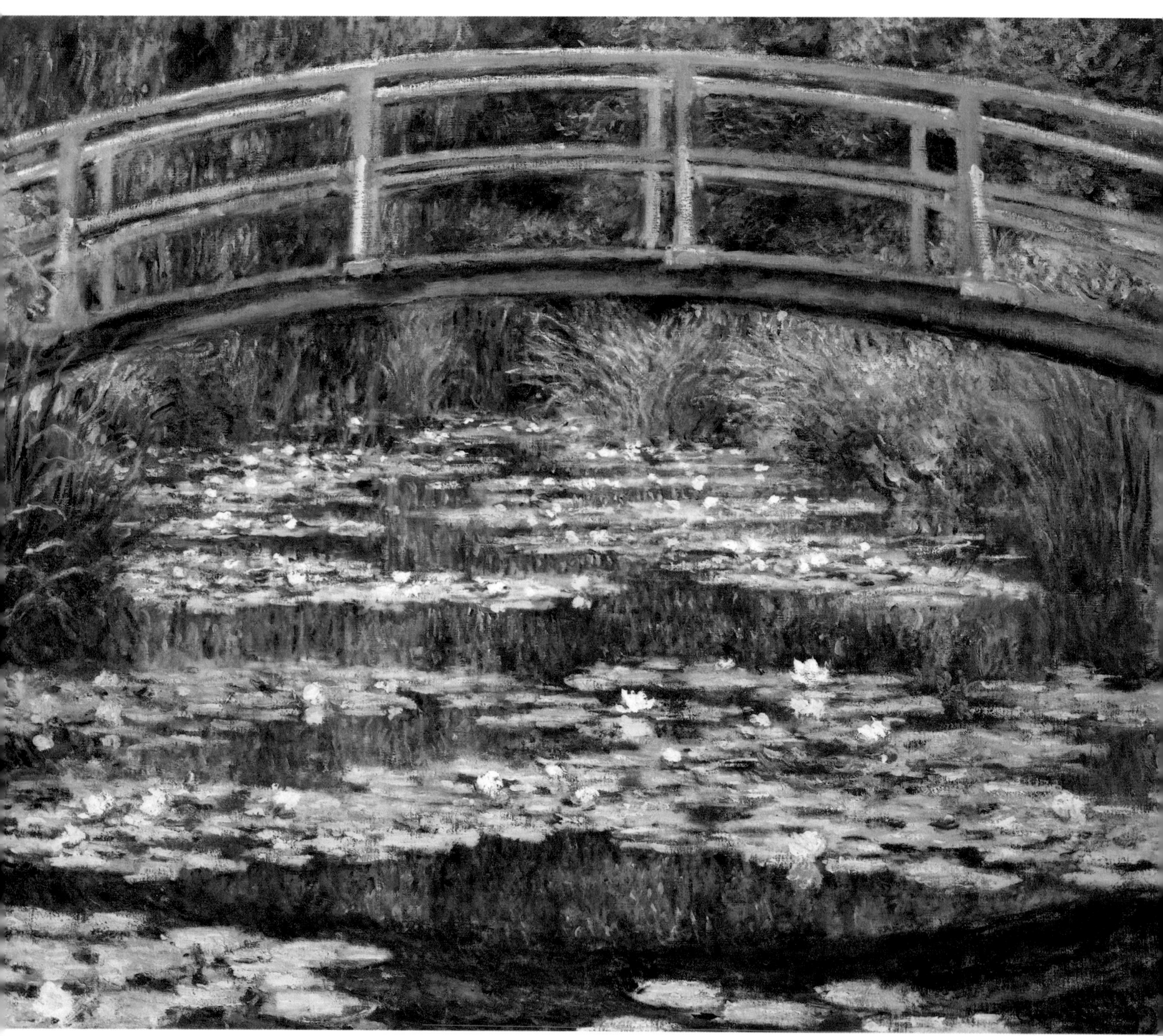

MICHAEL SWICKLIK

French Painting and the Use of Varnish, 1750–1900

Claude Monet, *The Japanese Footbridge*, 1899, oil on canvas
National Gallery of Art, Washington, Gift of Victoria Nebeker Coberly in memory of her son John W. Mudd, and gift of Walter H. and Leonore Annenberg

Picture varnishes traditionally have been applied as protective coatings over the paint film and as a means of giving a uniform surface to the work of art. The exact origin of varnishing paintings is not known, but by the sixteenth century it appears to have been a relatively common practice. Two kinds of varnish were used, those containing resin and oil (oil varnish) and those that simply contained resin dissolved in a solvent (spirit varnishes). It is believed that the oil varnishes were the first in common use. They would have given a thick, very glossy appearance to a varnish layer. By the seventeenth century, spirit varnishes are thought to have been more common. They could have been applied more thinly, giving a somewhat less glossy look to the painting.

As the style of French painting evolved from the opulence of the rococo in the eighteenth century to the controlled, polished surface of the nineteenth-century academic, through the frenetic brushwork of the romantic school associated with artists such as Eugène Delacroix, and to the loose, highly impastoed works of the impressionist painters, artists' techniques changed radically. The manner in which varnish was used was only one of many technical modifications, yet a very important one, as the amount of varnish applied to the surface of a completed painting and the addition of varnish to media or its absence have such significant consequences that they are an essential aspect of the appearance we now associate with each style. By examining the treatises of French academicians, the journals of Delacroix, and the words of the French impressionists as well as of dealers and critics, conservators and art historians can gain a sense of the changing use of varnish and understanding of the method prevailing at the time a particular painting was made.

THE EIGHTEENTH-CENTURY APPROACH

The founders of the French Academy sincerely sought to nurture good craftsmanship among painters by implementing a rigorous course of instruction. "Master painters," they declared, "in all their artworks made either at their ateliers or elsewhere are obligated to employ good colors and well fabricated, properly prepared canvases."[1] Yet by the middle of the eighteenth century their system was wanting in this very respect. The academy had, according to the historian Albert Boime, "split into cliques that significantly emphasized its administrative and honorary functions over and against its pedagogical responsibilities. Professional duties were neglected and the once rigorous system of instruction lapsed into an arbitrary and capricious eclecticism."[2] This state of affairs led to government-enforced reforms that included the formation in 1748 of the Ecole des Elèves Protégés. This school, an official effort to raise the level of technical training, was designed to present the craftsman's approach to painting and sculpture to the most promising students. With the renewed concern for the teaching of sound techniques to young artists, one painting professor, Jean-Baptiste Oudry (1686–1755), came under fire for neglecting his duties as a teacher. To compensate, Oudry delivered two lectures at the business meeting of the academy about issues of interest to the student painter. The first, in 1750, was on color. The second, and more important for our purposes, was delivered in 1752; this lecture, entitled "Underdrawing, Underpainting, and Retouching," was entirely about sound painting practices.

The academy's business meeting served as the forum for debate among members on both philosophical and practical matters. Therefore the delivery of a lecture at one of these meetings guaranteed an influential audience and enhanced the lecturer's credibility in official circles. Today "Underdrawing, Underpainting, and Retouching" is a valuable record of academic technique of the time and an ideal point of departure for a discussion of the uses of varnish in the eighteenth century.

Oudry's lecture was straightforward. He described how to prepare the canvas and then how to draw the sketch that would serve as a guide for the painting on top of the ground. It was not until he was well into his exhaustive treatise that he first mentioned varnish, suggesting it be used on top of the sketch:

I know that this practice of varnishing the sketch is not in general use but I am able to say that it does a great deal of good. When you take up this practice you will become conscious of your brush grabbing hold of the surface and operating with greater facility. You will see your colors flow with ease and cover perfectly. You will never have the disagreeable experience of seeing them sink into the sketch, nor consequently will you have the trouble of recalling them with oil. . . . It is necessary however to proceed with caution and varnish this sketch as thinly as you are able. Nothing then will prevent the work on top from forming a union with that underneath because the spirit of the turpentine which makes the base for this varnish evaporates instantaneously, leaving only that which is necessary to remove the spongy quality of the sketch.[3]

According to Oudry, what he called the "underpainting," or the main body of the paint film, should be placed on top of the varnished sketch. Once the underpainting was complete, it was again time for varnish. Oudry went on to say:

When the underpainting is complete over the entire painting and is left to dry completely, then it will tolerate varnishing. It must be varnished very lightly, with a very soft brush. . . . One must varnish the painting from one side to the other and to see clearly by this means what could be done to give the painting a beautiful harmony, a lightness of brushwork, or a particular finish. . . . If properly done the artist should never fear that this foundation would be able to form an obstacle to the intimate junction of the retouches with the more thinly painted areas of a freshly painted picture.[4]

This is Oudry's last mention of a varnish coating. He still expected, however, that the artist would need to add a few discriminate touches of color on top of this coating to give the painting its final harmony. It may well be that he intended another, thicker coating of varnish to be added after the final touches of paint, but he did not say so in his lecture.

Oudry promulgated the use of intermediate layers of varnish that were to be applied as thinly as the artist's capabilities permitted. He insisted that these varnish layers would not interfere with the union of the top and bottom layers of paint and would provide the artist with "a solid and durable technique."[5] Oudry thought it imperative that the artist not use too much varnish. Although his system for thin varnish layers was innovative, he was adamant in warning the artist not to add varnish directly to the paint medium so that the layers would dry more solidly and maintain greater durability.[6]

As simple as this counsel seems, it apparently was not simple enough for the majority of painters in this period. The connoisseur and biographer, Abbé Louis Gougenot, commented on Oudry's lecture:

One finds universal agreement with the research he has done on the care which one must bring to the choice of colors and to the procedure to which one must keep in employing them. . . . However, his advice on varnishing seems contrary to the general maxim—which is painting the layers directly on top of one another.[7]

A review of eighteenth-century artist's manuals indicates that Gougenot's observation was correct: most recommend that one layer be painted directly on top of the previous layer.[8] Even Oudry acknowledged that his method was not then generally practiced by contemporary artists. Gougenot also indicates a universal agreement that varnish should not be added directly to the paint medium. Both common practice and Oudry's specific instructions suggest that eighteenth-century use of varnish was far simpler than the methods involving combinations of varnish and oil developed in the nineteenth century.

The intellectual climate surrounding the reforms of 1748 also made discussions among artists about their materials commonplace during academy business meetings. One of these discussions provides special insight into the properties of varnish that the academy members found particularly desirable. An entry in the 1749 proceedings describes these properties:

> *Two particular associates have found the secret of composing a white varnish, without odor, clear and transparent, which saturates the colors and which is always able to be removed without damaging the painting. . . . These associates beseech the Academy to permit them to make a trial with their varnish on an appropriate painting under the watchful eye of its members in order to prove its properties.*[9]

The trial was approved, and approximately eight months later the members declared the varnish to have the good effects claimed for it and recommended its use.[10] Unfortunately, they did not specify the components of this varnish.

THE REFORMS OF THE FRENCH REVOLUTION AND THE NEOCLASSICAL APPROACH

French artists' approaches to varnishing remained essentially the same until the academic reforms initiated following the French Revolution. Among the most significant were those that established the Fine Arts Division of the Institute of France, as two organizations: a separate French Academy for honorary functions, and an Ecole des Beaux Arts for pedagogical functions. Although it would seem that the creation of a separately administered school would enable the student to be free of the constraints of the academy, that was not the case. The academy still controlled the philosophy of the professors at the Ecole. According to the rules of the institute, all the teachers had to be members of the academy.[11]

In the early years of the reformed institution, before 1830, the prejudices of the academy-member professors ensured that the Ecole curriculum reflected the ideals of Jacques-Louis David (1748–1825), who rose to artistic preeminence following the French Revolution and initiated the adoption of neoclassical style. One of the most important Davidian concepts for the technical training of an artist at the Ecole was "the dutifully finished work." Accordingly, only paintings exhibiting the highly polished surface now associated with the oeuvres of Adolphe-William Bouguereau, Jean-León Gérôme, Jean-Auguste-Dominique Ingres, and Jean-Louis-Ernest Meissonier, among others, were considered suitable for public exhibition. Sketchiness implied artistic indolence and sloth.[12] The ramifications of the Davidian concept for the methods employed by a young academic painter schooled in this system cannot be underestimated. The elimination of any brushwork to create a jewellike surface necessitated a technique quite different from that required to produce the lively, rococo style favored in the eighteenth century by academic salons.

Jean François Léonore Mérimée's *Art of Painting in Oil and in Fresco* is an important source for analyzing the changes in nineteenth-century academic technique that were brought about by the shift to Davidian philosophy. When he first published his manual in 1830, Mérimée (1765–1836) was secretary to the academy. In the introduction to Mérimée's book, Quatremère de Quincy, who at that time was the secretary to the Institute of France, recapitulated the findings of a commission he appointed to review the book: "We are of the opinion that we have carefully pointed out the great utility and advantages that must result to the art of painting from this publication. . . . The Academy approves of this opinion."[13] Mérimée's *Art of Painting in Oil* clearly had the strong approval of the academic hierarchy. Its credibility as representing the accepted academic technique of the time is comparable to Oudry's lecture in the eighteenth century.

A major point of departure from Oudry was

Mérimée's recommendation that varnish and oil be combined in the medium. According to Mérimée, this combination "gives greater brilliancy and transparency to the color and allows the production of more clear and transparent tints."[14] While it is true that Mérimée presented his techniques as his own rediscovery of the secrets of the old masters, particularly the combination of oil and varnish in the medium, it is curious to note that Oudry also considered himself to be revealing the true secrets of the masters in advocating precisely the opposite. Oudry spoke from his experience as a successful painter; Mérimée spoke as an official in the academy. Although Mérimée does offer some proofs of this discovery, they are not particularly convincing.[15] Rather, the text reads as if this is Mérimée's opinion of the way in which old master painters must have painted. For the academic artists who were interested in smooth, transparent, enamellike finishes, the greater translucency, brilliance, and glazing ability provided by the combination of oil and varnish were of paramount importance. Mérimée might well have found it politically advantageous to present the academic technique of the time as being the long-lost secret of the old masters.

Mérimée considered a number of media to be suitable. He referred to them as English varnish, oil-copal mixtures, Flanders varnish, and Italian varnish and gave recipes for preparing each. All contained both oil and varnish. Mérimée's deviations from Oudry's standards and those of other eighteenth-century academic artists were not confined to the preparation of media. Mérimée had his own opinions on all aspects of painting. Unlike the extremely thin layer of varnish that Oudry had recommended putting on top of the sketch, Mérimée recommended in some cases that a smooth white ground be prepared with a very viscous coating of varnish rubbed on with a stiff brush. And while Oudry did not mention the final varnishing of a completed painting, Mérimée advised:

One part of oil should be used for two of copal which should afterwards be diluted with oil of turpentine. . . . The best way of preserving pictures would be to varnish them lightly with copal at first and when this layer is perfectly dry to lay over it a couch of mastic. In a few years this will become yellow or chilled then it may be removed. The copal varnish being extremely hard will not suffer by the removal of this covering but will preserve the picture so well that even the glazing cannot be endangered in the cleaning.[16]

Mérimée recommended a series of thin, transparent glazes with a high proportion of varnish added to the medium—anywhere from 16.5 percent to 44 percent varnish in most cases, and, in some cases, 100 percent varnish. These practices and applications produce a surface that is easily worked by the artist, and they facilitated the development of smooth painting techniques. But Mérimée was also aware that such painting practices produced surfaces that were not very durable. His scheme of applying a relatively insoluble, thin, protective coating to preserve the glazes during cleaning is strikingly different in spirit from Oudry's belief that the entire technique should be "solid and durable."

The practices advocated by Mérimée facilitated production of the enamellike finish favored by the academic school. Despite his position in the establishment, however, not all painters followed his advice. There was much heated discussion, in fact, about the relative merits of the sketch compared to "the dutifully finished work," and while most painters adopted the academic preference for a highly polished finish, the more "romantic" painters objected to the academy in everything—approach, subject matter, and painting technique—and favored "sketchiness" as a final form of presentation. Presumably they had less need for Mérimée's recommendations.

The academy's preferred system of artistic education still relied heavily on a few chosen ateliers where the major responsibility for the technical training of the young painter fell to the master in charge. Naturally, advice varied from atelier to atelier, but those masters who were particularly good at preparing students for the academic competitions were inclined to teach Mérimée's methods.

The techniques taught by Adolphe-William Bouguereau (1825–1905) represented the epitome of mid- to late-nineteenth-century French academic painting. Bouguereau began as a student at the Ecole des Beaux Arts in 1848 and was granted a professorship there in 1875. Not only was he one of the most successful and popular of the academic artists, but as a teacher he was extremely influential in perpetuating the academic style. Because of his close ties to the academic mainstream, the techniques that he learned, used, and subsequently taught others offer excellent insight into the instruction offered at the Ecole and can be used to gauge Mérimée's accuracy in describing the academic technique.

Recently discovered notebooks that are still in the hands of his descendants contain Bouguereau's studio notes describing his working methods in detail. They are strikingly similar to those advocated by Mérimée. Bouguereau's notebooks show that with a stiff brush he would lay a layer of viscous varnish on top of his prepared canvases. For this layer he used a varnish consisting of a mixture of mastic, oil, and two types of drying agents. After painting in his sketch, he fixed it with a coating of copal and oil diluted with turpentine. For painting the body color, Bouguereau employed a medium consisting of one part gum elemi and five parts picture varnish to which he added several drops of oil and a siccative. He completed the picture by glazing with more of his painting medium, which he adjusted to contain a higher proportion of picture varnish and to which he added mineral spirits.[17] Essentially, both Mérimée and Bouguereau advocated a system with layers of varnish containing paint interspersed with an intermediate and very viscous coating on top of the sketch.

THE CHANGING APPROACH OF DELACROIX

While the change from Oudry's to Bouguereau's methods of employing varnish seem considerable, they are slight compared to the radical changes from Bouguereau's methods to those of the impressionists, who used no varnish at all in either the medium or on the surface of the completed painting. This shift requires examination of the techniques that made such changes possible.

In the nineteenth century the academic artist who wanted to experiment technically faced serious constraints. To achieve success in academic competitions and exhibitions, painters had to exhibit a highly polished, enamellike finish. Independent artists, who were likely to be proponents of the sketchy, romantic style, had to survive outside the academy. If they could, they were free to experiment at will, and many of them did so. Many, in fact, abhorred the academic look and deliberately adapted their style and technique to create an appearance that was obviously different. Eugène Delacroix (1798–1863) is one such artist, and his practices can be examined as a transition between neoclassicism and impressionism.

Delacroix was always opposed both to the philosophy and appearance of the highly polished surface that was the Davidian ideal. He also felt that this philosophy's stranglehold in the teaching institutions made it impossible for him to get technically sound artistic training there. Consequently, he was largely self-taught and an innovator and experimenter. Throughout his career, for example, he was known to have used unconventional combinations of media such as oil on tempera, wax on oil, and wax mixed with oil.[18]

Although this experimentation was often designed to facilitate the production of a painting with all the flourish of brushwork now associated with his style, Delacroix sometimes adopted particular techniques more from chance than from a thorough understanding of their effects. Frustrated because he could not solve technical problems, he consulted his trusted artists' colorman Etienne Haro.[19] When really uncertain, he tended to turn to the old masters. Many entries in Delacroix's journal discuss the painting methods of Veronese, Peter Paul Rubens, and other artists he particularly admired. Some entries even suggest that he turned to Mérimée's treatise for guidance.[20] Considering Mérimée's stated goal of revealing the secrets of the old masters, his treatise was a logical source for Delacroix despite its affiliation with the academic style.

Clearly, Delacroix was not able to solve all his technical problems through Mérimée; later journal entries describe continuing frustrations. An entry from 1857, for example, outlined comments on varnishes for the "dictionary on the Arts," a definitive treatise on all aspects of painting that Delacroix often discussed in his journal and had been preparing for years. "Varnishes," he wrote, "their deadly effects. Sparing use made of them on old paintings. Quote passages from Oudry."[21]

Oudry's lecture had been preserved in manuscript form in the Ecole des Beaux Arts, and apparently Delacroix had read it. Rejecting the practice of the nineteenth-century academy, he seemed to concur with Oudry that varnish should be used sparingly. Delacroix did not suddenly come to this conclusion; it developed from his constant experimentation. In fact, he later proposed an even more radical approach.

Little is known about Delacroix's use of varnish early in his career. His journal begins in 1823, and from that time until 1832, where there is a gap until 1847, there are no entries pertaining to this subject. An 1827 order for artists' materials from the shop of Haro's father requested large amounts of mastic, copal, and Venice turpentine—all of which were commonly used for varnishing.[22]

By 1849, Delacroix was experiencing great problems with the condition of some of his early large paintings. *Dante and Virgil*, for example, was in such poor condition that by the early 1860s it was completely transferred to avoid "imminent loss."[23] Although it was not actually restored until 1861, this painting was known to be in poor condition in the 1840s and had been worrying Delacroix for some time.[24] It appears that the paint loss caused Delacroix to reevaluate his varnishing technique. From a section of his journal that suggests he was reviewing Mérimée's book at the time, an entry reads:

> *While I have been working on my picture,* The Woman of Algiers, *I have discovered how pleasant, how necessary even it is to paint on top of the varnish. The only thing needed is to find some means of preventing the varnish underneath from being attacked when the top coat of varnish is removed at some later date.*[25]

Although Delacroix was painting with at least one intermediary layer of varnish, this statement indicates that he was experimenting but that complicated layering was not yet his common practice.

It is easier to establish Delacroix's use of varnish after 1849, as there are many journal entries on this subject. Most appear to concern the final varnishing or at least entire coatings of varnish at some intermediate step of painting rather than the additions of varnish to the media. He came to believe that "it was necessary to let the painting dry more thoroughly before putting on a new varnish."[26] Mérimée had warned against varnishing a painting too soon after completion, lest it crack, and this warning may have caused Delacroix some anxiety. After he had done his own retouchings on *Dante and Virgil*, he sent a letter to the minister in charge of the restoration pleading for restraint in varnishing: "I would urgently request of you that the painting not be varnished until after the most considerable lapse of time possible."[27]

Restorations of Delacroix's earlier paintings were actually more common in the 1850s than in the 1860s. Often these restorations included cleaning, and the results caused Delacroix still more anxiety about his use of varnish. Concerning the cleaning of the *Massacre at Chios* in 1854, he wrote in his journal: "I am inclined to agree that the painting has not gained by varnish removal without even having seen it. The painting would have lost the transparency of the darks—it is nearly without fail that this happens."[28] Delacroix elaborated on his objections a month later:

> *The effect is only too likely to occur of its own accord as the colors darken in the course of time. The dark colors become even darker in relation to the light colors which retain their value better. . . . Varnish sticks to the dark parts of a picture and is not easily detached, so that the dark parts gradually become more intense until a background that appeared only moderately dark when the picture was painted will in the course of time become sheer obscurity.*[29]

Delacroix's anxieties concerning both the premature cracking and the cleaning of his paintings eventually led to further experimentation with varnishing. In 1852 he wrote: "To mat the paintings, Haro made use of wax dissolved in rectified turpentine with a light addition of essence of lavender. This mixture rubbed with wool produces a varnish that does not have the inconveniences of other varnishes."[30] Here Delacroix suggested that a wax varnish, if adequately buffed, can substitute for a more conventional varnish coating. Presumably, the "convenience" of this varnish is that it is superior in preventing the tendencies of standard varnishes to discolor or cause a painting to crack. Another coating Delacroix tried in order to prevent the cracking he attributed to hasty varnishing was "a type of provisionary varnish of gelatin sold at the butcher shop that is dissolved in warm water and applied to the painting with a sponge."[31] He also experimented with a varnish made from garlic juice.[32]

Not surprisingly, these forays with other materials did not seem to solve Delacroix's problems. He had a predilection for unconventional media throughout his career that virtually guaranteed the deterioration of his paintings. As his frustration mounted, Delacroix blamed his old nemesis, David. In one journal entry from 1857 he wrote:

> *The most perfect technique is to be found in the works of the greatest masters: Rubens, Titian, Veronese, the Dutch painters; the special care they took in grinding colors, in priming and preparations, in drying the different layers of paint. The tradition entirely lost in modern painting. Hence bad results; neglect of preparations, bad canvases and brushes, execrable oils—impermanence—carelessness on the part of the artist. David was responsible for this carelessness because he affected to despise material means.*[33]

Delacroix went on to make reference to Oudry, already cited, and added, "Varnishes should be a kind of protective armor to the picture as well as a means of bringing out its brilliance."[34] Although Delacroix had come to believe varnish should be used sparingly, he still felt it necessary for protecting the painting.

By 1858, Delacroix's conservative approach to the use of varnish became, at least briefly, even more unyielding. For some time controversy had raged over the cleaning of paintings by Veronese and Rubens in the Louvre. Delacroix's friend Frédéric Villot was charged with overcleaning them, and when the painter Henri Joseph Constant Dutilleux asked Delacroix to comment, Delacroix reiterated his dislike of the extreme contrast between light and dark that he found typical after most picture cleanings. He did concede, however, that the result of the cleaning of the Rubens painting was really quite good. He concluded: "It is desirable that one never varnish. Our descendants would then without doubt have a more exact idea of our paintings."[35]

While Delacroix may not have acted on this conclusion by adjusting his technique, his statement indicates that the impressionists were not the first painters to question the automatic use of varnish. Clearly, Delacroix developed a conservative approach toward the use of varnish that he believed to approximate painters' methods before the nineteenth century. Moreover, since other independent artists of this period were also inclined to explore older methods, Delacroix's musings are more than just a painter's response to frustrations.[36] Reacting to the failings of academic techniques, they returned to earlier techniques and a more limited use of varnish, thereby laying the groundwork for the techniques later adopted by the impressionists.

THE PRACTICE OF *VERNISSAGE*

In addition to the attitude of the independents toward varnishing, one additional factor may have influenced the impressionists: the system devised by the French Academy to ensure that the paintings in its exhibitions had a final varnish coating.

In 1804, Pierre François Tingry, a Swiss writer on painting methods, declared, "Great masters rarely varnish their pictures after they are finished; they protect their tints by a coating of white of egg and do not varnish them until a year after."[37] This practice had apparently been common for centuries. On 12 January 1644 Nicolas Poussin wrote to his friend A. M. de Chantelou regarding a shipment of his paintings from Italy to Paris: "When you receive them you can stretch each one onto their stretcher, and with a sponge and clean water perhaps with some orange juice added, remove the temporary coating. When they are good and dry have them varnished by someone who knows how."[38]

In addition to confirming Tingry's assertion about the use of temporary varnishes, Poussin mentions another common custom—the use of a surrogate varnisher. For Poussin and undoubtedly other painters who followed, the matter was probably one of convenience: Poussin was in Italy, he did not want to ship his paintings varnished, so he needed to have them varnished in France. In nineteenth-century France, this assistance became increasingly formalized by the institution known as *vernissage*.

As the more widely appreciated understanding of *vernissage* is based on the British system, it may be illuminating to describe the English Royal Academy's procedure before discussing the French rite of *vernissage*, which is significantly different. Beginning in 1804, only members of the Royal Academy were allowed to enter the exhibition hall after their pictures were hung to retouch and varnish them before the opening. The practice could be viewed as a privilege, for it allowed academy members to adjust their own paintings in a manner that might make them more prominent than the paintings of nonmembers. But it also led to some extraordinarily unsound painting practices. It is well known, for instance, that J.M.W. Turner, in an effort to make his final enhancements, would sometimes add multiple layers of paint and varnish, one on top of the other, even before those underneath had a chance to dry. Despite the many attempts to abolish this practice and the technical abuses it generated, it remained in effect until 1852. Ironically, one reason for its continuance was that the works of Turner improved so dramatically from the results obtained on varnishing days that it would have hurt Turner to withhold the privilege. It cannot be mere coincidence that the date of its abolition—1852—was one year after Turner's death.[39]

In England, many academicians took advantage of its system, and on varnishing days one might have encountered a crowded exhibition hall with artists up on their ladders applying layer upon layer of paint and varnish while the critics milled about below. A varnishing day in France was likely very different. The earliest French reference to it is from an 1803 entry in the minutes of the newly formed Fine Arts Division of the Institute of France, which described "one day for hanging and varnishing."[40] The occasion was the Prix de Rome competition, and the aspirants were given a precise length of time to complete their work, after which the entries were locked up to dry.[41] In this case, it is unlikely that the artists would have then been allowed back in to the exhibition to retouch and varnish the paintings. In describing this portion of the installation, the artist Alexis Lemaistre said, "After the paintings were hung they were given a single coating of varnish."[42]

Perhaps developing out of the rules for competitions, a day was also set aside for varnishing prior to the openings of the official Salons that were the major yearly exhibitions in the academic system. Unlike the English system that allowed the alteration of every painting belonging to a Royal Academy member, in France the regulations stipulated that the paintings to be varnished were supposed to be only those that had been painted too recently to varnish when they were deposited at the exhibition hall. Typically, the painter had to deliver his painting six weeks before the opening of the exhibition.[43] As the artists almost always painted up until the last possible moment, there were inevitably a number of newly completed and, therefore, unvarnished paintings to be exhibited. Initially, there seems to have been no specific regulation prohibiting the artists themselves from participating at the Salon *vernissage*, but this practice became increasingly rare as the nineteenth century progressed. The artists were present at the hanging to ensure a favorable location for their paintings, but they let others do the varnishing, which they disdained as too lowly to perform in the presence of onlookers.[44] Generally, the varnishing was left in the hands of artists' colormen, who were trusted advisers on technical matters.

One fascinating aspect of the role of the artists' colorman as varnisher was that a single highly skilled colorman could perform this crucial finishing step for artists of vastly different styles—even for artistic rivals. Etienne Haro was one such varnisher. By the mid-1840s, he had, according to a contemporary, been "admitted for many years into the Galleries of the Louvre in order to varnish the paintings on exhibition there."[45] He was then the most influential and popular colorman among Parisian artists. He had a special relationship as an adviser to Delacroix, for whom he also often cleaned, relined, and varnished paintings. It seems extraordinary, considering the extreme difference in painting styles, that while Haro enjoyed such a strong relationship with Delacroix, he was performing many of these same functions for Jean-Auguste-Dominique Ingres. Haro was also known to have varnished for Edouard Manet and perhaps also for Jean-Baptiste-Camille Corot, Gustave Courbet, Jean-François Millet, Edgar Degas, and Alfred Sisley, all of whom he often advised on technical matters.[46]

Unlike the English system, which allowed the artist greater access to his work at the *vernissage*, the more restrictive French system made it less likely that technically unsound retouching would have been applied to the painting just before exhibition. With a single colorman charged with varnishing the paintings of a number of different artists—and by using the same pot of varnish—it is also less likely that the paintings on exhibition would have received a varnish toned in a manner specific to each artist. Unfortunately, although the abuses the French *vernissage* fostered were less severe than those in England, the system was not trouble free, as not all artists could avail themselves of the services of a colorman with the expertise of Haro, who assured a competent job. The following account of the nineteenth-century French *vernissage* proceedings, written in 1922, attests to the heartbreaking results a lesser-known artist might have experienced:

> *On the day of the vernissage, when the painters most want to present to the public their genius, they give to their color merchants the number of their paintings and one sees these worthy employees courageously slathering these paintings with varnish. Mounted on their ladders the colormen summon up the colors to a brightness resembling a poster. As it is necessary that they proceed quickly and time presses, they apply the varnish with large fat brushes, in abundance but unevenly. The brilliance which the paintings take on in this manner is frightening to behold. Like many modern paintings which contrast light impastoed areas to darker, flatter areas, at the junction between these areas the darks sparkle to such a degree that one is not able to see the painting at all.*[47]

THE APPROACH OF THE IMPRESSIONISTS

Perhaps some of the great impressionist painters, in their early years, had experiences like this. Denis Rouart recalled the following story about Degas:

> *Degas had sent his painting to the Salon. I no longer know in which year. The day of the* vernissage *he looked anxiously at his painting, not finding that it looked very well on the wall. It was very freshly painted (he had been working on it on into the night) and was evidently full of sunken-in areas and appeared very dull. He advised the varnisher who was just then passing by with his brush and pot of varnish "Go up and give my painting a coat of varnish." Whether the painting gained by the operation I don't know but upon seeing it again in his studio Degas decided to remove this varnish and to then repaint it. The result was disaster! In removing the varnish he naturally removed the better part of the painting.*[48]

Elsewhere Rouart identified the painting as *Mademoiselle Fiocre in the Ballet La Source*. According to John Rewald, this painting was first exhibited in the Salon of 1868.[49] Rouart's account suggests that Degas found some aspect of the varnisher's work unsatisfactory; otherwise he probably would not have tried to remove the coating.

Pierre Auguste Renoir recalled another incident as late as 1879:

> *The day before the opening a friend came and told me that he had just been to the Salon and that something queer seemed to have happened to my* Mademoiselle Samary. *I dashed to the Salon and found the picture almost beyond recognition—it looked as if it were melting away. It seems that the framer instructed the delivery boy to varnish another picture that he was delivering at the same time. The boy had a little varnish left over and decided to give me the benefit of it. I didn't varnish mine because it was still wet, but he thought I was being economical! The result was I had to repaint the whole thing in an afternoon.*[50]

It seems from these accounts that if purely practical considerations eventually encouraged impressionist artists to forego varnishing, dissatisfaction with the work of surrogate varnishers could have been one of them. As Renoir's recollection points out, the extended drying time that their higher impastos required probably made a general *vernissage* before exhibition undesirable.

In the early 1860s those artists who would become the impressionists were beginning to emerge from their atelier training and find their way in the art world of Paris. They may have known Delacroix's opinions on the dangers of varnish from the pamphlets published on the cleaning controversy,[51] or they may have sought them out. Delacroix's methods were so intriguing, for example, to Claude Monet and Jean-Frédéric Bazille that they peered through the window of a friend's apartment to watch him paint in his garden studio.[52] Certainly varnishing was a subject of discussion among these young artists. Renoir recalled: "I remember a great discussion which took place at Tortoni's between Wolff and another man. . . . It was Robert Fleury I believe. . . . They were arguing about whether it was better to varnish a painting immediately . . . or to leave it to time."[53] In any case, the approach to varnishing that the impressionists eventually adopted was similar to that which Delacroix suggested.

Edouard Manet and the Early Impressionists

Regardless of Delacroix's possible influence, other factors were at work in shaping the impressionists' approach toward the use of varnish. These artists had studied in the most progressive ateliers in Paris. Monet, Renoir, and Sisley all trained in the atelier of Charles Gleyre, and Manet had been a pupil of Thomas Couture. Neither of these masters was a staunch supporter of the academic tradition. Although Gleyre taught a technique that was similar to the system represented by the Ecole des Beaux Arts, he encouraged his students to experiment,[54] and Couture had devised a system that was much closer to Oudry than Mérimée.[55] Drawing on his early training in Couture's studio, Manet developed his own system, which, not surprisingly, was similar to Oudry's. He simplified his layering structure and abandoned the use of varnish in his medium.[56] As he was often the inspiration for the other artists, the influence of Manet (1832–1883) must be considered in speculating about the origins of the impressionists' attitude to varnish.

Despite Delacroix's warnings, there is little evidence that the young impressionist painters abandoned the final varnishing in the 1860s. The major vehicle for exhibition was still the official Salon, and by exhibiting there these painters would have almost invariably subjected their work to the *vernissage* had it been submitted unvarnished. Monet continued to submit his paintings already varnished. He wrote to Bazille in 1864, "My painting of flowers is finally varnished, framed, and on exhibition."[57]

There is at least one instance of a painting's being exhibited unvarnished, however; it is found in reference to a painting by Edma Morisot. Madame Marie-Josephine-Cornélie Morisot wrote to Edma on the occasion of the opening of the 1865 Salon:

> *It seems to me, particularly with the flowers, that your paintings have not been varnished. This is being too careless of the appearance of painting when the aim is to please the untrained eyes susceptible to the first impression. I think that it is not necessary that you disregard what is customary practice.*[58]

There are a number of ways to interpret this letter. The first question that comes to mind is whether Morisot actually intended this painting to be shown unvarnished—that intention would be remarkable at such an early date. It is conceivable, after all, that her varnisher simply forgot this picture in the *vernissage*. If the painting was deliberately left unvarnished, it would be the first known example of an impressionist artist doing so in an exhibition. It is safest to view this instance as an anomaly rather than as the start of a trend. The concern expressed by Madame Morisot over her daughter's unvarnished painting suggests that the taste of the day still strongly favored a glossy surface.

Careful consideration of the final varnishing practices of Manet during the same period makes the unvarnished painting exhibited by Morisot even more perplexing. In fact, awareness of Manet's methods in this period suggests that Morisot may have applied such a thin coating of varnish to her painting that it merely appeared unvarnished in comparison to the other paintings in the exhibition. Manet instructed Haro: "I would like you to go and varnish for me a painting which I have on exhibition at the circle of the Rue de Choiseul 12. I would like you to varnish it *very lightly* and with your best varnish."[59]

Manet's request for Haro's best varnish applied thinly suggests his concern about eventual discoloration. Obviously a thin layer of discolored varnish would be far less distorting to the colors than a thick one, and an excellent quality varnish would discolor much more slowly than one of poor quality. The instructions may also suggest a dislike of high gloss, for a thinly applied varnish would likely, although not inevitably, be more matte than a heavily applied layer. A thinly applied final varnish was also in keeping, as Delacroix had discovered, with the techniques of the old masters. Later, Renoir recalled that in the early years the impressionist painters tried "to induce painters to get in line and follow the masters."[60]

During the 1860s and 1870s the impressionists, while aware of the problems of discoloration, continued to accept the final varnishing as standard practice. In 1878, for example, Camille Pissarro wrote to the writer and collector Eugene Murer, "I am going to recommend to the colorman that he varnish your painting only with a varnish that is uncolored."[61] Pissarro's insistence that the varnish be uncolored may have arisen from his discovery of a "strange yellowness" on some of the paintings he had already sold.[62] Toned varnishes were commonly used to modify what was considered unacceptably intense color. In the 1870s the dealer Georges Durand-Ruel often applied them to make impressionist paintings more salable to a public that was hardly clamoring for these works.[63] When Monet was told of Durand-Ruel's interference, he was said to have replied, "You can imagine that I was not thrilled by this idea but what is one going to do—Even an artist has to eat."[64] As late as 1880, Monet appeared perfectly willing to varnish some of his paintings for a collector.[65]

A Clear Preference by 1880

By that time, however, most impressionists clearly preferred the unvarnished look. Constant references to the impressionists' "matte impastos" in a review of the 1876 exhibition by the critic Edmond Duranty suggest that these artists had forgone the custom of *vernissage* by this date.[66] The first conclusive evidence of the impressionists leaving their paintings unvarnished comes in their independent exhibition of 1881, which included works by Pissarro, Morisot, Gauguin, and Degas. The critic J. Karl Huysmans observed:

> *It is important to have these exhibitions of the independents frequently to fully appreciate the innovative uses of materials which they bring to their work. . . . They have corrected the shimmer of oil painting coated with varnish and adopted for the most part the English system, which consists of leaving the painting matte and covered with a sheet of glass. They avoid in this manner a glistening look with many shining areas and are content simply to remove the woolly and dull aspects from the painting.*[67]

Huysmans had reviewed the 1880 exhibition as well, and although it included works by the same artists, he did not comment on any divergence from the Salon style of varnishing.

In exhibiting their paintings glazed (covered with glass), the impressionists were replicating, in a sense, the saturating capabilities of varnish. They were not—yet—opting for a completely matte look. In all probability, they were concerned about critical acclaim and sales. Moreover, Berthe Morisot, Manet, and perhaps other impressionists were at the time experimenting with bare, unprimed canvas as an element in their compositions. They would not have wanted to compromise their experiments by saturating their canvases with varnish,[68] and glazing offered an intermediate approach.

Glazing also protected the paintings. Huysmans referred to glazing as "the English system," and glazing paintings on exhibition had been common practice in England since the mid-1870s. With academic painters working in England, such as Lawrence Alma-Tadema and James Tissot, it was prevalent.[69] At that time, glazing was also particularly popular, as the National Gallery had launched a massive glazing campaign to prevent damage similar to that caused by climatic extremes in its newly opened wing.[70]

Not all the impressionists participated in the 1881 exhibition. Monet and Renoir had decided not to exhibit, and it is instructive to examine their opinions on the use of varnish after 1880. It is also instructive to examine the opinions of the artists who did participate, and Pissarro especially, as he changed his aesthetic most drastically in embracing pointillism.

Pierre Auguste Renoir

The one impressionist artist reluctant to adopt the new unvarnished aesthetic was Renoir. Despite the near disaster his *Mademoiselle Samary* suffered in the 1879 Salon *vernissage*, he seems not to have objected to the use of varnish generally. He had not varnished the painting himself only because it was still wet, and by exhibiting paintings at the Salon every year until 1884 and again in 1890, where they would have been subject to *vernissage*, Renoir showed little appreciable concern for this issue.

If Renoir did experiment with unvarnished surfaces, he most likely did so during his so-called dry period, 1883–1889,[71] which roughly corresponds with his nonparticipation in Salon exhibitions. During these years Renoir was influenced by the look of fresco painting and experimented with removing a good part of the medium from his paints to create a dryer surface. Of his work he commented: "After having studied fresco, I had fancied I could eliminate the oil from the color. . . . Another reason that induced me to dry the oil out of my color was my search for a means of preventing the paint from darkening."[72]

This technique would have created a very lean, matte surface. As the reason for removing the medium was to keep the paint from darkening, it is likely that Renoir would have considered resaturating the paint with a coat of varnish counterproductive. Renoir's experimentation with this method of painting was brief. When he decided to abandon the technique, his reasons were unequivocal: "The surface became too dry and subsequent layers did not adhere well. . . . I later discovered that oil is the very thing which keeps the color from darkening."[73]

Shortly after returning to his standard technique of dipping his brush directly into the medium while painting, Renoir resumed varnishing as well. He wrote to Durand-Ruel on 15 April 1891: "I am going to send you two small canvases in order that you choose one and put it in the Brown sale. I am having frames made by Dubourg who will bring them to you. I count on your kindness to varnish and place into the sale the one you find most appropriate."[74] In another letter, dated 18 April 1891, he wrote, "I sent you a small case containing a small head of an infant for the Brown sale. There are with it two other small things which I put in to fill the case. I would be very obliged to you if you would varnish them for me because with all the sunken in areas it is impossible to see anything."[75]

Renoir apparently continued to desire an absolutely saturated surface throughout the rest of his career. Late in life he told the dealer Vollard: "I can't keep that bottle of oil full. I'm always afraid my pictures will be too thin. What a perpetual problem it is to paint rich and fat."[76] Marc Elder, one of Renoir's biographers, concluded, "He loved his paintings unctuous, paintings that should be varnished."[77] Unlike the other impressionist painters, Renoir seems not to have worried about the potential obscuring or discoloring effects of varnish coatings. He commented on Rubens' *Helena Fourment and Her Children*: "The white dress is full of dirt due to the layers of filthy varnish they have put on, but it's magnificent just the same. There's painting for you! Nothing can spoil splendid colors."[78]

Camille Pissarro

Camille Pissarro's views were diametrically opposite to those of Renoir. A review of an exhibition in 1882 reveals that Pissarro's paintings were exhibited under glass, presumably because they were unvarnished. Phillippe Burty commented, "Beneath glass Pissarro's paintings become like powerful pastels."[79] This exhibition was only one year after the 1881 independent exhibition at which Huysman observed glazed, unvarnished impressionist paintings. Clearly, Pissarro was an early convert to this style of presentation.

During this period Pissarro's paintings were sometimes mistaken by reviewers as pastels, an indication of how very matte Pissarro's surfaces were at that time. Writing to his son Lucien on 13 May 1883, Pissarro complained:

> *My* Market *on which I worked so much since last year is splendid in a white frame. Today's* L'Intransigent *mentions it. It is taken for a pastel. I haven't a single pastel—ah yes—a tiny one in a dark corner. They confuse everything, gouache, tempera, oil. What connoisseurs!*[80]

Had Pissarro been varnishing his paintings according to fashion, the reviewers would not likely have found identifying various media a problem.

By the early 1880s, Pissarro was adamant about his unvarnished aesthetic. On the reverse of the Louvre's *Paysage a Chapronval*, dated from this time, an inscription in the hand of Pissarro reads "*Veuillez ne pas vernir*" (please do not varnish).[81] He was even more resolute by the middle of the decade, when he adopted the pointillist technique introduced by Georges Seurat and Paul Signac. These artists, whose system of painting maximized the intensity and purity of color by juxtaposing small dabs of pure tones, would not have wanted to apply a varnish film that had the potential to discolor and thereby ruin the very effect they were seeking. Seurat himself confirms this point in a letter to Octave Maus in January 1887:

It is appropriate that I tell you of my horror of varnish. Often some paint shop proprietor will apply varnish without being told to, thinking he's doing the right thing and sending in his little bill. VETO. I'm against any varnishing of my canvases, either free or for a fee.[82]

In a brochure for the major neo-impressionist exhibition of 1886, Félix Fenéon, a writer and critic, succinctly confirmed this point in comparing the impressionist method to that of the postimpressionist:

Misters Pissarro, Seurat, Dubois Pillet, and Signac apply their colors flat; applied in broken touches their impastos are better able to maintain elasticity. They escape in this way the danger of the drying—craquelure. The sunken in areas disappear beneath the glass, just as they would beneath a varnish. Under the example of Alma-Tadema, James Tissot, etc. they put their canvases under glass; they thereby have little fear of the inevitable yellowing from even the most pure varnishes.[83]

While the unvarnished look had apparently become a matter of choice for the impressionists, it was a matter of dogma for the neo-impressionists, who by then also included Pissarro. Their painting method had become so precise that any deterioration causing any change was considered abhorrent. According to Fenéon, even their technique of placing one small dab of paint in close proximity to another was designed to prevent deterioration by cracking. As Huysmans suggested in his 1881 review, the glazing of the paintings provided the unifying effect otherwise achieved by varnish, which would even out discrepancies between matte and glossy areas. In all likelihood, it was their fear of discoloration more than a specific desire for matteness that prompted their preference for not varnishing.

The validity of Fenéon's assessment was confirmed by Pissarro. Before publishing his brochure on the neo-impressionist exhibition, Fenéon sent a proof directly to Pissarro to check for technical inaccuracies. Pissarro found Fenéon's statements "only too accurate,"[84] perhaps fearing that such detailed information would spawn imitators of their style.

Pissarro ceased painting in the pointillist style around 1891, returning to his earlier impressionistic style. But from this time until his death in 1903, there is no evidence that he resumed varnishing as well. It seems unlikely, as he had abandoned varnish long before he began painting in the pointillist style. Moreover, he continued to experiment with matte painting techniques through the 1890s. On his 1893 experiments with a casein borax mixture suggested to him by John L. Brown, Pissarro said with obvious pleasure, "The results are exactly like pastel."[85] During his later years, he would send as many as a dozen paintings at a time to his restorer, Portier, for cleaning. We do not know exactly what was removed from the paintings in the process, but when they were returned Pissarro considered them "resurrected," and described them as "grey, lusterless."[86]

Claude Monet

While Pissarro and Renoir represent opposite extremes in an approach to varnishing, Monet took a middle ground. In 1880 he had been willing to varnish a painting at the request of a client, but in the early 1880s he was also known on at least one occasion to have preferred a painting unvarnished.[87] In 1883 Monet explained to Durand-Ruel that he needed to redo some decorative panel paintings because they had to be unvarnished.[88] These examples do not really clarify the depth of Monet's commitment to the unvarnished aesthetic, but it likely increased as the decade progressed. In Monet's case, however, the impetus came from his preoccupation with the series paintings he had begun around 1887 rather than from a foray into pointillism.

In choosing the motifs for these series, Monet carefully considered their potential for an extended investigation of light, shape, color, and emotional effect. His descriptions of his intent always centered on capturing a distinct moment in time to show changes of light from one painting in a series to another. Paradoxically, although he was trying to record an instant in time, his working method became less and less spontaneous as he painted these series. He reworked some canvases years after he had painted them. Often, in retouching sessions he lined the canvases up one after the other and compared them to decide where to apply paint. Consequently, the paintings in the series must be considered not only representations of single distinct moments in time but also as collective works, with one painting inexorably linked to the next.[89] Monet's fascination with effects of light and the care with which he worked out the relationship of one painting to another suggest an interest in color effects every bit as strong as that of the pointillists. It was no surprise, then, to find that Monet was less inclined to varnish the series paintings than earlier works. In a review of an exhibit in New York in 1896 of a series of the Rouen cathedral paintings, Octave Mirbeau said that Monet "abhorred the trituration of his colors with varnish."[90]

The American artist Lila Cabot Perry remembered visiting Monet's studio in the 1890s and offered some fascinating insights that underscored Monet's concern for the preservation of his effects in the series paintings:

[Monet] said he was sure some of Rembrandt's pictures had been painted even more thickly and heavily than any of his, but that time with its leveling touch had smoothed them down. In illustrating this he took out from one of the grooved boxes in which he kept his pictures a view of the Rouen Cathedral that had been kept in the box practically ever since it had been painted and put [it] beside . . . one that had been hanging on the wall of his studio for some two or three years. The difference between the two was very marked, the one which had been exposed to the air and to the constant changes of temperature had so smoothed down in that short space of time that it made the other one with all its rugosities look like one of those embossed maps of Switzerland that are such a delight to children.

Perry's account suggests that Monet was greatly concerned about the longevity of the textures in his paintings.[91]

Another visitor to Monet's studio recalled seeing the artist actually squeeze out his tube colors onto blotting paper to absorb out some of the oil prior to painting,[92] as Mirbeau had also observed.[93] This method is often associated with Monet's desire for a matte effect; naturally, the removal of the medium from the paint would create a very lean and matte surface. But Perry's account of her visit suggests another possible motive: Monet may have hoped to reduce the leveling effect on his impastos by eliminating some of the medium that shrinks on drying. In removing the medium, Monet was approximating the methods used by Renoir in the 1880s; like Renoir, Monet could have painted dryly to prevent the darkening of his colors. Whatever his reasons, it seems clear that Monet was greatly concerned that the effects he worked so hard to achieve would remain unaltered.

Because Monet apparently eliminated both the final varnish and some medium from his series paintings, the final effect must have been quite matte. Unlike Pissarro, who painted with such diverse media as casein, pastel, and gouache while demonstrating a genuine interest in matte surfaces, it appears that Monet considered his technique as the most expedient means of preserving the appearance of his paintings. René Gimpel, one of Monet's dealers, believed that Monet rejected varnish because he thought the old masters had not used very much varnish themselves.[94] Other impressionists may have thought similarly. Elder offers what may be the best explanation for Monet's attitude. He records Monet's dismay at the deterioration of some paintings by Delacroix, Courbet, and Rembrandt in the Louvre:

The patina, the varnishes what horrors! Do you believe the gold colored Rembrandts—what nonsense! Do you believe that the collars of The Syndics *were not strikingly white when they were painted; Do you believe the limpid landscape in* The Carpenter's Family*? Varnish is death to the color!*[95]

Here Monet is in striking disagreement with Renoir, who did not find that the color changes induced by aged varnish spoiled Rubens' *Helena Fourment and Her Children*.

It is unlikely Monet used varnish after he began painting the series paintings. After 1900 his works became larger in size, but his concern about the effects of color became even more concentrated. At the end of his life, when he was negotiating the donation of his large series of *Water Lilies* to the Musée de l'Orangerie, Monet stipulated in the contract that they could never be varnished,[96] evidence of his determination that his later pictures remain unvarnished. Many of Monet's paintings are still preserved in an unvarnished state, especially the series paintings.

CONCLUSION

Comparison of two influential treatises on painters' techniques in the eighteenth and nineteenth centuries indicates quite different approaches in the use of varnish. Oudry's eighteenth-century lecture advocated the use of very thin intermediate layers of spirit varnishes while cautioning the artist to never add varnish directly to the painting medium. Mérimée recommended painting in thin glazes with varnish-containing media, perhaps adding a coating of viscous varnish on top of the ground and a final varnish containing oil. In the eighteenth century, Jean Felix Watin recommended only spirit varnishes for the final varnish. Both Mérimee's and Oudry's approaches facilitated the academic style of their time. The changes in technique that Mérimée's nineteenth-century manual suggested did not increase a painting's durability.

For artists working outside the academic mainstream, Delacroix in particular, the issue of durability seemed to take on increasing importance as the nineteenth century progressed. By the 1850s, Delacroix argued for a more cautious approach in the use of varnish, primarily out of concern for the longevity of his paintings. He looked back to the approach advocated by Oudry as more sound than the practice of his contemporaries.

The impressionist painters emerged from their atelier training in the 1860s aware of Delacroix's concerns and in the midst of a major cleaning controversy that made the effects of aged varnish prominent news and a *vernissage* system that guaranteed the artist little control. It would be difficult to imagine that the cautious approach toward varnish that they later adopted was not in some measure influenced by this climate.

Just as the impressionists' rejection of varnish cannot be seen as an isolated event in the development of artists' techniques, it cannot be generalized to include all the artists of the school from the beginning of their careers. Most impressionists cautiously accepted the use of varnish in the 1860s and 1870s. By the 1880s, however, many deliberately left their paintings unvarnished to achieve specific aesthetic effects. Yet, while Pissarro and Monet were committed to an unvarnished look, Renoir seemed to advocate precisely the opposite approach for most of his career. And even as Monet and Pissarro rejected varnish, they did so for different reasons: Pissarro because of his desire for a matte finish; Monet lest it discolor his effects. During Pissarro's pointillist period, he rejected varnish as a matter of dogma; for Monet it always seemed a matter of choice.

Research into the use of varnish by French painters is useful to the curator or conservator working in modern times. It explains more concretely the reasons that cleaning nineteenth-century French academic paintings is generally much more technically problematic than cleaning those from the eighteenth century. It indicates that with French paintings an intact original varnish layer should not necessarily be presumed to have been applied by the artist. Furthermore, in spite of the best intentions of the impressionists, the system in France by which paintings were varnished by color merchants, framers, and dealers almost guaranteed that paintings would receive a coating of varnish not long after they left the studio. Finally, this research suggests some guidelines for deciding whether to revarnish an impressionist painting after cleaning. Given the evidence, it is probably appropriate to revarnish most paintings by Renoir, while it is probably inappropriate to give the strong appearance of a coating of varnish to post-1880 paintings by Monet and Pissarro. With paintings by these two artists, the later the painting, the more inappropriate the revarnishing.

NOTES

This paper was made possible by the efforts of a great many people. I would like to thank Ross Merrill, David Bull, and Sarah Fisher for their administrative support at the National Gallery of Art, and my colleagues Carol Christensen, Paula DeCristofaro, Susanna P. Griswold, Ann Hoenigswald, and Cathy Metzger for their suggestions and encouragement. I especially appreciated the editing efforts of my wife, Mary Sebera, and of Janice Gruver of the National Gallery of Art conservation division. The contribution of my French colleagues, Isabelle Leegenhoek and John Wade, was also crucial. Most of all, I would like to thank the Mellon Foundation, which provided the funding that made this research possible.

Unless otherwise indicated, all translations are mine.

1. Quoted in Henri Testelin, *Mémoirs pour servir à l'histoire de L'Académie Royale de Peinture et de Sculpture*, ed. M. Ametole de Moutaiglon (Paris, 1853), 42.

2. Albert Boime, *The Academy and French Painting in the Nineteenth Century* (London, 1971), 5.

3. Jean Baptiste Oudry, "Discours sur la pratique de la peinture et ses procédés principaux, ébaucher, peindre a fond, et retoucher," paper presented to the French Academy, 2 December 1752, published from the manuscript in the Ecole des Beaux Arts in *Le Cabinet de l'amateur: Nouvelle série*, ed. Eugène Piot (Paris, 1849), 110.

4. Oudry 1849, 115.

5. Oudry 1849, 109.

6. Oudry 1849, 110: "Always keep from making your colors with both varnish and oil. This makes a painting that always stays sticky and cracks on drying."

7. Quoted in Henry Jouin, *Conférences de l'Académie Royale de Peinture et de Sculpture* (Paris, 1883), 403.

8. Le Pileur d'Apligny, *Traité des couleurs matérielles* (Paris, 1779); Pierre Joseph Macquer, *Dictionnaire raisonné universel des arts et métiers* (Paris, 1773); Jean Felix Watin, *L'Art de faire et d'employer le vernis* (Paris, 1772). Watin (300), for example, advises:

It is only necessary to varnish a painting in order to recall the colors and to conserve them and not to further color them or to give them a brilliance which obstructs one's ability to distinguish the subject. It is necessary also to avoid that which would make them dull; they should be, on the contrary, clear, light, and soft. With varnish made in alcohol the painting would crack; varnish made with oil would be too colored and too matte, and make the colors sticky; varnishes made with oil veil the colors like a drapery, obscuring them with a coating that cannot be cleaned off because one would necessarily remove the colors at the same time. These inconveniences lead us to reject all varnishes made with alcohol and oil for paintings, and lead us to adopt those made in turpentine for this purpose. . . .

To make the best varnish which provides perfect nourishment for the canvas, maintains the colors in their original state, and can always be removed without endangering the painting, compose your varnishes with mastic and turpentine.

9. Proceedings of the academy, 26 July 1749, *Procès-verbaux de l'Académie Royale 1648–1793*, ed. Paul Cornu, 10 vols. (Paris, 1909), 6:172, 173.

10. Proceedings of the academy, 7 March 1750, Cornu 1909, 6:200.

11. Boime 1971, 6–7.

12. Boime 1971, 20–21.

13. Quatremère de Quincy, introd. to Jean François Léonore Mérimée, *The Art of Painting in Oil and in Fresco* (1830), 3d ed., trans. William Benjamin Sarsfield Taylor (London, 1839).

14. Mérimée 1839, 86.

15. Mérimée 1839, 7–10. Mérimée's evidence for admixtures of varnish and oil in the medium are as follows: First, "the van Eycks mixed them because the idea of incorporating the two being so simple, we must infer that it would naturally, in the first instance occur to the mind of van Eyck" and "van Eyck and his followers' colors could not have simply been used with oil of a more or less drying quality but that they were mixed with varnish which is the cause of the surprising preservation which we witness in so many of the earliest pictures." Second, Leonardo used varnish in his medium, as testified by Pope Julius II, who visited Leonardo's studio and saw only chemical apparatus and utensils, which he understood were for the preparing of varnish. Third, the most certain way of knowing that the earliest painters mixed varnish with oil in their medium is by consulting those regularly responsible for restoring them. We learn from their researches that the color of those pictures that belong to the first epoch of oil painting are of a harder body than those of a later date and that they resist solvents much better; if they are rubbed with a file they show underneath a shiny appearance resembling that of a picture painted with varnish.

The first two of these reasons suggest to me paint that did not have varnish mixed with it; the third reason makes little sense.

16. Mérimée 1839, 91–92.

17. Louise d'Argencourt, *Bouguereau* [exh. cat., Musée du Petit Palais] (Paris, 1983), 77.

18. Louis de Planet, *Souvenirs de travaux du peintre avec M. Eugène Delacroix*, ed. André Joubin (Paris, 1929), 21–23.

19. Eugène Delacroix, *Correspondance général de Eugène Delacroix*, ed. André Joubin, 4 vols. (Paris, 1936). Letters between Etienne Haro and Delacroix discuss matters related to Delacroix's technique. See, for instance, letters of 6 June 1860, 5 August 1860, 10 September 1860, Joubin 1936, 4:183, 187, 196.

20. See, e.g., Eugène Delacroix, journal, 5 October 1847, *Journal de Eugène Delacroix*, ed. André Joubin, 3 vols. (Paris, 1932), 1:241–244. The entries surrounding the discussion of technique in October 1847 show remarkable similarities to Mérimée.

21. Delacroix, journal, 11 January 1857, Joubin 1932, 3:12.

22. Nathalie Sauvaire, "Rôle de la famille Haro dans l'oeuvre de Delacroix" (master's thesis, University of

Paris, 1978), copy in Bibliothèque Doucet, Paris. This receipt is preserved in the Cabinet des Dessins, Musée du Louvre.

23. Sauvaire 1978, 98.

24. Sauvaire 1978, 98. Letters concerning this matter are in the conservation archives, Musée du Louvre.

25. Delacroix, journal, 7 February 1849, Joubin 1932, 1:259.

26. Quoted in Sauvaire 1978, 100.

27. Quoted in Sauvaire 1978, 101.

28. Delacroix, journal, 27 June 1854, Joubin 1932, 2:206.

29. Delacroix, journal, 29 July 1854, Joubin 1932, 2:221.

30. Delacroix, journal, 4 October 1852, Joubin 1932, 1:490.

31. Delacroix, journal, 19 October 1853, Joubin 1932, 3:132.

32. Sauvaire 1978, 97.

33. Delacroix, journal, 11 January 1857, Joubin 1932, 3:12.

34. Delacroix, journal, 11 January 1857, Joubin 1932, 3:12.

35. Delacroix to Henri Joseph Constant Dutilleux, 8 August 1858, Joubin 1936, 4:42–43.

36. See, for instance, Gustave Courbet, *Courbet réconté par lui même et par ses amis*, ed. Pierre Courthion (Geneva, 1948), 209–210, for Courbet's criticism of contemporary artistic education and praise for the Renaissance system.

37. Pierre François Tingry, *The Painter and Varnisher's Guide* (London, 1804), 136.

38. Nicolas Poussin to A. M. de Chantelou, 12 January 1644, *Nicolas Poussin: Lettres et propos sur l'art*, ed. Anthony Blunt (London, 1964), 86.

39. William Sandby, *The History of the Royal Academy of the Arts* (London, 1862), 274–275.

40. Proceedings of the Institute of France, 14 May 1803, *Procès verbaux de l'Académie des Beaux Arts*, ed. Marcel Bonnaire, 2 vols. (Paris, 1940), 2:157.

41. Philipe Grunchec, *Le Concours pour la Prix de Rome de 1797 à 1863* [exh. cat., Ecole Nationale, Supérieure des Beaux Arts] (Paris, 1983), 26.

42. Alexis Lemaistre, *L'Ecole des Beaux Arts* (Paris, 1889), 349.

43. Jules Adeline, *Lexique des termes d'art* (Paris, 1884), 411.

44. Genvieve Le Pavec, interview with author, Paris, July 1985. Madame Le Pavec related this information from an interview she had had with the grandson of Pierre Louis Rouillarde, who exhibited in the Salons of the early 1870s.

45. Monsieur La Place, minister of finance, to Monsieur Calleux, director of Musées Royaux, 1847, cited in Sauvaire 1978, 110.

46. "Letters to Haro," MS, Bibliothèque Doucet, Paris. Letters from all of these artists to Haro concern various technical issues. The letters from Delacroix are published in Joubin 1936. Some of the letters from Ingres are published in André Joubin, "Haro entre Ingres et Delacroix," *Amour d'Art* 17, no. 3 (March 1936), 85–93.

47. Jean Gabriel Goulinat, *La technique des peintres* (1922), 2d ed. (Paris, 1926), 54.

48. Denis Rouart, *Degas: À la recherche de sa technique* (Paris, 1945), 9.

49. John Rewald, *The History of Impressionism*, 3d ed. (New York, 1961), 437.

50. Quoted in Ambroise Vollard, *Renoir: An Intimate Record* (New York, 1934), 96.

51. Frédéric Villot, "Restauration des tableaux du Louvre," *Annuaire des artistes et des amateurs* (Paris, 1860), 265–274; Emile Galichon, *Restauration des tableaux du Louvre, réponse à un article de Frédéric Villot* (Paris, 1860); Galichon, *Nouvelles observations sur la restauration des tableaux du Louvre, réponse à M. Ferdinand de Lasteyrie* (Paris, 1861). Emile Galichon's pamphlets practically repeat the contents of Delacroix's letter to Dutilleux.

52. Rewald 1961, 596.

53. Quoted in Vollard 1934, 82.

54. Gaston Poulain, *Bazille et ses amis* (Paris, 1932), 40–50.

55. Albert Boime, *Thomas Couture and the Eclectic Vision* (New Haven, 1980), 441–457. This discussion describes Couture's method, which is comparable to that of Oudry.

56. Anne Coffin Hanson, *Manet and the Modern Tradition* (New Haven, 1977), 143–177.

57. Claude Monet to Frédéric Bazille, 15 July 1864, in Daniel Wildenstein, *Biographie and catalogue raisonné de Monet*, 4 vols. (Paris, 1974), 1:420.

58. Marie-Joséphine-Cornélie Morisot to Edma Morisot, 8 May 1865, *Correspondance de Berthe Morisot*, ed. Denis Rouart (Paris, 1950), 68–69.

59. Edouard Manet to Etienne Haro, n.d., Bibliothèque Doucet, italics in original. The letter is filed among letters from the 1860s.

60. Quoted in Vollard 1934, 62.

61. Camille Pissarro to Eugene Murer, 1878, *Correspondance de Camille Pissarro*, ed. Janine Bailly-Merzberg, 4 vols. (Paris, 1980), 1:110.

62. Pissarro to Theodore Duret, 5 May 1874, Bailly-Merzberg 1980, 1:94.

63. René Gimpel, *Journal d'un collectionneur: Marchand des tableaux* (Paris, 1963), 95.

64. Quoted in Gimpel 1963, 128.

65. Alice Hoschede to Earnest Hoschede, 14 February 1880, Wildenstein 1974, 1:446: "M. Coqueret est venu ce matin demander pour vernir ses tableaux."

66. Edmond Duranty, *La Nouvelle Peinture: A propos du groupe d'Artistes qui expose dans les galeries Durand-Ruel* (c. 1876), new ed. (Paris, 1946), 23.

67. J. Karl Huysmans, *L'Art moderne* (Paris, 1883), 110.

68. Charles F. Stuckey and William P. Scott, *Berthe Morisot: Impressionist* (New York, 1987), 196.

69. Félix Fenéon, "L'impressionisme scientifique,"

L'art moderne, 19 September 1886, in Fenéon, *Félix Fenéon: Au-delà de l'impressionnisme*, ed. Françoise Cachin (Paris, 1966), 77.

70. William Gregory to Charles Eastlake, 25 October 1880, National Gallery, London. This letter discusses the glazing of all the paintings in these galleries.

71. Quoted in Vollard 1934, 118.

72. Quoted in Vollard 1934, 123.

73. Quoted in Vollard 1934, 123.

74. Renoir to Durand-Ruel, 15 April 1891, *Les archives de l'impressionnisme*, ed. Lionello Venturi, 2 vols. (Paris, 1939), 1:147.

75. Renoir to Durand-Ruel, 18 April 1891, Venturi 1939, 1:147.

76. Quoted in Vollard 1934, 202.

77. Marc Elder, Introduction to *L'Atelier de Renoir* (Paris, 1939), 25.

78. Quoted in Vollard 1934, 138–139.

79. Phillippe Burty, "Les Aquarellistes, les Indépendants et le Cercle des Arts, libéraux," *La République Française*, 8 March 1882; Bailly-Merzberg 1980, 158.

80. Camille Pissarro to Lucien Pissarro, 13 May 1883, *Camille Pissarro: Letters to His Son Lucien*, ed. John Rewald (New York, 1943), 32.

81. Joyce Hill Stoner, Winterthur Art Conservation Graduate Program, personal communication, 1985.

82. Georges Seurat to Octave Maus, January 1887, *Georges Seurat, 1859–1891*, ed. Robert L. Herbert [exh. cat., Metropolitan Museum of Art] (New York, 1991), 405.

83. Fenéon 1966, 77.

84. Camille Pissarro to Lucien Pissarro, 15 September 1886, Rewald 1943, 81.

85. Camille Pissarro to Lucien Pissarro, 17 October 1893, Rewald 1943, 212.

86. Camille Pissarro to Lucien Pissarro, 17 October 1893, Rewald 1943, 219.

87. Wildenstein 1974, 3:494.

88. Claude Monet to Durand-Ruel, 21 November 1883, Venturi 1939, 1:263: "J'ai dû encore les recommencer car invernis."

89. Grace Seiberling, *Monet's Series* (New York, 1981), 150–160.

90. Octave Mirbeau, *A Catalogue of Marvelous Paintings of the Cathedral Rouen* (New York, 1896), 9.

91. Lila Cabot Perry, "Reminiscences of Claude Monet from 1889 to 1909," *American Magazine of Art* 18 (March 1927), 122.

92. Gaston Bernheim de Villers, *Little Tales of Great Artists*, ed. and trans. Denys Sutton (Paris and New York, 1950), 79.

93. Mirbeau 1896, 9.

94. Gimpel 1963, 89.

95. Quoted in Marc Elder, *A Giverny chez Claude Monet* (Paris, 1924), 52.

96. J. P. Hoschede, *Claude Monet: Ce mal connu*, 2 vols. (Geneva, 1960), 2:25–26.

Contributors

Daphne Barbour, associate conservator of objects, received her M.A. in art history and Certificate in Conservation of Art from New York University's Institute of Fine Arts. Before joining the National Gallery of Art staff in 1987, she completed internships at several Smithsonian Institution museums and the Harvard University Art Museums. Her current research includes technical studies of Saint-Porchaire ceramics published in the National Gallery of Art catalogue, *Sculpture and Decorative Arts of Medieval, Renaissance, Classical, and Other Periods* (1992).

Sarah Bertalan received her B.A. in art history and languages from Hope College. She has worked in curatorial, administrative, and research positions at the Robert Lehman Collection, Metropolitan Museum of Art, and completed her M.A. in art history at the Institute of Fine Arts, New York University. After also completing a Certificate in Conservation at the Institute of Fine Arts Conservation Center, she held internships at the Philadelphia Museum of Art, Worcester Art Museum, and the Library of Congress. She was a Mellon Fellow at the National Gallery of Art from 1986 to 1988. Currently she is a free-lance paper conservator and consultant in Washington, D.C.

Carol Christensen joined the National Gallery of Art in 1981, where she is presently associate painting conservator, after receiving her M.S. degree from the Winterthur Art Conservation Program. She took a leave of absence in 1983 to work at the Gemäldegalerie, Berlin, where she was a Fulbright Scholar in the area of conservation studies. Although she has published on Raphael and Van Dyck, Gauguin has been her special interest for the past five years.

Antoinette Dwan holds a B.A. in English literature and art studio from the University of California, Berkeley, and an M.S. in art conservation from the University of Delaware/Winterthur Museum. She was a Mellon Fellow at the National Gallery of Art, 1984–1985, in the paper conservation department. She also worked at the National Museum of American History, Smithsonian Institution, the San Francisco Museum of Modern Art, and the Baltimore Museum of Art. At present she is a private conservator.

Lisha Deming Glinsman joined the National Gallery of Art in 1987 as a conservation scientist, where her work in the scientific research department has included x-ray fluorescence analyses on hundreds of Renaissance bronze objects. She received her B.A. in chemistry from the College of Saint Rose, Albany and has worked in industry and as a research chemist for the National Institute of Standards and Technology (formerly National Bureau of Standards). Currently she is working on statistical analyses based on the elemental surface composition of the National Gallery's Renaissance portrait medals.

Susanna P. Griswold holds an M.A. from the University of Michigan. She worked at the Palazzo Pitti, Florence, and the Detroit Institute of Arts, and was an assistant conservator at the J. Paul Getty Museum. From 1986 to 1988 she was a Mellon Fellow in painting conservation at the National Gallery of Art, where she is presently a conservator of paintings.

Michael Swicklik received his B.A. in art history from Colgate University and an M.A. and Certificate in Conservation from the State University of New York. He was associate conservator at the Kimbell Art Museum. A Mellon Fellow at the National Gallery of Art from 1984 to 1986, he is a conservator of paintings.